D1572837

A HISTORY OF THE SOUTH

VOLUMES IN THE SERIES

Volume VIII

THE SOUTH DURING
RECONSTRUCTION
1865–1877

A HISTORY

OF

THE SOUTH

Volume VIII

EDITORS

WENDELL HOLMES STEPHENSON

E. MERTON COULTER

The South

During

Reconstruction

1865-1877

BY E. MERTON COULTER

LOUISIANA STATE UNIVERSITY PRESS

THE LITTLEFIELD FUND FOR SOUTHERN
HISTORY OF THE UNIVERSITY OF TEXAS

PUBLISHERS' PREFACE

A HISTORY OF THE SOUTH is sponsored by Louisiana State University and the Trustees of the Littlefield Fund for Southern History at The University of Texas. More remotely, it is the outgrowth of the vision of Major George W. Littlefield, C.S.A., who established a fund at The University of Texas in 1914 for the collection of materials on Southern history and the publication of a "full and impartial study of the South and its part in American history." Trustees of the Littlefield Fund began preparations in 1937 for the writing of the history that Major Littlefield contemplated. Meanwhile, a plan had been conceived at Louisiana State University for a history of the South as a part of that institution's comprehensive program to promote interest, research, and writing in the field of Southern history.

As the two undertakings harmonized in essentials, the planning groups united to become joint sponsors of *A History of the South.* Wendell Holmes Stephenson, then professor of American history at Louisiana State University, and the late Charles W. Ramsdell, professor of American history at The University of Texas, were chosen to edit the series. They had been primarily interested in initiating the plans, and it was appropriate that they should be selected to edit the work. Upon the death of Professor Ramsdell in 1942, E. Merton Coulter, professor of history at the University of Georgia, was named his successor.

Publication of Volume VIII of the series marks the beginning of the final phase of historical planning and research which was begun more than a decade ago.

AUTHOR'S PREFACE

AMERICANS have generally called the fifteen years following the Civil War the Reconstruction period, and writers in this field until recently have let the reconstructing processes crowd out of their narratives everyday developments in the lives of the people. This custom has been especially true of those who have written about the South; for this region, being a war casualty, became the victim of a Federal government experiment. The biggest news was always what Congress was doing to the South, or what the agencies it had set up were doing; and these happenings were what Southern leaders thought about most, wrote about most in their private correspondence, and what the newspapers published. It is, therefore, easiest to present this most evident picture. There were, nevertheless, with all the political and constitutional abnormalities of the times, the ordinary activities of the people, as they sowed and reaped, went to church, visited their neighbors, sang their songs, and sought in a thousand ways to amuse themselves. The point of view set forth in this work is the *South* during Reconstruction—not *Reconstruction* in the South.

In the minds of Southerners, to reconstruct meant to put the Union of the states back as it was before the war. This understanding might well be expected of them, the most conservative of Americans, but it ignored realities which it were best Southerners had recognized. The dominant political element in the North soon showed it had no such intentions. Since no armistice was signed or treaty of peace made, it believed that there were no terms of surrender, either stated or implied, which it need respect. Northerners would seize this opportunity not only to remake Southerners in the many respects that had no direct relationship to the war; they would also remake the Union by not only degrading the Southern states but in the process also depriving all states of much of their power and bestowing it upon the central government. Here was the fruition of a growth in extremism evident in the North long before the war broke out, but now made easy by that war having been fought. This movement was not only concerned with the powers of government and its subserviency to the expanding economic interests of individuals but it was also a faint glimmering of a changing world, reflected most vividly in English liberalism and French radicalism.

The South set itself with determination against change, whether it be in the form of government under which it was forced to live or in the ways of life which its people had developed through generations. Southerners did not succeed in stopping a reshuffling of governmental powers in which all states, North and South, were losers; but they did prevent the Radical North from carrying out its cherished desire to remake them and their way of running their governments. When the North gave up its efforts in 1877 in failure, the South was permitted within reasonable limits to reconstruct itself, a process which may not yet be considered ended.

It is particularly true that in this period strong human emotions rose to such heights that they became one of the greatest fundamental facts in Southern developments. What happened was often of less significance than what the people thought and wanted, and so a study of the psychology of the South as far as it is possible looms into importance. The nearest approach to this uncertain science can be made through what Southerners said. What they believed to be the fact, therefore, became more important than what was actually the fact. For this reason, then, a great many direct quotations have been used in this work; and a greater part of the narrative has been made to progress through direct contemporary expressions than might be warranted in treating a less abnormal period of history.

No precise definition of the South is possible. When "South" or "Southerners" is used without a limiting adjective, it is normal to assume that the dominant point of view is intended. In this sense what Negroes or other minorities thought is, of course, not implied. True enough, it is not always easy to determine what the dominant point of view (or the minority opinion, for that matter) was; for certainly, apart from politics, there were many points of view. There were Baptists and Methodists and Catholics; there were saints and sinners; there were rich and poor; there were law observers and lawbreakers; there were rural people and city dwellers. Geographically, the South in Reconstruction times unifies itself for examination and treatment around the eleven states which made up the Confederacy more clearly than in any other period of its history. Reconstruction programs became the great common denominators. For that reason this work has placed emphasis on the old Confederacy, though the Border states have not been ignored.

As each generation feels constrained to rewrite the past, points of view and methods of approach necessarily change, and so revisionists arise. If they remain within the reasonable bounds of established facts, they may well make lasting contributions in fresher interpretations and in the presentation of new information; but if they depart from the old channels to attract attention in novel and unsubstantiated points of view, they themselves may soon be revised. The author of this work feels that there can be no sensible departure from the well-known facts of the Reconstruction program as it was applied to the South. No amount of revision can write away the grievous mistakes made in this abnormal period of American history. This writer, therefore, has not attempted it. Departing from the usual, however, he has sought to discover as far as possible what were the aspirations of Southern white Radicals and Negroes and what was their defense against charges made by traditional Southerners. It is hoped that evidences of this attempt will be found in the following pages. Also, he has made an effort to broaden the picture of the South during Reconstruction by giving greater attention to the lives of the people, white and black, in their many interests and activities apart from politics. In these respects more than in any others, this work would lay claim to have revised older treatments of the Southern Reconstruction period.

It ought to be said that the author has chosen to write this volume in the atmosphere and spirit of the times here portrayed rather than to measure the South of Reconstruction by present-day standards. In so doing he believes that he has added in this perspective a sort of historical fourth dimension which gives a balance attainable in no other way. If there be those who are disposed to condemn the South for not holding the point of view of the mid-twentieth century, especially on social and racial problems, and who also might be disposed to belabor the author for not measuring the South of that time by the mid-twentieth century standards, let them keep in mind that great changes have come in human concepts since 1865 and let them also remember what the author set out to do.

A great many people deserve the author's thanks, too many to particularize beyond mentioning Professor Wendell H. Stephenson, one of the editors of this series, to whom the writer feels a special obligation. In all the former Confederate states and in many other states from Massachusetts to Kansas, librarians and custodians of collections by making available their wealth of historical material aided in the making of this book.

E. M. C.

CONTENTS

ILLUSTRATIONS

CHAPTER I

THE COST OF WAR

THE CIVIL WAR was not worth its cost. It freed the slaves, upset a social and an economic order, strengthened the powers of the national government, and riveted tighter upon the South a colonial status under which it had long suffered. What good the war produced would have come with time in an orderly way; the bad would not have come at all. Its immediate effects on the South were glaring and poignant; those more fundamental were less evident and long-drawn-out. The war generation bore the brunt, and it was they who had to grapple hardest with the new problems.

As the war had been fought almost entirely in the South, here its destructions were wrought. What invasion feeds upon is the same everywhere—towns and cities, lines of railways, bridges and fences, forests and fields, factories and homes, livestock and granaries, and personal belongings. Of all the Federal officers General Sherman was most proficient in carrying the rigors of war to the people, and for this Southerners set him upon a permanent pinnacle dedicated to Civil War ruthlessness, and often gave him credit for the destructions of other commanders. The lone chimneys—Sherman's sentinels—reared themselves as conspicuous landmarks along the sixty-mile swath he cut across Georgia and up through South Carolina, and gave rise to the jest that Southerners had a peculiar custom of building chimneys without houses to go with them. A Northerner who had traveled through the South declared that Sherman had not left a building on the railway from Macon to Savannah,[1] and two years after the war Sherman agree-

1 John T. Trowbridge, *The South: A Tour of its Battle-Fields and Ruined Cities, A Journey through the Desolated States, and Talks with the People: . . .* (Hartford, 1866), 502.

ing and yet with kindly feelings toward the South recalled to his veterans what had happened: "Look to the South, and you who went with me through that land can best say if they too have not been fearfully punished. Mourning in every household, desolation written in broad characters across the whole face of their country, cities in ashes and fields laid waste, their commerce gone, their system of labor annihilated and destroyed. Ruin, poverty, and distress everywhere, and now pestilence adding to the very cap sheaf to their stack of misery; her proud men begging for pardon and appealing for permission to raise food for their children; her five million of slaves free, and their value lost to their former masters forever." [2]

The song "Marching through Georgia" gave special accent to Sherman's destructions in that state, but in fact he did his worst in South Carolina and left conditions there which a loyal Northern witness averred no pen could describe. Fearing he would be thought to be sentimentalizing, he added, "Yet that treatment was what the haughty little state needed." That North Carolina came out of the war with fewer scars led the same observer to remark, "More fire would have made more healthy spirit in this State." [3] Philip H. Sheridan's ravages of the Shenandoah Valley and four years of other warfare in Virginia made the Old Dominion a fearful sufferer. Tennessee and Mississippi lay in ruins wherever armies had marched. Alabama claimed destructions amounting to $300,000,000, and the cane planters alone in Louisiana suffered losses set at $100,000,000. War effects in uninvaded Texas were "less visible and less in reality" than in any other Confederate state. Total material destruction throughout the South has been estimated in billions of dollars. [4]

The most arresting ruins were those of cities, and of these Charleston's were the most pathetic, or "the most picturesque" as they appeared to one Northern traveler. [5] Another visitor from the North after viewing them looked into his heart and found pity.

[2] Augusta (Ga.) *Weekly Constitutionalist*, November 27, 1867.

[3] Sidney Andrews, *The South since the War: As Shown by Fourteen Weeks of Travel and Observation in Georgia and the Carolinas* (Boston, 1866), 111.

[4] William W. Davis, *The Civil War and Reconstruction in Florida* (New York, 1913), 319.

[5] Trowbridge, *South*, 514.

Here was "enough woe and want and ruin and ravage to satisfy the most insatiate heart,—enough of sore humiliation and bitter overthrow to appease the desire of the most vengeful spirit." [6] When Carl Schurz passed through in July, 1865, he saw, in addition to the ruins, rotting wharfs and weed-infested streets.[7] Columbia, South Carolina's other city, though smaller than Charleston, was more thoroughly destroyed. Everything in the business section had been swept away and two thirds of the rest of the city was gone. In the words of the inevitable Northern traveler, "It is now a wilderness of ruins. Its heart is but a mass of blackened chimneys and crumbling walls." [8] Atlanta was now as famous for its utter destruction as it had once been for its rapid growth, and Savannah could mourn over six blocks of ruins. "The burnt district" of Richmond, although wrought by the Confederates, was a casualty of war and as much a loss as if caused by the Federals. War passed through the streets of Fredericksburg and of Petersburg, and down in Alabama Selma lay in ashes. Over in Mississippi the little college town of Oxford had one business house left standing when the Surrender came. And so the story went; towns and villages throughout the fought-over Confederacy had their scars to show.

Two thirds of the South's railroads were utterly destroyed or crippled into inaction. The hairpin and corkscrew methods, heating the rails and twisting them around trees, had been most effective —140 miles of the Memphis and Charleston road as well as long stretches of other lines were examples of this treatment. Ruined bridges, stations, shops, and rolling stock added their quotas to the damages. The Savannah and Charleston line was completely destroyed; trains were not run on it again until five years after the war. The railroad destructions in South Carolina alone were at least $1,500,000.

Some of the old country mansions were burned, but more were stripped of their furnishings, as was Arlington, Robert E. Lee's home. In the low country, avenues of stately live oaks were with "unrespecting recklessness" cut down by soldiers for firewood.

[6] Andrews, *South since the War*, 1.
[7] *The Reminiscences of Carl Schurz* (London, 1909), III, 167.
[8] Andrews, *South since the War*, 33.

Later, plundered belongings turned up in Northern pawnshops, and Southerners long charged that "the houses of volunteer officers, and chaplains especially, in almost every New England and Northern village" were filled "with stolen plate, pictures, books, and even wearing apparel, and, in fact, everything from a piano to a pap-spoon, which . . . [were] proudly displayed as 'rebel trophies,' or 'confiscated' property." [9] A group signing themselves "Many Southern Ladies" published in Northern papers a plea asking for the return of their property and directed it to "the families of lawyers, ministers, captains, colonels, generals, professors in colleges, . . . [and to] thousands of privates in the army, and chaplains and governors of States." [10]

Added to the cost of war was the price of peace. All Confederate currency became worthless and all bonds were forcibly repudiated as part of the price of re-entering the Union. Money losses were not keenly felt as they had been cushioned by a steady decline in the value of Confederate currency; but bonds frequently represented a major portion of a lifetime savings. One hundred millions of insurance investments and twice as much bank capital evaporated. People who had bought public lands, once belonging to the Federal government but taken over by the states after the outbreak of the war, were now dispossessed, and many people who for any reason were not present when armies marched in upon their property suffered temporary or permanent confiscation on the ground of abandonment. During the war and the years following, farm lands drifted back to nature, and in only the three frontier states of Texas, Arkansas, and Florida was there an appreciably greater acreage under cultivation in 1880 than in 1860. Mississippi with almost 16,000,000 acres in 1880 had an increase of only 15,000, and none of the other Confederate states had yet reached the 1860 amount. South Carolina showed a decrease of more than 2,700,000 acres.[11] Livestock was especially susceptible to the hazards of war. Only in Texas, Florida, Louisiana, and Arkansas was there an increase in the number of horses in 1880 over 1860. The other states had not yet reached their 1860 level,

[9] New York *World,* quoted in Nashville *Republican Banner,* November 3, 1866.
[10] Sandersville *Central Georgian,* February 14, 1866.
[11] *Compendium of the Tenth Census, 1880* (Washington, 1883), I, 654, 675.

and in Georgia where horses had numbered 131,000 in 1860 there were in 1880 only 99,000. Other livestock followed much the same trend; its value in Alabama had not reached even in 1900 its level of 1860.

The greatest single possession the Southerner lost was his property in Negroes. Whether the money value of the slaves was one billion or four billion dollars, within which limits estimates have generally been made, freeing them has been characterized by a modern historian as "the most stupendous act of sequestration in the history of Anglo-Saxon jurisprudence." [12] As Southerners had reconciled themselves before the end of the war to the inevitability of freedom for their slaves, it was mockery in their eyes to give the North credit for doing a good and unselfish deed in emancipating them—an act Southerners themselves were about to perform. Queried a Southern editor, "Did our readers ever reflect that the slaves won their freedom by the products of their own labor? Did it ever occur to them that the Northern accumulation of Southern capital was a great savings bank in which half of every cent earned by the slave for a century had been deposited to his credit, and was checked out by John Brown and Mr. Lincoln to liberate him?" He concluded, "Such was the error of a system of exclusive industry, which thus furnished the means of its own annihilation, and left the country at one blow destitute of all that it had labored a century to acquire." [13] According to Benjamin H. Hill, the North did not check out its profits from slavery; the North freed the Negro "and kept the price of his slavery, and you [Northern people] alone hold the property that was in human flesh." [14] If freeing the slave was punishment for a crime, then, said another Southerner, "God knows the punishment of the late slaveholders is equal to the offense, however great its enormity." [15]

[12] Charles A. Beard and Mary R. Beard, *The Rise of American Civilization* (New York, 1930), II, 100. See also, William B. Hesseltine, *The South in American History* (New York, 1943), 483.

[13] *De Bow's Review* (New Orleans), V (1868), 693. All references to this magazine are in "After the War Series."

[14] *Report of the Joint Select Committee to Inquire into the Condition of Affairs in the Late Insurrectionary States* (Washington, 1872), VII, 797. Cited hereafter under the binder's title, *Ku Klux Conspiracy.*

[15] E. Carrington Cabell, "White Emigration to the South," in *De Bow's Review*, I (1866), 92. The author continued: "Their pecuniary loss is almost beyond calculation.

Although England paid for the slaves she freed in her dominions, Southern slaveholders had come to the conclusion by the end of the war that the United States would give no recompense. The wiser ones believed that it was inexpedient to agitate for it unless at the same time the losses of nonslaveholders be included, for otherwise they stood to become extremely unpopular with that class who had been their political support before the war.

Southerners had lost the ownership of their Negroes, but the freedmen still remained as economic wealth, however inefficient their work might have been as compared with slave labor. Though the Negro did not disappear with his servitude, yet the Southerner who had invested $1,000 in a slave suffered as great a loss personally as if he had invested that $1,000 in a Confederate bond.

Apart from the attempts to recover the value of cotton dishonestly seized by Federal agents, Confederate Southerners never received nor sought to collect war damages; for, indeed, only the Southerner who could prove that he had never aided the Confederacy could file a claim. These "truly loyal" Southerners early began a clamor to be paid for their losses—from a fund taxed out of the "rebels" if necessary. In 1871 Congress set up a Southern Claims Commission instructed to receive claims for a period of two years, and soon agents were busy ensnaring the deluded into paying them five dollars for filing the necessary papers. More than twenty-two thousand claims were received and for years thereafter their validity was investigated. Many Southerners who turned against their section after the war hoped that they might capitalize on this belated loyalty. In the hope of proving that they had been "rebels" during the war, Zachariah Chandler bought for $75,000 a mass of Confederate documents, known as the Pickett

---

The loss of property is universal. All have suffered. Thousands have been reduced from affluence to poverty. The loss of life, who can estimate? There is scarcely a Southern home that is not clad in mourning for some cherished member of the household. Districts of country larger than the areas of States have been rendered desolate by the hostile armies of invasion. The hope of Southern Independence, so fondly cherished by many, has been lost forever. Political power and influence have passed away, and the proud statesmen of the South cannot exercise the right of citizenship. What more could the bitterest enemy ask or desire?"

6

Papers, and it was stated that through proof here found the United States government saved enough to pay for the papers.[16] Most Southerners, knowing that their own claims were excluded, looked with disdain on this Commission and its work. They denounced it as "an organized fraud which has paid millions to men who were false to their country in her need, or perjured themselves for gold when the danger was past," and charged that no "true Southern man can get a claim out of this mill of mischief and fraud." [17] Yet for party advantage, Northern Republicans, now and then twisting the truth entirely around, warned the people that all "rebel" claims would be paid if Democrats got a majority in Congress. The Democrats retorted that none would be paid if they were in charge. A sum total of $60,258,150 was claimed; $4,636,920 was finally allowed.

It was estimated that there were 5,000,000 bales of cotton in the South at the Surrender, despite wartime restricted production, blockade-running, burning to prevent its falling into the hands of Federals, and seizure of $30,000,000 worth by Treasury agents. Cotton as a symbol of the South was something for the North to detest, but as a commodity of commerce, something to covet, and it was soon evident to Southerners that they were to be largely despoiled of this one ray of economic hope. By legislation passed during the war, Congress authorized the appointment of Treasury agents whose duty it was to thread their way throughout the occupied parts of the South and take possession of all abandoned property for the government. Though their chief interest was cotton, they took whatever they could seize and sell. With the coming of peace there was greater confusion, for Treasury agents now came in swarms. This led many returning Confederate soldiers and other Southerners to appropriate anything which had the character or suspicion of having been Confederate property—for it was subject to confiscation, and if the Southerner did not get it, the Federal Treasury agents would seize it.

[16] *Zachariah Chandler: An Outline Sketch of his Life and Public Services. By the Detroit* Post and Tribune (Detroit, 1880), 300–306. Chandler sold these papers to the United States government for what he paid for them.
[17] Greensboro (Ga.) *Herald,* May 1, 1879.

The brazen dishonesties practiced by these agents almost surpass belief. Said one editor, "The seizure and sale of cotton by Treasury agents at and near the close of the war was probably the most stupendous swindle which ever disgraced our Government." [18] Secretary Hugh McCulloch was forced by his conscience to remark of his brood of agents, "I am sure I sent *some* honest agents South; but it sometimes seems very doubtful whether any of them remained honest very long." [19] The methods of their dishonesties were diverse. Laws and regulations allowed them from 25 per cent to 50 per cent of the proceeds of their seizures; but such profits were insufficient to satiate their cupidity. They sold either to themselves or to others through collusion, for ten to thirty cents a pound cotton worth from sixty cents to $1.20 a pound, and transmitted to the government its proportion of the lower price. In Savannah alone, out of $21,000,000 worth of cotton sold, they handed over to the United States Treasury only $8,000,000. These "rogues and fortune-hunters," [20] who were "privateering on land in time of peace among the vanquished," [21] seized all cotton in sight whether it had belonged to the Confederate government or not, but they could be bribed to desist from taking private cotton. Conversely, now and then they would deface Confederate identification markings and, through agreement with a planter on whose land it might be found, share the profits with him. Many planters honestly owned cotton bargained for by the Confederacy but not received or paid for before the Surrender; and even when cotton had been paid for, the planter repossessed it if possible, for the Confederate bonds he had received for it had now become worthless. An agent in Texas forced a woman to sell for $75 a bale her 400 bales worth $200 each, under threat that he would seize it as Confederate cotton if she did not comply. Another agent who had an interest in a steamboat refused to let a planter move his cotton unless he shipped it on the agent's craft.[22] A Mississippi woman planter wrote Judge Advocate General Joseph Holt that

[18] *Weekly Columbus* (Ga.) *Enquirer*, June 4, 1872.

[19] Whitelaw Reid, *After the War: A Southern Tour, May 1, 1865 to May 1, 1866* (New York, 1866), 204–205.

[20] Trowbridge, *South*, 567–68.   [21] *De Bow's Review*, I (1866), 527.

[22] Walter L. Fleming (ed.), *Documentary History of Reconstruction* (Cleveland, 1906–1907), I, 30.

she hoped her cotton would not be seized as she had never borne arms against the United States, "though she has wished much she was a boy that she might do so." [23] Agents who could not find cotton seized horses and mules as Confederate property, and in some parts of the South they forced planters to pay the old Confederate tax-in-kind—the one tenth of certain farm products.[24]

The two greatest cotton thieves were Simeon Draper, general cotton agent for the Atlantic and Gulf states with headquarters in New York City, and William P. Mellen, agent for the interior with offices in Cincinnati. They seized cotton indiscriminately and then allowed the owner to recover part for a quitclaim on the remainder. This method was called "tolling." Sometimes a planter would find his cotton had to be "tolled" two or three times before it reached market. "Plucking" was another one of their inventions. In grading cotton generous samples from five or six bales would provide a bale of "pluckings." Draper, who had been bankrupt when he received his appointment, became a millionaire after a few years. There were "cotton rings" in all directions. Even respectable banking houses withheld deposits of Federal cotton money until forced by law to disgorge. In 1868 the Treasury Department recovered from Jay Cooke and Company $20,000,000 of cotton money due the government. William E. Chandler, Assistant Secretary of the Treasury, in charge of cotton seizures, entered upon his work poor but emerged worth hundreds of thousands of dollars. Many got rich, few were punished. One unfortunate was fined $200,000 and sentenced to prison for twenty years.

The presumption before the law was that all cotton had been Confederate owned, but any Southerner who could prove his loyalty during the war might receive recompense for his seized cotton. In 1872 Congress, becoming more liberal, passed a law to allow pay for private cotton seized after June 30, 1865, irrespective of the owner's loyalty, and as a result more than 40,000 claimants have received payment for their cotton wrongfully seized. The hope seems destined never to die in the breasts of Southerners that they may yet receive a small fortune for the cotton of their ancestors

[23] R. S. Holt, Yazoo City, Miss., to Joseph Holt, April 12, 1865, in Joseph Holt Papers (Division of Manuscripts, Library of Congress), XLVII, No. 6229.
[24] Fleming (ed.), *Documentary History of Reconstruction*, I, 27.

seized by cotton agents. Of the 5,000,000 bales on hand in 1865, 3,000,000 were seized.

The North came to put almost as great reliance in the power of cotton after the war as the South had done earlier; and though King Cotton had not won the war for the Confederacy, it paid the expenses of the North's rough handling of the South for a decade and a half after the Surrender. The Federal government collected from a prostrate South, through a special cotton tax, $68,000,000. The excuse for taxing cotton appears to have been based on the fact that the South was so desolated that there was nothing else on which to levy a lucrative tax—and since the South had caused the war it should pay for it. Treasury regulations during the war had put a tax on cotton, but not until the spring of 1865 did Congress establish a definite policy when it fixed the levy at two and a half cents a pound, increased to three cents in 1866. This was the most indefensible tax in American history. It was unconstitutional since it was not uniform on farm products and was in fact an export tax; it was unsocial and unwise since it beat down still further an impoverished people; it was levied upon a population still unrepresented in Congress; and it had much the appearance of a tax for revenge. According to a Northerner who had settled in the South, it was "one of Buck shot Stevens crazy hateful schemes" for punishing the South.[25] The best defense for it was the supposition that it was passed on to the consumer and paid by him.

After 1865 the price of cotton steadily declined to the point where the tax amounted to a fifth of the market price. In 1867 when cotton was selling for $65 a bale, $12.50 of this amount was paid to the United States government. Said a Northern settler in Alabama, "Two years cotton planting have ruined two thirds of the Northern men engaged in it, and mostly all of the Southern planters are broken." [26] Indeed, some of the most pronounced opposition to the tax came from Northern planters in the South, not only because it ruined their own chances but also because it worked a vast hardship on the freedmen whom the North was professedly

[25] Willard Warner, Prattville, Ala., to John Sherman, June 21, 1866, in John Sherman Papers (Division of Manuscripts, Library of Congress), CIV, No. 2470.

[26] Warner, Montgomery, Ala., to Benjamin Wade, December 9, 1867, *ibid.*, CXXIV, Nos. 28612–13.

bent on helping. According to a Northern planter in Alabama, the condition of the South was "deplorable—Insolvency and desolation every where" and the tax was much to blame. "It injures, *ruins* the very classes upon which the country depends for its rebuilding." [27] If the white planter did not thrive, how could he offer the freedmen work? It began to dawn on Northerners that they might lose the political support of the Negroes, especially so when a Negro organization in South Carolina demanded that the tax be repealed because it was "unjust and oppressive." [28] Said a friend of the Negro in 1867, "Congress has now given freedmen the ballot, while it takes away much of their bread and bacon." If the Negro had had his way he would have taken the bread instead of the ballot. "They cannot eat ballots, nor wear ballots." [29] Gerrit Smith, whose friendship for Negroes reached back to the time when they were slaves, declared that the small charities done for the Negroes by the Federal government were as nothing compared to the burden of the cotton tax imposed upon them.

The United States Commissioner of Agriculture considered the tax "disastrous and disheartening in the extreme," and to the native Southerner, who had learned to expect no mercies from his conquerors, it was "inexplicable." "We speak plainly," warned a farm editor, "when we say that so long as this course is continued, and human nature is unchanged, those who pursue it, will be hated in peace even worse than they were hated in war; and the indignation and sense of outrage felt by each Southern man, will be more or less intense, as his perceptions of equality and justice are more or less clear." [30] It was this inequality that so embittered Southerners; there was no tax on hay or grain. "Why is there a tax upon Southern cotton and a bounty upon New-England fish?" asked the editor of the *Land We Love.*[31] Another Southern editor replied,

[27] R. N. Barr, Claiborne, Ala., to Sherman, January 19, 1867, *ibid.,* CXXI, Nos. 27990–91.

[28] Greenville (S.C.) *Southern Enterprise,* September 4, 1867. See also, H. H. Armstrong, Notasulga, Ala., to Sherman, December 28, 1867, in Sherman Papers, CXXV, Nos. 28825–26.

[29] *De Bow's Review,* III (1867), 563; D. Heaton, New Bern, N.C., to Sherman, December 19, 1867, in Sherman Papers, CXXV, Nos. 28736–37.

[30] *Southern Cultivator* (Athens, Ga.), XXIV (1866), 144.

[31] *Land We Love, A Monthly Magazine Devoted to Literature, Military History, and Agriculture* (Charlotte, N.C.), IV (1867–1868), 358.

"If a tax of ten cents apiece on every orange raised in New England was levied by Congress it would be submitted to with becoming loyalty, but the same tax on pumpkins or onions would create a revolution." [32] The Southerner did not want relief from the North; he wanted an equal chance to make an honest living. As further proof of the utter iniquity of the law, cotton manufacturers were allowed a drawback equal to the tax, on all cloth they exported.

Despairing of getting the law repealed, planters sought to circumvent it. Since cotton was a curse to the South and agricultural reformers were at that time trying to induce planters to stop raising it, poet Francis O. Ticknor offered this advice:

> *To Congress:*
> *The Memorial of Thomas Grubb.*
> *Tax it! Tax it! don't relax it—*
> *Chain it; stamp it; d—n it, Tax it!*
> *Tax it deaf and dumb and blind—*
> *Out of sight and out of mind!* [33]

When the supply should be exhausted, the Northern cotton-mill men would come to their senses. Others cleverly suggested that, since manufacturing was good business, Southerners should immediately set up factories in every revenue district and manufacture cotton tax-free, for the tax was collected only when it moved out of the district.[34] Unsuccessful attempts were made to have the law declared unconstitutional; but, when in 1867 the South and its destiny passed into the hands of its Northern tormentors, Congress repealed the law, to become effective in February, 1868. For years thereafter unsuccessful efforts were made to have Congress refund the tax; but the impracticability of achieving justice was soon evident, for most of the records of tax payments were in the names of the commission merchants and so the planter was left without proof of his payment of the tax.

Shortly after the outbreak of the Civil War, Congress levied a direct tax of $20,000,000 but, as it could not be enforced in the

[32] Augusta *Weekly Constitutionalist,* April 10, 1867.
[33] *Southern Cultivator,* XXVI (1868), 39.
[34] Augusta *Weekly Constitutionalist,* October 3, 17, 1866; October 9, 1867; February 19, 1868; *De Bow's Review,* II (1866), 527–30.

Confederate states, it was necessary to await a brighter day. As soon as Federal troops got a foothold in the South, tax collectors began their work, seizing for taxes Arlington (Lee's home) and much property on the coast of South Carolina and elsewhere. Not until the Surrender could a concerted tax-collecting effort be made, and as the South was now prostrate, the tax could be collected only by seizing property and selling it. Pathetic sacrifices were worked. One estate worth $15,000 was sold for $300; another worth $24,000 brought $80, the amount of the tax, in each instance. The whole town of Fernandina, Florida, was sold for $10,608, but this sale was later disallowed. Agents collecting this tax engaged in much fraud. Often they bought property for the taxes and then sold it at a great profit. Agents in Florida collected $47,000 at an expense of $53,000! After 1866 the Federal government ceased to try to collect this tax, and in 1872 a law was enacted permitting owners of property still in the hands of the government to reclaim it.

The cost of war was not only expressed in iniquitous and unequal taxes upon the conquered, but also in the withdrawal of pensions from all Confederates who were veterans of past wars. This deprivation extended even to those people who should "manifest a sympathy" for the Confederate cause, and it went so far as to include women—even widows of Revolutionary soldiers. In 1867 a considerable number were restored to the pension rolls "as proof of their continued adhesion [sic] to the Union." [35] Of course, the veterans of the Confederate war never expected a pension, and they long professed to be too proud to accept one if offered; but as time went on Southerners, differing none from many Northerners, opposed the flood of pensions to Northern veterans, which became more corrupt the farther it flowed. Not only unwilling to help the Confederate veteran, but even designing his destruction as far as possible, Congress passed a law in January, 1865, denying the right to practice in Federal courts to anyone who fought for the Confederacy or who sympathized with it.

The South's losses in its human wealth were pathetic. It was forced to skip almost a generation of young men, dead of disease

[35] *American Annual Cyclopaedia and Register of Important Events of the Year 1867* (New York, 1868), 57; *Regulations Relating to Army and Navy Pensions, with Statutes* (Washington, 1871), 62.

or killed on the field of battle—or wounded into economic incompetency. More than a quarter of a million out of a white population of about five million did not return. Black was the prevailing color worn by women, mourning for kindred or simply for the Lost Cause. To surrendering soldiers paroles were given freeing them from arrest or molestation as long as they did not take up arms again, and during the summer of 1865 the Northern military prisons were emptied, though not fast enough to satisfy one Confederate prisoner at Johnson Island, who naïvely wrote in latter May, "I am tired of Prison life." [36] One hundred and seventy-four thousand soldiers were paroled and 60,000 prisoners were let out. Many of them walked back home. The wounded came back generally with the loss of an arm or leg. In some communities at least a third of the veterans lacked a limb. Mississippi spent in 1866 a fifth of her revenues on artificial arms and legs, South Carolina early appropriated $20,000 for this purpose, and fifteen years after the war Georgia was spending $35,000 a year.[37] A Georgian, early swallowing his pride, begged John Sherman, in Congress, to put Confederate veterans on the same basis as Federal soldiers in supplying artificial limbs. On some occasions Southerners with their two good arms were known to wear their coats with an empty sleeve or don military capes to show a sentimental respect for these unfortunates. The poverty of returning or returned veterans forced many of them to wear their grey uniforms with their necessary buttons. Federal authorities in the South frowned upon these buttons as symbols of a rebellious disposition and often caused great inconvenience by removing them. Negro troops took great pleasure in cutting off these buttons, but sometimes not without fatal results. Though military buttons were outlawed, no one seems to have objected to officers using their military titles.

At the end of the war only those Confederates who had been in the military service were protected by paroles; all civilian officials were subject to arrest and if they were important enough they

[36] W. L. Roddy, Johnson Island Prison, to David Faust, Philadelphia, May 28, 1865, in Sherman Papers, LXXXIII, No. 19352.

[37] *Maimed Soldiers in Georgia Supplied with Artificial Limbs, under the Act Approved September 20, 1879* (n.p., n.d.); James W. Garner, *Reconstruction in Mississippi* (New York, 1901), 122–23; Francis B. Simkins and Robert H. Woody, *South Carolina during Reconstruction* (Chapel Hill, 1932), 47.

might well expect it. President Davis and his cabinet fled southward, intent upon setting up a new authority west of the Mississippi or escaping to a foreign country. Governors, Confederate Congressmen, and other officials either awaited quietly at home to be arrested like Alexander H. Stephens or went into hiding like Robert Toombs. Joseph E. Brown, Zebulon B. Vance, and most of the other governors as well as such cabinet members as John H. Reagan, Stephen R. Mallory, and George A. Trenholm were arrested; and some military and naval officers who were declared not to be protected by paroles, such as Admiral Raphael Semmes and General Joseph Wheeler, were held. Judah P. Benjamin, John C. Breckinridge, Matthew F. Maury, and other important Confederates made their escape to foreign countries. Those arrested were imprisoned from Fort Pulaski in the Savannah River to Fort Warren in Boston Harbor, and were held for varying lengths of time.

Davis was looked upon as the greatest prize, although Lincoln felt that it would be fortunate for all concerned if he should escape to a foreign country; but on Lincoln's assassination the picture changed. Now a reward of $100,000 was offered for his arrest as an accomplice of J. Wilkes Booth in his mad act. On May 10 Davis was arrested in Georgia, and for the next few years the Federal government was plagued with the problem of disposing of him.

Booth was killed in a burning barn in Virginia and some of his fellow-conspirators were captured, tried by a military commission, and promptly executed. Many people began immediately to doubt that the man killed was Booth. An unnamed person had seen him in an unnamed foreign country; he had escaped through Florida. Within less than a year the Booth myth was flourishing.

Henry Wirz, who had been in command of the Confederate military prison at Andersonville, was personally charged with the more than 12,000 deaths which took place there, was arrested, tried by a military commission, and hanged. From this time on for a generation, Confederate prison "atrocities" were the most powerful political weapon that could be used in the North in securing Republican majorities.

The army of occupation in the South used military commissions to administer its justice, irrespective of whether the defendant had ever been in a military establishment or the regular courts were open; but in April, 1866, the Supreme Court declared this procedure unconstitutional in the famous *Ex parte* Milligan decision. The first application of this principle was made in the case of James Egan, a South Carolinian eighty years old and more, who had killed a Negro in September, 1865. Though the courts were open, he was tried by a military commission and sentenced to life imprisonment in the penitentiary at Albany, New York. Later he secured a writ of habeas corpus and the Federal Circuit Court in the Northern District of New York freed him.[38] As will appear hereafter, the Federal army was again to institute its military trials in the South, in open defiance of the United States Supreme Court.

The greatest loss that a people can suffer, greater than any material destruction, is their spirit. Some Southerners so suffered, but in the end the mass surmounted their deep despair, and in so doing the South won its greatest victory. At the end of the war the Southerners "stood in silent and submissive apprehension." [39] A brother of Joseph Holt, the Judge Advocate General, wrote him from Mississippi in April, 1865, "Our fields every where lie untilled. Naked chimneys, and charred ruins all over the land mark the spots where happy homes, the seats of refinement and elegance, once stood. Their former inhabitants wander in poverty and exile, wherever chance or charity affords them shelter or food. Childless old age, widows, and helpless orphans beggared and hopeless, are every where." [40] A traveler going from Chattanooga to Atlanta did not see a smile on a human face.[41] An editor envied the soldiers who had fallen and now slept the long sleep: "Those who strew flowers over the graves of departed heroes will feel that the quiet dreamers in the dust are far happier than those who still walk the rugged paths of a distracted world. . . . For them the wreath of wild flowers, for us the crown of thorns." [42] Disconsolately a Texan

[38] *The Federal Cases, Comprising Cases Argued and Determined in the Circuit and District Courts of the United States* (St. Paul, 1894–1897), Bk. 8, pp. 367–68.

[39] *American Annual Cyclopaedia . . . 1866* (New York, 1867), 511–12; Edward McPherson, *The Political History of the United States of America during the Period of Reconstruction* (Washington, 1875), 17; Reid, *Southern Tour*, 136.

[40] R. S. Holt, Yazoo City, Miss., to Holt, April 11, 1865, in Holt Papers, LXVII, No. 6226.

[41] John H. Kennaway, *On Sherman's Track; or, The South after the War* (London, 1867), 106.

[42] Augusta *Weekly Constitutionalist*, April 29, 1868.

envied "those who fell" and declared that it "would have been far better for us had our whole people been exterminated, fighting to the last for their rights." [43] The poet Paul Hamilton Hayne, believing that Northerners would hate the South forever, wondered "why in the mysterious providence of God we were allowed to be conquered by them." It was "the puzzle of puzzles." [44] As for pathetic old Edmund Ruffin, he would not struggle with the puzzle; having been denied the boon of a soldier's death, he himself ended his life. In the eyes of a Northern editor, the South's defeat was a piece of retribution and it should so consider it and "meet us as penitents in sackcloth and ashes." [45]

The old gentility and culture of Southern aristocracy—"proud, rich and cultivated" even in the eyes of its enemy—was gone, as completely swept away as the nobility in the French Revolution. Their splendid mansions were burnt down, their plantations were divided among the Negroes, and the owners were wanderers upon the face of the earth, glad to earn a dollar to keep themselves from starving. The proud Wade Hamptons had held their estate for three generations and now saw it fall into the hands of a South Carolina turncoat. A Georgia aristocrat, English-born, lost his fortune of $160,000; but undaunted he returned to his place of business in New Orleans as a cotton merchant, only to find that he could not compete with the new business methods. Not being able to make money enough to pay his office rent, he longed to go "to some place where I would be unknown and cultivate a small patch of ground for food until the wheels of life would stand still." Forced to economize to the utmost extent and at the same time keep up appearances, with scarcely the semblance of hope left as a support, he refused all social invitations as he would not develop obligations which he could never repay. Another old aristocrat now made his living raising flowers and selling them, while another peddled tea and molasses. [46] Another took to flower gar-

43 Louis T. Wigfall Papers (typescripts in University of Texas Library), May 19, 1867.

44 David K. Jackson (ed.), *American Studies in Honor of William Kenneth Boyd, by Members of the Americana Club of Duke University* (Durham, 1940), 232.

45 *Nation* (New York), III (1866), 31.

46 For examples cited in this paragraph, see *ibid.*, I (1865), 172; James S. Pike, *The Prostrate State: South Carolina under Negro Government* (New York, 1935), 107, 118–19; Godfrey Barnsley, New Orleans, to H. S. Gilmour, November 16, 1865; Barnsley,

dening, not for profit but as a retreat from an unkind present, remarking, "There is a great satisfaction in gardening as plants are always grateful for any kindness bestowed upon them." Carl Schurz on his trip through the South saw a distinguished-looking gentleman cutting down a fine old tree in the yard of a mansion in Mississippi, and on inquiry found that the gentleman owned the estate and was cutting wood to sell to passing steamboats. With a sad smile the woodchopper remarked, "I must live." A class of people who had made living an art was vanishing. As their fiery spirits faded, their custom of dueling disappeared, and with economic privations Southern hospitality was now forced to become more a tradition than a fact.

There were some now and then who had will-o'-the-wisp hopes of enjoying wealth again and others of experiencing it for the first time. Such were those who bore the name Jennings, for old William Jennings, of Birmingham, England, long ago had died without a will, and by this time the property he left was estimated to be worth $400,000,000. The Southern Jenningses formed a Jennings Family Association to keep alive this hope of getting their part and unwittingly to enrich the pocketbooks of lawyers.[47]

As the aristocrat had always had his detractors within his own gates, so there were some Southerners who looked with no great commiseration upon his fall. Said one, "Railing at the stirring and industrious who have got above them will do them no good. Going back to the past and summoning up the shades of illustrious ancestors will be of no avail. . . . To the hundreds of thousands of those descendants of high but broken-down families that are now bewailing their hard lot, we say, go to work!"[48] Another declared that the old idea, "to be wet-nursed by a negro wench made the

---

New Orleans, to daughter Julia, December 26, 1866; June 9, 1867; Barnsley, New Orleans, to Mrs. Hagleton, April 17, 1867; Barnsley, New Orleans, to George Barnsley, April 11, 1870, in Godfrey Barnsley Papers (University of Georgia Library); *Reminiscences of Carl Schurz*, III, 198–99. Thomas P. Collins, Crockett, Tex., wrote Thaddeus Stevens, February 19, 1866, telling how he had been worth $100,000 in 1861 and was now unable to pay his debts. He begged Stevens to treat the South honorably. Thaddeus Stevens Papers (Division of Manuscripts, Library of Congress), VI, No. 53871.

[47] Augusta (Ga.) *Daily Chronicle and Sentinel,* January 26, 1876.
[48] Augusta *Weekly Constitutionalist,* August 25, 1875.

gentleman," was now exploded and that "the sooner the South recognizes this fact, the better it will be for her." [49]

Now was the day when a new start was to be made by all— those formerly high and those formerly low. New leaders would arise, whose positions were not to be made by family trees, coats of arms, or wealth. It was neither unwise nor unmanly to acquiesce in what could not be remedied and to accept with as much cheer as possible the fortunes of war. Apart from the terrific task of adjusting the social fabric across racial lines, there was to be a new social order among white people. According to a Southern optimist, "in every people there is an inherent, invincible faculty of productive energy that neither the fiercest passions of man nor the mightiest convulsions of nature can overcome. . . . The child thinks the rainy day will never come to an end, and yet on the morrow the same child sports in the sunshine." [50]

From the standpoint of being invaded it was fortunate that the South was more agricultural than industrial, more rural than urban. Thus it suffered less than if its wealth had been concentrated in cities and factories. Its land could not be destroyed by war, its rivers still ran to the sea, and the sun still rose and set. It still had its ante bellum climate, summer and winter still followed each other as of old. The trees and the grass still grew, and seeds continued to sprout. Nature and nature's laws had not been disturbed. If the South would not lose its will to work and repair, its future was still secure. A planter in answer to a politician who had told him that Congress was about to pass a dreadful law against the South, asked, "Will it keep cotton from growing?" "No," said the politician. "Will it kill the corn?" asked the planter. "No," was the reply. "Then d——n the law," exclaimed the planter. [51]

Though Northern politicians and reformers might call themselves holy and the South evil, there were many other Northerners who had never warped their nature nor lost their human kindness. Though Santa Claus might become for a time a stranger to Southern children and those formerly opulent become "reconciled to

[49] Atlanta *Daily New Era*, October 3, 1867.

[50] Augusta (Ga.) *Daily Constitutionalist*, August 31, 1865.

[51] Augusta *Daily Chronicle and Sentinel*, May 18, 1871.

bread and water," there grew up organizations, in North and South, which gave much to relieve suffering and hunger. Conditions were worst for some months following the Surrender and again during the year 1867, when a mild panic was sweeping the nation, and all classes were almost equally hard-hit—aristocrats, middle class, poor whites, and Negroes.

Aid was given first by the United States Army, which divided its supplies with the needy, and then by the Freedmen's Bureau; but relief was soon coming from people as widespread as was commiseration for human suffering and ability to help. Famine conditions in 1867 called forth the greatest efforts. Holding meetings to arouse interest, addressed by Horace Greeley, Henry Ward Beecher, and Peter Cooper, the New York Southern Relief Association sent thousands of bushels of corn into the South; the New York Southern Famine Relief Commission raised $200,000; Philadelphia set up its Southern Famine Relief Fund and called in vain upon Congress to appropriate $1,000,000; St. Louis raised over $126,000; Baltimore held a Southern Relief Fair and collected over $100,000; from California came $45,000 in gold and from Kentucky much corn; and Dr. J. Marion Sims, a South Carolinian in France, sent his check for $1,000. Relief organizations in the North and in the border states raised almost $3,000,000 during the two years following the war. The Southern states themselves, as soon as they could organize their governments, made large appropriations for relief.[52]

A more socially-minded Congress than America had at this time would have made appropriations for relief; but, dominated by such leaders as Benjamin F. Butler and Thaddeus Stevens, bent upon their plans of revenge, it refused all appeals. Sarcastically the New York *Times* observed that Congress was too busy "to give much attention to such commonplace matters as starvation and distress. We want the Southern people well under martial law; we want to make sure that all their negroes have the right to vote, and

[52] *Land We Love*, II (1866–1867), 378–82; *De Bow's Review*, I (1866), 663–64; III (1867), 493–94; IV (1867), 160; *American Freedman, A Monthly Journal Devoted to the Promotion of Freedom, Industry, Education, and Christian Morality in the South* (New York), I (1866), 165; Sandersville *Central Georgian*, May 1, 1867; Little Rock *Weekly Arkansas Gazette*, October 30, 1866; J. G. de Roulhac Hamilton (ed.), *The Correspondence of Jonathan Worth* (Raleigh, 1909), II, 904 ff.; Alice B. Keith, "White Relief in North Carolina, 1865–1867," in *Social Forces* (Chapel Hill), XVII (1938–1939), 337–55.

then we will enquire whether they are starving or not. . . . The best way is, now we have them down, to keep them down. . . . If we should feed them we would make them insolent, and they might think it unreasonable in us to stick bayonets in them afterwards, in order to make them sincerely sorry for their rebellion." [53] When government was later restored in the Southern states according to Congressional desires and Radicals were in charge of states, then Congress made appropriations for relief (in 1874); but it was conveniently near election time and took on more the appearance of an attempt to influence votes. In Alabama relief for spring flood damages was not distributed until the fall political campaign, and one agent told sufferers that they could receive aid only if they voted the Republican ticket. Another charged each Negro a twenty-five-cent fee and gave him two pounds of bacon which could have been purchased for less than that price.

The South suffered heavy damages both in spirit and in property, but it was able in time to repair both. Its woes were in a great part incident to war and conquest and not due to the malice of invading armies. Wars are no respecters of persons, either of victors or vanquished. Southerners were not consumed with bitterness for Federal commanders, excepting Sherman and Butler, nor for the soldiers who followed them. In fact, they placed some of the blame upon a few of their own commanders, and especially did many who had come under the sway of General Wheeler condemn him and declare that he and his men were the greatest "set of thieves and cutthroats out of jail." Yet there was long a vocal element in the South who laid all their troubles on the war and who did not realize that the South would have had hard times even if there had been no war. They did not take into consideration the fact that the North also had suffered. Time has always been a great healer and with its passing Southerners were able to forget their war enemies—and a new generation was to forget largely the war itself. The ills of Reconstruction, which the South now could only faintly sense, were destined to come in full measure to grow and rankle when memories of the war had faded into a glorious experience. Congressional Reconstruction brought for the South what

[53] Quoted in Augusta *Weekly Constitutionalist*, February 27, 1867; and in Americus (Ga.) *Tri-Weekly Sumter Republican*, February 23, 1867.

the Civil War was never able to accomplish—unification of the people. Had Southerners been allowed a normal existence, more than likely the bitter internal dissensions of the war would have left after peace strong party conflicts—and there might never have developed the aroma of the Lost Cause. It is one of the ironies of history that the term Reconstruction, which the Southerners so frequently used during the war to mean a return to the old Union as it was and which they would have been glad to accept at the Surrender, was afterwards made to mean something so grotesquely different as to cause the term to be abhorred for generations.

CHAPTER II

THE WAY BACK

THE SURRENDER was a term early used by Southerners to mark the end of their efforts to set up a new nation, but Davis on his retreat southward after the fall of Richmond had not yet accepted that meaning. He would have broken up the Confederate armies into guerrilla bands and have harried the country into honorable terms for the South. Lee refused to listen to such a plan, and General William J. Hardee rather than accept it said, "So help me God, I am willing and ready to fight to put an end to it"—a statement applauded thus by a Georgia editor: "His sentiment is characteristically noble, and will be honestly re-echoed by every law abiding citizen in the South." [1] Balked in this move, Davis, who had a premonition of what was in store for the South, hoped to escape to the regions beyond the Mississippi, where Edmund Kirby Smith still commanded large forces, and continue the Confederacy there. At least one Southerner agreed: "Let our soldiers look to the great West, where Liberty and Right are yet unclouded by defeat or dissension, and where the star of the Southern Confederacy is as bright now as on the night of the first Manassas." [2] On May 10, 1865, Davis was captured and the Confederacy collapsed without the protection of a treaty of peace.

In so quickly giving up the new nation which they had set up, Southerners were not to pursue for generations a course like that which the Irish, Poles, or Czechs had taken. Four years were not sufficient to hallow the Confederacy and make of it an undying ideal. Southerners were of the same race and language as the rest of the United States, and they had a common heritage. They were

[1] Augusta *Weekly Constitutionalist*, May 24, 1865. See also, *Southern Cultivator*, XXIII (1865), 83.

[2] Augusta *Weekly Constitutionalist*, April 26, 1865.

now ready to resume their position in the old government, and it is a remarkable fact that not one Southerner thereafter took up arms against the United States. "We are thoroughly whipped . . . ; and now we want you to quit reproaching us," was the common feeling, and a Northern observer agreed that the "war spirit is gone, and no fury can re-enliven it."[3] John H. Reagan, in Fort Warren Prison, begged his fellow Texans to accept the new day; other leaders, civil and military, newspaper editors, and conventions of the people expressed the same feelings. A farm editor advised, *"Let the war end!* with all its bloodshed and horrors; and let the glorious and thrice-blessed arts of Peace and Industry flourish! Let us trust in God, and go forth bravely to conquer the difficulties of the 'shadowy Future!' We can soon be a great and prosperous people, if we WILL be so!"[4] The nobleness of General Grant at Appomattox "won more hearts to his cause than would a hundred victories; and its record will be the brightest page in his historic fame," thought a Georgian.[5] A meeting of the citizens of Clarksville, Tennessee, declared that they accepted "frankly and honorably the new position established by the termination of the war," and they repelled "with contempt and indignation" any feeling that they were less honorable because they had remained true to their pledge to fight for independence, "claiming that steadfast faithfulness to a failing cause is a better ground for confidence in their present engagements, than would have been afforded by a vacillating and double-faced subserviency, prompted by the hopes of emolument and fear of loss."[6] Said a Floridian, "We all, North, South, East and West, have *one country, one destiny, one duty.*"[7]

The evidence of Southern surrender was not *ex parte.* Federal military officers and Northern travelers agreed that the South had honorably laid down its arms. The commander of Florida found "only the most entire spirit of submission" to his authority; a general in Georgia was sure that "an officer, without arms or escort, could arrest any man in the State"; and the Secretary of War declared in November, 1865, that national authority was "effectually and peacefully exercised over the whole territory of the United

[3] Andrews, *South since the War*, 4.   [4] *Southern Cultivator*, XXIII (1865), 137.
[5] Augusta *Weekly Constitutionalist*, May 24, 1865.
[6] Memphis *Argus*, October 17, 1865.   [7] *De Bow's Review*, I (1866), 92.

States." [8] A Federal agent in Mobile said the Southerners were whipped "& own it and are ready to do any thing even to negro suffrage (which they hate) for a return to the prosperity of old"; [9] and *mirabile dictu* to the ears of Southerners, Harriet Beecher Stowe, after spending some time in Florida, could say that "the Southern people are no more inclined to resist the laws or foster the spirit of rebellion than Vermont is. They desire only peace and the restoration of the Union." [10] Another Northerner, after traveling through the South, said with a touch of pathos, "The South has had enough of war for a long time to come; it has supped full of horrors. The habiliments of mourning, which one sees everywhere in its towns and cities, will cast their dark shadow upon any future attempt at secession, long after they have been put away in the silent wardrobes of the past." [11] And the common story was the docility of Confederate soldiers; a Federal general enthusiastically declared that "these Rebel soldiers are an honor to the American name." [12]

There was now generous appreciation of the South's surrender, even by its former worst enemies. Henry Ward Beecher in the flag-raising ceremony in Charleston in April, 1865, begged the North, the moment the Southerners dropped their arms, to "stretch out your own honest right hand to greet them. Recall to them the old days of kindness." [13] And Gerrit Smith said, "The South has suffered enough, and she deserves to be soothed and comforted, and no more afflicted, by us." [14]

It would be too great a strain on human nature to expect that everybody, North and South, had these generous feelings, or that the South enjoyed its defeat. It could not be expected that Southerners would give up their manly feelings or their innermost convictions; they had never thought of surrendering their honor. "Is

[8] "Condition of the South," *Senate Executive Documents*, 39 Cong., 1 Sess., No. 2. Serial No. 1237, p. 53; "Report of the Secretary of War," 1865. *House of Representatives Executive Documents*, 39 Cong., 1 Sess., No. 1, Serial No. 1249, p. 2.

[9] F. W. Kellogg, Mobile, Ala., to Zachariah Chandler, June 19, 1865, in Zachariah Chandler Papers (Division of Manuscripts, Library of Congress), III, Nos. 617–18.

[10] *Scott's Monthly Magazine* (Atlanta), VI (1868), 492.

[11] Trowbridge, *South*, 585.

[12] Reid, *Southern Tour*, 206.

[13] Lyman B. Stowe, *Saints, Sinners and Beechers* (Indianapolis, 1934), 294–96.

[14] Fleming (ed.), *Documentary History of Reconstruction*, I, 142.

it possible," asked editor James D. B. De Bow, "that the North demands a miracle? In the conflict of arms, must *convictions* go down as well as *standards?* Can men, indeed, be made, as Hudibras has it

> '. . . *Orthodox*
> *By blows and knocks?*'

I may *think* treason every day in the year, but without an *overt act,* there can be no traitor!" [15] In the words of a South Carolinian, the Yankees have "left me one inestimable privilege—to hate 'em. I git up at half-past four in the morning, and sit up till twelve at night, to hate 'em." [16] Northerners could well understand that Southerners did not like being conquered, nor was it reasonable to expect that they should; yet editor Edwin L. Godkin of the *Nation* thought the South was too obedient to be honest, that it was attempting to disarm the North for ulterior reasons, because the friendly attitude of the South contradicted "all the teachings of history and all our experience of human nature." [17] Thus, indeed, was it hard to please all the South's critics. Charles Étienne Gayarré, the Louisiana historian, spurning the duplicity charges, declared, "There never has been in us any marked treachery, or sneaking equivocation." [18]

For fear Southerners might appear too agreeable, some tormenters hoped to goad them into violent action or language by forcing them to salute the United States flag or walk under it, to prove such statements as these: "They are more bitter than ever," said of Louisianians; or of Georgians, "there is [sic] more rebels in the state now than when the state seceded." A Federal agent in Virginia made this analysis of those who denounced the Yankees: "First—Women, whose tongues are busier than their hands—second—old men whose ideas have become crystallized so that they cannot conceive of anything new—third—Fools whom everybody knows to be fools." [19]

[15] *De Bow's Review,* II (1866), 107. [16] Trowbridge, *South,* 577.

[17] *Nation,* I (1865), 516.

[18] Charles Gayarré, New Orleans, to Charles Sumner, February 28, 1866, in Charles Sumner Papers (Widener Library, Harvard University), Box 77, No. 58.

[19] Michael Hahn, New Orleans, to Sumner, October 5, 1865, *ibid.,* Box 74, No. 137; L. Black, La Fayette, Ga., to Stevens, December 18, 1865, in Stevens Papers, V, No.

A penetrating test of what was in the Southerner's heart was to be found in his attitude toward the assassination of Lincoln. This crime produced widespread sadness over the South; it was a "dreadful crime" and Booth was an "atrocious assassin." "Mr. Lincoln had, to a certain extent," said a Georgia editor, "won upon our people; they believed in him they would find a lenient judge and strong protector, and sorrowed all the more for him when he fell, cruelly murdered." [20] A Northerner who wandered widely over the former Confederacy seeking "The South as it is," declared, "I have never heard Mr. Lincoln mentioned by any Southerner except in terms of respect and liking." [21] Yet, some must have rejoiced.

President Andrew Johnson, being a Southerner, had a fundamental understanding of the South. He, therefore, needed no special investigations before formulating and proceeding with his Southern policy; but to provide himself with the latest information he sent agents to the South during the first year after the war. The first to leave was Carl Schurz, reformer to the extent of revolutionist, German-born, and lacking a common sense produced by American upbringing. Flighty in mind, he consulted through a medium the spirits of Schiller and Lincoln, and was informed by the latter why Johnson had summoned him to Washington and also that he would later be a United States Senator. Beginning with a prejudice against Johnson's views, he was soon startled by learning that the South was "not impressed with any sense of its criminality" and that it did not see that all its old ways must be made new—that a social and political revolution was under way. The Negro must have the right to vote to help along the revolution, he believed. In no part of the civilized world was there "such an accumulation of anarchical elements as [in] the South." Having already exposed most of his views and findings in the newspapers before returning, he received a cold reception from the President, who did not even ask him for a written report. Unasked, he wrote

---

53414; J. W. Sharp, Superintendent of Freedmen's Bureau, Dinwiddie Courthouse, Va., to Stevens, February 9, 1866, *ibid.*, VI, No. 53832; Myrta L. Avary, *Dixie after the War* (Boston, 1937), 22.

20 Augusta *Weekly Constitutionalist*, September 27, 1865; Avary, *Dixie after the War*, 85.

21 *Nation*, I (1865), 110.

one which Johnson's enemies in Congress called for, to be used against the President.[22]

A little later, Benjamin C. Truman, the President's New England secretary, spent eight months in the South. He found practically no hostility there against the North; Congressional Radicals were not interested in this report. In November, 1865, General Grant made a hurried trip south as far as Georgia to supplement an already rich understanding of the South. He found a "very fine feeling manifested" and thought that the South should be entrusted with its government as soon as possible. These views did not please Congress, but Grant's standing made it impolitic to say so. Harvey M. Watterson, father of "Marse Henry," the famous newspaper editor, also made a trip into the South for the President, and found conditions favorable to Southern restoration.[23]

One of the foremost characteristics of a civilized people is its need and desire for government. It was a fearful sight to see law and order disintegrate with the collapse of the Confederate armies; the land was filled with rumors of foreign interventions, of treaties of peace—nothing was too wild to be believed. Sherman's original terms of surrender offered to Joseph E. Johnston looked to a continuation of the state officials under the old Confederacy, but such terms were disallowed in Washington. Yet governors acting along these lines called their legislatures together to provide for conventions to repeal secession ordinances or to send commissioners to Washington to make terms. Incoming Federal troops prevented the legislatures from meeting except in Mississippi, where the legislators were speedily dispersed. In South Carolina some people, believing that old things had passed away "and all things have become new," called for new men to keep government going and

[22] "Condition of the South," *loc. cit.,* 37; *Reminiscences of Carl Schurz,* III, 155–56, 201–209; Fleming (ed.), *Documentary History of Reconstruction,* I, 55. Schurz landed at Hilton Head, South Carolina, July 15, and visited South Carolina, Georgia, Alabama, Mississippi, and Louisiana.

[23] "Report of Benjamin C. Truman," *Senate Executive Documents,* 39 Cong., 1 Sess., No. 43, Serial No. 1237, pp. 1–14; Fleming (ed.), *Documentary History of Reconstruction,* I, 29, 44; William A. Dunning, *Reconstruction, Political and Economic, 1865–1877* (New York, 1907), 49–50; *Ku Klux Conspiracy,* I, 31; "Condition of the South," *loc. cit.,* 106–108. Truman arrived in Alabama in September, 1865, and spent nearly eight months in the South, visiting all the Confederate states except Virginia, North Carolina, and South Carolina.

warned that it should be "no reproach to say of a man that you have never heard of him before," while others thought people in high position were "the ones to inaugurate a movement which . . . [would] end in arousing the whole State into action in regard to the subject of re-union." [24]

To prevent anarchy the army of occupation marched in and dispersed itself in small groups widely over the country with each state comprising a department under a major general. Even if the army had been forbearing it would have had difficulty in preserving order everywhere; but with soldiers singing "John Brown's Body" and exciting the Negroes, and with a previously submerged lawless white element now unrestrained, for a short interim there was little law and order in some parts of the South.

At the end of the war the tendency was for the best element in the Federal army to get mustered out first, leaving a less reliable soldiery to police the South. Many of these troops remaining were Negroes, the number in October, 1865, amounting to 85,000. Many of them were scattered widely over the South where they became almost without exception a vicious influence. Elated over their high station, their uniforms and guns, they took special delight in insulting white people and in instilling dangerous notions into the heads of the freedmen. Occasionally they had bloody clashes with the whites and ravished white women. In Nashville they collided with the police and were disarmed and turned over to the provost marshal; in Beaufort, North Carolina, a Negro soldier raped a white girl and was arrested and sent to Fort Macon near by where other Negro troops threatened to turn the guns of the fort on the city; and near Augusta, Georgia, marauding troops demolished the home and threatened the lives of a family who objected to the Negroes drinking out of the well bucket instead of the proffered gourd dipper. In Newberry, South Carolina, a Confederate soldier returning after the war to his Texas home was beset by Negro troops and murdered because he attempted to protect two white girls from their insults.[25]

[24] Charleston *Courier*, April 24, 25, May 3, 1865.

[25] *Harper's Weekly* (New York), X (1866), 442; "Report of the Secretary of War," 1865, *loc. cit.*, 53; Trowbridge, *South*, 251; Andrews, *South since the War*, 206; Avary, *Dixie after the War*, 141, 377–87; Augusta *Weekly Constitutionalist*, January 3, 10, February 21, 1866; Charles W. Ramsdell, *Reconstruction in Texas* (New York, 1910),

Southerners felt especially aggrieved that they should be thus humiliated by their former slaves and by self-obtruding blacks from the North. Was it to show the Southern people that a fundamental revolution was in the making for them? Even Northerners felt the shame of it. Said one, "I am at a loss to see what possible good their presence here is now. If to humble the Southern pride, that end has been fully accomplished. I have heard black soldiers make the most insulting remarks to Southerners, who are too glad to get by with only that to take notice of them." [26] General Grant, seeing no good purpose served in having Negro troops in the South, advised their removal. Before the end of 1866 practically all had been withdrawn.

The most immediate problem confronting the South as well as the government in Washington was to set the Southern states to functioning again as members of the Union. Lincoln, in common with other Northerners during the war, had held that a state could not secede; the Confederate states had merely refused to perform their duties as members of the Union. In line with this doctrine Lincoln had in 1862 tried to re-establish Federal authority in Tennessee, Louisiana, and Arkansas by appointing military governors; and Louisiana elected two Congressmen, who were seated. To set up more definite regulations for rebuilding loyal state governments, Lincoln issued a proclamation on December 8, 1863, granting pardons to all who would take an oath of allegiance, excepting the more important Confederate leaders, and declaring that when one-tenth the number who had voted in the Presidential election of 1860 should establish a loyal government in a state, it would be recognized. Tennessee, Louisiana, and Arkansas set up governments under this plan, but Congressional leaders who disagreed with this easy plan denied them recognition by refusing to admit their Congressmen and to count their votes in the Presidential election of 1864. In fact, Benjamin Wade and Henry Winter Davis devised a more difficult plan in opposition to Lin-

82; Garner, *Reconstruction in Mississippi,* 104 ff.; James S. Allen, *Reconstruction: The Battle for Democracy (1865–1876)* (New York, 1937), 56; Nashville *Republican Banner,* January 10, 13, 1866.

[26] *Nation,* I (1865), 393.

coln. Therefore, by the end of the war there had been no completion of the political reconstructing of any of the states, which Congress would recognize, and there had been no agreement as to how it should be done. One of Lincoln's last acts was to suggest after Appomattox that the Confederate legislature of Virginia meet and take the state out of the war; but, as this move was later interpreted, it did not mean that the Confederate state government in Virginia would be recognized.

The case of Virginia was peculiar. When this state was disrupted in 1863 by the admission of West Virginia, the so-called loyal government of Virginia, which had been functioning in what had now become West Virginia, moved to a small area surrounding Alexandria and there ridiculously paraded itself as Virginia under the governorship of Francis Pierpont—ignoring, of course, the Confederate state government in Richmond. Lincoln recognized this government as Virginia and after his assassination President Johnson took the same position.

Now with the war over and Lincoln dead, the constitutional status of the former Confederate states was as much disputed as ever. Various theories were advanced, differing according to their advocates' degree of hostility to the South. The South was well satisfied now to accept the old Lincoln theory that the states had never been out of the Union; thereby they would enjoy from the beginning the inestimable advantage of being under the protection of the Constitution. Johnson held this doctrine, often called the Presidential theory. Another idea, slightly differing and described by its name was the suspended animation theory. Those who wanted less constitutional protection for the seceded states—as Charles Sumner—adopted what they called the state suicide theory, which they held would throw the states back into a territorial status. Such extremists as Thaddeus Stevens argued that the states, having lost the war, became conquered provinces; they could claim no rights whatsoever. How bitterly the South looked upon those enemies who had turned upon their former doctrine and now declared that the states had been out of the Union and still were out! "Such an assertion," said a Tennessee editor, "would have sent Northern men to some dungeon three years ago, and yet these ranting maniacs in the halls of Congress in the strictest rules of parliamentary order and Congressional rhetoric now assert their 'treason.' " [27]

Just as the war had begun when Congress was not in session, so it ended; and just as Lincoln had waited three months before he allowed a special session of that body to meet, so Johnson waited eight months for the regular session to assemble. Neither was anxious to be bothered by Congress. Recognizing Virginia, Tennessee, Louisiana, and Arkansas as already provided for, Johnson, being advised that Lincoln's old proclamation of December 8, 1863, was now insufficient, issued on May 29 a new amnesty proclamation. It was much like Lincoln's in excluding the high Confederate leaders from pardon; but it differed in having a greater number of excepted classes, fourteen in all, and especially in the exception from pardon of all Confederates worth more than $20,000. By its terms it made pardons available for the great mass of Southerners if they simply took an oath to support the Federal government. The oath was generally administered by army officers, though county officials might also do so. People flocked forward in such numbers as to make taking the oath appear a pleasant little exercise. Men, women, and children without regard to age or previous conditions swore allegiance and received their certificates as souvenirs of the occasion.

To a business or professional man a pardon was of the greatest importance; without one he was completely estopped. He could not buy or sell, preach a sermon or practice law, apply for a copyright or patent, vote or participate in the government in any fashion, or be certain if he married that it was legal, and he could not recover his property if it had been confiscated. The proclamation provided that those denied general amnesty should receive pardons directly from the President if their cases were found to merit them. Applicants must first be recommended by persons of prominence. Those most often vouching for applicants were governors of states, military officers (sometimes by General Grant), United States Supreme Court Justices, United States Senators, prominent Southern Unionists, and even now and then by the President. Applications next went to the United States Attorney General who made his recommendation to the President, and if

[27] Memphis *Daily Bulletin*, December 12, 1866.

the latter agreed he directed the Secretary of State to issue pardons. This circuitous route made it possible to buy influence from someone along the line and as a result a suspicion of corruption was sometimes cast on this humanitarian activity. Accompanying these applications were long letters of explanation which might be a manly defense or in a few instances a recantation. Undoubtedly the President must have got a secret satisfaction out of receiving the obeisance of former proud Southerners who had made him in his younger days feel keenly their high position. Out of the more than 15,000 applications, Johnson granted about 13,500 before general pardon legislation or proclamations intervened, and more than half of those granted went to people who were begging forgiveness for owning more than $20,000 worth of property.[28]

Expecting through his pardon proclamation to build a loyal people on whom to base his restored state governments, the President as commander in chief of the Federal armies immediately appointed a provisional governor for North Carolina and during the next two months provided the other six former Confederate states with provisional governors—Virginia, Tennessee, Louisiana, and Arkansas being considered already reconstructed. All were Southerners identified with the states over which they were to rule, but they were men whose Union principles had been evident during the war. Only one had ever held a Confederate position, Judge Benjamin F. Perry of South Carolina. They were in a sense military governors and their salaries were in most instances paid by the War Department.[29]

[28] Jonathan T. Dorris, "Pardon Seekers and Brokers: A Sequel of Appomattox," in *Journal of Southern History* (Baton Rouge), I (1935), 276–77, 284; "Pardons by the President," *House of Representatives Executive Documents*, 40 Cong., 2 Sess., No. 16, Serial No. 1330; L. York, White Hall, La., to General Lorenzo Thomas, May 22, 1866, in Andrew Johnson Papers (Division of Manuscripts, Library of Congress), XCV, Nos. 11162–63; Jonathan T. Dorris, "Pardoning the Leaders of the Confederacy," in *Mississippi Valley Historical Review* (Cedar Rapids), XV (1928–1929), 3–6, 14; C. Mildred Thompson, *Reconstruction in Georgia, Economic, Social, Political, 1865–1872* (New York, 1915), 118. These pardon papers are still closed to the public, out of consideration for the descendants of the applicants as well as to protect the reputations of certain contemporary Northerners. They are now in The National Archives.

[29] William M. Robinson, Jr., *Justice in Grey* (Cambridge, 1941), 602–603; "Provisional Governors of States," *Senate Executive Documents*, 39 Cong., 1 Sess., No. 26, Serial No. 1237, p. 3. Johnson appointed the following provisional governors: William W. Holden, North Carolina; Benjamin F. Perry, South Carolina; James Johnson,

The duty of these military governors was to maintain as much formal rule as possible until they could organize constitutional conventions to accept the results of the war and set going new state governments. After taking the oath of allegiance, most local and state officials continued in office during this period. Who should vote was a question of great moment at this time. Chief Justice Salmon P. Chase, who made a trip through the South immediately after the war, came back obsessed with the same idea which he had before he left—that the Negroes should be allowed the suffrage. Other visionaries thought so, and some Southerners, like Reagan, believed that though it would be a dangerous move, it would be less perilous ultimately, as a refusal might call down upon the South the full vengeance of a Congress dominated by Radicals. The plan of universal suffrage and universal amnesty was now beginning to be heard. President Johnson, a Southerner, feeling that it might be well for the same reason to allow the most intelligent Negroes to vote, finally decided against Negro suffrage.[30] He stated in his proclamation appointing provisional governors that the suffrage should be the same in each state as it had been before secession. Four years of extreme Unionism and exposure to the North had not changed Johnson's fundamental understanding of the South and its Negro problem.

With only white people who had taken the oath of allegiance voting, all the provisional-government states except Texas elected constitutional conventions which met and ended their work before November, 1865. Their immediate task was to accept the results of the war which Johnson had decided upon: to repeal (or declare null) their secession ordinances, free their slaves, and repudiate their war debts. All agreed except South Carolina, which refused to repudiate its debts. Debt repudiation had both its advantages and disadvantages. It would teach future generations not to attempt another war of disruption and it would free the present generation of a great financial burden—as an instance, Georgia would be relieved of $18,000,000 of her $20,000,000 debt. Yet

Georgia; William Marvin, Florida; Lewis E. Parsons, Alabama; William L. Sharkey, Mississippi; and Andrew J. Hamilton, Texas.

[30] Fleming (ed.), *Documentary History of Reconstruction,* I, 174; Ramsdell, *Recon struction in Texas,* 88; Memphis *Daily Bulletin,* December 12, 1866.

repudiation set a dangerous example for the future, and it well might weaken a state's financial credit; and more particularly in this instance it would work a social and economic revolution. by bringing about the destruction of the Southern upper classes who held this debt. Most of the states bitterly contested it, yet Texas, late in holding her convention, repudiated not only her war debt but also her civil debt, unrelated to the war.[31]

Dealing with the secession ordinances cost no money but it affected state pride. Long contests took place over the wording of the repeal measures, whether to consider secession null and void from the beginning, which would dishonor the Confederate tradition, or declare it no longer operative. North Carolina declared secession null and void; Mississippi, Texas, South Carolina, and others merely repealed their ordinances. Freeing the slaves was merely agreeing with an accomplished fact; but the wording of the clauses was important in any future demand for compensation. Though Lincoln had always been willing to pay for the slaves, the South had good reason to believe that Congress never would have agreed. Convinced of its justice, yet the South soon forgot this unpaid debt.

Now was an excellent opportunity for these constitutional conventions to work revolutionary changes in their fundamental law, to bring on that new order which was taking shape in the minds of Northern extremists. Yet no remarkable progress in constitutional development was recorded; for Southerners—whether they were of the upper class, who played no part in these conventions, or of the masses who were in charge—had not considered that losing the war meant accepting a revolution. Though none of the constitutions was entirely remade, yet all were given a more democratic slant. Where property qualifications for holding office still existed, they were set aside; South Carolina by abolishing parishes and refusing to count Negroes for representation transferred more power from the low-country aristocracy to the upcountry gentry, and the same basis with like results was adopted in Alabama;

---

[31] Speculators bought up Confederate bonds and aided in the movement to prevent repudiation. There were various issues of paper currencies not only by the Confederate central government and the Confederate states, but also by cities and other agencies. All indebtedness was repudiated.

South Carolina transferred the election of Presidential electors from the legislature to the people; and, generally, officials heretofore appointed, such as judges, were made elective. In no convention was there the slightest chance that Negroes would be given any degree of suffrage, though in South Carolina Wade Hampton and others thought it might be entrusted to the most intelligent.

Under these new constitutions elections were immediately held for regular state governments. A few months of peace having given the South its bearings and more courage to assert its traditional self, a swing developed toward the leaders it had always known and trusted. In Georgia a call went up for Alexander H. Stephens, still in prison, to be the next governor; [32] and a Southerner in advocating a Confederate veteran for a county office declared that he was "in favor of conferring places of honor and of profit upon those who honored us by their gallantry upon the battle field." [33] A Northerner traveling through the South at this time agreed and remarked, "For my part, I wish every office in the State could be filled with ex-Confederate officers." [34] Though these elections resulted generally in the success of old Whigs, who had opposed secession but had joined in the war, they showed distinctly the determination of the South to uphold its traditions.

The new state governments were soon fully organized with legislatures meeting, courts sitting, and governors performing their duties, although in some of the states, as in Alabama, the provisional governors were tardy in giving up their power. All state officials must have taken the oath of allegiance and received pardon, and Federal officials, such as revenue collectors, marshals, custom officers, and postmasters, were required to take the ironclad oath that they had never willingly aided the Confederacy in any manner. Some of the former did not receive pardons until after their elections, and so scarce were those who could take the ironclad oath that many of the latter had to be appointed in violation of the law.

These new Johnson organizations were a little less than normal state governments, so considered by the armies of occupation and by Johnson himself, and utterly repudiated by Congress. The army,

[32] Columbus (Ga.) *Daily Enquirer*, October 28, 1865.
[33] Sandersville *Central Georgian*, January 3, 1866.
[34] Andrews, *South since the War*, 95.

which now operated through four territorial departments in the South, was omnipresent, ready to impose its will against the states, disallowing their laws and interfering with their courts. The commander in Mississippi attempted to disband the state militia but was prevented from doing so by the President. Johnson hardly gave the state governments a fair chance as he did not restore the writ of habeas corpus until 1866 and did not declare the war ended until autumn of that year.[35] Congress, which had felt slighted in not being given a part in devising state restoration, refused to seat the Congressmen from these states when it met in December, 1865.

Yet these states with empty treasuries heroically set to work to repair the damages of four years of war. Their first duty was to ratify the Thirteenth Amendment, freeing the slaves; this they all did with the exception of Mississippi which declared it unnecessary since her constitutional convention had freed the slaves within her own borders. To relieve the people from private debts which were hard pressing them, legislatures passed relief laws staying collections, suspending court sessions, and extending the time for redeeming real estate lost through forced sales.[36] Relief from debts owed for slaves or slave hire was considered a Federal question and was finally settled when the Supreme Court declared Negro notes valid, despite the pleas of a North Carolina Unionist who said "that is asSackly [exactly] what we want is to Stop the old Rebbels from collecting the nigor notes." [37] In order to complete state rep-

[35] "Report of the Secretary of War," 1866, *House of Representatives Executive Documents*, 39 Cong., 2 Sess., No. 1, Serial No. 1285, pp. 5–6; Augusta *Weekly Constitutionalist*, September 20, 1865; Macon (Ga.) *Daily Telegraph*, February 13, 1866; Atlanta *Daily New Era*, January 15, 1868; Fleming (ed.), *Documentary History of Reconstruction*, I, 193; Robinson, *Justice in Grey*, 608 ff.; McPherson, *Reconstruction*, 15–17.

[36] T. J. Pretlow, Southampton, Va., to Stevens, December 27, 1865, in Stevens Papers, V, Nos. 53467–70; Augusta *Weekly Constitutionalist*, October 10, 1866; Simkins and Woody, *South Carolina during Reconstruction*, 46; Thompson, *Reconstruction in Georgia*, 88; Walter L. Fleming, *Civil War and Reconstruction in Alabama* (New York, 1905), 354; Garner, *Reconstruction in Mississippi*, 120.

[37] J. J. Sharp, Edgecombe County, N.C., to Sumner, April 6, 1869, in Sumner Papers, Box 94, No. 14; Gideon J. Pillow, Memphis, to Sumner, April 6, 1869, *ibid.*, Box 91, No. 68A; Greenville *Southern Enterprise*, February 28, 1867; Greenville (S.C.) *Enterprise*, May 1, 1872; *Weekly Columbus Enquirer*, April 30, 1872. Contracts made in Confederate currency were held to be valid to the extent of the specie value of the currency at the time of the contract. Americus *Tri-Weekly Sumter Republican*, March 17, 1866.

resentation in Congress, the legislatures chose their Senators without delay. Acting normally, though without regard for Northern susceptibilities, they picked outstanding leaders, Confederate generals, high Confederate civil officials—even the Vice-President of the Confederacy—most of whom had not yet been pardoned. In answer to the inevitable criticism, a Georgian exclaimed, "what a miserable representation we will have in Congress if only those are sent who did not voluntarily aid the 'rebellion.' " [38]

The legislation which attracted greatest attention was embraced in the so-called Black Codes. The Negro as a slave had been property; he had no rights, civil or political. The mere act of setting him free still left him without these rights; he was still not a citizen. It was a problem of the first importance to nurse him into the responsibilities of a free citizenship among a population which had always been free. He must be protected against the whites and himself no less than the whites against him. Just as a group of Natchez Negroes said in May, 1865, "We are your friends, and it cannot profit you to keep us weak," [39] so a convention of Clarkesville Tennesseeans said of the Negro, "We . . . deem it the duty of every good citizen to exercise all the offices of a kindly sympathy in ameliorating his condition," and further suggested "that by us alone can the new system be hopefully inaugurated and carried out, and that the less we are subjected to interferences from without, the more promising will be our undertaking." [40] George Fitzhugh declared, "We are not perfectionists, like the Northern people, and should not expect, or try, to make Solomons, nor even Fred Douglasses of the negroes"; but he believed the Negroes should be given an opportunity to make a living and progress as they were able. It was either tutelage or extermination through their own weaknessses.[41] There can be no doubt that the fundamental purpose in the minds of the lawmakers was to advance the fortunes of the Negroes rather than retard them or try to push them back into slavery. Undoubtedly in doing this the South would

The Federal courts held valid the ordinary acts of government of the Confederate states. Garner, *Reconstruction in Mississippi*, 64 ff.

[38] Augusta *Weekly Constitutionalist*, October 25, 1865.

[39] New Orleans *Tribune*, May 30, 1865. [40] Memphis *Argus*, October 17, 1865.

[41] *De Bow's Review*, I (1866), 578.

be protecting itself against the lawlessness of Negroes unrestrained and it would be advancing its own material development as well as that of the Negroes in inducing them to work. That some Southerners hoped these laws would obstruct the Negroes more than help them is doubtless true.

Many Northerners, especially Radical Congressmen, saw in the Black Codes a brazen attempt to cast the Negroes back into slavery. Alluding to the Mississippi Code, the Chicago *Tribune* threateningly told "the white men of Mississippi that the men of the North will convert the State of Mississippi into a frog pond before they will allow any such laws to disgrace one foot of soil in which the bones of our soldiers sleep and over which the flag of freedom waves." [42]

These laws grew out of experience with free Negroes and slaves, from apprenticeship laws in force in the North, from Freedmen's Bureau rules and regulations of the War Department, and from the experience of the British in the West Indies and of Russia with her serfs. Some of the constitutional conventions had appointed commissions to study the subject and have a code ready when the legislatures should meet. The Mississippi Code was the first, most elaborate, and most severe; Georgia and Alabama had few laws regarding Negroes, and Arkansas and Tennessee at first passed none whatsoever. The more elaborate codes dealt with vagrancy, apprenticeship, labor contracts, and the civil status of Negroes. In no cases were Negroes allowed to sit on juries, and in most of the states their testimony was not accepted in court if a white person was the defendant. The former was proper and necessary for the maintenance of justice, but it was poor logic which dictated the latter. No law could force a jury to believe Negro testimony, but at times it might be valuable in establishing facts, and by allowing it where Negroes were defendants it actually gave Negroes greater protection than whites. Negroes wanted especially this right. [43] Said one, "To be

[42] Quoted in J. G. de Roulhac Hamilton, "Southern Legislation in Respect to Freedmen, 1865–1866," in *Studies in Southern History and Politics Inscribed to William Archibald Dunning* (New York, 1914), 148.

[43] "Report of Benjamin C. Truman," *loc. cit.*, 12; "To the People of Texas," August 11, 1865, in John H. Reagan Papers (Texas State Library, Austin; typescripts in University of Texas Library); Kennaway, *On Sherman's Track*, 79; Fleming (ed.), *Documentary History of Reconstruction*, I, 252. Examples from various Black Codes (but

sure, sah, we wants to vote, but, sah, de great matter is to git into de witness-box." [44] Whatever anyone might have thought about these codes, the question was in fact academic, for they were never actually put into effect. The Freedmen's Bureau and the United States Army prevented their enforcement, and later when the Radicals got control of the Southern governments they removed them from the statute books.

In the upheaval following the war, normal conditions could hardly be expected, yet a year and a half afterwards the Secretary of War was surprised at the small amount of lawlessness.[45] Apart from the bloody Memphis riot [46] in May, 1866, and the New Orleans outbreaks [47] the following July, both of which were race clashes, there was no epidemic of crime in the South. Said a Georgia editor, "It would be utopian to expect an absolute absence of lawlessness, as long as the millenium remains but a promise, and man's fallen nature makes the millenium a remote conjecture." [48] With their exaggerated sense of honor, traditional in their make-up,

---

mostly from Mississippi): Negroes were allowed to sue and be sued, to buy and sell property (except in Mississippi they could rent or lease land only in cities, though they could buy land anywhere), and to have their slave marriages legalized. They were forbidden to carry firearms or other deadly weapons, to make seditious speeches, to treat animals cruelly, to sell liquors, or to preach without a license. Contracts for labor must be in writing, and Negroes quitting without good cause should forfeit their wages. Negroes under eighteen years of age not supported by parents must be apprenticed to "a suitable person," the former owner having preference. The master must not inflict cruel punishment. Vagrants, without reference to color, should be fined. The use of the terms "master" and "servant" in the apprenticeship laws was bitterly attacked in the North as showing that the South was attempting to restore the Negroes to slavery, but such critics forgot that their own apprenticeship laws used the identical terms.

[44] Andrews, *South since the War,* 180.

[45] "Report of the Secretary of War," 1866, *loc. cit.,* 6.

[46] This riot had been precipitated by a clash between Memphis policemen and Negro troops. Forty-six Negroes were killed and more than eighty injured.

[47] The New Orleans riot was caused by an attempt of the 1864 constitutional convention to reassemble in order to seize power in the state for the Radicals and Negroes. Forty-one people were killed and about 160 were wounded, mostly Negroes and their Radical friends. The Conservatives believed an attempt was being made "to bring on civil war amongst the races." Carrollton (La.), *Times,* August 4, 1866. The New Orleans *Picayune* warned, "Let what will come, of this they [Negroes] may be assured, the white races of Louisiana will remain masters." Quoted in Carrollton *Times,* August 4, 1866.

[48] Augusta *Weekly Constitutionalist,* October 24, 1866.

Southerners were quicker than Northerners to commit murder, but lesser crimes though more disgusting flourished in the North —"Forgeries, defalcations, social scandals, indecent domestic complications, clerical short-comings, prurient horrors of nameless kinds." [49]

To those who opposed Johnson's program of restoration, news of Southern violence was welcome. The *Nation* for two years after the war ran a section to record and call special attention to crimes in the South, especially crimes against Negroes. Ordinary lawbreaking and any indiscreet expression were exaggerated and published in the North, and much was manufactured without foundation. A Freedmen's Bureau agent in denying racial clashes, added, "God knows the question is vexed enough without adding fuel to the flames." [50] News of Southern violence was of great political value in the North, a fact which led a Southerner to remark sarcastically that "a number of riots are desired in a number of prominent points in the South, such as Richmond, Mobile, Memphis and New Orleans. If twenty or thirty negroes, martyrs to liberty, can be killed at each of these places, so much the better for the Radical cause." [51]

Even before Congress met in December, 1865, there was rising opposition among Congressmen to Johnson's dealings with the South. Such Radical leaders as Sumner and Stevens had been whetting their anger and laying their plans.[52] When Congress met, they

[49] Communication from D. G. Wooten to *Scribner's Monthly* (New York), XVIII (1879), 622. The Southern press took delight in publishing news on Northern crimes under such headlines as these: "The Auburn Horror," "A School Marm Shoots a Livery Stable Keeper Because he will not Marry her," "A Five Act Tragedy in Real Life— Crime in Indiana." The Augusta *Weekly Constitutionalist*, February 27, 1867, said, "We have, on several occasions, demonstrated that for every murder in the South, we could produce fifty murders in the North; for every theft in the South, a hundred burglaries in the North; for every corrupt official in the South—heaven alone knows how many rogues in any one New England State."

[50] Little Rock *Weekly Arkansas Gazette*, August 25, 1866.

[51] Augusta *Weekly Constitutionalist*, August 15, 1866.

[52] Judge J. C. Underwood, Alexandria, Va., to Sumner, July 17, 1865, said that letting the South back into the Union would be "a cruel cruel breach of faith & honor to the Freedmen." Sumner Papers, Box 74, No. 22. Thomas I. Durant, New Orleans, to Sumner, October 1, 1865, said the admission of the Southern states whether with or without Negro suffrage would be a serious blunder—"a probationary system is indispensable." *Ibid.*, No. 134.

took their revenge on the President by refusing to admit the Congressmen from the Southern states, and by appointing a Joint Committee on Reconstruction to investigate the South and let Congress know when states were ready to be readmitted. Angered by the South's Black Codes Congress passed a new Freedmen's Bureau Act, which greatly increased the powers of that body,[53] and the Civil Rights Act, which made the Negro a citizen and gave him all civil rights enjoyed by whites. The President vetoed both bills, but Congress passed the second over his veto. Now open warfare broke out between the President and Congress.

Many Southerners were surprised and angered at the turn of events; they had done all that they had been asked to do, and now they saw their states refused admission into the Union. They had ratified the Thirteenth Amendment, which only states could do; yet Congress in other respects did not now regard them as states. This was one of the many inconsistencies that characterized Congressional action during the next decade. An irate Virginian, having no Congressman to serve him, asked Stevens for some free government documents, since "you will not let our so-called representatives get into your circus"; [54] and a Georgian, signing himself "Confederate," poured out his wrath, "Pass as many of your low down laws as you please and confiscate our whole country— do you suppose our honor will be impaired? Miserable Scoundrel —Hell's dominions are too good for such men. Now call me *disloyal*. Yes *I am disloyal* to any *damned* Government ruled by such men as you are, and 'glory that I still live to hate you.' " [55]

Having disagreed with Johnson's reconstructing of the South, Congress was therefore compelled to bring forth a plan of its own, which was submitted in the form of an amendment to the constitution and ultimately became the Fourteenth. It embodied the Civil Rights Law and much more; it was in fact revolutionary. It defined citizenship, made the Negro a citizen, and gave him civil rights. Although it did not confer on him suffrage outright, it penalized any state which did not allow him to vote. It denied to

[53] This body had originally been created in March, 1865, as a bureau in the War Department.

[54] Thompson Powell, Halifax County, Va., to Stevens, February 22, 1866, in Stevens Papers, VII, No. 53895.

[55] "Confederate," Atlanta, Ga., to Stevens, May 1, 1866, *ibid.*, No. 54069.

many Confederates the right to hold office and provided that only Congress could remove their disabilities. It repudiated the Confederate debts and guaranteed the Federal. In June, 1866, this amendment was submitted to the states, including the Southern states, which Congress refused to consider states for any other purpose than ratifying constitutional amendments. Encouraged by Johnson every Southern state except Tennessee indignantly rejected this amendment, agreeing with the Mississippi editor who said that however much the Southern states might want to be back in the Union, they were "not prepared to become parties, to their own degradation." [56] The South had come to distrust the integrity of Congress, and doubly so in this plan, as Congress had not promised the Southern states admission into the Union even if they ratified the amendment. Tennessee, which had fallen into the hands of the amazing "Parson" William G. Brownlow and his Radicals, was by him browbeaten into a doubtful ratification by a remarkable performance. For this "heroic and patriotic" act Tennessee was readmitted into the Union, but the course of her Radical government for the preceding year had been more a recommendation for her admission than her ratification of the amendment. One of Brownlow's enemies declared that "except the lowest order of yankees, free negroes and East Tennessee tories, I have met no man, woman or child, who attempts an apology for or to extenuate the course of this infamous miscreant." [57]

Political party developments had by this time crystallized along clear lines. President Johnson, who had always been a Democrat though an unyielding Unionist, had lost the support of the Radical elements in the Republican party and was seeing many conservative Republicans slip away. This defection was brought about by the President's forthright political methods, by his moderate course in dealing with the South, and by the clever political leadership of his bitter enemy, Thaddeus Stevens. The Democrats in the North who had looked askance at Johnson for the past four years now turned to him and became his principal supporters.

[56] Aberdeen (Miss.) *Daily Sunny South,* December 3, 1866. C. W. Dudley, Bennettsville, S.C., to William E. Chandler, June 29, 1866, said that to crush Southerners into despair could "never make them good citizens." William E. Chandler Papers (Division of Manuscripts, Library of Congress), II, Nos. 294–97.

[57] Sandersville *Central Georgian,* November 28, 1866.

The South was big with future political possibilities. Northern Democrats need not have expected the automatic support of Southern Democrats; Democrats in the Confederacy had developed no debts to Northern Democrats.[58] Furthermore, there was no good reason at the end of the war to expect that the old Whig tradition in the South was dead and that old Whigs would naturally join the Democrats. In fact, in the first elections after the war the antebellum division of Whigs against Democrats was evident. The South had always known a two-party system; why should it not have one now? The gradual disappearance of this reasonable expectation and hope was due entirely to Northern folly. Blinded by their course of vengeance the Northern Radicals, by making loyalty alone their touchstone of worth, threw away their chance to build up an intelligent and respectable following in the South —especially from the old Whig element. The riffraff which had been able to keep out of the Confederate armies, the ignorant Negroes, Confederate deserters, and political turncoats could qualify for Radical blessings; the intelligent, the honest, the steadfast were lumped together and declared evil. There had been an excellent chance to drive a wedge into the latter class; the Radicals did not take advantage of it and therein lay a principal cause of the ultimate failure of their plan of Reconstruction.

To make it easy for the old Whigs and the Democrats to unite after the war and to ward off Northern hostility, Southerners began calling themselves Conservatives. They soon brought themselves to support Johnson and thereby formed a combination with Northern Democrats. At first they remembered Johnson for his uncompromising hostility to the Confederacy and for his extreme sayings, but as he developed his Southern policy they quickly came to his support. They forgave almost all when Johnson defended their honor by denying the charge that the South, in taking the oath of allegiance, "had blistered its lips with a lie," and in appreciation of this defense a Georgian said that "little as it may be, that one utterance has made him more friends in the South than

---

[58] Said the Memphis *Daily Bulletin*, December 12, 1866, "The difference between the people of the South and those of the North consists in the fact that we care not which set of rascals holds the offices if they will do us justice, enfranchise our people, and relieve us of insufferable burdens."

all the pardons he has granted and all the property he has restored."[59] An admirer frankly wrote Johnson, "I thought you a
radical in politics, & feared you would be a fanatic in power," but
he was now delighted to find him otherwise.[60] A Radical in Tennessee wrote to a Northern Radical, "The President used to be called
a 'Dam traitor' he is now 'our President.' "[61] In 1866 Johnson
made a trip South and received an honorary LL.D. degree from
the University of North Carolina.[62]

The first Southerners who became uncompromisingly Radicals
were few and of doubtful local standing. Expressing his opinion of
North Carolina Unionists, a Northerner believed "a conquered
Rebel will, to my thinking, be much more easily converted into a
good citizen,"[63] and a Southerner felt that there were enough
loyal men in his state "to fill all federal offices but there are not
loyal men enough to elect them."[64] Another found that a Southern Unionist was a person who had hated secessionists but who
also hated the Yankees as much.[65] In the early days Radicals in
Virginia were whipped together by John Minor Botts, James W.
Hunnicutt, and Judge John C. Underwood, by Parson Brownlow
in Tennessee, by Andrew Jackson Hamilton in Texas, and by
various leaders in other states.

To unite the Johnson followers a convention was held in Philadelphia in September, 1866, which brought Northerners and
Southerners together in political equality for the first time since
the war. Delegates from throughout the South attended. Soon
thereafter the Radicals made a countermove by holding two conventions in the same place, one for the Northern Radicals and one

---

[59] Augusta *Weekly Constitutionalist*, September 27, 1865. "It is in the power of the
Southern people, by a just and temperate course to add greatly to the list of the
Northern supporters of the President." *Ibid.*, March 7, 1866.

[60] J. T. Trezevant, Memphis, to Johnson, June 11, 1866, in Johnson Papers, XCVI,
Nos. 11342–43.

[61] John Seage, Murfreesboro, Tenn., to Chandler, May 16, 1866, in Zachariah
Chandler Papers, IV, Nos. 680–81.

[62] David L. Swain, Chapel Hill, N.C., to Johnson, June 9, 1866, in Johnson Papers,
XCVI, No. 11331.

[63] Andrews, *South since the War*, 111.

[64] G. W. Welker, Greensboro, N.C., to Stevens, December 2, 1865, in Stevens Papers,
V, Nos. 53344–46.

[65] Trowbridge, *South*, 328.

for the Southern Radicals, with much fraternizing. These moves were part of the campaign for the election of Congressmen in November. The Radicals won this Congress by a two-thirds majority —an ominous sign of future trouble for the former Confederate states.

Reconstruction had now been thrown into a snarl, and one of the most difficult problems which ever confronted the American nation must be settled by a people somewhat less than normal. The misconceptions which each section had held of the other in ante-bellum times had not been cleared away by four years of war. Victory is no less likely to produce psychological disturbances in mass thinking than is defeat, and also the victor may suffer as much spiritual damage as the vanquished. Northerners blamed the South for the tens of thousands of empty places in their homes, left by fathers, sons, and brothers killed on battlefields or taken away by Southern prison life; likewise they held the South responsible for high taxes and a large national debt. Revenge is a natural human trait; that Northerners should not have had some of this feeling would be little less than miraculous. Yet Southerners failed to sense these facts. They tended to act as if they alone had been sufferers. They looked only at their own empty chairs. They refused to believe that they had been responsible for the war, and they knew they had not only felt the pangs of defeat but with it they had also lost much of their material accumulations of the past hundred years. Refusing to see that a mighty cataclysm had shaken the profound depths of national life, they did not expect that many things would be made anew but rather looked for them to be mended as of old—that Humpty Dumpty might after all be put back on the wall in the South, even if not in the nursery rhyme. The psychological element present in Reconstruction neither side would recognize.

CHAPTER III

SHORT CUT TO CIVILIZATION

NEGROES were wronged by Reconstruction as much as were the whites. Their destiny as a race was played with by visionaries and by designing politicians and was given a trend which was not to be deflected within any calculable period of time. Policies were dictated not by what the Negroes were but by what the conquerors thought they ought to be.

Slavery had not been an unmixed evil for the Negroes; it had brought them from barbarism and sometimes slavery in Africa to America and subjected them to the white man's civilization, the product of a thousand years of freedom. They had, indeed, not come of their own volition; certainly they would never have arrived through free immigration. It was often remarked by disinterested observers that the lot of the slaves in America was better than that of the Negroes left behind in Africa; and when the slaves became free they seemed to agree that they had won by the transaction, for they never chided anyone because they had been brought to America. They were proud of being Americans and they resented being removed. "This is your country," said a convention of Georgia Negroes addressing their white neighbors, "but it is ours too; you were born here, so were we; your fathers fought for it; but our fathers fed them." [1] If slavery had held horrors for them, they immediately forgot them. In freedom they did not harbor resentment for any ill-treatment they might have received in slavery, for Negroes seldom took revenge upon their former masters. Instead, the freedman might well pity his old master. This spirit Irwin Russell, the Mississippi poet, well expressed in his poem "Mahsr John":

[1] *American Freedman,* I (1866), 12.

47

I heahs a heap o' talkin', ebrywhar I goes,
'Bout Washintum an' Franklum, an sech genuses as dose:
I s'pose dey's mighty fine, but heah's de p'int I's bettin' on:
Dere wuzn't nar a one ob 'em comes up to Mahsr John.

. . . .

Well, times is changed. De war it come an' sot de niggers free,
An' now ol' Mahsr John aint hardly wuf as much as me;
He had to pay his debts, an' so his lan' is mos'ly gone—
An' I declar' I's sorry for my pore ol' Mahsr John.[2]

Nor did the whites come out of the war with resentment and ill will toward the Negroes. They knew that Negroes had not won their freedom, that they had not conspicuously asked for it, and that some had actually not wanted it. Southerners were profoundly thankful for the manner in which the slaves had conducted themselves and their masters' business during the war; and the Negroes themselves took some pride in their part in that conflict. "We never inaugurated a servile insurrection," a Negro convention proudly boasted. "We stayed peaceably at our homes and labored with our usual industry, while you were absent fighting in the field, though we knew our power at the same time, and would frequently speak of it." [3]

Slaves, especially household servants, had developed a courtesy and a certain gentility in manners which remained habitual with them in freedom. When Jefferson Davis, a half-dozen years after the war, visited his old Mississippi plantation, now owned by his former slave Ben Montgomery, he was received with affection and deference. Even in their heyday of power and glory, South Carolina freedmen, now transmuted into high state officials, respected their old masters and expected to be addressed by their first names. Negro belles, made so by the turn of political fortunes, forgot their airs and entered back doors when they visited the homes where in slavery they had been nursemaids. But many who had not come under the cultural influence of the planters soon left off "missus" or "massa" and began calling their employers by their last names. as, indeed, well became a people growing into the ways of freedom.

[2] *Scribner's Monthly*, XIV (1877), 127.   [3] *American Freedman*, I (1866), 12.

James D. B. De Bow, the editor of the famous review, in making a trip through Virginia two years after the war observed that many freedmen "retained their old-time courtesy, but a majority of both men and women were evidently staggering under the weight of their own importance, and were ludicrously inflated and pompous." [4]

Yet slavery left the Negro illiterate and untrained for the responsibilities of freedom, with such human weaknesses as lying and thieving exaggerated. He loved idleness, he had no keen conception of right and wrong, and he was "improvident to the last degree of childishness." General Lee testified that the Negroes were an "amiable and social race" who liked "their ease and comfort" and who looked "more to their present than to their future condition." [5] They were early warned "that a continuous jubilee is not the lever by which they are to provide for the support of themselves and families." [6] As a race they were spendthrift and gullible, though some were amenable to the advice to save their money. Easily influenced by peddlers and storekeepers, Jewish and Gentile, they bought brass finger rings worth fifty cents apiece for $5.00 or $6.00, and earrings, breast pins, and gaudy cotton handkerchiefs at correspondingly high prices. They also had a great liking for tobacco, whisky, and mackerel.

As many of their greater likes and lesser vices were called forth by the prohibitions in slave days, the indulgences of these now took on the additional value of being marks of freedom. The importance of riding a horse or mule could hardly be exaggerated in the eyes of a freedman, a fact which helped the Negro to make up his mind to steal riding animals. To possess a gun and be followed by a dog which he could call his own greatly helped him to enjoy his new freedom; and to carry a pistol distinguished the "young colored gentleman" from the "gun-toting" generality of Negroes who sometimes carried their guns to the fields to produce a thrill or to shoot a rabbit. A disgusted Northern Radical declared, "A

---

[4] De Bow's Review, IV (1867), 595. See also, Frances Butler Leigh, Ten Years on a Georgia Plantation since the War (London, 1883), 131.

[5] Report of the Joint Committee on Reconstruction, at the First Session Thirty-ninth Congress (Washington, 1866), Pt. II, 130.

[6] Charleston Courier, April 25, 1865.

young colored gentleman seems to think he is not fully dressed unless he has a pistol buckled to him, or hid away in his pocket, and when in company, uses the most trivial pretext to draw it out." [7] The cheapest deadly weapon was the razor, which was called into use more frequently by whisky and women than for the purpose for which it was made. Negroes progressed rapidly in lawlessness, made easy by owning deadly weapons; and, although much fighting was done among themselves, now and then they became a menace also to white people. It was charged that in North Carolina in 1867 a fourth of the Negro population went armed with guns, pistols, and bowie knives, although the whites did not pretend "to wear fire arms." There was widespread fear in the South in 1865 that the Negroes would engage in a general uprising at Christmas. In Chicot County, Arkansas, in 1872 armed Negroes took three white men from jail, riddled them with bullets, and went about burning and pillaging.

Another mark of freedom which seized many Negroes in the summer of 1865 was to abandon the slave cabin and set out in any direction. This was the surest test of freedom, for heretofore to leave the plantation required a pass. No more could the master give them orders, and they would soon be out of hearing of the old plantation bell. The Negroes were now going somewhere to attend to the desires or unfinished business of slave days, to look for a relative, to see the soldiers, to "Joy my freedom," but especially to go to town to receive something or just to sit and wait. Arriving at their destination, they sat on goods boxes and whittled sticks or took possession of curbstones or doorsteps or perchance the shade of trees, being forced slowly to move by the relentless sun. In the beginning the army and Freedmen's Bureau made distributions of food, but soon a pestilence of petty thievery broke out, and the soldiers began to drive the Negroes back to the country. [8] A Northerner traveling in the South in the summer of 1865 was convinced that "the race is, on a large scale, ignorantly sacrificing its own good

[7] Macon (Ga.) *American Union*, March 19, 1869.

[8] *Nation*, I (1865), 393; II (1866), 492; Raymond (Miss.) *Hinds County Gazette*, November 29, 1867; Augusta *Weekly Constitutionalist*, June 7, 21, 1865; Reid, *Southern Tour*, 532; Edward King, *The Great South* . . . (Hartford, 1875), 341. One Negro in South Carolina is said to have walked one hundred miles for a half bushel of corn. Simkins and Woody, *South Carolina during Reconstruction*, 225.

for the husks of vagabondage." [9] Just as the whites from now on marked all time from the Surrender, so the Negroes, using the same date, varied the expression to "since dis time come." Very soon many Negroes drifted back to the old plantations and made arrangements with their former masters on the basis of freedom.

Since in slave days the Negroes had been supplied with all the necessities of life, in freedom they expected to continue to receive support without seeing that they must continue to work. Though not to all, freedom meant to many Negroes freedom from work. Encouraged by Northern reformers and schemers, they came to think of themselves as a chosen people and of their country's obligations to them as something which could never be fully met. "So far, since the freedom of the slaves," said a disillusioned Northern Radical, "the Negro has had but one object—self. He accepts the labor of his white friends and as a matter of course, and he works for nobody but himself. He cries out for equality before the law—equal rights and privileges—yet, is the last to grant the same thing he asks for." [10]

As the Negroes failed to receive as freely as they expected, the inherent human weakness to steal asserted itself. Armed with the lingering feeling of slave days that what belonged to their masters belonged to them also, they became a menace to anything which could not be locked up or nailed down. A Northerner who came south to become a planter declared, "Stealing is no name for this trying vice. It is wholesale robbery of everything in their power to help themselves to." His wife added, "The Negroes are the worst thieves that the Lord ever permitted to live. They steal everything they can lay their hands on." [11] Their favorite objects of theft were hogs, chickens, cattle, horses and mules, cotton, and all sorts of vegetables and fruits. An Alabama planter said he had quit raising hogs and was forced to pay twenty-five cents a pound for meat selling for five cents before the war; and he added, "We dare not turn stock out at all." [12] Others abandoned raising vegetables and

[9] Andrews, *South since the War,* 349–50.

[10] Macon *American Union,* July 6, 1871.

[11] Charles Stearns, *The Black Man of the South, and the Rebels; or, The Characteristics of the Former, and the Recent Outrages of the Latter* (New York, 1872), 55.

[12] Fleming (ed.), *Documentary History of Reconstruction,* II, 279. See also, *Southern Magazine* (Baltimore), XVI (1875), 513–19; *Daily Columbus Enquirer,* January 17,

garden crops. The absence of stock laws in most of the South made it easy for Negroes to steal livestock as it ran loose in the fields and woods. For some years after the war scarcely an issue of a Southern paper failed to carry notices of rewards for stolen horses and mules —"a mouse colored mare mule," "a dark bay mare," "a horse mule." Cotton stealing became systematic. Negroes picked cotton in the fields or stole it after it was picked and, waiting until darkness, took it to small stores or groggeries, called "dead fall houses," usually on the edge of swamps or in other out-of-way places, and sold it to dishonest merchants. To break up this thievery of cotton and other farm products some states passed laws forbidding merchants to trade in such articles after sundown. Negro thieves did not draw the color line; they stole from one another as readily as from whites. Honest Negroes living around Chattanooga quit raising chickens because the thieves "just pick 'em up and steal 'em in a minute!" [13]

Although Negroes supposedly had a great affection for a mule, yet they were given to treating cruelly any animal within their power. The planter's habit of obliging his Negro workmen in certain small matters led him to be generous in lending his mules for Sunday rides. Negroes ran and whipped the animals so mercilessly that soon voices were raised against lending them. "These dashing cavaliers would rush by as fast as couriers on the eve of battle," said an indignant Georgian. "One wagon, with a poor team, came dashing down a hill, the driver laying whip like Jehu behind time." "If you can't stop," he advised, "sell your stock, rent your land, and quit farming. You can't buy horses for negroes to ride to death, and make any money." [14] Called forth largely by the behavior of the Negroes, laws against cruelty to animals were passed in some of the states.

A definite contribution which freedom gave to Negroes was an opportunity to develop their social activities. The women retired from the cotton fields, for no lady worked in the fields, if, indeed, anywhere. Their first great ambition was to wear a veil and carry

1866; Macon *Daily Telegraph*, February 13, 1866; Charles Nordhoff, *The Cotton States in the Spring and Summer of 1875* (New York, 1876), 70.

[13] Trowbridge, *South*, 252.   [14] Greensboro *Herald*, May 22, 1879.

a parasol. If they lived in towns the passing of a train was an important social event and they adorned themselves in brass jewelry and glass beads and assembled at the station to watch. If Negroes were to take on the ways of the society which they saw about them, and build up family life, then their women must be less active as fieldworkers and give more attention to homemaking. And marriages, which were in slave days arrangements of convenience, must be made legal and sanctified. Black Codes had provisions legalizing slave matings and giving Negroes a reasonable time to make up their minds on their permanent attachments. Having had in slave days more freedom in this field than "since dis time come," Negroes found it difficult to treat marriage as a permanent arrangement, and for some years after the war there were few marriages. In thirty-one Mississippi counties there were in 1866 only 564 marriages; in 1870, the habit of marrying having taken a stronger hold, there were 3,427.[15] The law legalizing slave marriages in Alabama was so much disregarded that when the Radicals with their Negro support gained control, they repealed the old law and dated Negro marriages from 1867, thus wiping out much adultery, bigamy, and desertion. Though there was some evidence among Negroes of the truth of Kipling's famous dictum that the female of the species is more deadly than the male, Negro women generally liked their husbands strong even to the extent of wife-beating. One of the effects of freedom on Negro women seems to have been a diminution for a time, at least, of their maternal instincts. A Briton passing through the South a year after the war declared he did not see a Negro woman who did not want to be relieved of the care of her children;[16] and another Briton, long a resident of the South, said that children were "looked upon by most of them [their mothers] as a burden and if the mothers did not intentionally kill them their habitual neglect produces the same effect."[17] Yet freedom did bring family life to the Negroes, and among the better class the family Bible began to make its appearance, into which

[15] Robert Somers, *The Southern States since the War, 1870–1* (London, 1871), 251.
[16] Kennaway, *On Sherman's Track*, 70.
[17] Barnsley, New Orleans, to J. K. Reid, January 11, 1868, in Barnsley Papers; *Nation*, IX (1869), 164.

the names and birthdays of the children were written. The ages of the older ones were guesses and the writing at first was mostly done by Yankee schoolteachers.

The servility implied in having only one name, the Negro gradually remedied when freedom came. He now assumed a right not even possessed by the whites, to pick any name which suited his fancy. If he fitted into the "good old darky" class he took the name of his old master as his family patronymic; but if he were greatly impressed by the new order he probably chose the most sonorous and awe-inspiring names he could find—hence the great number of George Washingtons, Andrew Jacksons, and Abraham Lincolns. Names were like wives in that they were frequently changed.

Race did not completely predispose all Negroes to assume an equality among themselves. Freemen of ante-bellum days now considered themselves an aristocracy among the freedmen, the *nouveau libre;* the upcountry Negroes, generally of a higher type, looked down on the low-country masses; the dark Negroes disliked the mulattoes; the town Negroes considered themselves the social superiors of the country Negroes; and the background of higher stations in slavery such as household servants and artisans as against field hands, had a tendency to divide Negroes socially in freedom. Of course, the records of a Negro's life were so unfixed and his moving around was so constant that these social standards at best were only tendencies.[18] Social equality with white people, wherever it was advocated, was not a native growth; it was cultivated by visionaries and dangerous politicians.

The festive spirit was native with the Negro, bursting forth in his war dances in Africa, expressed in slavery through his religion, and in freedom not only in his religion but also in many societies and lodges, mostly secret, and in holidays which he found and which he made. He loved gala and regalia. First in his affection was the Fourth of July, which he and his Radical Republican mentors seized from the Southern whites and made almost an exclusive possession, more for political than patriotic purposes. Only

[18] Alrutheus A. Taylor, "The Negro in the Reconstruction of Virginia," in *Journal of Negro History* (Washington), XI (1926), 248–49; Stearns, *Black Man of the South,* 62, 478–79; Fleming (ed.), *Documentary History of Reconstruction,* II, 265.

little less important than the Fourth was Emancipation Day, which he celebrated at various times from January 1, aided by New Year enthusiasm, to June "teenth" (nineteenth), reinforced by watermelons.[19] Many secret societies, charitable and benevolent, and lucrative to the promoters, grew up with striking names. There were the "Workers of Charity," "Shekinak Society," "Sisters of Zion," "Knights of Wise Men," "Daughters of Ham," "Independent Pole Bearers," "Sons of Relief," "Sisters of Sympathy," "Young Men Never Lies Society," and many others.

Unfortunately for the Negroes freedom meant the loss of certain attentions which they received in slavery, designed to keep them healthy and clean and to prolong their lives. Freed from restraint "since dis time come," they tended to become slovenly and careless of their health and cleanliness. A British traveler declared that now "nothing on earth can make them wash." [20] Disease, especially smallpox, was spread by soldiers, white refugees, and wandering Negroes, and the mortality among the freedmen became alarming. A resident of New Orleans observed, "The *friends* of the negro race have presented them Pandora's box—The mortality has been and will be frightful." [21] In Charleston, where in antebellum times the death rate was about the same for whites and Negroes, the difference grew to twenty-four per thousand for whites and forty-three per thousand for Negroes after the war. In Macon, Georgia, 500 Negroes were said to have died during December, 1865. Dr. Josiah C. Nott, who made a scientific study of Negroes, declared that they were huddled in shanties around Mobile, "stealing, burning fences for fuel, dying of disease and want, and yet you cannot get a cook or washerwoman at twenty dollars a month." [22]

Such were some of the characteristics of the Negroes. The freedmen were not responsible for what they were; for what they were not the South was no more to blame than the North. The problem

[19] The date might be January 1, when the final proclamation was issued, or the time when actual freedom came to the Negro, that is, when army commanders established it after the war.

[20] Charles W. Dilke, *Greater Britain: A Record of Travel in English-Speaking Countries during 1866 and 1867* (New York, 1869), 28.

[21] Barnsley, New Orleans, to R. Maury, December 2, 1865, in Barnsley Papers.

[22] *De Bow's Review*, I (1866), 269.

of the Negro was one of the greatest produced by the war, yet the North in dealing with it increased rather than diminished its difficulty. By assuming the Negro to be entirely different from what he actually was, the North acted as if there really were no problem at all. Immediately after the war Stevens seems to have had in mind the necessity of some constructive plan when he asked Sumner where he could find in English a correct history of the Russian serfs and the terms of their liberation, but he soon gave up any such idea.[23] Instead of studying his condition—intellectual, social, and economic—and working out a five-year or a ten-year or even a lifetime program, the Radical leaders took up the Negro as a makeweight in their own political and economic schemes. Having ravished the race in their own interests, they left the Negro worse off than when they picked him up. He was now left on the doorstep of the Southerners, who were to bear the responsibilities of his presence but were not permitted freedom in solving the riddle. The South knew from the beginning that a principal factor in Reconstruction was the Negro; even the writer of doggerel knew it:

Nigger man! nigger baby!
Nigger woman! nigger lady!
Nigger with the Grecian bend!
Nigger! nigger to the end! [24]

Instead of helping the Negro the Radical leaders praised him. They sought to capture his sympathy and support, not by providing him with an education and land at national expense, but by telling him how civilized he already was and how well prepared he was to take over the rulership of the country he occupied. Such a program bankrupted the Radicals of their integrity, but it cost no money. A Radical general thought the Negroes would soon be the intellectual superiors of the white race,[25] and *Harper's Weekly*, after time enough had elapsed since the war to permit a considered judgment, said, "That, with every disadvantage and discouragement, the slaves of yesterday have shown themselves to be citizens more orderly and valuable than the majority of the master race

23 Letter, October 7, 1865, in Sumner Papers, Box 74, No. 140.
24 Montgomery *Weekly Advertiser*, October 6, 1868.
25 Augusta *Weekly Constitutionalist*, September 25, 1867.

that sneered at them, is indisputable." [26] After the war the North enslaved the Negro to its own schemes no less than the South had done before to its interests. "Let us have done with it," said a Northern newspaper, "and give the negro a chance to help himself"; [27] and a Southerner agreed it was time to put a stop to "the officious influence of those traffickers in a certain sort of spurious humanitarianism that seems to have followed the negro with fatal persistency through all his later history in this country, and which comes mainly from his so-called Northern friends and benefactors." [28]

To build a house without foundations was first on the Radical program. The freedmen should be given the vote to protect themselves and to guarantee the results of the war—those results being in the secret minds of the Radicals the perpetuation of their political power, and in the minds of their economic allies the maintenance of a high tariff and an easy road to exploitation of the country's resources. If the Radicals had thought that the South had been conquered sufficiently to join their party, they would have had no interest in giving the Negroes the vote. The Negro leaders of this movement openly declared that the freedmen "votes will weigh, as a single mass, on one side of the balance" and that the whites "must be prevented from organizing for any political purpose." [29] The visionary reformers seemed to think that the ballot had miraculous properties, that the most ignorant and irresponsible Negroes could raise themselves by this simple device to dizzy heights of social betterment. One advocate held that Negroes were morally and intellectually "as well prepared for it as the mass of poor whites in the South," [30] and another was sure that intelligence and education were no test of patriotism, for, if so, how could Lee, Stephens, and other Southern traitors be explained.[31] The fact that the North "rejected and scorned" Negro suffrage for itself was considered by the Radicals insufficient reason why it would not be good for the South. There were so few Negroes in the former

[26] *Harper's Weekly*, XV (1871), 1074.
[27] Chicago *Tribune*, quoted in Augusta *Weekly Constitutionalist*, April 21, 1869.
[28] D. C. Wooten, Austin, Tex., quoted in *Scribner's Monthly*, XVIII (1879), 623.
[29] New Orleans *Tribune*, June 7, 23, 1865.
[30] Trowbridge, *South*, 589.
[31] *Harper's Weekly*, IX (1865), 306.

section that their voting could have no effect, but in the South there were great opportunities for it to work changes. Only six Northern states permitted it; Connecticut, Wisconsin, and Minnesota rejected it in 1865; and Kansas later voted it down by a 50,000 majority.

Many Northerners saw how illogical and dangerous Negro suffrage would be. They observed how it stultified those people who for a generation had been telling of the extent to which slavery had degraded the Negroes, but who, immediately after emancipation, insisted that freedmen were civilized enough to rule not only themselves but their former white masters as well. To the mind of Oliver P. Morton of Indiana, " 'to say that such men . . . just emerging from this slavery, are qualified for the exercise of political power is to make the strongest pro-slavery argument I ever heard.' " [32] General Sherman believed the Negroes should first be put through a period of training, and the scientific mind of Louis Agassiz rebelled at the thought of Negroes' voting. In the light of anthropological knowledge as it existed in 1865, almost no reason could be found to support Negro suffrage. What had been the fruits of the Negro race tree?—slavery and degradation. Agassiz wrote in 1863, "I cannot, therefore, think it just or safe to grant at once to the negro all the privileges which we ourselves have acquired by long struggles. History teaches us what terrible reactions have followed too extensive and too rapid changes." [33] The United States Commissioner of Agriculture believed that one of the greatest goods that could be done to the Negroes would be to disabuse their minds of "the delusions of political preferment." [34] Henry Ward Beecher thought that civilization for the Negroes could not "be bought, nor bequeathed, nor gained by sleight of hand. It will come to sobriety, virtue, industry and frugality." [35] To an Englishman who traveled through the South, Negro suffrage was "putting the fool's cap on Republican principle." [36]

[32] *Land We Love,* IV (1867–1868), 262.

[33] Quoted in James F. Rhodes, *History of the United States from the Compromise of 1850* (New York, 1896–1906), VI, 38. See also, *Memoirs of General William T. Sherman* (New York, 1875), II, 373–74.

[34] *Report of the Commissioner of Agriculture,* 1867 (Washington, 1868), x.

[35] Augusta *Weekly Constitutionalist,* September 16, 1868.

[36] Somers, *Southern States since the War,* 228.

The desire for Negro suffrage did not originate with the freed-men—others opened Pandora's box out of which this evil flew. A few Negroes actually opposed it. The Negro wanted property and instead he was given the vote. When once he had it, its power over him grew fast and worked further against the peace and contentment he needed. It made him vain and idle and put into his head dangerous desires, impossible of fulfillment. In a Southerner's judgment, "He would be more or less than human if he exhibited any conspicuous humility, for never, since the world began, was a poor fellow so suddenly elevated into a seat of power, so lavishly granted such possibilities for mischief, so grovellingly worshiped by a formidable faction of the master-race." It was a wonder that his very head did not "burst with its amazing grandeur and every little kink of wool turn to a golden diadem." [37] In mock earnestness the white man now began to wish he were a Negro:

> Oh! if I was a nigger,
>   I'd do just as I please,
> And when I took a pinch of snuff,
>   All Yankeedom would sneeze.
> Then Congress too would worship me,
>   And bow down at my feet,
> And swear that since the world began,
>   There was nothing half so sweet.[38]

The Negro suffrage movement in the South was brought in by Northern travelers, teachers, soldiers, Freedmen's Bureau agents, and special organizations. Though the masses never embraced suffrage with complete enthusiasm, the leaders among the Negroes quickly took it up and began encouraging it among their race. Negro meetings and conventions, usually promoted by interested whites, became common throughout the South, and suffrage was always put high on the lists of rights demanded. Probably the first of these meetings took place in Nashville on August 24, 1865, to be followed the next month by a large gathering in Raleigh with delegates present from almost half the counties of North Carolina. This convention demanded the right to testify in court, to serve on

[37] Augusta *Weekly Constitutionalist*, August 12, 1868.
[38] Carrollton *Times*, November 9, 1867.

juries, and to vote; and it solemnly announced, "These rights we want, these rights we contend for, and these rights, under God, we must ultimately have." This convention, like most Negro gatherings, partook of a politico-religious nature with shouts and sobs and at times with fights waxing hot over such trivialities as who should be the seventh vice-president. In October a meeting held in Mobile sent Sumner a special invitation which he declined. In January, 1866, a Negro convention in Augusta petitioned the legislature for the usual rights. This meeting was under the control of the Equal Rights Association, an organization founded in the North and widely extended over the South. In 1869, after suffrage had come to the Southern Negroes, a national Negro organization was established in Washington, with Georgia's *nègre terrible,* Henry M. Turner, acting as temporary chairman. Two years later this organization met in Columbia to promote Negro rights and solidarity.[39]

The first impulse of most Southerners was to disbelieve that anyone could be so diabolical as to give the Negro the vote and hand the South over to him to rule. "To give the negroes the privilege of the elective franchise NOW," said a Memphis editor in the fall of 1865, "would be little short of madness"; [40] and an Augusta editor denied that the Negro was fit to govern himself, "much less the whites." [41] "Good God! the thought is horrible," said a Charlestonian. "Give us peace or exterminate us at once." [42] Benjamin H. Hill thundered out that the South would never consent to Negro government "whether with or without the aid of the mischief-making adventurers from abroad, or selfish apostates

[39] New Orleans *Times,* June 23, 1865; Andrews, *South since the War,* 120–31; Allen, *Reconstruction,* 73; A. Saxon, Mobile, Ala., to Sumner, October 25, 1865, in Sumner Papers, Box 74, No. 156; *American Freedman,* I (1866), 11–14, 86; *Daily Columbus Enquirer,* February 9, July 17, 1866; Raleigh *Tri-Weekly Standard,* January 17, 1867; Sandersville *Central Georgian,* April 11, May 23, 1866; Henry L. Swint, *The Northern Teacher in the South, 1862–1870* (Nashville, 1941), 31; Tallahassee *Weekly Floridian,* June 27, October 31, 1871; Washington *New National Era,* October 26, November 2, 1871; Charles H. Wesley, *Negro Labor in the United States, 1850–1925* (New York, 1927), 169–70.

[40] Memphis *Argus,* October 17, 1865.

[41] Augusta (Ga.) *Daily Press,* February 12, 1869.

[42] Tallahassee *Sentinel,* July 22, 1867.

from their own blood at home." [43] A more mild-mannered Southerner counseled, "Let us see that our colored friends have a plenty of good food and clothes and fuel to sustain life, before we summon them to the electoral college to settle grave affairs of State and determine the destiny of nations." [44] A Northern traveler said that the Negroes were "densely ignorant, and comprehend nothing of the meaning of politics," and that he had never met a Southerner, rebel or Unionist, who favored Negro suffrage; [45] and a Northerner resident in the South declared he would never consent to Negroes being "rulers over me and my children." [46]

History afforded glaring examples of Negro rule, both past and in the making. Who could complacently look at its record in Haiti, Santo Domingo, or Jamaica!—and Southerners were now contemplating much the unhappy lot of these countries. "It is murderous to be compelled to live where every thing around you, justly calls up these dark & gloomy apprehensions," said a South Carolinian. [47] Most applicable to the South was the situation in Jamaica, where the slaves, set free a generation earlier, were at this very time carrying out a murderous uprising against their former masters, now ruined. Remembering Jamaica's plight, a Georgian in 1865 hoped that the "Christmas bells will never ring as a tocsin, but rather in mellifluous tones well out: 'Peace and good will, good will and peace, peace and good will to all mankind!' " [48] Even kindly advice came from England to the government in Washington that it make not the same mistake the British had made in Jamaica—that it not let its Southern lands run to waste and become a place where the Negroes might "squat and vegetate." [49]

Yet in the face of what appeared so universally to be a catastrophe, there were some Southerners who felt it was best that they

[43] Benjamin H. Hill, Jr., *Senator Benjamin H. Hill of Georgia: His Life, Speeches and Writings* (Atlanta, 1893), 808.

[44] *De Bow's Review,* I (1866), 140.

[45] *Nation,* II (1866), 493.

[46] Stearns, *Black Man of the South,* 427.

[47] Dudley, Bennettsville, S.C., to Chandler, June 29, 1866, in William E. Chandler Papers, II, Nos. 294–97.

[48] Augusta *Weekly Constitutionalist,* December 6, 1865.

[49] London *Times,* quoted in Augusta *Weekly Constitutionalist,* March 21, 1866. See also, *ibid.,* January 31, 1866.

themselves give the suffrage to the Negro and thereby avert the full force of the Radicals. There was some possibility that by so doing they would win the gratitude of the freedmen and secure the control of their votes. Fear of this development disturbed the Radicals and made even Johnson consider it undesirable since it would dim his hope of displacing with the middle class the old planter leadership. The South did not act, and the North won the Negro's political heart so completely that for some years few freedmen could ever be persuaded by their white friends to vote the Democratic ticket. A Negro would follow his old master's advice "in matters of labor and investment in which he was personally concerned," but would bitterly oppose him in politics.[50] A Georgian in reasoning politically with his former slave said, "Mike, you have known me all your life. Don't you believe I would tell you what is right?" "Yes, Mas Henry, I know what you say is right," he replied; but still he voted the Republican ticket.[51] A Mississippian declared he "would as soon reason with a shoal of crocodiles or a drove of Kentucky mules." [52]

If Southerners had been less prejudiced and more realistic, they would have followed the instincts of Lincoln. They would have given the suffrage to those Negroes worthy of it and thereby would have helped "to keep the jewels of liberty within the family of freedom." In so doing they would not have compromised with the true principles of democratic government.

Although it was impossible to reason many Negroes into Democrats, it was almost as difficult to make the mass of them vote at

[50] Fort Warren Letter, August 11, 1865, in Reagan Papers; Reagan to J. W. Throckmorton, October 12, 1866, *ibid.*; Augusta *Weekly Constitutionalist*, February 21, 1866; Fleming (ed.), *Documentary History of Reconstruction*, I, 117; George Campbell, *White and Black. The Outcome of a Visit to the United States* (London, 1879), 182; Reid, *Southern Tour*, 143–45, 288–89; Fleming, *Civil War and Reconstruction in Alabama*, 386–91; King, *Great South*, 81. The *Nation*, IV (1867), 286, said the Negro would be courted by everybody "and many Democratic Politicians will have negro blood in their veins—while on the stump, at any rate."

[51] Augustus L. Hull, *Annals of Athens, Georgia, 1801–1901* (Athens, 1906), 293.

[52] James B. Ranck, *Albert Gallatin Brown, Radical Southern Nationalist* (New York, 1937), 275. A Mississippi planter said, "The negroes whom I employ will always come to me for help in their troubles; they deposit their money with me; they think I am the best man in the world. But when it comes to the election they will take the word of the most notorious low-lived vagabond who calls himself a Republican before they will mine." Nordhoff, *Cotton States*, 81.

all. In some regions the general impression prevailed that they should be paid for voting, and liquor and barbecues were frequently resorted to as persuaders. "Without all this, the negro will not vote," a Republican admitted.[53] Negroes began to see the emptiness of voting, and one in South Carolina advised: "Colored men of the South, it were time we were turning our attention to other duties than following the lead of irresponsible politicians." [54] Yet in some regions Negroes became intoxicated with their freedom, and sought to vote before laws had been passed allowing it. It has been said that the first Negro suffrage in the South was in May, 1865, in the election of the mayor of Fernandina, Florida, supervised by Treasury agents; also about this time a so-called election of a Negro Congressman took place among the colored population in Leon County, Florida. Joe Oats, the successful candidate, a dishonest scamp, playing upon the gullibility of his colored constituents, took up a collection among them for his trip to Washington. After spending the money on a journey that carried him probably as far as Georgia, he returned to make a report on the laws which he had got passed.[55]

When the wheels of misfortune turned their rounds and propelled the Negroes not only into voting but also into holding office as well, amidst an atmosphere reeking with a corruption produced mostly by their white allies and mentors, Negro officeholders were given a reputation for ignorance and dishonesty that was long to dog the progress of the race. They were put into places of responsibility before they were ready; no malignant enemy could have done the Negro race a greater disservice. Indeed might the Negroes have cried out: Save us from our friends.

Certain Northern visionaries honestly thought that the solution of the Negro question lay not only in forced social equality but also in the disappearance of both races through miscegenation;

[53] Nordhoff, *Cotton States*, 19. See also, A. L. Harris, Savannah, to Sherman, November 29, 1867, in Sherman Papers, CXXIV, Nos. 28522–25; Tallahassee *Sentinel*, May 3, 1867; Fleming (ed.), *Documentary History of Reconstruction*, II, 44.

[54] Augusta *Weekly Constitutionalist*, November 25, 1868.

[55] Alrutheus A. Taylor, *The Negro in Tennessee, 1865–1880* (Washington, 1941), 1–24; Hamilton J. Eckenrode, *The Political History of Virginia during the Reconstruction* (Baltimore, 1904), 65–66; J. G. de Roulhac Hamilton, *Reconstruction in North Carolina* (New York, 1914), 120.

the political tricksters knew better, but for a time they favored the program as part of their scheme to capture and hold Negro votes. Well might Southerners look with abhorrence on miscegenation, as, indeed, did most Northerners, with one of the latter expressing some levity in this parody on "Yankee Doodle Dandy":

> *Yankee Doodle is no more,*
> *Sunk his name and station;*
> *Nigger Doodle takes his place,*
> *And favors 'malgamation.*
> *Nigger Doodle's all the go,*
> *Ebon shins and bandy,*
> *Loyal people all must bow*
> *To Nigger Doodle Dandy.*[56]

Bishop Gilbert Haven of the Northern Methodist Church saw the millennium nearing when he predicted that the "hour is not far off when the white hued husband shall boast of the dusky beauty of his wife, and the Caucasian wife shall admire the sun-kissed countenance of her husband as deeply and as unconscious of the present ruling abhorrence as is his admiration for her lighter tint." [57] In addition to a few Negro reformers, only the dregs of both races favored intermarriage. A South Carolina Negro boasted that "when 'the Yankees' came he would go to 'quiltings,' sit beside white girls, and have a white wife." [58] Laws as well as antipathy prevented racial amalgamation.

There was much muddled thinking, in both sections of the nation, on what constituted social equality. Many Southerners erroneously believed that Negro suffrage meant social equality; with more reason they felt that to admit Negroes without segregation to conveyances, schools, hotels, and other public conveniences would be dangerous. To prevent these intrusions, they passed the so-called "Jim Crow" laws. Many Northerners, forgetful of the fact that their Negroes were few, believed that their own admixtures

[56] New York *Vindicator*, quoted in Carrollton *Times*, September 22, 1866.
[57] Hunter D. Farish, *The Circuit Rider Dismounts: A Social History of Southern Methodism, 1865–1900* (Richmond, 1938), 212–13.
[58] *Ku Klux Conspiracy*, I, 521.

bore no relation to social equality; that, as Greeley argued, there was no more social equality in Boston than in New Orleans.[59] Many Negroes very naturally and with good reason wanted the right to go and come in the company of whites in public places, to ride on streetcars and trains, to enjoy public parks, to attend public meetings, to go to public schools, to join temperance societies, and to become members of lodges like the Good Templars.[60] The reformers believed that such associations would lead to social equality. "Nothing removes prejudice so rapidly as laws prohibiting distinction or discrimination," declared an emissary of the new day in Georgia.[61] In the heyday of Negro rule in South Carolina, such rights bolstered by Negro suffrage did bring about social equality to some extent.

If social equality meant, as it evidently did mean, that the races would have the right to associate together in the same social functions, the mass of Negroes did not want it. Negroes of substance and intelligence wanted to build up their own society, and they objected to the presence of whites just as the whites disliked mingling with Negroes. Low whites were ejected from a Negro dance hall in Macon, Georgia, and the city court fined one of them $10.[62] A Louisiana Negro declared, "Social equality is a humbug. There are many men of my own color with whom I would not associate, and not a few whites in the same category." [63] One old colored man expressed his philosophy in this quaint way, "White folks dat'll eat wid me ain't fitten fuh me to eat wid." [64] Stephens, who knew many freedmen and was well respected by them, said he

[59] Americus *Tri-Weekly Sumter Republican*, December 13, 1866; Rome (Ga.) *Weekly Courier*, October 1, 1873; Kennaway, *On Sherman's Track*, 82; Fleming (ed.), *Documentary History of Reconstruction*, I, 281.

[60] New Orleans *Tribune*, June 10, 1865; Atlanta *Weekly Sun*, October 16, 1872; Elberton (Ga.) *Gazette*, August 7, 1872; Howard K. Beale, "On Rewriting Reconstruction History," in *American Historical Review* (New York), XLV (1939–1940), 819.

[61] E. Belcher, Augusta, Ga., to Sumner, April 7, 1870, in Sumner Papers, Box 99, No. 42.

[62] Macon *Daily Telegraph*, February 13, 1866. J. N. Glenn, Conyers, Ga., wrote Sumner, June 11, 1870, that "the Negroes poor creatures none but the verry [*sic*] worst of them desire it [social equality]." Sumner Papers, Box 99, No. 56.

[63] New Orleans *Weekly Times*, December 19, 1874. See also, Atlanta *Christian Index*, August 17, 1871.

[64] Avary, *Dixie after the War*, 192.

believed the Georgia Negroes wanted no social equality or mixed race relations of any kind.[65]

Radical politicians in the South soon saw that arguments for social equality lost them votes among both races, and they began to declare the whole movement had been trumped up by the Democrats to injure the Republicans. A Radical meeting in Morganton, North Carolina, in 1867, attended by 2,000 blacks and whites, resolved that "no sensible person of any complexion desires or expects social equality; and that we do hereby denounce, as a base slanderer, any man who insinuates that it is one of the objects or purposes of the Republican party to bring about social equality between the white and colored races." [66]

One of the cruelest frauds practiced upon the Negro by his supposed benefactors was the inferential promise of land and other property. Its positive purpose was to humble and strike terror into the hearts of the whites, for according to this scheme the white man's land was to be confiscated and given to the Negroes. The basis of this threat was the Confiscation Act of 1862, which provided for the seizure of "rebel" property but which Lincoln refused to enforce. During the war certain so-called abandoned property was seized by the armies, especially in South Carolina and Georgia, and given temporarily to the Negroes; but with the end of the war Stevens hit upon his plan to confiscate lands of Confederates owning more than 200 acres, estimated to amount to almost 300,000,000 acres. It was to be distributed to the freedmen in 40-acre lots, and the remainder was to be sold to provide pensions for Federal soldiers and to pay the national debt.

Thus was the Negro, who needed property before all other things, given the promise of it. The news was spread by soldiers, Treasury agents, teachers, Freedmen's Bureau agents, and other Northern emissaries. A representative of the Northern Methodists' God declared: "Both retributive and compensative justice demand that property in the South should change hands, and a just God will see to it that those who have been robbed of their earnings for generations shall not fail to obtain their share. Everything is

[65] *Speech of Hon. Alex. H. Stephens, of Georgia, on the Civil Rights Bill, Delivered in the House of Representatives, January 5, 1874* (Washington, 1874), 12.
[66] Raleigh *Tri-Weekly Standard*, August 31, 1867.

now drifting in that way, and in the golden age coming the planters of the South will be black men." [67] Radical Negro leaders began to insist that there could be no republican government unless the planters' property were seized. Rebels "have forfeited their rights to the protection of society," said a Louisiana Negro. "It is enough for the republic to spare the life of the rebels,—without restoring to them their plantations and palaces." There might be "amnesty for the persons, no amnesty for the property." [68] As time wore on Negroes became anxious for the distribution—for their forty acres and a mule. A Memphis editor said of Arkansas, and might have extended his statement to include the rest of the South: "Scarcely a grown-up man or woman of African extraction, in town or country, but believes that he or she will very shortly be placed, by virtue of a Congressional edict, in possession of the comfortable homes and broad acres of his or her whilom master or mistress." [69]

Negroes became upset and unruly and threatened to seize what they could—in fact, some of their riots were called forth by these agrarian desires. News was spread that all horses and mules ridden into Tallahassee by whites would be seized and given to the freedmen. [70] To disabuse the minds of Negroes the United States Commissioner of Agriculture declared that there would be no "dividends of confiscated estates." [71] Sane Negro leaders, such as James H. Harris, warned his people, "You will not believe these evil-minded men who persuade you that you will get a portion of your master's land." [72]

Continuing to hold confiscation as a promise to the Negroes for their votes and as a club over the whites to humble them, Stevens in 1867 introduced his confiscation bill in Congress, embodying his pledge made in 1865, with the additional feature of providing recompense to all loyal citizens for damages done to them by the war. As for the justice of this, stern old Stevens said, "He who can patiently listen to that putrid humanity which we now see propagated, has more command of himself than I have." [73]

[67] Farish, *Circuit Rider Dismounts*, 172. See also, *De Bow's Review*, I (1866), 324.
[68] New Orleans *Tribune*, April 19, May 6, 1865.
[69] Memphis *Avalanche*, quoted in Augusta *Weekly Constitutionalist*, May 29, 1867.
[70] Tallahassee *Sentinel*, September 30, 1867.   [71] *De Bow's Review*, V (1868), 80.
[72] Raleigh *Tri-Weekly Standard*, September 3, 1867.
[73] Americus *Tri-Weekly Sumter Republican*, June 1, 1867.

Although the South did not know it, there was not the slightest chance that Congress would pass a confiscation bill; it had never been in a Republican party platform and it was strongly opposed by many Congressmen. Senator Henry Wilson of Massachusetts, stern enough against the South otherwise, declared that Southerners had suffered and been disappointed "more than any body of men in the history of the world," and that he would not stand for confiscation. "I don't want an Ireland or Poland in America." [74] And Greeley declared that he knew of nobody in the North who wanted confiscation, except Stevens and turncoat Ben Butler.[75]

There were much deeper reasons held in the North against confiscation than humanitarian considerations; there was that much more compelling reason of self-interest. Confiscation was a revolutionary doctrine much too dangerous to be played with. It was a doctrine that might very readily spread over the North, and "very soon under its debauching influence, immense numbers at the North will be clambering in the name of 'Agrarianism,' 'Equalization,' and other taking names, for their neighbors' possessions." [76] Using William Aiken of South Carolina and James W. Wadsworth of New York as examples of Southern and Northern businessmen, a Philadelphia editor made this pertinent application of the confiscation doctrine: "The labor which rendered Aiken's fields fertile and brought to him a large return was just as lawfully obtained, just as liberally compensated for under the laws and rules governing in the community, and no more arbitrarily regulated, than the labor which made Wadsworth's vast estate what it is and put money in his purse. . . . No claim upon the products of labor on behalf of Southern laborers can be made without asserting a

[74] Greensboro *Herald*, August 31, 1867.

[75] Aberdeen *Daily Sunny South*, December 3, 1866; Americus *Tri-Weekly Sumte Republican*, December 13, 1866.

[76] Augusta *Weekly Constitutionalist*, July 3, 1867. See also, Atlanta *Daily New Era*, October 8, 1867; Roger W. Shugg, *Origins of Class Struggle in Louisiana* . . . (University, La., 1939), 243. A Northern writer said that "the masses may demand a redistribution of Northern property, for their benefit, such as the Radicals will then have made in the South for the benefit of the negro." L. B. Woolfolk, *The World's Crisis* (Cincinnati, 1868), 649. A confiscation of Southern property "would win for us throughout the civilized world the character of obdurate barbarians," said the *Nation*, IV (1867), 375.

68

similar claim for Northern laborers." [77] The Troy (New York) *Times* said that "if Mr. [Wendell] Phillips' reasoning [for confiscation] be good for the South it must be good for the North also, and it proposes to begin the division of property at Boston"; to which the Boston *Commercial Bulletin* replied, "We are not quite ready to 'divide up' here in New England, though the dividend would probably be represented by a figure quite tempting to spendthrifts and small politicians." [78]

Here was the complete answer to the question of how much of a revolution the responsible North had in mind in reconstructing the South. The South was being held down, not to establish communism there, but to assure a more capitalistic exploitation of the North. Stevens' controlling principle was not to help the Negro. If it had been, he would not have attempted the trick of confiscation; he would have worked out a Federal aid program whereby the government would have bought from Southerners their surplus land and given it to the Negroes or sold it to them on a long-term payment plan. How humanitarian it really would have been if the money denied Southerners for their slaves could have reached them by this other method, and the freedmen have received their worth in land! The Negro's high hopes were left to fade away; how much better for him, had they never been raised!

[77] Quoted in *De Bow's Review*, IV (1867), 587.   [78] Quoted *ibid.*, 588.

CHAPTER IV

THE FREEDMEN'S BUREAU

THE nearest the United States government came to a program of rehabilitation for the South was the establishment in the War Department of a Bureau of Refugees, Freedmen, and Abandoned Lands whose major activities were designed only for the Negroes, however, and even for them it was not to supply that economic security which the old masters had given. The law setting it up came into being the day before Lincoln's second inauguration, and provided that the Bureau should continue for the duration of the war and one year thereafter. Its powers and duties were increased in a bill which President Johnson vetoed on February 19, 1866, but which in rewritten form was passed over his veto the following July.

By the last-named measure the Bureau should disband at the end of two years. Subsequent legislation extended its life to 1872 but curtailed its activities. For administrative purposes the South was divided into districts, each consisting usually of one state, though in some cases there might be two states, as in the case of Kentucky and Tennessee. At the head was a commissioner, with an assistant commissioner for each state. Under each assistant commissioner were numerous agents and clerks. All were required to take the ironclad oath, declaring that they had never voluntarily aided the Confederacy in any fashion or particular. The Commissioner was General Oliver O. Howard of Maine, who continued in the office throughout the life of the Bureau. Among other accomplishments, he had marched through Georgia with General Sherman, and had therefore come in contact with many destitute Negroes. When the Bureau legislation was debated in Congress it was feared that this organization might become a rest-ing place for broken-down preachers and played-out reformers, too lazy to work and slightly too honest to steal; but actually more deserving patriots received most of the positions. The law contemplated the use of soldiers and military officers extensively and even exclusively if deemed best. In South Carolina as well as in Florida the army was at first almost completely in charge of Bureau activities; whereas in Georgia and Alabama the local state officials carried on the work in the beginning. As the Bureau became better established throughout the South, the personnel changed considerably, and now Northern Treasury agents, reformers, and school-teachers took almost complete charge. As most of the Southern local officials who at first acted as agents were unable to take the ironclad oath, they were dismissed. Assistant commissioners were generally high army officers. The Bureau operated in all the former Confederate states and also in the border slave states, though it did not reach Texas until December, 1865.[1]

The duty of the Bureau was to look after the interests of the Negroes and of the "loyal [white] refugees." None of the latter were of the planter class, however far they might have "refugeed" or however destitute they might be. Soon even the most loyal white refugees were convinced that they were only the stepchildren of the Bureau if not, indeed, outcasts. The Bureau's immediate task was to prevent people from starving, especially the improvident and excited Negroes filling the towns and cluttering up army camps and the whites in the devastated wake of the armies, and here the Bureau was least partial in its activities. Almost all of this relief was given during the fall and winter following the Surrender and during 1867, the year of destitution. The Bureau gave out a total of almost 22,000,000 rations, of which the freedmen received about 15,500,000. During the first year, whites in Alabama received more rations than did the freedmen. Even so, the Bureau failed to reach a great many destitute people, for its agents were located only in towns and cities but not in all of them. This fact was an important cause leading the Negroes to flock to the towns,

1 Paul S. Peirce, *The Freedmen's Bureau: A Chapter in the History of Reconstruction* (Iowa City, 1904), 44, 48; Andrews, *South since the War*, 24, 259; *American Freedman*, I (1866), 87; James G. Randall, *The Civil War and Reconstruction* (Boston, 1937), 731.

leaving the old and infirm behind for their destitute former masters to feed—an obligation the Bureau insisted must be met even though all the younger Negroes who could work had left. Southerners felt the injustice of such requirements. Although the Negro had been freed from his slavery to the white man, yet by such rules the old master must continue in his servitude to his old slaves. Most former slaveowners as far as it lay within their power were glad to provide for their old servants, yet justice required that the United States government take up the old master's obligations now that the Negro had been freed of his.

Another service of immediate importance performed by the Bureau was to give free transportation to freedmen and refugees making their way back home or going to places of employment. Most of this aid was given in 1865 and 1866, during which time 2,000 refugees and 30,000 freedmen were assisted.

There was a vision faintly grasped and then allowed to fade, which if carried out, would have been of inestimable worth to future generations—hospitalization and socialized medicine. True enough, it was provided primarily for Negroes, but if it had continued it might well have been extended to all races and throughout the land. Freed from their masters' care the Negroes fell a prey to disease, especially to deadly smallpox, becoming a menace to all about them. The Bureau set up forty-five hospitals and during the first year after the war treated 143,000 freedmen and 5,600 refugees.[2]

The original law of March 3, 1865, setting up the Freedmen's Bureau, by inference left the impression that the freedmen were to be provided with land, their greatest necessity as well as their greatest desire. The Bureau was made the custodian of all abandoned and confiscated land and empowered to divide it into forty-acre tracts, to be rented to refugees and freedmen for three years, after which they might buy it at slightly more than sixteen times the yearly rent. Even if nothing else had intervened, few could have bought the land at this price. The scheme was either a grim trick or a naïve hope.

The amount of land which came into the possession of the Bureau

[2] Swint, *Northern Teacher in the South*, 5; Peirce, *Freedmen's Bureau*, 87–104; *De Bow's Review*, III (1867), 194–95.

was only 800,000 acres (including 1,500 pieces of town property) which, although it comprised less than one fifth of one per cent of the land in the Confederacy, consisted generally of the choice plantations. This land was seized for nonpayment of the direct Federal tax levied at the beginning of the war, or confiscated because the owner had aided the Confederacy or because he had supposedly abandoned it. Legally, abandoned property was so designated because the owner had left it to aid the Confederacy, but zealous and dishonest agents considered anything abandoned which was not being occupied by the owner. In the summer of 1865 Christopher G. Memminger having left his Charleston home to spend a vacation in the mountains of North Carolina soon learned that it had been seized as abandoned. Federal agents confiscated for their own use law libraries and robbed mansions of old family portraits later "to look down from the walls" of Yankee residences. Much of the land seized for taxes was in the Beaufort, South Carolina, region. It was divided into twenty-acre lots which permanently came into the possession of the freedmen, though enough whites later returned to dominate the region socially and economically, but not politically for a long time.[3]

Most of the so-called abandoned property was ultimately returned to the owners, as President Johnson's pardons carried with them the restoration of property. Negroes who had settled down on this land as renters were given time to gather their crops and allowed to collect the value of any permanent improvements they had made; but the owner could often offset these claims by counterclaims for wood cut or other uses that reduced the value of the property. It did not seem to be generally known that confiscated property could be held only during the lifetime of the original owner, for the Federal Constitution declares that "no Attainder of Treason shall work Corruption of Blood, or Forfeiture except during the Life of the Person attainted." In pursuance of this principle, the heirs of John Slidell recovered after his death confiscated property amounting to over $275,000 and rents of $10,000 accumulating in the period after his death and before the

3 Charleston *Courier*, September 11, 1865; Peirce, *Freedmen's Bureau*, 129; Henry D. Capers, *The Life and Times of C. G. Memminger* (Richmond, 1893), 378; Reid, *Southern Tour*, 48; Campbell, *White and Black*, 117.

return of the property. The heirs of Robert E. Lee were paid $150,000 for Arlington which the Federal government had early in the war seized not as confiscated property but for the non-payment of the direct tax, the claim being paid on the ground of a defect in the procedure of seizing it.[4] Thus was justice done the Southerner, but in so doing the freedman saw his hopes of becoming a landowner go glimmering. Instead, he was given the ballot, which he could neither eat nor wear nor use intelligently.

The Bureau entered the laudable field of providing the freedman a job as a free laborer and seeking to protect his rights as a worker. If this supervision had been carried out by people who knew as much about Negroes and conditions in the South as did the Southerners, there should have been no complaint; but the supervising agents were largely Northern placemen and former Federal soldiers. Though not uniformly visionary, many of them were enough so to bring down upon themselves the opposition not only of planters but even of some of the freedmen. During the war Negroes had been forced by Federal armies to labor on seized plantations and some of the rules used were adopted after the war both by the Freedmen's Bureau and by the planters.

Southerners, knowing Negroes better, felt that they should be allowed to deal with the freedmen without interference. De Bow declared that when he was superintendent of the Census in 1850 he made a study of free Negroes, and that he found them "immeasurably better off" in the South than in the North.[5] Free Negroes, therefore, offered no new problem. "The best friend today that the freedman has," said a Southern editor, "is the Southern man." The Radical politician loved him because the Negro "makes his capital"; the Bureau loved him "because the freedman is his bread and butter"; and the "professional philanthropist weeps" because

[4] Charleston *Courier,* September 8, December 27, 1865; Atlanta *Daily New Era,* November 15, 1867; Trowbridge, *South,* 377, 534–35; McPherson, *Reconstruction,* 13; Greenville *Enterprise,* May 1, 1872; Little Rock *Weekly Arkansas Gazette,* February 3, 1874; Randall, *Civil War and Reconstruction,* 691; New Orleans *Weekly Times,* July 18, 1874. See also, Pargoud *v.* United States, 13 Wallace 156 (1871), and Armstrong *v.* United States, 13 Wallace 154 (1871).

[5] *Report of the Joint Committee on Reconstruction,* Pt. IV, 134.

"every tear over Cuffee is as good to him as gold." [6] The United States Commissioner of Agriculture was sure that the least apprehension of an attempt to revive the system of slavery was entirely groundless; [7] and De Bow declared that if Southerners were "let alone, to manage affairs in their own way, and with their intimate knowledge of negro character, and that sympathy with him and his fortunes, which is but the natural result of long and close association, every thing . . . [would] be done, in good time, for the social, physical, and political advancement of the race." [8] In some communities the planters formed county-wide associations to make sure that no one gave the Negro workman less than what they considered to be his just rights.

Continuing to work on the same plantations for the same masters appeared to the freedmen too much like slavery, and as long as they could go to town and get Bureau rations they expected to enjoy their freedom. They did not like to be summoned to work by the old slave devices of blaring horns and clanging bells and they did not like the term "overseer" any longer. And some of them began to dislike their old friend King Cotton. Said one, "If ole massa want to grow cotton, let him plant it himself. I'se work for him dese twenty years, and done got nothin' but food and clothes, and dem mighty mean; now I'se freedman, and I tell you I ain't going to work cotton *nohow*." [9] To protect himself and the freedman, too, the planter as well as the Freedmen's Bureau, insisted on written contracts, but the freedman not always understanding them and soon forgetting what he might have understood did not like to sign them. He wanted to be a free agent to take advantage of any opportunity which might come his way; never

[6] Augusta *Weekly Constitutionalist*, September 19, 1866.

[7] *Report of the Commissioner of Agriculture*, 1867, p. x.

[8] *De Bow's Review*, I (1866), 7.

[9] *Nation*, I (1865), 426. See also, Trowbridge, *South*, 367. Robert Somers, the Englishman, who traveled over the South in 1870–1871, said he found on one plantation a bell with a rich sweet tone and that he would have given "a quarter-dollar at any time to hear its soft and melodious peal sounding over the great silent valley"; but it reminded the Negroes of slavery, and now the most they would endure from the bell was the sound of a gentle tap with the finger. He observed the Negroes had been "elevated by some 'patent hoist' unknown to ordinary human experience." Somers, *Southern States since the War*, 130.

having had a chance heretofore, he could not well be blamed for wanting to seize any flood tide that might come along. Now having something which the planter must have, he could use his labor as a club to be swung in many directions.

During the fall of 1865 labor conditions were much upset, and the Bureau warned the freedmen that they must work or starve. Assistant Commissioner David Tillson of Georgia announced: "Rations will not be issued, or other aid given, to able bodied refugees or freed people who are offered, or who can find, opportunities to labor for their own support and who neglect or refuse to do it." [10] The unfortunate rumor had been spread by soldiers and certain Bureau agents that there was to be a distribution at Christmas—forty acres and a mule, and some wag added "and a white man to do the work." Naturally, a Negro was loath to bind himself to work a year for someone else when he himself was about to become a planter.

The contracts were of many kinds and with the passing of years they were changed fundamentally. For the remainder of the year 1865 after the Surrender, some Negroes were willing to work for no more than they had received in slavery—food, clothing, a cabin, medical attention, and the care of the old and the young. As freedom developed others were given the wages of slavery and in addition from an eighth to a third of the crop. Some planters with extreme liberality gave them half of the crop and this grew into the custom in Mississippi. The plan of including food, at first widely used, was based on an understanding of the Negro's tendency to prowl; he would spend half his time going after his food if it were not provided. Economists of the day estimated a proper distribution to be one third for labor, one third for land, and one third for supplies which would include work stock, farm implements, and seed. According to this estimate laborers were getting a much bigger return than they deserved. They assumed none of the risks and yet they received generally a half of the crops, having furnished nothing but their labor. The principle was wrong, as the Negroes labored only on what they shared. For helping to keep the plantation in order, clearing land and hedges, draining wet lands, work-

10 *Daily Columbus Enquirer,* October 28, 1865.

76

ing in vegetable gardens, they must be paid wages. Though the planter had some control over his plantation, it was less than complete. An Englishman who saw such an economic order for the first time observed, "The soul is often crushed out of labour by penury and oppression. Here a soul cannot begin to be infused into it through the sheer excess of privilege and licence [sic] with which it is surrounded." In some communities, and especially during the first period of freedom, wages were paid, ranging from $8.00 to $15.00 a month for men and less for women. Food and cabins were included. All contracts must be approved by Freedmen's Bureau agents, who used their best efforts to make the terms as liberal as possible for the freedmen. Enterprising printers provided blank forms for these labor contracts.[11]

The chief disadvantage of the wage system was the difficulty of holding the Negroes on the plantation when they received their pay, as they felt an impelling desire to spend it before engaging in further labor. As a result, most of their wages were withheld until the end of the year; and then the old difficulty reappeared, for this larger sum must be spent before they would sign another contract. Another disadvantage, which worked against the Negroes, was the inability of planters always to pay the promised wages. Crop failures, low prices, the inattention of the Negroes themselves, and other agricultural hazards sometimes left the planters without money. To protect themselves against some of these uncertainties, it was argued that planters should make contracts for shorter periods than a year.

As the Negroes had never had an opportunity to develop a sense of responsibility, they saw little reason to abide by their contracts— which to them were a restriction on their freedom. Their besetting sin was to leave their work at any time it suited their fancy—to slip away on short trips or to leave permanently. Where advances

11 For the quotation, see Somers, *Southern States since the War*, 129; for sources on other points, see Barnsley Papers, June 20, 1865; *Daily Aberdeen* (Miss.) *Examiner*, January 17, 1867; *Southern Cultivator*, XXIII (1865), 100–102; XXIV (1866), 4–5; XXVI (1868), 14; *De Bow's Review*, V (1868), 213; Jessie M. Fraser (ed.), "A Free Labor Contract, 1867," in *Journal of Southern History*, VI (1940), 547–48; Wesley, *Negro Labor in the United States*, 132; Aberdeen *Daily Sunny South*, December 3, 1866; *Daily Columbus Enquirer*, November 1, December 31, 1865; Trowbridge, *South*, 366.

were made to them in return for part of their share of the crop when it should be gathered, some of them still expected their original allowance and reported to the Bureau that they were being cheated. A Northerner who had come South to attempt to farm declared that Negroes would keep their contract "only so far as it suited them to do so; and any attempt on our part to enforce its provisions, were pronounced by them the acme of oppression, as worse than the 'rebs' served them." [12] Undoubtedly some planters took advantage of their Negro workmen, but anyone who would cheat a Negro would likely cheat a white man just as quickly. A Mississippi planter declared that agriculture in the South was at the mercy of irresponsible labor: "The *positive* fact is, that, until laws are passed to regulate the position of employer toward employee, and *vice versa,* there can be no reliability in planting, and, consequently, no success." [13] Some planters were quite successful in managing their labor supply. Gideon J. Pillow, who turned planter after the war, stated that he had 400 freedmen working well for him and that he could get 1,000 if he wanted them; and Andrew J. Donelson said the Negroes on his Mississippi plantation were entirely satisfied; he had no trouble either with the Negroes or with the Freedmen's Bureau.[14] A Northerner traveling through the South in 1865–1866 observed, "Judging from what I saw in Georgia, Alabama, Mississippi and Louisiana, I should say that a great majority of the freedmen are now receiving tolerably good treatment and tolerably good wages." [15]

The Negroes debated in their minds and on the rostrum what system they liked best. In one forensic display in Georgia the question debated was stated thus, "Which is better for the laboring man, to work for wages or a part of the crop?" [16] The more industrious and intelligent who were unable to become landowners rejected both these systems and sought to become renters, where in the beginning the landlord could control neither their labor nor their crops. They paid the landlord either a money rental

[12] *Daily Columbus Enquirer,* March 23, 1866. See also, Leigh, *Ten Years on a Georgia Plantation,* 75; Stearns, *Black Man of the South,* 363.

[13] *Plantation* . . . (Atlanta), II (1871), 546.

[14] *De Bow's Review,* I (1866), 224; Augusta *Weekly Constitutionalist,* September 20, 1865.

[15] *Nation,* II (1866), 493.   [16] Macon *American Union,* January 26, 1871.

or more often a part of the crop. Usually the planter furnished everything except labor and took half the crop. This represented a great gain in the eyes of the Negroes, for under this system with no supervision they received as much as they had made under the share system. The Negro was as independent of the landlord as if he owned the land. To the planters this was a dangerous trend. To lease land to Negroes of character was all right, "but to locate Tom, Dick and Harry at farming in their own account, concerning whom there is no evidence that they will work systematically or live honestly, is to set up a moral pest-house—a source of temptation to idleness, discontent and dishonesty right around you. . . . Let negroes by diligence and frugality get a fee-simple title to land if they wish to farm on their own account. The habit acquired in earning the land will then stick to them, and their example will stimulate others." [17]

The enforcement of contracts as well as the protection of all the other rights of freedmen, both real and fancied, was under control of the Freedmen's Bureau and was carried out by special Freedmen's Bureau courts. In theory these courts were to provide justice where the regular courts had not yet been set up or where the latter were attempting to enforce the Black Codes. They came and went in the various states without uniformity, depending on the whim of the assistant commissioner. Alabama escaped them for a time in the beginning; they were discontinued in Georgia and in Tennessee in 1866. Such courts usually consisted of three people, a Freedmen's Bureau agent and two citizens of the vicinity if suitable ones could be found. There was no pretense of carrying out judicial hearings according to the rules of evidence used in regular courts and no attempt was made to apply the law. This was necessarily so, as the judges were untrained. They took up all matters relating to freedmen and if a white man were concerned especially in the matter of contracts the Negro usually came out winner. Many of the cases related to contracts, but petty crimes also made up an important part of the business,[18] and here the

[17] *Plantation*, II (1871), 216. See also, Nordhoff, *Cotton States*, 72; Robert P. Brooks, *The Agrarian Revolution in Georgia, 1865–1912* (Madison, 1914), *passim*.

[18] Nashville *Republican Banner*, May 27, 1866; Augusta *Weekly Constitutionalist*, May 23, 1866; *Daily Columbus Enquirer*, May 24, 1866; David Tillson, *Bureau of*

freedmen were likely to receive sterner justice. Worse crimes were punished by regular military commissions more often than through the regular courts, until the *Ex parte* Milligan decision temporarily abolished this form of military interference.[19]

Actuated more by fear that the South would educate the Negroes and thereby gain their support rather than that it would not, the North undertook the task, and in this work the Freedmen's Bureau played an important part. Northern visionaries foresaw a much wider problem than educating merely the Negroes; the whole South, besotted for generations with its slavery, was barbarian and must be remade in the image of the North. James Russell Lowell declared that it had "no public libraries, no colleges worthy of the name, . . . no art, no science, still worse no literature but Simms'—there was no desire for them"; [20] and William Lloyd Garrison's *Liberator,* averring that no "portion of Europe for the past hundred years has been more hopelessly sunk in ignorance," asked, "Now, how can these masses of human beings, black and white—for there is virtually no difference in moral conditions at present—be raised to a fit position in the republic?" [21] A religionist answered that since the war had corrected the Southerners the government must now instruct them. It "should teach the South line upon line, precept upon precept, by military garrisons, by Bureau courts, by Congregational churches, by Northern settlers, by constitutional amendments, by christian missionaries, by free schools, lectures, newspapers and reading rooms, what be the first principles of social order, political eminence, moral worth and industrial success." [22] The *Nation* argued that education would make Southerners Republicans; [23] and the whole movement took on the character of a continuation of hostilities

---

Refugees, Freedmen and Abandoned Lands, Circular No. 4 (n.p., April 6, 1866); Kennaway, *On Sherman's Track,* 67; Trowbridge, *South,* 340, 446; Fleming (ed.), *Documentary History of Reconstruction,* I, 347.

[19] Augusta *Weekly Constitutionalist,* January 16, 1867. During Military Reconstruction, the *Ex Parte* Milligan decision was largely ignored.

[20] Paul H. Buck, *The Road to Reunion, 1865–1900* (Boston, 1937), 23. A New England Society was organized in Nashville and Sumner was invited to a meeting. Henry Stone, Nashville, to Sumner, December 14, 1867, in Sumner Papers, Box 84, No. 2.

[21] Boston *Liberator,* August 4, 1865.

[22] Atlanta *Christian Index,* March 22, 1866.

[23] *Nation,* VII (1868), 386.

left off at Appomattox. "A teacher costs less than a soldier," remarked a Northern editor.[24]

Federal aid sensibly directed would have been a befitting element in reconstructing the whole South; but such a program was never seriously considered. Attention was given to making the Negroes political and intellectual allies of the North and to blotting out racial lines in the South. A Boston teacher told Negro students in Richmond, "You boys who are laggards at school will drive donkeys on the streets of Richmond, while those that are industrious, studious and obedient, will own the mansions and stores on Main street." [25] The spearhead of this educational movement for the Negroes was carried forward first and with great vigor by aid societies organized all over the North, some of which began their work before the end of the war. A year after its close there were 366 societies and auxiliaries, each of which was responsible for sending from one to seven teachers to the South. They soon coalesced into two groups, the American Missionary Society for all sectarian activities, and the Freedmen's Union Commission for nonsectarian efforts.[26]

The main educational work of the Freedmen's Bureau was to aid schools set up by these organizations rather than to set up schools of its own. It afforded military protection wherever needed; it provided schoolhouses; it gave free transportation to teachers; and it met most of the expenses of these schools. Throughout the five years of its existence it expended $5,262,511 on Negro schools. This money came from the confiscation and sale of property that had belonged to the Confederate government and from the rentals of abandoned property before it was restored to its owners. Representing the former kind of property were blockade-runners, three of which sold for $50,000, warehouses, iron foundries, cotton, and hospitals. Returns from abandoned property soon dried up. The aid societies were also liberal in supporting these schools; for years the American Missionary Society expended annually $100,000. Much of this money was raised by the auxiliary societies located

24 Editor of the *Freedmen's Record*, quoted in Swint, *Northern Teacher in the South*, 84. See also, Charleston *Courier*, July 18, 1865.

25 Boston *Liberator*, June 16, 1865.

26 *National Freedman* (New York), II (1866), 133–36; *American Freedman*, I (1866), 1; Swint, *Northern Teacher in the South*, 5–22.

widely in the small Northern towns, but large industries also contributed with their humanitarianism doubtless reinforced by the expectation that the freedmen's purchasing power would ultimately be increased.[27]

In charge of the educational activities of the Freedmen's Bureau was John W. Alvord as general superintendent with his office in Washington, assisted by a superintendent in each state. All schools were required to make reports to the Bureau. In 1866 when the schools had become well established, there were 1,389 teachers in 964 schools instructing 90,000 students. Three years later the number of teachers had risen to 9,503, of whom probably 5,000 were natives of the North.[28]

It was the Northern teachers who determined the character of these schools and thereby greatly disturbed the Southerners. They were almost entirely women, "strong minded women and weak minded women"; "all either fanatics or knaves—in the proportion of about five of the latter to one of the former"; and their sole mission was "to stir up strife and sow the tares of hate and evil in the minds of their pupils." [29] Such were the opinions of most Southerners. Refusing to receive these teachers socially, they forced them to take refuge in the homes of Negroes and enjoy their society.

Although they were self-sacrificing and altruistic, their fanaticism blotted out the common sense necessary to the success of their work. A North Carolinian wrote President Johnson that they "conduct themselves in such a way as to disgust our folks, they

[27] William K. Boyd, "Some Phases of Educational History in the South since 1865," in *Studies in Southern History and Politics*, 280; Peirce, *Freedmen's Bureau*, 76; Buck, *Road to Reunion*, 166–67; Farish, *Circuit Rider Dismounts*, 180; Swint, *Northern Teacher in the South*, 3, 24–34. It should be remembered that Negro education was not universally provided in the North; Indiana had no provision for it until 1869, and then it must be in separate schools. Horace M. Bond, *Negro Education in Alabama: A Study in Cotton and Steel* (Washington, 1939), 32.

[28] Luther P. Jackson, "The Educational Efforts of the Freedmen's Bureau and Freedmen's Aid Societies in South Carolina, 1862–1872," in *Journal of Negro History*, VIII (1923), 1–40; *American Freedman*, I (1866), 21, 82, 90–91; Swint, *Northern Teacher in the South*, 35. There were 4,000 Negroes in school in Macon, Georgia, in 1866. *Nation*, II (1866), 228. Statistics of Negro pupils were highly inaccurate, because the same names were often counted more than once as they appeared in different lists. Swint, *Northern Teacher in the South*, 7.

[29] Atlanta *Daily Opinion*, September 5, 1867.

boast what they can do, talk abusingly about sins of slavery and glorify the North." [30] They left the North with the song on their lips:

> *We go to plant the common schools,*
> *On distant mountain swells,*
> *And give the Sabbaths of the South*
> *The ring of Northern bells.*[31]

One of them wrote, soon after arriving in Savannah, "I am just at this time feeling as if it would be pleasant, had I the power, and an *iron heel* strong enough, to grind every one of the Secessionists deep into the earth." [32]

Because the South believed that the Negroes would be made better people through education and because it feared the kind of education the Northern missionary teachers would give, many Southerners immediately following the Surrender advocated teaching the freedmen. The Negro was not to blame for his freedom; he had a kindly feeling toward his former master; the South could even forgo the education of its own white children for a time in order to save the Negro from error, prejudice, and superstition. Governor James L. Orr of South Carolina, former Governor Andrew B. Moore of Alabama, Jabez L. M. Curry, Bishop Holland N. McTyeire, and many other leaders of Southern thought favored this course. Bishop Stephen Elliot of Georgia, fearing the evil influence of Northern missionaries, declared, "Every person imported from abroad to instruct or teach these people is an influence, unintentional perhaps, but really, widening the breach between the races. This work must be done by ourselves—done faithfully, earnestly, and as in the sight of God." [33] A Georgia editor said he had always believed "that it was the duty of the State to provide for the instruction of all its inhabitants, of whatever color, even when the blacks were slaves." It certainly should not be left to Northern missionaries, "who have such crude ideas of us as a people, and many of whom are in the South at present for no other purpose than that of filling their pockets with what

[30] C. F. Sufdorff, Garysburg, N.C., to Johnson, July 28, 1866, in Johnson Papers, XCVIII, Nos. 11814–17.
[31] Stearns, *Black Man of the South,* 542.
[32] Swint, *Northern Teacher in the South,* 63.   [33] *De Bow's Review,* II (1866), 313.

little filthy lucre they may be able to gather from the unsuspecting colored man." [34] An Arkansas editor feared the Northern Jacobins would teach the freedmen "the deluding doctrines of Equality and Fraternity." [35]

Education, if provided by Southerners, made freedmen better workmen, whether the worker himself was receiving it or his children. As Negro families were more content to remain on the plantation if their children could attend a school, numerous planters provided schoolhouses and teachers at their own expense. Wade Hampton established a schoolhouse as well as a church for his plantation and gave this advice in a public speech, "Let us be scrupulously just in our dealings with him [the Negro], let us assist him in his aspirations for knowledge, and aid him in its acquisition." [36]

If the Negro were to be correctly educated, it must be done by Southerners. A call, therefore, went up for Southern teachers to take up work in the Freedmen's Bureau schools and in schools set up by Southerners, such as the school provided in Charleston by the Rev. A. Toomer Porter. From Alabama came this advice: "Let the colored people be educated and as far as we are able let the Southern people help them to build their schoolhouses and teach them too." [37] In some regions the entire teaching force of the Freedmen's Bureau schools consisted of native whites. The widows of Confederate soldiers, their children, and even Confederate soldiers became teachers in Negro schools. College graduates from many of the state universities engaged in this work; and some of the Northern aid societies bore testimony to the aid and interest of Southerners. At one time almost half of the teachers in the Freedman's Bureau schools were native whites.[38]

It should not be inferred that all Southerners favored educating Negroes or that those who favored educating them agreed with the instruction of Northern teachers. Illiterate whites generally

[34] Augusta *Weekly Constitutionalist*, April 3, 1867.

[35] Little Rock *Weekly Arkansas Gazette*, September 18, 1866.

[36] *De Bow's Review*, VIII (1870), 338.

[37] Montgomery *Advertiser*, quoted in Fleming (ed.), *Documentary History of Reconstruction*, II, 181.

[38] Farish, *Circuit Rider Dismounts*, 177–80, 184; Swint, *Northern Teacher in the South*, 122–42.

disliked Negroes and opposed educating them. "Fools and fanatics alone" and not the "more intelligent and respectable portion" were the opponents. Yet there were some respectable Southerners, who from the beginning did not believe in Negro education, as Governor Jonathan Worth of North Carolina and Josiah C. Nott, who declared, "As a class, the negroes who cannot read or write are more moral, more pious, more honest, and more useful members of society than those who have received education." [39] In the eyes of some, to try to educate a Negro was to try to make him a white man, which was as impossible as to "reverse the Gulf stream, or thaw the ice at the poles." [40] Some of the most pronounced opposition to the education of Negroes came after the Northern teachers had done their worst in the South by turning the Negroes against the white people, a kind of education which Curry later said "was unsettling, demoralizing," and "pandered to a wild frenzy for schooling as a quick method of reversing social and political conditions." [41] When the Negroes thus educated and enfranchised voted against the white man's interests, violence broke out against Negro schools, Northern teachers were driven out, and schoolhouses were burnt.

When Negroes were first offered education, they seized the opportunity with an avidity scarcely equaled by their zeal for their "forty acres and a mule." They felt that they could not be completely emancipated until they had attended a school; they looked upon education as having miraculous powers. Negroes "were to be seen at every street corner, and between the hours of labor, poring over the elementary pages." [42] The porter in the store or hotel was studying his speller when not busy with his work, and the washerwoman propped her reader on the fence while she labored over the washtub. They came to the schools, from the cradle to the grave; in one school it was noted that there were four generations of Negroes. [43] One old Negro student remarked, "I'm jammed on to a hundred, and dis is my fust chance to git a start." [44] Some teachers found that the most effective way to punish a colored

[39] De Bow's Review, I (1866), 269.   [40] Scott's Monthly Magazine, VII (1869), 255.

[41] Fleming (ed.), Documentary History of Reconstruction, II, 208.

[42] Scott's Monthly Magazine, VI (1868), 647.

[43] Fleming (ed.), Documentary History of Reconstruction, II, 182.

[44] Trowbridge, South, 337-38.

child was to refuse to hear his lesson or refuse to let him come back to school. In one Georgia town where the whites were in a majority, the Negro school had 150 pupils, whereas the white school had only 35.[45]

Education was, in fact, a fad which soon lost its novelty for the majority of Negroes. In most of the Southern states the only tax that touched the Negroes was a poll tax, generally $1.00, which was used for their schools, yet most of them did not pay it; and when schools attempted to charge fifty cents a month, few Negroes appeared. Ten years after the Surrender a Northern traveler estimated that the Georgia freedmen spent in a half-year for liquor as much as they had paid for schools since emancipation. He stated that the freedmen in Atlanta had spent $3,000 going to a circus that had recently been there.[46] In 1870 not one tenth of the Negro children were in school; [47] but some of this nonattendance must be based on lack of schools as well as lack of interest. A Southern editor said in 1869 that the Negroes were "not so eager now to acquire an education as they professed to be sometime since. It is with difficulty they can be coaxed to school in great numbers, while in some places schools which have been generally sustained by Northern missionaries are about to close for want of students; or, disgusted with the lack of attention and gratitude, the teachers prefer returning whence they came." [48] One disillusioned Northern teacher gave as her testimony "that the more one does for them the more they expect to be done." [49]

Schoolhouses varied from palatial homes seized as abandoned property, such as the Memminger home in Charleston, to old slave markets, as in Savannah, and hovels everywhere. The methods of teachers varied widely, as indeed did the character of the schools. There were industrial schools, night schools, Sunday schools, and the elementary day schools. In some schools books were used, especially the *Freedmen's Book,* made up of accounts of famous Negroes

[45] *National Freedman,* II (1866), 123; Sandersville *Central Georgian,* July 3, 1867.

[46] Nordhoff, *Cotton States,* 105.

[47] Peirce, *Freedmen's Bureau,* 83; John W. Alvord, *Letters from the South, Relating to the Condition of the Freedmen, Addressed to Major General O. O. Howard* (Washington, 1870), 5, 38.

[48] *XIX Century* (Charleston), I (1869), 236.

[49] Greensboro *Herald,* August 19, 1869.

such as Toussaint L'Ouverture, poems and orations by Negroes, and praise of heroes like John Brown; also charts with illustrated words were used. Often there was little more than oral discussions, reciting John Greenleaf Whittier's antislavery poems, and singing "The Battle Hymn of the Republic" and other songs of that nature.[50] As might well be expected Negro children were densely ignorant, some answering that Columbus wrote the Ten Commandments and others holding that Uncle Sam wrote them. One grateful pupil insisted that Jesus Christ was "Massa Linkum." Instead of the three R's being taught, later critics claimed that the three P's were emphasized—Politics, Pulpit, Penitentiary. Certainly industrial education was not as common as it should have been. Booker T. Washington, thirsting for something worth while, found the teachers trying to instill the traditional New England education into the children of a people who needed practical training. Washington found himself and what he wanted in the Hampton Normal and Agricultural Institute in Virginia. This school was set up by General Samuel C. Armstrong, the son of a Hawaiian missionary, who declared, "An imitation of Northern models will not do." [51]

The Bureau and its Northern supporters expected that by introducing education into the South through the Negroes they would set the style of all education there, and when once the Radicals should secure control, there would be set up a free school system open to whites and blacks without distinction of race or color. The Freedmen's Bureau schools grew up haphazardly, without system or intelligent direction. They, therefore, did not serve as the origin of the common school system in the South and they left little to mark their passing or to recall that they had ever existed, except a few units which grew into institutions of higher learning, as Fisk University, Atlanta University, St. Augustine in Raleigh, and Hampton Institute. Indeed, some Negroes came out of the Bureau schools knowing who wrote the Ten Commandments, and what was even more important, how to read their

[50] R. C. Waterson, Richmond, to Sumner, May 10, 1866, in Sumner Papers, Box 78, No. 50; *American Freedman*, I (1867), 174; Trowbridge, *South*, 251, 510; Peirce, *Freedmen's Bureau*, 75; Bond, *Negro Education in Alabama*, 115.

[51] King, *Great South*, 603. See also, *ibid.*, 604; *American Freedman*, I (1867), 167–68; Peirce, *Freedmen's Bureau*, 85; Wesley, *Negro Labor in the United States*, 150.

labor contracts and how to add up their money; and a considerable number, how to teach their race according to the New England method.

From 1868 to 1872 the Bureau continued to function in its schoolwork and in making collections of bounties and pensions for veteran Negro soldiers and sailors. This latter duty was given to the Bureau to protect the Negroes from dishonest claim agents who charged them outrageous fees for performing the simple service of filling out the proper blanks. From 1867 to 1870 the Negroes received $7,683,000 from this source.[52]

Another work for which the Bureau was not legally responsible but for which it early took the credit and later the blame, was the so-called Freedmen's Bank. It was granted a charter by Congress as the "Freedmen's Savings and Trust Company" March 3, 1865—the very day the Freedmen's Bureau was provided for. Its president throughout almost its entire existence was John W. Alvord, the general superintendent of education in the Freedmen's Bureau, and its agents were usually connected with the Bureau or had formerly been so. It was only natural, then, that the bank should appear in the minds of the freedmen to be part of the Bureau, and, therefore, a part of the United States government. The purpose of this bank was constructive and entirely laudable—to teach the freedmen thrift, to save their money. With headquarters in Washington, it had thirty-two branches scattered throughout the South; and many freedmen became proud depositors and, as they believed, even creditors of Uncle Sam. They put almost $20,000,000 into this institution before it crashed in 1874.

The corruption that permeated the South as well as the whole country gradually entered the bank. Its bookkeeping became shamefully lax, and its loans were made to favored parties with little or no security. Shortly before the failure Alvord retired in favor of the unsuspecting Fred Douglass who reaped the infamy. The deposits at the time of the failure were $3,299,000. A moral obligation and every consideration of good policy and helpfulness

[52] "Report of the Secretary of War," 1869, *House of Representatives Executive Documents*, 41 Cong., 2 Sess., No. 1, Pt. II, Serial No. 1412, p. 11; *Nation*, XII (1871), 3; McPherson, *Reconstruction*, 349–50; *American Annual Cyclopaedia . . . 1870* (New York, 1872), 315; Montgomery *Weekly Advertiser*, December 8, 1869; Peirce, *Freedmen's Bureau*, 55–74.

to the Negroes required the United States government to repay the losses, but no compensation was ever granted. The depositors were able finally to reclaim 62 per cent of their deposits when all assets had been liquidated.[53]

The Democrats hoped to make political capital out of the failure by declaring that the Freedmen's Bureau and the Freedmen's Bank were "a pair of Republican twins worthy of their progenitors and patrons, and both . . . destined to enjoy a loud-smelling immortality." [54] In the election of 1876 the promise was made: "If the Democrats get in power the thieves will have to give up their plunder and the negroes will get their money back." [55]

The Freedmen's Bureau had a fundamentally important task to perform in the South, of more personal consequence to the inhabitants, black and white, than the political and constitutional reconstructing which so thoroughly engaged the attention of Congress. It could have given a trend to race relations which would have helped to solve a problem made for the South when the first Negroes were landed in Jamestown. In this most fundamental of all Southern problems it made a conspicuous failure. It worked to bring about suspicion which ripened into racial hostility. While Radical Reconstruction was in the making, many Bureau commissioners and agents acted as spies and representatives of the Congressional leaders; and when elections under this new Reconstruction were held, many who had been connected with the Bureau reached office. Governor Robert K. Scott of South Carolina had been assistant commissioner there; and in Florida the Bureau officers practically took control of the state.[56] From every state they got

53 Walter L. Fleming, *The Freedmen's Savings Bank: A Chapter in the Economic History of the Negro Race* (Chapel Hill, 1927), 19–163; Montgomery *Weekly Advertiser,* January 6, 1875; Washington *New National Era,* January 12, 1871; Wesley, *Negro Labor in the United States,* 144. Playing upon the rising desire of some Negroes to save their money, a few sharpers from Boston, who came South to sell Bibles and lecture on temperance, concluded that they could grow rich quicker another way. They organized the Freedmen's National Bank at Sandy Hill, South Carolina, and exchanged for United States money notes "resembling blacking-box labels, but printed in gaudy colors." They were able to make away with about $4,000 before the fraud was discovered. Augusta *Weekly Constitutionalist,* May 23, 1866.

54 Augusta (Ga.) *Weekly Chronicle & Sentinel,* June 7, 1876.

55 Rome *Weekly Courier,* September 20, 1876.

56 General James B. Steedman, writing Johnson from Jackson, Mississippi, June 26, 1866, said it was evident "that the Bureau officers with a very few exceptions constitute

themselves elected to Congress. Thus was a farce played upon representative government; these Northerners could not represent the South, for, as a Northern newspaper stated, they were "mere representatives of New York or New England interests." [57]

Apart from a few assistant commissioners the personnel of the Bureau was susceptible to charges of personal dishonesty and corruption. Even General Howard himself was not above reproach, and although committees of investigation exonerated him, it could not be successfully denied that his records were carelessly kept, that he was lax in carrying out the law, and that his use of Bureau funds was not always correct. Distrustful of the Bureau activities from the beginning, President Johnson appointed Generals James B. Steedman and A. R. Fullerton to make an investigation. They traveled over the South and made their reports in the summer of 1866. They found the agent at Newbern, North Carolina, exercising the "most arbitrary and despotic power" and "practicing revolting and unheard-of cruelties on the helpless freedmen under his charge." [58] The law allowed agents to rent for themselves abandoned lands, on which they worked the freedmen and frequently cheated them out of their wages or part of the crops. Generals Steedman and Fullerton declared that some of the agents taught the freedmen "to distrust all white men but those who had immediate authority over them," and "under the guise of friendship, took advantage of their credulity, and fraudulently appropriated their crops." [59] The agents were notorious in appropriating fines and forfeitures for their own use. Steedman and Fullerton believed a special investigator could find in every state *"stealings,* which in our opinion are very large." [60] The meanest villainy was to foment freedmen strikes

---

a Radical close corporation, devoted to the defeat of the policy of your administration." Johnson Papers, XCVI, Nos. 11505–06.

[57] Philadelphia *North American,* quoted in Augusta *Weekly Constitutionalist,* April 15, 1868.

[58] *Daily Columbus Enquirer,* May 20, 1866. See also, *ibid.,* May 13, 1866.

[59] Augusta *Weekly Constitutionalist,* June 20, 1866. See also, *Southern Cultivator,* XXIV (1866), 134; *Daily Columbus Enquirer,* August 17, 1866. Said a Texan of his state, "As usual, the officers of the institution are generally engaged in solving the problem of free labor by running plantations on their own account." *Ibid.,* August 12, 1866.

[60] Steedman and A. R. Fullerton, Montgomery, Ala., to Johnson, June 14, 1866, in Johnson Papers, XCVI, Nos. 11395–96.

in the busiest period of the season, and settle the trouble at $20 a head, with the result that the Negroes would be forced to return to work at the same wage and the agents would pocket the fees. Well might the Negroes themselves cry out against their friends and protectors. John Wallace, a Florida Negro, said of the Bureau: "Instead of a blessing it proved the worse curse of the race." [61] Southerners long remembered and detested this organization with its agents, hangers-on, and schoolmarm teachers: "Lucky Job! . . . He was merely tried by the officious advice and interference of only three intermeddling friends, while we, poor devils at the South, as pennyless as he, are annoyed with more than three million just such intermeddlers." [62]

[61] John Wallace, *Carpetbag Rule in Florida: The Inside Workings of the Reconstruction of Civil Government in Florida after the Close of the Civil War* (Jacksonville, 1888), 41.
[62] *Southern Cultivator*, XXIII (1865), 162.

CHAPTER V

THE NEGRO AS LABORER AND LANDOWNER

THE ante-bellum slogan "Cotton is King" might well have been changed after the war to "Labor is King." Under slavery the South had a constant labor supply and from a superficial viewpoint an inexhaustible supply. In fact, the slave embodied a mass of labor, years of it, ready to be drawn out as the planter needed it. Labor in slavery frequently went to waste, as the slave was not actually used in rainy times, wintry days, or slack periods. Labor was like the air or the sunshine—it was on hand to be used at will.

When the slave was set free, this labor supply vanished; it had been confiscated and given back to the Negro to use as he pleased. The South did not realize then, nor did it for years thereafter, that since labor was an article which must be bought, it should be used sparingly and to the best advantage. Southerners thought of their free Negro laborers as happy-go-lucky erstwhile slaves who must be humored and not pushed too hard. The Negro's character itself, molded for generations in slavery, practically forced the Southerner into this attitude, even if he had rebelled against it. The Negro, therefore, worked for about half what free laborers in the North received, because he did not earn more. The thought of farm hands in the North receiving as much as $32 a month staggered the imagination of Southerners—such wages for Negro laborers they correctly believed would have bankrupted agriculture in the South. This would have been so not only because the Negro did not earn that much, but also because the Southerners had not disposed their farm operations on the basis that labor was dear, cost money, and therefore should be used sparingly. Northerners farmed more intensively, drawing the line between good land and worn-out land, using every labor-saving device possible, and sticking to crops that required the least labor.

Since slavery to the Southerner meant compelling the labor of another, he became convinced when freedom came to his slaves that they would not work. It was illogical to assume that a free Negro would labor of his own volition. The fact that the Negro took his fling with freedom and was slow to make contracts not only confirmed the planter in these views but also demoralized Negro labor for many years.[1] A favorite topic of conversation on which there was general agreement was that a free Negro did not work as well as a slave. A careful observer, after traveling through the South in 1873 and 1874, concluded that plantations were producing only from a third to a half of their ante-bellum cotton crops.[2] On an Arkansas plantation in 1859 thirty-five slaves—men, women, and children—picked more than 10,000 pounds of cotton in fourteen weeks; in 1869 an equal number of freedmen in the same length of time picked less than a third of that amount. In Alabama the black counties had not by 1900 reached the annual yield produced in slave days. This latter fact is, nevertheless, not proof that the free Negro was a worse workman than a slave: The mass of Negro labor became less concentrated in farm work, and Negro women eschewed the fields when freedom came. But, the fact that in 1878 the total cotton crop for the first time equaled that of 1860 did not mean that the Negro had come to work as well as before the war, for a great deal of the increase was produced by small white farmers who had turned their attention to cotton.[3]

Basically the freedman did not like to take orders; that reminded him of slavery. "The hardest work before the North now is to teach the Negro what constitutes his freedom," said a Northern traveler.[4]

[1] De Bow's Review, I (1866), 324, 328. Said the Eatonton (Ga.) Countryman, quoted in Southern Cultivator, XXIV (1866), 87, "Not one negro in our whole knowledge, made a contract until the federal authorities compelled him to do so."

[2] King, Great South, 272. It has been estimated that a freedman would spend about $100 a year, whereas the expense of keeping a slave for a year was about $16. Allen, Reconstruction, 194.

[3] Report of the Commissioner of Agriculture, 1867, p. xiii; Somers, Southern States since the War, 6. In 1860 the whites raised 12 per cent of the cotton; in 1883, 44 per cent. Bell I. Wiley, "Salient Changes in Southern Agriculture since the Civil War," in Agricultural History (Baltimore), XIII (1939), 67.

[4] Andrews, South since the War, 97.

The South was long in learning that it should adopt a different attitude in giving orders to freedmen. A Northerner who had turned Southern planter found his Negro workmen "most *exceedingly and aggravatingly* provoking"; they had "an *utter unwillingness* to obey implicitly any order given them." In the midst of the planting season they decided they wanted a holiday, and although he offered them two later on, they insisted on taking the day off when they wanted it.[5]

Negroes on public works around Charleston labored on an average of only four days a week. If a Negro was sent out to work alone, "there was every probability that he would go to sleep or go fishing." An Alabama planter declared they would do "only what they can't help, and no more"; a North Carolinian judged that "a freedman is a *free man*—so free, indeed, that neither law nor gospel can hold him, when some fancy or whim suggests to him a change of location or service"; and a Georgian expressed his opinion of Negro labor by this notice:

$50 Reward
Is offered for information that will enable me to make a living,
and make the ends meet on my farm, by the use of negro labor.

Mrs. Frances Butler Leigh, the daughter of Fanny Kemble Butler, tried to run the old plantation under free labor but after ten years she gave up. When she wanted a task performed, she "first had to tell the negroes to do it, then show them how, and finally do it" herself. Another testified, "I can do a thing twice while they are getting ready to perform it." [6]

When the Negro received the ballot, according to a widespread feeling, he became a less reliable workman. He must go to political meetings, day and night, and when he voted he must take off a few days for the occasion. A disgruntled South Carolinian declared, "Old Ned has 'laid down the shovel and the hoe,' and has applied

[5] Stearns, *Black Man of the South*, 171, 328, 415. See also, *Report of the Commissioner of Agriculture*, 1867, pp. 420–23.

[6] The following citations appear in the order of the quotations to which they refer: Reid, *Southern Tour*, 504; *Southern Cultivator*, XXIV (1866), 213; XXVI (1868), 33, 207; Leigh, *Ten Years on a Georgia Plantation*, 57; *Southern Cultivator*, XXIV (1866), 210.

his muscles to the hinges of the ballot-box." [7] Some of the radically inclined Negro leaders advised the freedmen not to work for "secessionists and copperheads" when they had work to do for themselves "or for loyal, just, liberty-loving white citizens." [8]

Testimony on the Negro's dependability as a worker naturally varied. The most successful slaveowners became after the war the most successful employers of freedmen. Not forgetting the fundamental character of the Negro as they had learned it in slavery, they overlooked his weaknesses and kept in mind the fact that although there were "a great many bad negroes in the South—lazy, worthless wretches—" still there were "also many good ones." A Georgian with a sense of humor advised those who would successfully work Negro laborers not to swear at them in their presence, "but if you must get mad and have a swearing spell, walk off to the woods, lay hold of a stump, beat it with your fist, and curse it if you will to your heart's content. If you are not then a sorer and wiser man, then you had better quit farming and try something else." Another offered this advice, wiser and more practical, "Don't *promise* and never pay. Give what is right and don't deceive the negro. Don't go out to look up hands, by any means. Let them hunt homes and they will not be so arrogant, and self inflated." An Alabama planter declared that the freedmen were working "much better than any supposed," and President Johnson's secretary after spending months traveling over the South said that a large majority of them "returned voluntarily and settled down in the old cabins of their former quarters." [9]

Freedom brought to the mass of Negroes a greater variety of work than they had engaged in as slaves. If a freedman no longer wanted to serve as a farm hand, he might enter many other kinds of labor and might even become a proprietor of a little establishment all his own. The businesses that appealed to freedmen most and were easiest to set up were barbershops, blacksmith shops, bootblack parlors, shoeshops, and tailor shops. Some freedmen set up small

[7] *Southern Cultivator,* XXVIII (1870), 198.

[8] New Orleans *Tribune,* September 27, 1865.

[9] The following citations appear in the order of the quotations to which they refer: *Southern Cultivator,* XXIV (1866), 81; XXVI (1868), 13; *Weekly Columbus Enquirer,* April 6, 1869; J. H. Watts, Montgomery, to Mrs. Wigfall, March 6, 1866, in Wigfall Papers; "Report of Benjamin C. Truman," *loc. cit.,* 9.

stores and around the Chesapeake Bay many became oystermen. As skilled laborers, some became carpenters and brickmasons, and received as much as $3.00 a day. In fact, the economic opportunities of Southern Negroes surpassed those of the North. There was no labor movement in the South as there was in the North to whip up a feeling of labor consciousness and by drawing the color line, deny to the Negro a place. Forgetting for the time his resentment against Southern white people, Frederick Douglass declared that the South offered the Negro "greater and more numerous opportunities for usefulness. In all the handicrafts that are shut against the colored man at the North, he may freely work at in the South. He meets with little resistance there as a carpenter, blacksmith, shoemaker, brick layer, shipwright or joiner." "At the North the negro . . . [could] hardly walk the street without insult by the low and vulgar," whereas in the South, declared Douglass, he went his way unmolested.[10]

Why did the North not tap the great Southern reservoir of cheap Negro labor? There were great public works being started, and the transcontinental railroads were in the process of construction. Carl Schurz thought the Negroes should be given an opportunity to help build the railroads and settle in the West; [11] instead, Chinese laborers were brought in. Racial prejudice in the North and the West rather than the reluctance of the South to give up the Negro led to his rejection.

Although there was little labor consciousness among Southern whites, there were soon some rumblings among the blacks. Some Negro leaders, looking upon themselves as representing the great labor supply in the South, rather naturally attempted to organize and direct this power. Soon after the war the Negro longshoremen in Charleston organized and carried out a few successful strikes; the washerwomen of Jackson, Mississippi, formed an association for higher wages; and Negro ironworkers in Alabama organized a union. In 1866 the Colored Mechanics' Association was formed in Nashville,[12] and three years later the Mechanic Labor Asso-

---

[10] Washington *New National Era,* August 3, 1871.

[11] "Condition of the South," *loc. cit.,* 45.

[12] Simkins and Woody, *South Carolina during Reconstruction,* 370–71; Allen, *Reconstruction,* 166; Taylor, *Negro in Tennessee,* 145.

ciation of Georgia was set up in Macon. The last organization showed strong racial and labor consciousness and it sought to extend branches into every county in the state, to raise wages, and to control the supply of labor. It flirted now and then with the idea of calling strikes in cotton-picking times. It was not to be exclusively a farm labor organization; it recommended that Negroes fit themselves to enter "all professions and every branch of employment." "We need," it added, "colored lawyers, doctors, philosophers, editors, etc." To enhance labor scarcity and to elevate the race, this convention disapproved, "first, of females performing field labor of the same kind and quantity as that performed by men," and it called on the men to "take their wives and daughters from the drudgery and exposure of plantation toil as soon as it . . . [was] in their power to do so."[13]

The National Labor Union had already made a place in its conglomerate ranks for the Negroes, but this group, becoming more a political party than a labor organization, speedily disintegrated. In December, 1869, two months after the Macon convention, the first exclusively Colored National Labor Convention assembled in Washington. Here was an attempt of the Northern and Southern Negroes to coalesce and stand behind a single program. A North Carolina Negro was made chairman. Its next session was in Columbia in 1871, and its third and last meeting took place in New Orleans, presided over by Frederick Douglass.[14] It fell a victim to Negro politicians and preachers.

Although the world lay before the freedman to go where he pleased, the land of his slave upbringing seemed to appeal to him most. For a half century there had been in the minds of people, North and South, the scheme of colonizing the Negroes in the land of their origin, and the Negro government of Liberia had been set up on the west coast of Africa for their reception. Now, the Negro in freedom was even more eager to stay in America than when he had been a slave. The Colored National Labor Convention in its Columbia meeting strongly resented the present

---

[13] Macon *American Union,* October 29, 1869.

[14] Washington *New National Era,* May 11, 1871; Montgomery *Alabama State Journal,* December 16, 1870; Allen, *Reconstruction,* 167; Wesley, *Negro Labor in the United States,* 177–78, 186 ff.

efforts to return freedmen to Africa. Alluding to the American Colonization Society, it resolved that "our ancient enemy, not content with pursuing us forty years before our liberation and enfranchisement, is still upon our track, and is doing all the mischief it can by teaching our people that this is not our permanent home, and that we must go to Africa, or elsewhere." [15]

The allure of the fatherland far across the seas had a sentimental appeal to dreamers and impractical men as well as to certain severely practical and scheming Negroes. A group in Halifax, North Carolina, felt the call and asked to be sent to Liberia, but Henry M. Turner, ubiquitous preacher, politician, and crook, eschewing Liberia wanted support for an undertaking which might possibly settle upon Fernando Po as a jumping-off-place for carrying the gospel up the Niger. During the two years following the war 2,000 Negroes from South Carolina set sail for Africa; in 1868 the *Galcona* carried away 446 Negroes, principally from Savannah and Columbus, Georgia, with their white friends' wishes that they have "a pleasant voyage and comfortable houses in the El Dorado of the East"; and ten years later the "Liberian Exodus Association" sent out of Charleston its ship *Azor* with a cargo of 230 black emigrants for Africa.[16]

More successful would have been colonization schemes for the New World and more specifically for some part of the South itself. There was some consideration given to Florida and Louisiana, but the utter opposition of the white people in those regions as well as other considerations made the segregation of Negroes anywhere in the South chimerical.[17]

Although the Negroes did not want to go back to Africa or even to the North, they were not averse to making wide migra-

[15] Washington *New National Era*, January 19, 1871.

[16] Petition in Elihu B. Washburne Papers (Division of Manuscripts, Library of Congress); Carthage (Tex.) *Panola Watchman*, November 24, 1875; Simkins and Woody, *South Carolina during Reconstruction*, 234; Macon *Daily Telegraph*, May 16, 1868; Greenville (S.C.) *Enterprise and Mauntaineer*, April 24, 1878.

[17] *Southern Cultivator*, XXIII (1865), 157; Greenville *Southern Enterprise*, September 11, 1867. J. R. Hill, Albany, Ga., writing to Charles Sumner, May 6, 1869, said that "the settlement of the colored people on the public lands in the States or Territories is purely Utopian. Here they were brought up in extreme ignorance and poverty. Their attachments for home & kindred surpasses those of any other race and here they should be allowed to remain." Sumner Papers, Box 94, No. 73.

tions within the South itself. One of the first agitations discoverable within the mass of blacks in the South Atlantic region was a movement toward the coast, caused, as far as any reasons could be found, by news of Sherman's distributions of land in the South Carolina and Georgia low country, and by the more salubrious climate there.

A potent and exasperating cause for the most considerable movement of Negroes was the labor agent. He made his way slyly through the towns and villages and the larger plantations, spreading the good news of higher wages in other places. Those regions might be the next plantation but most likely they were far away.[18] Turner, special colored adviser for his flock in Georgia, did valiant service in quieting the stirring freedmen. He told them: "The cow and calf each one is to have, and the cotton trees which you have to climb to get to the cotton ball [sic] is all a hoax. These men who throng the air and darken the heaven to get hands will say anything to get you there. . . . There are colored men employed to go around and tell you stories that know nothing about it." [19] A most effective defense against the activities of labor agents was the report spread throughout the Southeast that Negroes who went away were being enticed to the coast where they were loaded on ships, taken to Cuba, and sold into slavery. Some of the Freedmen's Bureau agents discouraged labor agents, and Georgia passed a law making it a misdemeanor for a person to entice away the workmen of another.[20]

The course of empire for the Negroes went westward—to the Mississippi Valley and especially to Mississippi, Louisiana, Arkansas, and Texas. Land was richer and consequently wages were higher. Instead of the bale of cotton to four acres and the $7.00 a month wages in South Carolina and Georgia, it was a bale to the acre and $15 a month in this new El Dorado. Labor agents embellished the scene far beyond the facts; they pictured in Texas

[18] Sometimes Negro sergeants in the United States Army took advantage of their position when Negro soldiers were being mustered out, by exacting a fee from planters who wanted to hire them. Reid, *Southern Tour*, 562.

[19] Augusta *Weekly Constitutionalist*, February 20, 1867.

[20] Macon *Daily Telegraph*, February 13, 1866; *Acts of the General Assembly of . . . Georgia . . . 1866* (Milledgeville, 1867), 153–54; Brooks, *Agrarian Revolution in Georgia*, 30.

a city inhabited only by Negroes—2,000 of them. Arkansas, under Radical rule, set up a Colored Immigration Aid Society to draw off the Negroes from the Southeast, largely to increase voting strength. Considerable numbers of Negroes drifted westward. In 1867 it was estimated that 1,000 Negroes from South Carolina were passing through Atlanta every week; and in 1873 Georgia lost probably 20,000 of her colored workmen.[21]

This movement was called forth principally by a desire for higher wages and it was confined entirely to the old slave states. There was another westward movement of Negroes about the same time which had as its objective merging with the stream of settlers going to the mythical Golden West, there to become land-holders and make a great civilization. Here was the opportunity to escape the bonds of race and color that would forever hold the Negroes in the South to restricted limits. A few Negro leaders and some erstwhile abolitionists sought to awaken the freedmen to this land of opportunity, and a few railroad companies ran cheap excursions to the frontiers of this new Canaan. Now and then a Negro convention was held to further the cause. It did not succeed because the Negro seemed to desire to go West no more than to Africa, and the West supported by the North was not so far away that it was unaware of the color line.[22]

Yet there suddenly broke out in 1879 a strange mass movement of Negroes to Kansas, drawing most heavily from Mississippi but setting up fields of agitation as far away as North Carolina and Virginia. It came to be called the Exodus, its pilgrims the "Exodusters," and its leaders "Moseses of the Exodus." No Moses stood out prominently above the others, unless it was Ben (Pap) Singleton of Tennessee. It has been estimated that from 15,000 to 60,000 Negroes struggled into Kansas, sacrificing all earthly possessions to get there, to starve or become public charges—and to

[21] King, *Great South*, 300; Trowbridge, *South*, 460; Robert H. Woody, "The Labor and Immigration Problem of South Carolina during Reconstruction," in *Mississippi Valley Historical Review*, XVIII (1930–1931), 196–200; Thomas S. Staples, *Reconstruction in Arkansas, 1862–1874* (New York, 1923), 340–43; Wesley, *Negro Labor in the United States*, 214.

[22] Washington *New National Era*, June 15, 1871; *Daily Richmond Enquirer*, October 30, 1866; Richmond *Enquirer & Examiner*, November 28, 1867; Taylor, *Negro in Tennessee*, 106–24.

receive little more welcome than the Children of Israel had got at the hands of the Philistines. This "Kansas Fever" attracted wide attention and led to much speculation as to the cause; even Congress ordered an investigation, with each political party hoping to make capital out of the findings. The Republicans insisted that the Negro was fleeing intolerable persecutions in the South, lack of economic opportunities, unequal justice in the courts, and the suppression of the spirit of the race by the whites. Democrats were sure that it represented a deep Republican trick to shift Republican votes to doubtful states, giving additional weight to this reason by recalling that many Negroes had gone to the especially doubtful state of Indiana. They also charged the railroads with stirring up the Negroes to go somewhere so that they might collect their fares. There was little political significance in the Kansas Exodus. More likely it was the "40 acres and a mule" longing over again, the laudable desire of the Negro to own property and have an equal opportunity with other people. Finding Kansas not different in these respects from the South, a great many returned to the land of their birth.[23]

Corollary to the dictum that a Negro would not work was the equally positive belief that the Negro would soon become extinct. What else could be expected of a people who had been forced by slavery to keep clean just as they had been forced to work? Hinton Rowan Helper, who in ante-bellum times had greatly displeased his fellow Southerners by his book *The Impending Crisis,* agreed with them after the war in his book *Nojoque,* in which he predicted that the Negro would decay and disappear; but if the Negro should not so oblige this prophet, he advocated the forcible extermination of the race. If the Negroes should not of their own accord become extinct, Southerners would not follow Helper in extinguishing them; but they were still sure that they must look elsewhere for their labor supply.

There were more white men than Negroes in the South, yet

23 Henry King, "A Year of the Exodus in Kansas," in *Scribner's Monthly,* XX (1880), 211–18; *Nation,* XXVIII (1879), 239–40; Benjamin H. Hill, *The Union and its Enemies* (Washington, 1879), 9; *American Annual Cyclopaedia . . . 1879* (New York, 1884), 354–58; "The Proceedings of a Migration Convention and Congressional Action respecting the Exodus of 1879," in *Journal of Negro History,* IV (1919), 51–92; John G. Van Deusen, "The Exodus of 1879," *ibid.,* XXI (1936), 111–29.

farmers long neglected even to think of themselves as constituting a labor supply. The tendency was for the poorer whites to become owners of small patches which they tended, or more likely they became tenants—still leaving the field of the day laborer unoccupied. Forgiving the North for the war, many Southerners immediately set their hopes high on enticing Northern laborers to the South. These might not only make good workers but they might also help the South maintain the white man's civilization. "If a Conservative," said De Bow, "he will have his convictions confirmed; if a Republican, the chances are that association with the life-long object of his mistaken sympathy, will convert him to our side." [24] Alexander H. Stephens' half brother Linton and many other Georgians signed an invitation to "all good people of the North, whether farmers or mechanics, whether Protestants or Catholics, or of no church—all classes—to come and settle among us, for our mutual good; assuring all such, again that they shall have thrown around them, the same law, the same protection, and the same justice in every respect as are 'meted out to us.' " [25] Few accepted. Wages were lower in the South, the Negro was unattractive to white workmen of whatever origin, and it was still believed that a white man could not work well in the hot Southern climate. A few idlers from the great cities were induced by labor agencies to come South, but they were uniformly unsatisfactory.

The springs from which an unending labor supply had flowed to the North for many years lay in Europe. European immigrants had helped to make the North great and powerful, and had, perhaps, turned the scales against the South in the war. To bring to the South immigrants primarily, but Northerners too, most of the Southern states set up immediately after the war immigration commissioners and chartered various immigrant aid societies. These commissioners were provided with funds sufficient to publish booklets descriptive of the opportunities offered in their respective states and also in some cases to send agents to the principal European ports where immigrants embarked for America. They distributed booklets written in the language of the people

[24] *De Bow's Review*, IV (1867), 150.
[25] Marietta (Ga.) *Journal*, May 19, 1871.

and sought to induce them to come to the South immediately on landing in New York City.

The immigration aid societies were primarily land companies, which located lands for sale cheap or bought up such lands for resale to the immigrants. Some of these societies were less than state-wide. There was an immigration society in Newberry, South Carolina, which brought to that community 272 immigrants within the year ending in June, 1869. The nationalities of these immigrants were characteristic of the general desires throughout the South—Germans, Swedes, Danes, Dutch, and French. To these must be added English, who came in considerable numbers to Virginia. After the Franco-Prussian War Southerners developed substantial hopes that many Frenchmen would migrate to the South, especially those in the lost provinces of Alsace and Lorraine. Feeling that there was danger in accepting indiscriminately all Europeans who might offer themselves, these commissioners gave especial attention to skilled workers such as blacksmiths, carpenters, shoemakers, and machinists.[26] Ready to accept anybody, a North Carolinian who had lost his patience with the freedmen cried out, "Send us forty cargoes of Hindoos, Hottentots, Malays, Chinamen, Indians, anything; we can not be worsted." [27]

If immigrants were not captured while they were yet in Europe they must be seized upon immediately on their arrival at Castle Garden in New York Harbor before they should disperse or be taken in charge by interested Western agents. To serve the South especially in this regard the American Emigrant Company was chartered by the state of New York, and capitalized at $1,000,000. Its headquarters were in New York City, but branches were established throughout the South and agents were scattered over Europe. This company offered its services in securing any kind of workmen whom Southerners might order. The American Emigrant Company and other similar agencies usually charged the planters $5.00 for each workman secured. To make it easy

[26] *Report of the Joint Committee on Reconstruction*, Pt. III, 95–98; *XIX Century*, I (1869), 46–47; *American Farmer* (Baltimore), I (1867), 374; *De Bow's Review*, I (1866), 8, 335; Greenville *Enterprise and Mountaineer*, June 2, July 14, 1875; Galveston *Tri-Weekly News*, August 11, 1865; Montgomery *Weekly Advertiser*, April 21, 1868; Dalton *North Georgia Citizen*, May 4, 1871; *Plantation*, II 1871, 33–34; III (1872), 24.

[27] *American Farmer*, III (1868), 24.

for laborers and prospective settlers to reach the South, railroads reduced fares for such people by one half or more. In 1868 a number of railroads in Georgia, Alabama, and Tennessee reduced their fare to one cent a mile.[28]

With all its efforts, the South failed to attract many European immigrants. Virginia and Texas were the most successful, but their success was little due to their endeavors. Actually, there were fewer people of foreign birth in the South in 1880 than in 1860. The success the South attained at the time it was putting forth its greatest efforts may be seen in these facts: In 1868 there were 213,000 immigrants who arrived in the United States, of whom 78 went to Arkansas, 713 to Virginia, 564 to Louisiana, 127 to Georgia, and similar numbers to other Southern states, while 65,000 went to New York, 34,000 to Illinois, 16,000 to Wisconsin, and similar numbers to other Northern and Western states.[29]

For many reasons the South did not attract European immigrants. Almost all such people landed in the North, and as many of them had kinsfolk or acquaintances in Northern or Western states, they naturally were attracted thither. Land was easy to get in the West and, though the South advertised its cheap lands and reduced its railroad fares to the point where it argued that an immigrant could arrive in the South and buy a farm for what it would cost him to reach the West, the argument did not prevail. The Negro repelled immigrants; he represented even to the most lowly European a social scale they did not care to approach; and when the Radical Reconstruction of the South placed Negroes in high places and permeated the governments with corruption, the South had less than nothing to attract respectable people. Southerners had a mistaken impression of what a European immigrant was looking for. They wanted him to take the place of a

[28] De Bow's Review, I (1866), advertisement; IV (1867), 579–80; Augusta Weekly Constitutionalist, January 30, 1867; December 23, 1868; June 23, 1869.

[29] Southern Magazine, XIV (1874), 587; De Bow's Review, IV (1867), 160; King, Great South, 792; Marietta Journal, January 12, 1872; Buck, Road to Reunion, 153; De Bow's Review, VI (1869), 249–50. In 1875 Governor Augustus H. Garland of Arkansas was busily promoting a meeting of the Southern governors in New Orleans to encourage immigration to the South. Little Rock Weekly Arkansas Gazette, December 20, 1875; January 10, 17, 1876.

Negro workman, live in Negro cabins, and eat Negro food—cornbread and bacon. Also, the reputation of the South as a sickly region with a hot climate soon reached the immigrants' ears.[30] In fact, it was a sort of natural law that immigrants followed latitude and not longitude when they moved in great numbers to a new land. A South Carolina planter secured a group of German laborers; he fed them better than his other hands and according to his account "even gave them coffee and sourkrout [sic]—when, what would they do but demand butter for their bread and milk for their coffee, and the next thing the whole crowd left" him.[31]

The South had one more scheme for solving its labor troubles. The Negro was out of the picture; Northerners had not made him "a good statesman, but they [had] utterly ruined him as a plodding laborer." Planters infinitely preferred "the sturdy Irish and indefatigable Germans; but if they will not come, we must take the Chinese," said a Southerner. True enough, the Chinaman was a heathen and worshiped idols but he respected "the sanctity of the most fragile chickencoop." [32] Here were the main arguments back of the movement to attract the Chinese: He would either eliminate the Negro as a workman or bring him to his senses; he must be taken because Europeans would not come; he was industrious and would work for small wages; and he was an intelligent laborer and might well help to industrialize the South. What was even more desirable, he might be dominated politically and thus through the lowly Chinaman the South might reach political emancipation.

The first Chinese made their appearance soon after the war and became workers in the cane fields of Louisiana. Before long they were laboring on railroad construction. On the Alabama and

[30] Fernandina *Florida Mirror*, November 30, 1878; *Weekly Columbus Enquirer*, December 7, 1869; *Land We Love*, VI (1868–1869), 303–16; Woody, "Labor and Immigration Problem of South Carolina," *loc. cit.*, 196–212.

[31] *Daily Columbus Enquirer*, June 20, 1866.

[32] Augusta *Weekly Constitutionalist*, June 2, 1869. In advocating Chinese labor a correspondent of the *Weekly Columbus Enquirer*, October 12, 1869, said the Negroes were "a class of people who regard us as their enemies, and are influenced and directed in their almost every act by Northern miscreants and Southern traitors, and we should get them from among us, unless they can be brought to their senses by opening their eyes to what is for their interest and the interest of the country."

Chattanooga Railroad 600 or 700 were earning $15 a month. The first of these Celestials came in from Cuba, but after 1869, when the Union Pacific Railroad was completed, many of them came over that route from California.[33]

The Chinese movement was somewhat a fad; most Southerners were convinced that these people would become a greater curse to the South than the Negro had been. As it was best that Chinese should associate only with their kind, they could never be spread out over the South in small numbers. Hence only the large plantations could use them. Said a Louisianian, "A few speculators engaged in importing Chinese laborers, and a few old fogies who still hanker after the questionable title of 'large planters,' are the main advocates of Asiatic immigration." [34] There might even be danger in the politics of a Chinese if he should get the vote. "If Chinamen come, as they can and may come, by millions," said a South Carolina editor, "they will find always a radical party ready to cooperate with them to set up Budah [sic] or any other god for the sake of sharing the spoils. . . . We may see a temple erected in all the great cities to Chinese gods, and aspiring politicians patronizing them." [35]

Impelled by Northern labor opposition to Chinese and also by the fear that the South might use them politically, Northern politicians immediately fell in with the movement against them. They suddenly discovered that the Chinese were of a lower civilization. Soon Congress adopted a new naturalization policy, ever after adhered to and at which wonderment has never died down: only white and black people might become American citizens through naturalization. The most educated Chinese was barred from citizenship but "the lowest specimens of the negro tribes of Africa—of ignorant and beastly black barbarians, who never donned a garment, who live on reptiles and fruits, and to whom a letter in any alphabet is as inexplicable as the shades on the moon's surface . . . might become an American citizen." [36] When

[33] At a Chinese labor convention in Memphis in 1869, Tye Kym Orr, a Chinese, praised Oriental labor and suggested that Southerners would have an excellent opportunity to Christianize their Chinese workmen. Montgomery *Weekly Advertiser*, July 27, 1869.

[34] *Plantation*, I (1870), 392.   [35] Greenville *Southern Enterprise*, April 21, 1869.

[36] Editorial in *Weekly Columbus Enquirer*, July 12, 1870.

Southern state governments through Radical Reconstruction were turned over to Negroes and their white Radical allies, all governmental efforts in the South to bring in laborers were immediately abandoned.

Although George Fitzhugh, proslavery advocate and antebellum philosopher, argued that the Negro was inherently communistic and opposed to private property because in Africa he had not known that institution and in slavery had experienced little of it, nevertheless the most persistent and vociferous desire of the freedman was for private property in land. Indeed, the Negro would not have used his private property as wisely as the more intelligent whites, but none except a few of the educated had ever heard of Karl Marx and his communistic system. It entered not in the slightest into the minds of the Southern Negroes. Any expressions of theirs which seemed similar were only coincidental. Furthermore, there was not the slightest trace of a class struggle in the South. Race consciousness was so all-consuming that it cut through class like a battle-ax. And this was so, not entirely because of the whites; there was race consciousness and some race solidarity among Negroes as well.

The Negro wanted land. Some revolutionary West Indian Negroes attempted in Louisiana to bring about the seizure of the large estates there and have them "democratized"; but they never succeeded in popularizing their doctrines. The Negro was looking for his forty acres and a mule as he wandered around carrying his halter. One Georgia Negro not finding his mule, in his simplicity wrote Charles Sumner asking for the loan of $500 with which he would buy two mules, and a Virginia Negro secured 500 names to a petition "asking Congress to appropriate money to buy lands and sell us, and give us time to pay for the same." [37] Negroes accepting at face value Congressional solicitude for their welfare had good reason to expect land at the hands of Congress, and the agitation among Southern Negroes for a Congressional appropriation to buy land was long in subsiding. Some asked for $1,000,000, others asked for $10,000,000. Transcontinental railroads received from the Federal government about 200,000,000

[37] J. K. Williams, Augusta, Ga., to Sumner, March 15, 1867, in Sumner Papers, Box 81, No. 5; G. H. Seldon, Kinsale, Va., to Sumner, April 23, 1870, *ibid.*, Box 99, No. 47.

acres, yet after the war not one free acre did the Negro receive except through the ineffective homestead system. The Federal government might well have made the freedman the ward of the nation or "a child of the republic," as it had done the Indians earlier. It could have devised means of ultimate landownership, including farm utensils, mules, and other necessities for operating farms.

The nearest the Federal government came to answering the Negro's prayer for land was a modification of the Homestead Law, called forth as much by vengeance against the Southern whites as to be an aid to the Southern blacks. There were over 46,000,000 acres of public lands in the five Southern states, Florida, Alabama, Mississippi, Louisiana, and Arkansas. This land was now thrown open to Negroes in eighty-acre tracts, former Confederates being excluded for a year from the benefits. In a supplementary bill the House provided that the 5,000,000 acres of public lands which had been given to Southern railroads before the war should be forfeited, but the Senate, fearing the effect that such legislation might have on grants to Western railroads, rejected the bill. As Southern public lands had been picked over for many years, the most desirable tracts had been taken up; some of what was left could have been had for as little as twelve and one-half cents an acre but found no purchasers. Yet for the next ten years there was more lively homesteading in the South than in the West— in the sense that a bigger proportion of this land was taken up than was entered in the West. There were 40,000 entries, but there were by no means that number of homes set up, and of those set up there were whites as well as Negroes entering them. Many of these entries were made by speculators working through dummies. Yet at the time Mississippi Negroes were carrying out their Exodus to Kansas, there were five and a half million acres of public land in Mississippi which could be had at the rate of 160 acres for $18.[38]

If the Federal government seemed far away and too busied

---

[38] "Report of the Secretary of War," 1869, *loc. cit.*, I, 11; Paul W. Gates, "Federal Land Policy in the South, 1866–1888," in *Journal of Southern History*, VI (1940), 304, 307–10; Peirce, *Freedmen's Bureau*, 131; "Proceedings of a Migration Convention," *loc. cit.*, 52.

with the nation's business, the radically reconstructed state governments might have aided the Negroes in securing lands within their borders. Most of the Southern states under this regime with great prodigality aided the building of railroads, but only South Carolina adopted a program of landownership for Negroes. It appropriated $500,000 to be used in buying land to be resold in small lots, but so reeking with corruption was the whole procedure that little good came out of it, and South Carolina Negroes continued to cry out for land—begging for 80,000 rural homesteads of 10 acres each. In Georgia there was a movement for a bond issue to purchase 100-acre tracts for Negroes. Undoubtedly some of the Radical zeal for extremely high taxes in the South was born of the feeling that the land would be taxed out of private ownership into the possession of the state, which could then pass it on to the Negroes.[39]

These landless freedmen became impatient for the day of division, and though Sherman declared that he had had no intention of giving them the land on the coast when he issued his forty-acres order, they still looked and hoped for their land. They refused to believe Governor William Marvin of Florida when he said, "The President will not give you one foot of land, nor a mule, nor a hog, nor a cow, nor even a knife or fork or spoon." [40] Nor did they believe that they were being tricked by designing politicians when these false hopes were aroused. "The man who tells you to wait until a division of the land gives you forty acres," said a well-wisher of the Negro, "is the worst enemy you could have. He is deluding you that he may rise upon your shoulders." [41] Still they longed for the feel of their own plows tilling their own soil.

This longing for land made them an easy prey for traveling

[39] Macon *American Union*, August 18, 1870. A Radical politician made a speech in Little Rock in 1867 advocating the taxing of landholders so severely they would be forced to give up their lands. Little Rock *Weekly Arkansas Gazette*, December 17, 1867.

[40] Davis, *Civil War and Reconstruction in Florida*, 359.

[41] Washington *Daily New Era*, February 27, 1868. Said the editor of the *Plantation*, II (1871), 521, in discussing the debt of the North to the freedmen: "Let it hunt out the blood-money, and require that it shall be expended in the purchase of forty acres of land and a mule each for the children of those who were captured in Africa by Northern men and sold to the wicked Carolinians!" See also, Montgomery *Alabama State Journal*, June 19, September 25, 1869.

shysters and tricksters, who soon after the Surrender swarmed over the South, picking the carcass clean of what the war had left. Some sold for $5.00 each slips of paper purporting to be certificates for parts of the old plantations on which the Negroes had been slaves; others charged $1.00 each for red, white, and blue pegs which when used to enclose land, the Negroes were told, would give title to it. For the illiterate Negroes, adding a grim joke to injury, these extortioners included a so-called deed, reading thus: "Know all men by these presents, that a naught is a naught, and a figure is a figure; all for the white man, and none for the nigure. And whereas Moses lifted up the serpent in the wilderness, so also have I lifted this d——d old nigger out of four dollars and six bits. Amen. Selah!" [42]

Groups of Negroes here and there became tired of waiting for their division. "Hounded on by human beings with white complections but leprous souls," said a Southern editor, "these benighted creatures tamper with destiny and juggle with satan." [43] Three hundred Negroes, more or less, broke out in open riot in 1869 on the Ogeechee River rice lands in coastal Georgia. They drove out the white owners, seized control of property, and showed their intention of running that part of the state as their own. They were subdued by Federal troops. The next year a better organized and more serious outbreak against constituted authority took place in the vicinity of Louisville, Georgia. A clever Negro named Cujo Fye was the leader of this movement to organize clubs among Negroes whose purpose was to protect them against arrest, debts, and taxes, to effect their release if placed in jail, to guarantee their right to vote, and ultimately to gain control of land. A mob estimated at a thousand broke down the doors of the Louisville jail and released one of their members. United States troops suppressed the movement. There were frequent rumors throughout the South of Negro uprisings designed to seize control of property. [44]

[42] Fleming, *Civil War and Reconstruction in Alabama*, 447.

[43] Augusta *Weekly Constitutionalist*, December 20, 1865.

[44] Augusta *Daily Press*, January 9, 1869; *Weekly Columbus Enquirer*, January 5, 29, 1869; August 30, 1870; Augusta *Weekly Chronicle & Sentinel*, September 7, 1870; Greensboro *Herald*, August 26, 1875.

Most whites favored Negro ownership of land if they got it in a legal way. Albert Gallatin Brown of Mississippi said to a group of Negroes, "I look to the day when every honest man among you will own land." "But I warn you," he added, "that you must woo the coming of that day by habits of industry, frugality and earnest desire for peace and good will among men." [45] The statement, often retailed, that Southerners did not want the Negro to own land, and that they successfully kept him from it to a large extent, is based on very slight fact. Land for sale was so plentiful and so cheap that it would have been practically impossible to deny the sale of it to a Negro who could pay for it. In most cases where the planter refused to sell land to a Negro, it turned out that the Negro wanted a choice spot in the midst of the plantation, or was making some other unreasonable demand which would have been as quickly denied to a white man. But there is no doubt that most planters had misgivings when strange Negroes sought to settle down on strategically located plots of land, where they might turn their holdings into nests of thieves to steal from the near-by plantations.

There were Southerners, with whom even some Northerners agreed, who did not believe that the Negro should become the outright owner of land anywhere, because it did not appear to be the logical way for the Negro to reach ultimately the position of economic security. They feared that without some restraining supervision, Southern Negroes like West Indian Negroes would drift back into a bush civilization, subsisting on the easy products of a salubrious climate and a rich soil. A New York *Herald* correspondent after traveling over the South came to the conclusion that "the experiment of making the uneducated plantation Negro a planter on his own account is an utter and unmitigated failure." [46] There was a certain political significance in a Negro's owning land. As long as he was a laborer his employer could hold an uncomfortable and restraining hand over him when he cast his ballot. Though the employer's advice often went for nothing in the Negro's politics, yet it was a force which

[45] Greensboro *Herald*, August 31, 1867.
[46] Quoted in Thompson, *Reconstruction in Georgia*, 59.

some of the Negroes could not ignore all the time, and which most of the Negroes did not ignore in some states in the later Reconstruction period.

With all their handicaps, disappointments, and false hopes corruptly raised in their hearts, Southern Negroes made commendable progress in securing the ownership of land. As an example, Georgia Negroes in 1880 owned 586,664 acres out of a total area of 37,700,000 acres. Practically all of this was acquired after the war, unlike the situation in Virginia where a large free Negro population by 1860 had come to own 60,000 acres. Negroes had gained from the white man their passion for private ownership of property and they went forward with it unaided by that authority which should have given them something else before the ballot.

CHAPTER VI

A BREACH OF FAITH

PRESIDENT JOHNSON'S plan of dealing with the South called for no fundamental changes, nor did it in this time of confusion contemplate seizing the opportunity to increase the powers of the national government. In his opinion the war had been an unpleasant and unfortunate episode in the life of the nation, and should be forgotten as soon as possible. This was not the idea, however, of the rising consciousness in the North which was politically directed by the Radical Republicans in Congress, and which was beginning to crystallize in schemes to be applied to the South as well as to the whole country.

Radicalism may be concerned as much with methods as with ends. It may be advocacy of revolutionary changes in laws and ways of government, without being designed for the common good. The spirit of change was in the air throughout the civilized world—whether in England, France, Prussia, or America. Attacks were being made on existing institutions whatever they might be. In England, the disestablishment of the Irish Church was an expression; in Prussia, the destruction of local autonomy; in France, the rise of the commune; in America, the plans for change were somewhat confusing. Some thought the Radical program meant one thing, others believed it meant the opposite.

As the Radicals played with social and political equality in the South and talked of confiscation of Southern property, Southerners began to believe that Radicalism meant the destruction of all human rights based on worth, culture, and traditional civilization—that it was communism or a cult based on the destruction of individual values and the degradation of the states.

It began to have a glimmering resemblance to the later cults called Fascism and Nazism. Southerners sensed a revolutionary spirit in the air; they were shocked that Congress passed unconstitutional laws, did violence to the Constitution itself, and never sought to be consistent in its own acts.

To the submerged Negroes this program of political and social equality and of confiscated lands meant a New Order; but at first they did not know that it was never fully intended for them beyond securing their political support. The Radical leaders had no intention of starting an epidemic of communism in the South, for which the South was thankful. "It is fortunate for us," said a Southern editor, "that the earnest, conscientious fanatics, such as those who for a season inaugurated the Commune of Paris, and are now threatening Europe, did not establish themselves among the blacks. The results might have been fearful." [1]

There was a strange combination that made possible Radical success. Northern capitalism, led by New England, joined hands with "the ultra infidelic rascals like Wade, Sumner, Stevens, *et id omne genus,*" [2] and gave them the backing of its influence and money. These political Radicals gained as their chief desire public office; the economic Radicals secured as their part high tariffs, friendly tax laws, free lands, government loans, freedom from governmental control, and rights to exploit the nation's natural resources. Therefore, Radicalism was not revolution for the masses, but conservatism for the few. "The Radicals, like the old Federalists," said an observer of the national picture, "are an aristocratic party, but tinctured with the fanaticism of the age." [3] The few genuine Radicals bent on revolution for the masses were hoodwinked and were carried along with this movement until they sensed where it led.

The Radical program could not be worked out through President Johnson, hence the early break with him. The Southern states with their old-time American ideas must not be allowed to

---

[1] *Plantation,* II (1871), 552.

[2] Henry Cooke to Jay Cooke, October 12, 1867, quoted in Ellis P. Oberholtzer, *Jay Cooke, Financier of the Civil War* (Philadelphia, 1907), II, 28.

[3] Woolfolk, *World's Crisis,* 512.

return to the Union until "the political and social condition of the South" was made "to be the same with that of the North." [4] Many who did not agree with the Radical program, whether it was for the masses or for the few, were made to support the party through fear that the South was about to restore slavery, that it would repudiate the Federal debt, that it would start the war again, that it would exterminate the Negroes. In fact, the spearhead of the Radical movement to take the South in hand was a play upon these fears, and closely allied to them, upon a feeling of vengeance against those who were charged with responsibility for so many Northern woes. According to this view the Southerners did not seem to realize that they had been whipped, that they had lost the war; the governments Johnson had set up were failures, they could not maintain law and order. The war had closed too soon, at least according to this Radical nursery rhyme:

> *High diddle, diddle,*
> *The Radical fiddle—*
> *The War closed a little too soon*
> *The little dogs laugh*
> *While Butler and staff*
> *Ran away with another teaspoon.*[5]

To establish this great force of argument, the Radicals used various means. The Joint Committee on Reconstruction held many hearings ostensibly to get a true picture of Southern conditions, but in reality to discredit the Johnson governments. The questions it asked either pointed to a strange mentality on the part of the quizzer or to the feeling that Southerners must have had a strange mentality: Would a Southern jury convict Jefferson Davis of treason? Would Southerners prefer Confederates in their elections over Union men? Would they give the Negro the vote? Unless this Committee felt that the war had left the Southerners a little less than human, the answers to these questions were self-evident. A question frequently asked was whether

[4] *Nation*, II (1866), 460.

[5] Aberdeen *Daily Sunny South*, January 4, 1867. Asked the *Nation*, IV (1867), 71. "What nation so completely defeated as the South has been has ever had as good terms offered it by the victor?" "Is there no common sense left amongst the adherents of the 'Lost Cause'?"

the South would try to repudiate the Federal debt. This was a clever question calculated to arouse fears in the minds of Northerners holding Federal bonds, but there was no reason otherwise for asking it unless, indeed, there was point in the facetious remark of a Virginian to Charles Sumner that, as he had got whipped in the war, certainly no one should expect him to pay for the cost of his whipping. Even the *Nation* bore witness that "nothing worthy of note has come from any Southern source indicating that a desire to evade or prevent the punctual payment of the national debt is prevalent amongst the Secessionists." [6]

Violence in the South was played up on the highest keys. Freedmen's Bureau agents, Federal officeholders, Northern schoolteachers, designing place hunters both Southern and Northern were constant purveyors of atrocity information to Stevens, Sumner, Wade, and other Radical leaders. Albion W. Tourgee, an Ohio-born North Carolinian, had scarcely arrived in his new state before he began telling Northerners about a millpond out of which seventeen dead Negroes had been fished. The more he was pressed to locate the pond the smaller it became until it finally evaporated together with the seventeen drowned Negroes. Stevens was told by an Arkansan that after a "rebel" had disputed with a freedman, "that night the negro cabbens [*sic*] were seen to be on fire, the next morning I saw a Sight that ap[p]al[l]ed me 24 Negro Men Women and Children were hanging to trees all round the Cabbins [*sic*] the next Night the[y] Burned Down a fine African Church which Cost the Freed Man about $5000." [7] John C. Underwood, wearer of the judicial robes for the Federal District Court in Virginia, wrote Greeley in 1866 how a little Negro girl's back had been burned by Virginia fiends, but even so there might be good in such a horrible crime: "If the Republicans of New York will induce Barnum to send on & get the little girl Martha Banks & show her burnt back to the people as a specimen of rebel reconstruction I believe it would be worth ten thousand votes this fall." To distribute pictures of the burnt back with a "spirited description" would have a profound effect, espe-

6 *Nation*, VII (1868), 24.

7 William D. Mallet, Pine Bluff, Ark., to Stevens, May 28, 1866, in Stevens Papers, VIII, No. 54112.

cially on the "impulsive Irish." He added, "I do not believe the sight of the true cross would produce a more thrilling effect." Later he wrote Greeley, "Indeed, God only knows the hardships of a live union man in this den of rebel lions." [8]

An Alabaman begged Stevens, "for God's sake give the Rebels no quarter"; [9] Joshua Hill, long-standing Georgia Unionist, told Greeley that intolerance in Georgia was "almost as great as it was in the days of the rebellion"; [10] and a Virginian wanted to know why Congressmen, who refused to "tolerate rebels" in their body permitted "rebels to govern loyal men" in the South.[11] Texas was held up as the most horrible example of unbridled crime, and here the Radicals were on firmer grounds as to its extent but not its cause. Most of the crime in Texas had no reference to politics or to the war. It represented the growing pains of a frontier region inadequately policed and still encumbered by its Indians. Its crimes related to horse stealing, cattle rustling, saloon shootings, Mexican brawls, and Indian pillagings, out of which welter came such outlaws as Sam Bass and such law enforcers as Lee Hall. Comanches and Apaches raided the Texas settlements without mercy; a group of Indians one night came within three miles of San Antonio and stole 130 horses. President Johnson's secretary, Benjamin C. Truman, estimated that there were 5,000 men in Texas "depending entirely upon robbery and murder for a precarious subsistence." [12] Within three years after the war there were over a thousand murders in the state, but whites suffered more than Negroes.

[8] Letters, Alexandria, Va., August 8, 1866, Richmond, November 27, 1867, in Horace Greeley Papers (New York Public Library), "Letters to him, 1866–1872."

[9] Henry W. McVay, Florence, Ala., to Stevens, March 1, 1867, in Stevens Papers, IX, No. 54365.

[10] Letter, Madison, Ga., September 22, 1866, in Greeley Papers, "Letters to him, 1866–1872." A Georgian sent Stevens this account of atrocities in his state: "There are parties of rebels now going about through the state murdering loyal citizens in their houses at night and shooting them from the bushes during the day. Thirty-seven good citizens were murdered in this way in about 3 days." The murderers were "said to be composed chiefly of slaveholders sons who are mad at the loss of their slaves." J. McKee, Dawsonville, Ga., to "Dear Brother Stevenson," April 16, 1868, in Stevens Papers, XI, No. 54798.

[11] A. Watson, Fredericksburg, Va., to Stevens, May 3, 1866, in Stevens Papers, VII, No. 54076.

[12] "Report of Benjamin C. Truman," loc. cit., 3.

Yet politicians and army officers attempted to make Texas crime appear racial and political. George A. Custer, whom the Sioux Indians later by massacring made famous, discovered that Texans were still buying and selling Negroes as late as 1866, and affirmed two years later that the United States flag was not tolerated in the Northern part of the state. He declared that Governor Hamilton told him if the United States did not take over Texas he "would pull up stakes and leave here." [13] Another army officer, James S. Brisbin, fearing a reduction of army personnel if times became too peaceful, told of the astounding disloyalty of Texans: "If I had not already been a radical I must of necessity have become one after seeing and hearing what I have within the last three weeks. It is useless to palliate excuse or cover up the sins of these people, the truth is they are unrepentant rebels and many of them ought to be hung. They hate the union and proscribe men on account of their opinions. A more irate and senseless set cannot be found in [sic] the face of God's earth." [14]

There was crime in the South, as even Southerners admitted, and there was crime everywhere throughout the world, civilized and uncivilized. Undergoing an upheaval following four years of disastrous war, the South actually had less crime than such a situation would have suggested. General John Tarbell, who spent some months in the South in 1865 and 1866, testified before the Joint Committee on Reconstruction, "The South I left is not at all the South I hear and read about in the north. From the sentiment I hear in the north, I would scarcely recognize the people I saw, and except their politics, liked so well." [15]

Congress refused to recognize the Johnson state governments in December, 1865. Yet for months it talked and investigated and still worked out no plan of its own until it put forth the Fourteenth Amendment, which the South so promptly rejected. Now there ensued more talk which led old editor De Bow to ask, "Must we fight four years and talk ten years more about the

[13] George A. Custer, Austin, Tex., to Chandler, January 14, 1866, in Zachariah Chandler Papers, III, Nos. 649–54; Custer, Austin, to Chandler, January 8, 1868, ibid., Nos. 644–48.

[14] James S. Brisbin, Austin, Tex., to Chandler, October 5, 1866, ibid., IV, Nos. 719–22.

[15] Report of the Joint Committee on Reconstruction, Pt. III, 157.

fight?" [16] Congress continued to talk but at the same time it consolidated its position against Johnson by passing laws to control
its own sessions and to set going impeachment investigations
against the President. Finally in 1867 it was ready to act with
bills so ill-considered and badly worded that it took four to
make plain what should have been said in the first. These acts
were passed on March 2, 23, July 19, 1867, and March 11 of the
following year. The first three were the handiwork of John
Sherman, strangely enough regarded by many Southerners as
their special defender though he was the brother of the General.
Chief among his assistants in this work was wig-wearing, club-
footed old "Thad" Stevens, frank and bold, with his grimly
sharpened hatchet-face, soured on all the world except his Negro
housekeeper, believed to be his concubine, and her race, and urbane
Charles Sumner, canting and visionary, who "would shed tears at
the bare thought of refusing to freedmen rights of which they had
no comprehension, but would filibuster to the end of the session
to prevent the restoration to the southern whites of rights which
were essential to their whole conception of life." [17]

The first act, asserting what had not been proved, that "no
legal State governments or adequate protection for life or property now exist in the rebel States," grouped them into five military districts and set the army over them ostensibly for their
protection.[18] The make-believe Johnson state governments were
permitted to exist only so long as they were considered of any
advantage to the military commanders. Whenever the people
should come to their senses by making governments "in conformity with the Constitution of the United States," by enfranchising all Negroes and disfranchising an uncertain number

[16] *De Bow's Review,* III (1867), 216.

[17] Dunning, *Reconstruction,* 87. Sumner got much enthusiasm for his position from
letters written by Southern Radicals, white and black. For example, see Mattie E. Long,
Morgantown, Ga., to Sumner, October 14, 1868, in Sumner Papers, Box 87, No. 85.

[18] These were the districts: I, Virginia; II, North Carolina and South Carolina; III,
Georgia, Florida, and Alabama; IV, Mississippi and Arkansas; and V, Louisiana and
Texas. Later some rearrangements were made. As Tennessee had already been readmitted into the Union, it was not included in military Reconstruction. A movement was
started in Congress to include Kentucky in military Reconstruction on account of the
strong Southern position she took after the war. See E. Merton Coulter, *The Civil War
and Readjustment in Kentucky* (Chapel Hill, 1926), 312–39.

of "rebels," and by ratifying the Fourteenth Amendment, they might be admitted into the Union. Virginia made preparations to comply immediately, but there was good reason to believe that the majority of the states would prefer to live indefinitely under military rule rather than submit to these humiliations.

To give life to and set into motion this Congressional plan of getting the states back into the Union, a second act was passed on March 23. The commanding general was required, before the following September 1, to make a registration of the voters, who must take a long and complicated oath. Then an election for a constitutional convention must be held, and if the constitution it drafted should be ratified in an election in which at least a half of all registered voters participated, and if this document pleased Congress, then the state should be admitted into the Union. To clarify the complicated oath required of all voters, to establish the complete dominance of the military commanders over all civil authority in violation of the *Ex parte* Milligan decision, and to give registration boards absolute power to deny registration to any person, Congress passed on July 19 a third law. This act ended with the strange catchall expression that the three laws should "be construed liberally, to the end that all the intents thereof may be fully and perfectly carried out." Though this law specifically disfranchised all people who had ever held a civil office of any sort, in reality it made possible the disfranchisement of any person, because "no person shall be registered unless such board shall decide that he is entitled thereto."

As the plan for military Reconstruction unfolded, the South could scarcely believe what it heard and read—was it a ghastly trick or a nightmare that would disappear with the morning? It had put its faith in the President and accepted the plan which he had proposed; it had accepted the terms of the national government which had conquered it; and it had pleased some of its former worst enemies such as Gerrit Smith and Henry Ward Beecher. It had even been so unwise as to put its faith in the Constitution, forgetting that it had seceded originally because it had found little protection in that document in ante-bellum times. However little it might have expected to find now, after four years of warfare, the South still could not forget its respect

for law. "Every proposition in these Military Bills has been originated since the war," charged Benjamin H. Hill of Georgia;
"not one of them was demanded during the war, or was made a
condition of the surrender." There had been a breach of faith.[19]
It was time the South should cease to put its trust in the word of
the government, or hold out any hope for effective aid from its
Northern friends. A Mississippi editor asked, "Is it not time that
our people had ceased to follow this will-o-the-whisp [sic] of a
'reaction at the North'? How much further will they permit
themselves to be led by it into bogs and quicksands which grow
deeper as they advance in its pursuits?" [20] Even in the North
there was strong opposition to military Reconstruction: "Who
can be deluded into the belief that this is a reconstruction that
will last?" asked the New York *Times;* [21] and the Springfield
(Massachusetts) *Republican* wanted to know what except dislike
would be "gained by the temporary ostracism of the largest and
most intelligent portion" of the South.[22]

Newspapers throughout the South echoed such sentiments as
those of the Georgia editor who wrote: "Military rule may be
imposed on her [the South], every device of State torture may be
applied, these will be the shame of those who employ them, not
hers—but she will never confess a falsehood, nor affix the brand
of infamy on her own brow!" [23] The Southern leader who attacked
military Reconstruction with the greatest force and effect was
Benjamin H. Hill. In his twenty-two articles entitled "Notes on
the Situation," written for the Augusta *Chronicle & Sentinel,* and
recopied widely by newspapers over the South, and later reprinted
in a pamphlet, he dissected the Military Reconstruction Acts
with precision and sound learning. He showed their utter un-
constitutionality, their prostitution of the military forces to the
extinction of civil liberties, their degradation of the executive and
judicial departments. He called upon the President to refuse to

19 Hill, *Senator Benjamin H. Hill*, 747. Of course, the Radical Congressional group
argued that the President had had no right to commit the government to any plan;
that it was the right and duty of Congress to reconstruct the South.

20 Jackson (Miss.) *Clarion*, quoted in Atlanta *Daily New Era*, September 13, 1867.

21 Quoted in Augusta *Weekly Constitutionalist*, February 19, 1868.

22 Quoted in Tallahassee *Sentinel*, August 8, 1867.

23 Augusta *Weekly Constitutionalist*, February 27, 1867.

carry out these laws and advised the people to ignore military Reconstruction and continue to elect their state officials. His most bitter invectives he saved for those Southerners who accepted military Reconstruction and became important leaders in it.[24]

Certain that the Military Reconstruction Acts were unconstitutional Mississippi sought through the United States Supreme Court to restrain President Johnson, who was equally sure they were unconstitutional, from enforcing them. In the case of *Mississippi* v. *Johnson,* the judges turned their backs on the brave argument of their *Ex parte* Milligan decision and retreated behind technicalities to keep from handing down a decision—it was a political matter in which they could not assume jurisdiction and, besides, the President could not be interfered with in the performance of his duties. Georgia thinking she saw a loophole sought to restrain Secretary of War Edwin M. Stanton, but the court again dodged behind technicalities—the matter was political and the Secretary of War was an agent of the President and, therefore, could not be interfered with. In two other cases there seemed greater likelihood that the Supreme Court would be forced to take up the Reconstruction Acts. William H. McCardle, editor of the Vicksburg *Times,* was arrested for a wordy attack on the military authorities of Mississippi and held by a military commission for trial. Through a writ of habeas corpus, his case soon reached the United States Supreme Court on appeal, and that body was preparing to hand down a decision when Congress quickly took away its jurisdiction. Another Mississippi newspaper editor, E. M. Yerger of the Jackson *News,* was accused of murder and was about to be tried by a military commission when he succeeded in getting his case into the United States Supreme Court. The judges were relieved of the uncomfortable duty of making a decision when the army handed Yerger over to the civil authorities.

Whether the Reconstruction Acts were constitutional or not, there were some Southerners who decided it was more sensible to be realistic and accept what they could not prevent—thereby in

[24] The most convenient place to find these articles is in Hill, *Senator Benjamin H. Hill,* 730–813.

the long run lightening their load. In every state there were men of substance and leadership who held this point of view and they carried with them varying numbers of the common people. Joseph E. Brown of Georgia advised that peace be made with the adversary quickly. "Gentlemen need not flatter themselves," he said, "that they have the privilege of choosing between the present proposition and continued military government." If the South rejected this plan, probably the next step would be to turn the country over almost completely to the Negroes, and confiscation, "the sleeping lion" on the speaker's table in Congress, might be reawakened into reality.[25] Undoubtedly many Southerners were scared into acquiescence by this "sleeping lion." Albert Gallatin Brown, James L. Alcorn, and Ethelbert Barksdale in Mississippi advised acceptance, and so did Roger A. Pryor, who had gone from Virginia to New York City to make a living. Others, especially Confederate military heroes, considered their military code required acquiescence in peace, now that they had surrendered their arms. John S. Mosby, fearless raider in war, was in peace an appeaser. Pierre G. T. Beauregard, hero of all Creoles, advised submission "but with that calm dignity becoming our manhood and our lost independence." [26] General James Longstreet, already laboring under the stigma of his delayed attack in the battle of Gettysburg, said, "Accept the terms that are offered us by the conquerors! There can be no discredit to a conquered people for accepting the conditions offered by their conquerors. Nor is there any occasion for a feeling of any humiliation." [27]

There were other affairs than politics to engage the attention of people; why not get Reconstruction over with and return to the normal existence of making a living? "The South can promise herself nothing," said a Georgia editor, "until restoration and union is [sic] effected. She is now suffering in all her interests, both public and private, on account of her disintegration. Once again restored in the union . . . peace and prosperity will again

[25] *Speech of Ex-Gov. Joseph E. Brown, of Georgia, Delivered in Milledgeville, Ga., June 6th, 1867, on the Present Situation and Future Prospects of the Country* (n.p., n.d.), 1–8.

[26] Augusta *Weekly Constitutionalist*, April 10, 1867.   [27] *Ibid.*, April 3, 1867.

flow to her borders." [28] Eschew politics, said Hiram Warner of Georgia: "Looking to their present and future material interests, our people should act upon their own judgment, regardless of politics or politicians." [29]

Some of these Southerners had no further interest or purpose than the restoration of their states to a normal political existence; others had an itch for office and they believed co-operation with the Radicals was their easiest and quickest road to success. Outstanding in the latter class were Brown of Georgia, Alcorn of Mississippi, Holden of North Carolina, Orr of South Carolina, and General Longstreet of Louisiana. It seemed more than a coincidence that many of the most prominent Southern Radicals had been outstanding secessionists, which led Hill sarcastically to say that the purpose of the Military Bills could not have been to punish the "rebel" secessionist fire-eaters of 1861.[30] In fact, the first interest shown by Congress in passing amnesty bills was to relieve Southern Radicals of their disabilities. The lovers of turmoil knew no loyalties. In this respect, then, they were both the cause and the consequence of the war. Conversely, many who did not believe in secession and who refused to fight either by becoming bushwhackers or deserters, now also became Radicals. Those who had a grievance against the ante-bellum ruling class; who felt social inferiority; who disliked the rigors of war; who opposed conscription, impressment, and the suspension of the writ of habeas corpus during the war; in fact, almost "every one that was in distress, and every one that was in debt, and every one that was discontented"—all these tended to gather themselves unto the Radicals. It must not be inferred that all who acquiesced in military Reconstruction became Radicals; many stayed out of politics altogether, others voted against the program, and even some who voted for it did so to end the question as soon as possible. In denial of the rumor that he was a Radical one South-

[28] Cartersville (Ga.) *Express,* quoted in Atlanta *Georgia Weekly Opinion,* November 16, 1867.

[29] *Ibid.,* September 17, 1867.

[30] Hill, *Senator Benjamin H. Hill,* 756, 760. Nordhoff, *Cotton States,* 53, found that some of the most corrupt Radicals in Louisiana had been fire-eating secessionists in 1861.

erner exclaimed, "God knows I had rather they had said I had stolen one of my neighbor's sheep." [31]

For the true Southern Radicals, Hill could at first find no name but could only say, " 'O ye vile, *unnameable* things!' " But there soon came into existence, whether invented in the South or imported from the Pacific Coast, a name ever after to stick and be an embarrassment in polite society, even unto the second and third generations—Scalawag. Whether it had been used for the filthy sheep, the scaly pig, or "the venomous, shabby, scabby, scrubby, scurvy cattle," or "the mangy dog," "it only partially" revealed "the baseness of the renegade." [32] Scalawags were singled out by name and impaled. As for Longstreet, who joined the Republican party, "It would have been well for his fame if he had been buried in the same grave with the cause for which he had fought so well"; [33] or as a Northern editor saw him, "To poverty and immortality he has preferred ostracism and wealth, and there is not a genuine man of either party but despises his swift recantation and swifter search for spoils." [34] Brownlow of Tennessee, who was not a true Scalawag as he was not a turncoat, was characterized by George D. Prentice as "a thing as much out of nature as Barnum's wooly horse, or his giants and dwarfs, or his calf with two heads and eight legs," whose blood was "hell broth, which Satan will one day sup with a long spoon." [35] Southerners

[31] Greensboro *Herald*, October 12, 1867.

[32] *Land We Love*, VI (1868–1869), 87. "Our scallawag is the local leper of the community. Unlike the carpet bagger, he is a native, which is so much the worse. Once he was respected in his circle; his head was level, and he would look his neighbor in the face. Now, possessed of the itch of office and the salt rheum of Radicalism, he is a mangy dog, slinking through the alleys, haunting the Governor's office, defiling with tobacco juice the steps of the Capitol, stretching his lazy carcass in the sun on the Square, or the benches of the Mayor's Court." Tuscaloosa (Ala.) *Independent Monitor*, September 1, 1868, reproduced as frontispiece in Fleming (ed.), *Documentary History of Reconstruction*, I.

[33] Augusta *Weekly Chronicle & Sentinel*, November 11, 1874.

[34] Brooklyn *Eagle*, quoted in Greensboro *Herald*, April 15, 1869.

[35] Quoted in E. Merton Coulter, *William G. Brownlow, Fighting Parson of the Southern Highlands* (Chapel Hill, 1937), 306. Brownlow was probably the most bitterly hated man in the South. The Nashville *Gazette*, quoted in the Tallahassee *Sentinel*, April 2, 1867, said that Brownlow was dead "and that the personage at the Capitol is no other than Old Nick himself, who has assumed temporarily the shape and the fea tures of the ex-Parson."

preferred in office "the blackest man that can be found to the whitest renegades of the South . . . those who have dishonored the dignity of the white blood, and are traitors alike to principle and race." [36]

Southerners in their anger became unreasoning. Even in its early stages before the Radical program began to reek with corruption, they would not admit that a person could honestly support it through a positive belief in it or because of a conviction that it was better to accept what he could not prevent than to bring upon himself a worse fate. Many respectable, intelligent, realistic Southerners supported the Radicals in the beginning and drew the opprobrium of Scalawag.

Another class of Radicals in the South were not of the South, and, therefore, were less reprehensible; they had come out of a shady or obscure life in the North, bringing all their earthly belongings in a carpetbag—hence they were Carpetbaggers. In North Carolina they were sometimes called Squatters, and in Georgia the terms Skowheganite or Skowhegan Skunks were used. Scalawags thought they ought to be called simply Newcomers. Carpetbaggers were Northerners who came south to play politics and secure offices; Southerners did not apply this term to Northerners who entered the economic life of the community and eschewed political activities. Lincoln had opposed the idea of Northerners drifting south to secure offices, and Greeley described them as "stealing and plundering, many of them with both arms around negroes, and their hands in their rear pocket, seeing if they cannot pick a paltry dollar out of them." [37] Some had come in the wake of the army, others had come as teachers and Freedmen's Bureau and Treasury agents, and still others had simply come as prospectors. They early made friends with the Negroes to secure their votes, and by sometimes marrying Negresses, they showed less racial prejudice than Scalawags, and correspondingly increased their success in politics. Many Negroes were to learn too late that they had misplaced their confidence. John Wallace, a Florida Negro, said his race would have made "better citizens and more honest legislators if they had not been contaminated

36 Augusta *Daily Constitutionalist,* August 15, 1867.
37 *Ku Klux Conspiracy,* I, 522.

by strange white men who represented themselves to them as their saviors." [38] A few Carpetbaggers were Negroes who, using their racial assets, were able to supplant white Carpetbaggers. The Southerner's attitude toward Carpetbaggers was a normal human reaction and should not be contrasted with the welcome frontier communities of the West gave newcomers, who were presumably honest men.

Negroes composed a third division of the Southern Radicals, and as the ballot was not their chief longing, there was some fear that they would not vote at all or that they would be dominated by Southern Conservatives. To instill political life and to capture their votes, the Radicals organized them and any willing whites into the Union League of America (the U.L.A.) or, as it was often called, the Loyal League.[39] This organization had been started in the North during the war and had been brought south by soldiers, Freedmen's Bureau agents, and other Northern emissaries. The Negroes, traditionally much impressed with societies and rituals, flocked in. Meetings were secret and initiations were carried out with great mystery and impressive ceremony, beginning in total darkness punctuated now and then with flashes of light. The United States flag, the Bible, the Constitution, the Declaration of Independence, and such symbols as the sword, the anvil, the sickle, and the ballot box were displayed. Then followed the swearing of oaths, speechmaking, and the singing of "Hail Columbia" and other songs. The sign of recognition was the tolling off of the Four L's—Lincoln, Liberty, Loyal, League. Though the initiation fee varied, in some places it was $5.00 and monthly dues were ten cents. This organization was at its height from 1867 to 1869. In North Carolina there was a women's auxiliary with its members sworn to marry only members of the League.

The League was said to have in its heyday between 200,000 and 300,000 members. At first there was a considerable membership of whites, but racial antipathy soon drove them out. Meetings took on the nature of night schools in which the Negroes

[38] Wallace, *Carpetbag Rule in Florida*, 3.

[39] In Florida there was a secret society called the Lincoln Brotherhood, and in North Carolina the Heroes of America (H.O.A.) were strong. Both were Radical organizations.

were not only taught to vote the Republican ticket, but also to hate their white neighbors. Evil ideas which they gained at these meetings led them into insolence toward whites, disorders, burning of barns and ginhouses, and lawlessness such as "scouring the woods with fire arms shooting down cattle and hogs even within sight of the owners' houses." These meetings were extremely effective in bringing the Negroes to the ballot boxes and tyrannical in forcing them to vote the Republican ticket. Negroes had exchanged economic slavery with economic security for political slavery without economic security. A correspondent of the New York *Sun* said a Negro told him "that he did not dare to vote as he wished to; that he had got his freedom from slavery, but that he had no freedom to vote except at the dictation of the League." [40]

Organizing the League among Negroes had almost as profound an effect on the whites as had John Brown's raid in 1859. They resented and feared its dangerous teachings. John B. Gordon declared that the "burning of Atlanta and all the devastation through Georgia never created a tithe of the animosity that has been created by this sort of treatment of our people." [41] This fact had much to do with putting life into the Ku Klux Klan, and the Klan did much to destroy the League.

As the first elections under military Reconstruction would normally come in the latter part of 1867, great activity broke out in organizing parties for the contest. The Radicals held conventions in every state, "black and tan" and "lily white" intermixed, and wooed the Negroes by making them chairmen and members of committees. Now for the first time the Republican party took definite form in the South. Holden in North Carolina spread the word: "Let our loyal people, and especially the colored people, trust no man who will not promptly and proudly say he is a Republican," [42] and a Georgia Carpetbagger warned the Negroes to "be sure to vote for a Radical. Vote for the man whom the Rebels denounce most bitterly, and you will be pretty

40 Quoted in Marietta *Journal,* March 17, 1871.
41 Stanley F. Horn, *Invisible Empire: The Story of the Ku Klux Klan, 1866–1871* (Boston, 1939), 170.
42 Raleigh *Tri-Weekly Standard,* April 4, 1867.

128

sure to be right." [43] In some places the Negroes were told that they would be fined $500 each and exiled to a foreign country if they did not attend political meetings.[44]

White people were inveigled and threatened into the Republican party, and the laboring class especially was sought. "The poor white men have no business in the Democratic party, which, in times past, made slaves of them," warned an Alabama editor.[45] "Now elevate yourselves, toiling white men and black men," a Northern orator advised a Raleigh audience; but good strategy played down any reference to social equality and led to vehement denials that it was part of the Republican plan.[46] The threat of confiscation was often used against planters who refused to hire Republican Negro workmen, and it was often charged that Congress would not admit any state organized by the Democrats. To carry Republicanism to the South, Senator Henry Wilson of Massachusetts and Congressman William D. (Pig Iron) Kelley made speaking tours through that region in the summer of 1867.

The Democrats, or Conservatives as they usually called themselves, were equally busy. They consolidated their white strength and made in some places almost frantic and pathetic appeals to the Negroes for their support. A Georgian addressed a colored audience thus: "We are all creatures of one good Being. We are all brethren, children of one Father. He has made us differently —we, to work in one part of his vine yard—you, in another. But all to receive the wages of our work." [47] An Alabaman appealed to the Negroes: "The whites here who have been raised up with you—who have run foot-races with you, played marbels [sic] and gone 'possum hunting with you, are better friends than any Yankee that ever lived, or died." [48] In Terry, Mississippi, the

[43] Griffin (Ga.) *American Union*, August 16, 1867.

[44] Leigh, *Ten Years on a Georgia Plantation*, 98.

[45] Montgomery *Alabama State Journal*, July 3, 1869.

[46] Raleigh *Tri-Weekly Standard*, May 2, 1867.

[47] Elias Yulee, *An Address to the Colored People of Georgia* (Savannah, 1868), 30.

[48] Continuing, he asked whether the Radicals and mean whites had "any land to rent you, any houses for you to live in, any thing for you to do, or any money with which to pay your wages?" Mobile *Advertiser*, quoted in Sandersville *Central Georgian*, August 7, 1867.

whites and the Negroes held a Fourth of July celebration together, with equal representation on the necessary committees. The whites furnished the food and the Negroes cooked it. This meeting was to give "mutual assurance of a cordial, good understanding between the white man and the colored men of this neighborhood." [49]

There was some Negro response in a like spirit of friendship. A Negro in a political gathering of 2,000 of his race in Columbia said, "Try friends first, and when they have deceived you there will be time enough to seek the sympathy of strangers." [50] A Georgia Negro gave this testimony: "I know those amongst whom I was raised; I do not know those who come to me and take me by the hand at night, and give me advice in the dark, and when it is light do not notice me on the street." [51] Southern newspapers gave wide publicity to friendly expressions from Negroes.

President Johnson, believing that the Military Reconstruction Acts were unconstitutional, but also believing that he should respect them until the courts should declare them void, set up the required five military districts and appointed commanders for them.[52] Congress having abolished the state militias, these commanders might use, ignore, or destroy the state governments they found in their districts, and rule without reference to law, courts, or custom. This was military government as far as they chose to make it—all in violation of the Supreme Court's decision in the *Ex parte* Milligan case and in defiance of official statements of the President, Congress, and the Supreme Court implying that the war was over. Some commanders were more reckless with their power than others, but all of them interfered with the state governments to some extent. They put ignorant Negroes on juries; in many cases they denied the courts the right to func-

---

[49] Raymond *Hinds County Gazette,* June 21, 1867.

[50] Greenville *Southern Enterprise,* March 28, 1867.

[51] Griffin *American Union,* August 23, 1867.

[52] The President appointed John M. Schofield for the First, David E. Sickles for the Second, George H. Thomas for the Third, Edward O. C. Ord for the Fourth, and Philip H. Sheridan for the Fifth. Thomas was immediately transferred to the Department of the Cumberland and John Pope took charge of the Third. Various other changes were later made.

tion and set up military commissions to take their places; and they expelled officials high and low and filled their places with soldiers. They removed the governors of Virginia, Georgia, Mississippi, Louisiana, and Texas. The most despotic of these "military satraps" were E. R. S. Canby, John Pope, and Philip H. Sheridan.

Yet to many Southerners such military government appeared preferable to rule by Negroes, Carpetbaggers, and Scalawags which the commanders were charged with setting up. According to the editor of the *Land We Love*, "There is not one of the five Districts in so unhappy a condition to-day, as is Tennessee *in the Union*"; [53] and a Northern editor remarked, "There is a responsibility in a 'Pope' and a 'Schofield,' while there is none in a Scipio or a Sambo." [54] Jacob Thompson, back from his exile in Europe and Canada, declared that he would rather live under General Edward O. C. Ord in Mississippi than "with the negroes in the ascendant." [55] As fewer than 20,000 soldiers were assigned to the whole South, military occupation prevailed largely as an unseen power though an ever-present trouble. A Confederate veteran believed, "Could the Boys in Blue stand on Southern soil side by side with me and my faithful comrades today, they would cast their votes in favor of the government for which they fought, and for which their comrades died—a white man's government, a Union of white men." [56] This feeling was not in vain, for more often than not the Federal soldiers formed their friendships with the Conservative Southerners, much to the chagrin of the Carpetbaggers and Scalawags. Southerners invited soldiers to their homes and to dances and receptions. In one Georgia town a Carpetbagger complained that the soldiers of occupation were no sooner off their trains before "rebels" were buying them drinks; and another declared, "The soldiers now here partake completely of the spirit of the rebels, seem to feel licensed

[53] *Land We Love*, III (1867), 86.

[54] New York *Express*, quoted in Augusta *Weekly Constitutionalist*, November 13, 1867.

[55] Percy L. Rainwater (ed.), "Letters to and from Jacob Thompson," in *Journal of Southern History*, VI (1940), 107–108.

[56] Richmond *Whig*, quoted in Augusta *Weekly Constitutionalist*, November 13, 1867.

to commit depredations that rebels would not dare to do." [57]

As the second Military Reconstruction Act required all commanders to make a list of voters before September 1, 1867, they immediately set about the task. They divided their territory into registration districts and appointed a registration board of three members, one of whom some commanders insisted must be a Negro. Since all "registers," as they were called, must take the ironclad oath, most native white Southerners were unable to qualify. Thus soldiers, Freedmen's Bureau agents, and Negroes secured the positions. General Pope, in the Third District, paid registers from fifteen to forty cents for every name secured, depending on the distance traveled to get it, and he allowed travel expenses of five cents a mile on railroads and steamboats and ten cents a mile in the country. It was, therefore, good business to enter onto the record as many names as possible, and so it came about that sometimes Negroes were registered two or three times, under different names. Some Negroes not understanding what registration meant, believed it represented another free distribution of something to eat or wear; they brought buckets and baskets to put it in and hurried lest it give out before they arrived.

As only those could vote whose names were on the registration lists, it was important to scrutinize with great care any native white who applied. According to the law, no person could register who had "been disfranchised for participation in any rebellion or civil war against the United States," or who, having held a civil office, had later engaged in rebellion. The purpose was to erect as large a black electorate as possible and to eliminate old Confederate leadership both from voting and officeholding. What laws disfranchised a person for having participated in rebellion was never made clear by Congress, but in the third Reconstruction Act it declared that the decisions of the registers were final. If they chose to disbelieve a white man in the face of the most conclusive proof, they could deny him the right to vote, and there was no appeal. It has been estimated that about 150,000 white Southerners were disfranchised. When the registration of voters was completed, it was found that Negroes were in a majority in South Carolina, Florida, Alabama, Mississippi, and Louisiana.

[57] Griffin American Union, November 29, 1867.

The total number registered was 627,000 whites and 703,000 Negroes.[58]

The second step was to hold elections to decide whether constitutional conventions should be called and at the same time to elect delegates to such conventions. It was a solemn moment in the course of civilized government and society in America when now for the first time a great mass of ignorant voters two years out of slavery were to take charge of the processes of government and constitution making. Southerners, who stood to suffer most, were almost stupefied. Some advised against voting at all and thereby allow such ignorance and incompetency to be enthroned that Congress would not admit the states; others argued that everyone should vote for delegates but vote against holding the convention; while more realistic leaders begged the people to vote both for the convention and for the most intelligent candidates.

So completely was election machinery in the hands of Radicals that there was no need for them to engage in corruption and sharp practices, yet in some places they could not resist their opportunities. Negroes came in droves and encamped for days around the ballot boxes, making it difficult for whites to vote. It took time for Negroes to undergo this unusual experience; some had forgotten the names under which they had registered, and others had lost their ballots. The outstanding characteristic of this election was the refusal of the white people to vote. In South Carolina and Florida about a tenth of those registered voted, about a third in Alabama, and in no state did many more than half vote. Most of the whites who voted cast their ballots for the conventions, a fact which, however, did not make them Radicals. With all the novelty in voting, and with all the urging of Loyal Leagues, there were a great many Negroes who did not vote—in Alabama, almost 33,000 out of 104,000 who were registered. In all the states except Texas, where elections were not held until 1868, conventions were authorized.

[58] William A. Russ, Jr., "Registration and Disfranchisement under Radical Reconstruction," in *Mississippi Valley Historical Review*, XXI (1934–1935), 163–80; Rhodes, *History of the United States*, VI, 83. Contemporaries estimated the number of disfranchised from 300,000 to 500,000. Augusta *Weekly Constitutionalist*, June 24, 1868.

Practically the entire membership in every state was made up of Radicals, and in South Carolina and Louisiana a majority of the delegates were Negroes. The number of Negro delegates varied from nine in Texas to seventy-six in South Carolina. In most of the conventions from South Carolina to Louisiana, Carpetbaggers dominated the proceedings though they were not in a majority, and they put the stamp of the North upon most of the constitutions which were made. As these conventions met, day after day drawing out their sessions and frequently making a burlesque of orderly procedure, most respectable Southerners looked upon them as mongrel menageries, even though they realized their destiny was being played with. Most of the Negro delegates could not read, some of them were fugitives from justice, some were expelled for their truculence and disorderliness, and others were jailed for theft; but the great majority were harmless and took orders explicitly from their Carpetbagger mentors. The loud-talking and troublesome few set off all Negro officeholders then and thereafter to a bad start, and gave them the reputation of being uniformly unscrupulous troublemakers or inane ninnies. Such were Joe Oats in Florida, Pinckney B. S. Pinchback in Louisiana, G. T. Ruby in Texas, and Tunis G. Campbell and Aaron Alpeoria Bradley in Georgia. Of Bradley, the best his Radical friends could say was, "The arrogant presumption, ignorance, bullyism and impertinence of this negro, is becoming intolerable." [59] Shortly he was expelled unanimously, and another Radical speeded his departure thus: "At last this worthless and brawling negro has been expelled from his seat in the Convention." [60]

These conventions were outrageously extravagant and many of their members were dishonest. A delegate living only 100 miles from Little Rock drew travel expenses for 900 miles; and a member of the North Carolina convention living 30 miles from Raleigh collected expenses for 262 miles. The Florida convention voted to begin salaries a month before the delegates convened. Taking over the functions of legislatures, these conventions wrestled with such problems as outlawing the terms "nigger" and "Yankee";

[59] Atlanta *Georgia Weekly Opinion*, January 7, 1868.
[60] Atlanta *Daily New Era*, February 13, 1868.

they changed the names of counties reminding them of Confederate heroes such as Lee and Davis; they spent many days debating measures designed to raise money for their salaries; the Texas convention, dragging itself out over two sessions, became snarled in the rivalries of two factions led by the two Hamilton brothers, Andrew Jackson and Morgan C., and wasted months without discussing a constitution. According to the historian of Texas Reconstruction, "The two sessions of the convention had cost the state more than $200,000 for five months of wrangling, not more than one month of which was spent in actual consideration of the constitution." [61] In Florida the convention split into separate bodies and occupied halls in different cities.

Conventions in some of the states took up a great deal of time in discussing relief from old debts. Stay laws or outright repudiation of debts contracted before the Surrender worked in various directions. The Radicals designed them for political effect, hoping to draw into their party great numbers of whites who would thereby vote for the ratification of the constitution. In fact, relief provisions would have helped the planter class as much as the poor whites, and would not have benefited at all the Negroes who had no debts.

The constitutions finally turned out were much better than the Southerners had ever hoped for; in fact, some of them were kept for many years after the Southern whites again got control of their governments. Almost uniformly they were more democratic than the documents they supplanted, made so by increasing the electorate through Negro suffrage, requiring the total population as the basis for representation, reducing the terms of office, and by adding such principles as homestead exemptions and nonimprisonment for debt. They called for free education for all and favored the economic development of the South. They added new offices such as lieutenant-governorships and sought to set up Northern practices such as township government. Running through all of them was a greater centralization of power in the hands of the governor, who in most constitutions was given the power to appoint local government officials. In Louisiana this power was so great as to make the governor a potential dictator.

[61] Ramsdell, *Reconstruction in Texas*, 260.

A Northern commentator declared that power was more centralized in Louisiana than in France under the Empire: "No ruler
of a civilized community," said he, "ever possessed greater power
than the governor of Louisiana under this constitution." [62]

The suffrage and officeholding provisions were revolutionary
but in harmony with military Reconstruction, and, therefore, not
surprising. Every state gave Negroes the right to vote, and six
placed on the whites restrictions growing out of their support
of the Confederacy. North Carolina, South Carolina, Georgia,
Florida, and Texas in no way obstructed white men either in
voting or holding office; Virginia and Mississippi put no effective
restrictions on voting but excluded from office practically all
sympathizers with the Confederacy; Alabama and Arkansas denied the right both to vote and to hold office to all male citizens
who had ever held a civil office and later had aided the Confederacy or who had opposed the adoption of military Reconstruction; and Louisiana, most severe of all, denied suffrage and
office practically to all who had aided the Confederacy. The three
last-named states frankly and blatantly disfranchised and disqualified for office Democrats, white and black, without reference to
whether they had or had not aided the Confederacy. Specifically
included in the constitutions of Texas and South Carolina was the
import of the Fourteenth Amendment, which denied no one the
right to vote but which disqualified for office certain classes which
had previously held office; but, whether stated or not, these restrictions applied to all states. Disabilities and disqualifications
were taken out of both the Mississippi and Virginia constitutions
in the election on their ratification, so that only Alabama, Louisiana, and Arkansas actually applied suffrage and officeholding restrictions against white people.

The next step in military Reconstruction was to submit these
constitutions to the people for ratification. This was done early
in 1868 in all the states except Virginia and Texas. Now was the
crucial time in Radical Reconstruction. All efforts put forth up
to this time were in vain if these documents were rejected. This
moment was serious for the Southerners too; if these constitutions

[62] Nordhoff, *Cotton States,* 44.

were adopted the South would come under alien rule. Therefore, their bitter opposition was not so much against the contents of these documents as against the impending Negro-Scalawag-Carpetbag domination of the new state governments. For that very reason the Radicals wanted these constitutions adopted; signs were ominous that the Democrats might win the presidency in 1868 unless a Radicalized South could be brought to the rescue.

In the election not only were the constitutions submitted for ratification, but full sets of candidates to fill the offices were voted on at the same time. The rules of suffrage were not those in the document being voted on, but the rules Congress had set up in the Military Reconstruction Acts. This was an unconstitutional procedure as far as the suffrage qualifications were concerned for those voting for state officials; but Congress was now in a hurry to get the states back into the Union and could not wait for another election for state officials after the constitutions had been ratified. The elections were carried out in an amazingly loose fashion; they extended over a period of fifteen days in some of the Arkansas counties and in Alabama they ran from two to five days. To strengthen the validity of these constitutions, Congress had provided in the second Military Reconstruction Act that at least one half of all registered voters must participate in their ratification. This procedure played into the hands of those opposing ratification, for anyone who did not cast a ballot voted against the document, whether through choice, sickness, or death. A Conservative who stayed away from the polls voted against it; a Radical who died voted against it. In some states the Conservatives chose to muster their full strength and vote the document down by positive action; in others they carried on a campaign to keep people from voting at all. Mississippi voted it down by the first method and Alabama rejected it by the second. Congress could not well force Mississippi into the Union, but it dragged Alabama in by breaking faith with the South and itself, too, in passing the fourth Military Reconstruction Act, which repealed the one-half provision in the second. All the other states, except Virginia, who hesitated to submit her Radical document to the people, and Texas, who had not yet made one, accepted their constitutions in 1868 and set up governments which ratified the Fourteenth Amendment. Congress quickly readmitted them into the Union.

CHAPTER VII

BLACKOUT OF HONEST
GOVERNMENT

CONGRESS had set up new state governments because, as it claimed, the Johnson states were illegal and did not protect life and property. New leaders under new constitutions now took charge; the elimination of the old Southern leaders, from top to bottom, had been the heart of the Congressional plan. Would Congressional governments succeed better than Johnson governments—or even nearly as well?

Intent upon filling the thousands of offices made vacant, the delegates of the constitutional conventions maneuvered themselves into the best ones, and set up machinery which controlled the rest. In some of the states a few Conservatives slipped into minor offices. Governors were empowered to fill most of the local offices by appointment; legislatures could declare offices vacant and provide for filling them to their liking; and returning boards, a new Radical device for counting ballots, could manipulate the votes to bring about any desired result. In addition to the state offices, there were Federal positions to be filled, both elective and appointive—Congressmen, judges, customs collectors, revenue agents, and postmasters. As noted, all elective offices the Radicals controlled and all appointive offices fell into their hands when President Johnson gave way to Grant in 1869. Now all Southern officialdom became a powerful Radical machine. Even Federal judges became miserably partisan and corrupt. John C. Underwood in Virginia thoroughly disgraced himself in the proceedings relative to the trial of Jefferson Davis and by his political manipulations; Richard Busteed in Alabama debauched his bench through a rich harvest of bribes in cases brought before him by collusion; and Edward H. Durell in Louisiana became so completely a part of the corruption in that state that he resigned to escape impeachment.[1]

Most of the people who filled the many offices were untrained and untried—Scalawags, Carpetbaggers, and Negroes. Had the times been normal their duties would have been onerous and complicated; with the times out of joint they took the easy road and speedily buried themselves in corruption. Carpetbaggers filled a majority of the higher offices. In the first elections in the seven states admitted in 1868, four of the governors, ten of the fourteen United States Senators, and twenty of the thirty-five Representatives were Carpetbaggers. Throughout the whole period of Reconstruction nineteen Carpetbaggers went to the Senate. Some of the outstanding ones who held high offices were: in South Carolina, Daniel H. Chamberlain, native of Massachusetts and educated at Harvard and Yale colleges, mostly honest, but succumbing ultimately to party necessities, and B. Frank Wittemore, also from Massachusetts, thoroughly corrupt, and expelled from Congress; in Mississippi, Adelbert Ames, son-in-law of Benjamin F. Butler, resigning the army to enter politics, crusading and inept, fleeing the governorship to escape impeachment; in Louisiana, Henry Clay Warmoth of Illinois, entering the political scene poor and retiring rich, and William Pitt Kellogg, born in Vermont and growing up in Illinois, leading his adopted state government into a blackout of honesty; and in Arkansas, Powell Clayton, passing from a disgraced governorship to the United States Senate.[2]

Although the Carpetbaggers played an important part in every

---

[1] These judges had been appointed before the Radicals took charge of the South. Avary, *Dixie after the War*, 237–44; Fleming, *Civil War and Reconstruction in Alabama*, 744; John W. Burgess, *Reconstruction and the Constitution, 1866–1876* (New York, 1902), 270–71. Nordhoff, *Cotton States*, 85, said the Alabama election law set up "one of the most perfect machines for political fraud that I have ever heard of." In Plaquemines Parish, Louisiana, one name out of every seven and one-half people in the white population was put on the registration books, but one name out of every three and one eighth of the colored people received a place on the list. Many of the names were, of course, fictitious; out of forty-eight names drawn on a jury, thirty-six were nonexistent. *Ibid.*, 66.

[2] Dunning, *Reconstruction*, 120; Reginald C. McGrane, *Foreign Bondholders and American State Debts* (New York, 1935), 313; C. Mildred Thompson, "Carpet-Baggers in the United States Senate," in *Studies in Southern History and Politics*, 161–66. Warmoth, whose salary as governor was $8,000 a year, admitted making over $100,000

state, they were not uniformly strong. In Virginia, North Carolina, Georgia, Tennessee, and Texas, the Scalawags came to be dominant, and, therefore, all that was reprehensible in Radical rule in the South should not be placed on Northern importation. The pestilences of the times knew no limits either geographical or racial; native-born white Southerners became as corrupt as Carpetbaggers, and only in South Carolina and Louisiana did the Negroes ever have a majority in any legislature.

And yet the most spectacular and exotic development in government in the history of white civilization was to be seen in the part the Negroes played in ruling the South—longest to be remembered, shuddered at, and execrated. An English traveler could hardly believe his senses as he saw the Negroes made "King, Lords, and Commons, and something more," and in South Carolina he observed "a proletariat Parliament . . . the like of which could not be produced under the widest suffrage in any part of the world save in some of these Southern States." As a Southerner saw the South's predicament, "What a white commune was in France we all have seen; what a negro commune is in America our eyes have also witnessed. Both made war on intelligence and social distinctions, both brought chaos in their train." [3]

Though the Northern Radicals instituted Negro suffrage and officeholding in the name of justice, they were thoroughly insincere in their protestations; for in the first place few of the Northern states allowed the Negroes to vote and none ever promoted a Negro into any office, however intelligent the Negro or however lowly the position. Furthermore, the Radical national government, unrestrained by state laws or suffrage requirements, waited long to appoint Negroes to office in the North. Seeing these inconsistencies, a delegation of Negroes, representing both North and South, begged President Grant in 1869 to select some Northern Negroes. [4] A Southerner prayed that "some Boston

---

his first year in office. By 1872 his wealth was estimated at $500,000 to $1,000,000. Fleming (ed.), *Documentary History of Reconstruction*, II, 39. So outraged did some communities feel that they refused to let officials take their seats. Stearns, *Black Man of the South*, 212–40.

[3] Somers, *Southern States since the War*, 41; *Southern Magazine*, XIV (1874), 587.

[4] Montgomery *Alabama State Journal*, May 22, 1869.

Sambo may be appointed postmaster in that city so that the Puritans of that place may get a dose of the physic they have prepared for the South." [5] Why had no Negro been elected to office in the North? "Why has such a negro, for example, as Frederick Douglass," asked a Southerner, "never been sent by the Radicals of New York to represent his city of Rochester in the Legislature of the State or in the Congress of the nation?" [6] Until a Negro should sit in Congress, representing a Northern state, "and a score of colored men shall sit in the Legislature of each of the New England States, then, and not till then," said a Missourian, "will the black man be as well treated in those Radical regions, as he is now treated in the rebel States of the South." [7]

Carpetbaggers were as little desirous of promoting Negroes into high office in the South as their Northern colleagues were in their states; and Scalawags, actuated by racial antipathies more than Carpetbaggers, objected to Negroes holding any offices. Both were quite desirous that Negroes vote—but not for Negroes. A Georgia Negro wrote Charles Sumner that there was no other place in the Union where there were so "many miserable hungry unscrupulous politicians . . . and if they could prevent it no colored man would ever occupy any office of profit or trust." He later wrote, "I am tired of being used as stepping-stones to elevate white men alone to office and would like to vote for some competent colored man" to go to the United States Senate.[8] A convention of Negroes in Macon resolved in 1868 that they did not recommend the colored man "to be satisfied with being a mere pack horse, to ride white men into office, whether he [sic] is the exponent of our sentiments or not; no, it would be better that we did not have the Ballot." [9] Even so, Negroes frequently held offices far beyond their capacity to administer them.

In South Carolina, Florida, Mississippi, and Louisiana the Negroes reached the zenith of their power, but in no state was a Negro ever elected to the governorship, though in South Caro-

[5] Dalton *North Georgia Citizen*, May 27, 1869.

[6] Augusta *Weekly Chronicle & Sentinel*, September 16, 1874.

[7] *Missouri Republican*, quoted *ibid.*, June 8, 1870.

[8] Belcher, Augusta, Ga., to Sumner, April 5, 1869, in Sumner Papers, Box 94, No. 9; Belcher to Sumner, February 3, 1870, *ibid.*, Box 96, No. 99.

[9] Macon *American Union*, October 9, 1868.

lina, Mississippi, and Louisiana Negroes became lieutenant governors. In Mississippi the lieutenant governor, Alexander K. Davis, frequently acted as governor during the absence of Ames; and in Louisiana, Lieutenant Governor Pinchback succeeded to the governorship if it be admitted that in the jigsaw puzzle of politics in that state Governor Warmoth was legally impeached and removed. All other state offices in some state at one time or another were filled by Negroes—but in only one state was a justice of the Supreme Court a Negro. South Carolina elevated to this position Jonathan Jasper Wright, a colored Carpetbagger from Pennsylvania.[10] The great majority of Negro officeholders were local officials—such as constables, justices of the peace, county superintendents of education, etc.—though in all the states there was a sprinkling of Negroes in the legislatures, ranging in number from only one in Tennessee to a majority in some of the sessions of the South Carolina legislature. It was a bitter comment among Negroes that Brownlow, the most Radical of native Southerners, saw to it that few of their race attained office in Tennessee.

White members of most state legislatures disliked the presence of Negroes; in Georgia in 1868 resentment gained the ascendancy and the white members, Radicals and Conservatives, banded together and expelled them. In later sessions when they reappeared at the behest of Congress and the army, the editor of the legislative manual merely recorded their names without the customary biographical sketches, explaining that there was nothing to say about them beyond their having been waiters, bootblacks, and cotton-field hands. He slyly admitted another motive: "though Congress could compel him to associate with negroes in a deliberative body, sit beside them in railroad cars, etc., neither Congress, Military Government, a triple Reconstruction nor even another amendment to the national patch-work, the United States Constitution, could compel him to publish their biographies in this book." [11]

A considerable number of Negroes were appointed to Federal

[10] Robert H. Woody, "Jonathan Jasper Wright, Associate Justice of the Supreme Court of South Carolina, 1870–77," in *Journal of Negro History*, XVIII (1933), 114–31.

[11] Alexander St. Clair-Abrams, *Manual and Biographical Register of the State of Georgia for 1871–2* (Atlanta, 1872), vi.

positions in the South, such as postmasters and mail agents; but the highest Federal service performed by Negroes was in Congress. Southerners looked with some degree of complacency on Negroes going to Congress, for there Northerners would see Negro rulers in operation and would be forced to associate with them. Since Negroes would not make corn, or cotton, or sugar, it might be that they would make laws. "We want negroes to be so thick in Congress," said a Virginian, "that a man standing on the wharf at Aquia Creek, with a favorable wind, could smell them. We want their wool to be knee-deep in the halls of Congress, and we do not want any one there who is not five times blacker than the ace of spades." [12]

In the summer of 1868 a South Carolina Radical inquired of Charles Sumner whether he thought it would "injure the republican party in the North and West if [we] were to send some colored men to Congress." [13] It was apparently not considered bad politics, for during the next dozen years seven Southern states sent as Senators and Representatives twenty-eight Negroes. The greatest number at any one time was eight in 1875. The states sending Negroes were North Carolina, South Carolina, Georgia, Florida, Alabama, Mississippi, and Louisiana. Mississippi sent the first one in the person of Hiram R. Revels, as Senator, born a free Negro in North Carolina. Only two Negro Senators ever served in Congress, both from Mississippi. Pinchback, the Louisiana mulatto, succeeded in getting himself elected both to the House and Senate for overlapping terms, but he was not seated in either place. Some of these Negro Congressmen did creditable service, but others became either echoes of their Radical masters or disgusting troublemakers. Their service did not recommend their race to the South or even to the North, for not until the twentieth century did a Negro sit in Congress from any Northern state. [14]

It would have been remarkable had Negroes shown any con-

[12] Richmond *Times,* quoted in *Southern Cultivator,* XXIV (1866), 61.

[13] W. B. Nash, Columbia, S.C., to Sumner, August 22, 1868, in Sumner Papers, Box 87, No. 18.

[14] Samuel D. Smith, *The Negro in Congress, 1870–1901* (Chapel Hill, 1940), 3–9, 45, 137–44; William A. Russ, Jr., "The Negro and White Disfranchisement during Radical Reconstruction," in *Journal of Negro History,* XIX (1934), 171–92.

spicuous ability as lawmakers and rulers, though they were better than there was reason to expect; but even so, much of their performance was either grotesque or puerile. Psychologically and in every other respect the Negroes were fearfully unprepared to occupy positions of rulership. Race and color came to mean more to them than any other consideration, whether of honest government, of justice to the individual, or even of ultimate protection of their own rights. Negroes on juries let color blind them, and they rejected the wisest counsel, Northern and Southern, against banding together politically, instead of dividing on issues and policies of government. Of course, many white Conservatives made it difficult for them to do otherwise; but Negroes proscribed their own race if any voted Democratic—their preachers excommunicating them, their womenfolk bringing all their feminine powers to play against them, and Loyal Leagues intimidating and doing violence to them.[15] Their idea of the new order was

> De bottom rail's on de top,
> An' we's gwine to keep it dar.[16]

Radical leaders impressed their views on the Negroes. An Alabama editor said, "The Radicals are now trying to persuade the Southern negroes that it was very cruel and inhuman to rescue them from the dinner pot—that it would have been much better for them had their forefathers been eaten in Africa. Perhaps it would. If they intend to let carpet-baggers and scallawags lead them by their noses forever we are sure it would have been. Any man had better be eaten than a 'born fool' forever or the father of a generation of fools." [17]

[15] As an example of a sensible attitude, a Negro candidate wrote, "I am for peace and harmony, and utterly opposed to any discussions having a tendency to excite bad feeling between any classes of society; and in canvassing the District I shall so conduct myself as to merit that respect and kindness which has always been shown me." Greenville *Southern Enterprise,* April 1, 1868.

[16] King, *Great South,* 453.

[17] Montgomery *Weekly Advertiser,* August 18, 1875. This is part of a Radical handbill to impress Negroes: "Every man knows that the Republican Party, under the lead of God, President Lincoln and General Grant, freed the whole colored race from slavery; and every man who knows anything, believes that the Democratic party will, if they can, make them slaves again." Dalton *North Georgia Citizen,* September 10, 1868.

Most Negro officeholders were more to be pitied than blamed, but a few blatant, dishonest, insolent megalomaniacs discredited all. A Carpetbagger characterized Henry M. Turner, preacher, politician, and presider at many Negro conventions, as "a licentious robber and counterfeiter, a vulgar blackguard, a sacrilegious profaner of God's name, and a most consummate hypocrite." Yet the Negroes elected him to the Georgia legislature—"if he had received his deserts, he would have gone to the Penitentiary"; he was "a thief and a scoundrel, and yet they voted for him." "If the colored people have not the elements of morality among them sufficiently to cry down such shameless characters, they should not expect to command the respect of decent people anywhere." [18] One Southerner told Sumner that he treated Negroes kindly, "but to Sit still and allow an ignoramus to represent me in government Councils I am not a going to do it & you know that no senseble [sic] man will." [19] Another, seeing the humorous side of a Negro candidate, said, "Ike has no 'book larnin', but he bakes an excellent wheat pone, and knows how to drive a hack." [20]

General William S. Rosecrans, amidst a Confederate atmosphere at White Sulphur Springs, asked General Lee, in writing, whether he thought the South must in reality be ruled by "the poor, simple, uneducated, landless freedmen" under the corrupt leadership of whites still worse. Lee and thirty-one other prominent Southerners signed an answer declaring their opposition, basing it on no enmity toward freedmen, "but from a deep-seated conviction that at present the negroes have neither the intelligence nor other qualifications which are necessary to make them depositories of political power." [21] The minority report of a Congressional committee declared, "History, till now, gives no account of a conqueror so cruel as to place his vanquished foes under the domination of their former slaves. *That was reserved for the radical rulers in this great Republic.*" [22]

18 Macon *American Union*, December 29, 1870; June 15, 1871.

19 Unsigned letter, Ft. Gaines, Ga., to Sumner, October 5, 1868, in Sumner Papers, Box 87, No. 74.

20 Tallahassee *Sentinel,* September 2, 1867.

21 Augusta *Weekly Constitutionalist*, September 16, 1868.

22 *Ku Klux Conspiracy*, I, 438. "Now, we have as our rulers the vilest of mankind, whom no gentleman would allow to enter his kitchen," said the *Land We Love,* VI (1868-1869), 174.

South Carolina and Louisiana, apart from Haiti, were the world's classic examples of Negro rule, but worse than Haiti, for the black emperors of that benighted country ruled over black people who had never known any other kind of rule but bad. The general character of Negro government in these states was dismal and devastating in the extreme. It meant that the protection which civilized communities had received from their governments was at an end. Heretofore, if conditions should become too bad there was always an irreducible minimum of intelligence to which an outraged people could turn for redress; in these states that irreducible minimum miraculously had been reduced to nothing, for no appeal could be made to ignorant Negro majorities. One of the first questions put to a stranger coming to New Orleans to see the sights was whether he had seen the Negro legislature in action; and *Appletons' Hand-Book of American Travel* advised tourists that a peep into the statehouse in Columbia would "be intensely interesting and should not be missed by those who desire to see the negro in the role of a statesman." [23]

Specifically, the South Carolina House in 1873 consisted of 124 members, of whom 23 were Conservatives. Of the remaining 101 Radicals, 94 were Negroes. The Negroes thus outnumbered the whites more than three to one, though the Negro population of South Carolina was only slightly larger than the white. The Negro legislators were of all shades, from the lightest mulattoes to the blackest negroids, fresh from the kitchen and the field, in clothing ranging from secondhand black frock coats to the "coarse and dirty garments of the field." The white members did or said little, stunned by what they saw and heard—voluble, jabbering Negroes, always raising points of order and personal privilege, speaking a half dozen times on the same question, and repeating themselves constantly without knowing it. A South Carolinian viewed the scene for a time and as he turned away exclaimed, "My God, look at this! . . . Let me go." A Northern newspaperman who came down to see this amazing spectacle declared it was "barbarism overwhelming civilization by physical force" and "a wonder and a shame to modern civilization." A black parliament

---

23 Charles H. Jones (ed.), *Appletons' Hand-Book of American Travel, Southern Tour* . . . (New York, 1874), 132.

representing a white constituency—the only example in all history! [24]

Saddled with an irresponsible officialdom, the South was now plunged into debauchery, corruption, and private plundering unbelievable—suggesting that government had been transformed into an engine of destruction. It was fortunate for the South that its officials were bent on private aggrandizement and personal gain, rather than on a fundamental class overturning which would have resulted in confiscations and an upset of civilization. This condition was, therefore, nothing more than the Southern side of the national picture. Corruption permeated government from the statehouse to the courthouse and city hall—though in local government there was a tendency for more honesty to assert itself under the closer scrutiny of the people. Yet it is probably true that New Orleans suffered as much from misgovernment as Chicago and Boston did from fire.

The variety of means used to debauch government and plunder the public treasury bespeaks the vivid imaginations and practical ability of the perpetrators. Every seceded state came under the withering hand of Radical rule, but it was reserved to South Carolina, Louisiana, and Arkansas to suffer most. Legislatures piled up expenses against their impoverished states to fantastic heights. In Florida the cost of printing in 1869 was more than the entire cost of the state government in 1860; and the legislature sold for five cents an acre 1,100,000 acres of public land held in trust. The Georgia legislature bought from a favored agent in Atlanta an unfinished opera house for $250,000, previously sold for much less, to convert it into a capitol building. In Arkansas a Negro was given $9,000 for repairing a bridge which had originally cost $500. Brownlow of Tennessee, too palsied to sign his name, gave wide authority to others to attach his signature to state bonds with results easily imagined. In South Carolina the legislature bought for $700,000 land worth $100,000 for resale to Negroes; it issued $1,590,000 worth of bonds with which to redeem $500,000 worth of bank notes, and paid $75,000 to take a state census in 1869, although the Federal census was due to be taken the following year, which cost only $43,000; it voted extra compensation of $1,000

[24] Pike, *Prostrate State*, 10–16.

to the speaker for his efficient service when he lost $1,000 on a horse race; it paid for lunches, whiskies and wines, women's apparel, and coffins charged by the legislators to legislative expenses; and Governor Scott while drunk was induced by a fancy lady in a burlesque show to sign an issue of state bonds. The Louisiana legislature was extremely ingenious in devising means of spending the state's money: Before the war its sessions had cost on an average of $100,000 but under Radical rule they cost about $1,000,000, half of which was for the mileage expenses and salaries of the members and clerks; its printing bill under three years of Warmoth's rule was $1,500,000 although previously it had never amounted to more than $60,000 for a year; to provide a capitol building it paid $250,000 for the St. Louis Hotel, recently sold for $84,000; it chartered the Mississippi Valley Navigation Company and purchased $100,000 worth of stock in it, though it never organized to do business; it chartered a Society to Prevent Cruelty of Animals, whose activities turned out to be rustling stray animals in New Orleans and holding them for $5.00 a day charges to the owners and arresting horses left standing in the streets while their riders were transacting business in the shops; and the chief justice was a party to the sale of a state-owned railroad for $50,000 on which had been expended more than $2,000,000, refusing to sell it at a higher price to bidders whom he did not favor. The cost of clerks and assistants amounted to as much as the total expenses of wartime sessions; legislatures created new offices and increased the salaries of the old ones and created new counties for the spoils that went with them; governors pardoned criminals for pecuniary and political reasons, and legislation was regularly bought and sold, one Louisiana legislator demanding the price of his vote though he had been absent—and so the record of corruption could be extended ad infinitum.[25]

Whether or not the purpose of Radical Reconstruction was to

[25] *Ibid.*, 49, 191–97, 199, 213; Nordhoff, *Cotton States*, 31, 43, 47, 56, 59, 60, 62; Ella Lonn, *Reconstruction in Louisiana After 1868* (New York, 1918), 30, 34, 50, 87; Davis, *Civil War and Reconstruction in Florida*, 648–50, 666–67, 670–71; Robert H. Woody (ed.), "Behind the Scenes in the Reconstruction Legislature of South Carolina: Diary of Josephus Woodruff," in *Journal of Southern History*, II (1936), 78–102, 233–59; Simkins and Woody, *South Carolina during Reconstruction*, 113, 134–40; Coulter, *William G. Brownlow*, 376–77.

place "the negro and the almighty dollar in the sanctionary of the Constitution," [26] there was ample evidence in Southern state documents of the intention to do both. Yet these constitutions were considered then and since as proof of the desires of the framers to promote true democracy and economic recovery. Whatever the motives, the results were devastating to honest government, for they opened up to dishonest speculators, Northern and Southern, the exploitation of Southern credit in the name of railroad development. In these robberies stand high the names of George W. Swepson and Martin S. Littlefield in North Carolina and Florida, Hannibal I. Kimball in Georgia, and John C. and Daniel N. Stanton in Alabama. In every state there were individuals or groups that seized their opportunities.

The process was simple and appeared entirely divorced from corruption; in fact, it was nothing new, for it had been used in the South before the war and directly following, before the Radicals had secured control of the government. It consisted merely in the state lending its credit to private companies in their efforts to construct railroads, by buying their stock, by guaranteeing the payment of railroad bonds, and by giving them a fixed sum for each mile constructed, and in the last two methods taking a mortgage on the railroad. A Georgia Conservative said, "[It] is now quite apparent that the public mind has, with very considerable unanimity, accepted 'State aid' as the true policy of the State"; [27] and an Alabama Radical agreed that it was *in no sense a party measure*." [28] It was only through the dishonesties of state officials that the great stench in railroad aid arose. In violation of law they delivered bonds before the railroads were built, and the dishonest promoters sold these bonds for what they could get and never built the roads. Sometimes legislatures also loaned more per mile than the roads were worth when finished, so that even with the roads turned over to the states, considerable losses were suffered. The amount usually allowed was from $10,000 to $15,000 a mile, to be paid as ten-mile units were completed. Counties also lent their credit. A Chicago editor declared that guarantees were claimed "and generally ob-

26 Minority report, *Ku Klux Conspiracy,* I, 525.
27 Augusta *Weekly Chronicle & Sentinel,* July 20, 1870.
28 Montgomery *Alabama State Journal,* December 18, 1869.

tained for anything which had two parallel bars of iron, however light, upon any apology for a road-bed," and, he might have added, for nothing at all.[29] Every state suffered under these dishonesties except Mississippi, where there was a constitutional provision against state aid, but the legislature got around it by making outright gifts to certain favored companies.[30]

North Carolina authorized almost $28,000,000 of railroad bonds and actually delivered over $17,500,000; on account of ill-kept records, Alabama could never determine the amount of her issues, but it has been estimated from $17,000,000 to $30,000,000; a ring of twenty men controlled the charters of eighty-six railroads in Arkansas and got state loans to the amount of $5,350,000, to which was added $3,000,000 in levee bonds that railroads could claim by making their roadbeds serve as levees; Georgia lent to railroad companies $5,733,000; and so the story goes.[31] It should be remembered that these issues were not total losses, for where they were not delivered there could be no loss, and where the railroad had been built the state when forced to foreclose on defaulted bonds became the owner of the road. Some of the states after the raids had been made passed constitutional amendments forbidding aid to private companies.

Railroad rings used other means to reap rich harvests, such as bribing legislatures to sell their railroad holdings for practically nothing, as in South Carolina and in Florida, or as in Georgia which used the state-owned Western and Atlantic Railroad for political purposes, and later leased it under circumstances of great favoritism. Speaking of railroad legislation in Alabama, General James H. Clanton said that in the statehouse "and outside of it, bribes were offered and accepted at noonday, and without hesitation or shame," and that the effect of these dishonesties was "to drive the capital from the State, paralyze industry, demoralize labor, and force our best citizens to flee Alabama as a pestilence,

[29] *Railroad Gazette: A Journal of Transportation* (Chicago), IV (1872), 87.
[30] Garner, *Reconstruction in Mississippi*, 289.
[31] *Weekly Columbus Enquirer,* July 25, 1871; Augusta *Weekly Chronicle & Sentinel,* July 19, 1871; Somers, *Southern States since the War,* 82 ff.; Nordhoff, *Cotton States,* 30, 58; McGrane, *Foreign Bondholders and American State Debts,* 294–95; Albert B. Moore, "Railroad Building in Alabama during the Reconstruction Period," in *Journal of Southern History,* I (1935), 421–34, 437–38.

seeking relief and repose in the wilds of the distant West." [32]

The legislatures which engaged in these corruptions, railroad and otherwise, were controlled by the Radicals, but Democratic Southerners also took advantage of openings, though they had fewer chances. Nathan Bedford Forrest became much involved in Alabama railroad scandals but he was honest enough to impoverish himself in his efforts to recompense his creditors. Alabama Radicals sought to excuse themselves of their villainies by claiming correctly that the idea of state aid was "of Democratic origin." [33] Speaking of a state-aid bill before the legislature in 1869, a Radical charged that many "of its strongest lobbyists and largest beneficiaries" were "rampant, reactionary Democrats." They added, "Yet these very men, who expect to make money out of it, will use the argument that the Republican party had a majority in the Legislature, and will falsely, but hopefully, charge it upon Republicans as a partisan crime against the state." Democratic Southerners were forced to buy desired legislation other than for railroads—even for securing a charter for a college. And there were Democratic officeholders who partook of the same financial characteristics as Radicals. A Democratic official in Montgomery County, Alabama, defalcated to the extent of $50,000; in 1866 the Democratic treasurer of Mississippi stole from that state $61,962; and the whole administration of Governor Robert Lindsay of Alabama (1870–1872) in lack of honesty differed little from the administrations of the Radicals between whom it was sandwiched.[34] In Georgia a Democratic editor emboldened himself sufficiently to

[32] *Weekly Columbus Enquirer*, March 15, 1870. Governor Warmoth of Louisiana considered corruption a normal condition in his state. "Why, damn it," he remarked, "everybody is demoralizing down here. Corruption is the fashion." Quoted in Shugg, *Origins of Class Struggle in Louisiana*, 227.

[33] Montgomery *Alabama State Journal*, December 18, 1869; March 25, 1870.

[34] Nordhoff, *Cotton States*, 74, 75, 90; Montgomery *Weekly Advertiser*, January 6, 1875; James D. Lynch, *Kemper County Vindicated, and a Peep at Radical Rule* (New York, 1879), 19; Somers, *Southern States since the War*, 132; Fleming, *Civil War and Reconstruction in Alabama*, 616, 740, 753 ff. The Montgomery *Alabama State Journal*, December 27, 1872, charged against the Democrats that "our common school fund has been squandered, and education languishes throughout the state; our lands are without a market; our warrents are being hawked about the streets, and can be sold only at a ruinous discount; our officers are unpaid; our treasury is empty, and our state is on the verge of bankruptcy."

make this charge: "It is a mortifying fact that the extravagance of Bullock's administration—we say nothing as to the corruption—benefitted about as many Democrats as Republicans." [35] It might also be added that Southern Democrats participated in the Salary Grab of 1873.

Through chartering the Louisiana Lottery in 1868 the Radicals set up an institution of such malodorous reputation that Alexander K. McClure could say it was "lavish in its gifts, ostentatious in its charities, and generous in public enterprise, but the Church could as well draw its financial sustenance from the bawdy-house or the gambler's den, and hope to promote vital piety, as can the politics, charity, or enterprise of New Orleans draw tribute with self-respect from the lottery swindle."[36] Although this lottery had been chartered by a Radical legislature, it was owned and operated by Southerners and its periodic drawings were presided over by the Confederate heroes, Pierre G. T. Beauregard and Jubal A. Early. This evil institution stirred up such hatred throughout the country that it led people to believe lotteries were exclusive Radical inventions.

Lotteries had been chartered widely over the United States in early days, but they had been generally outlawed before the outbreak of the Civil War. Immediately afterwards they returned to the South and were chartered by the Johnson governments and by the Democrats after Radical rule was ousted. Lotteries always announced that they had been set up for a laudable purpose, however much the private gain might be. South Carolina organized one to promote immigration; lotteries for the distribution of land were set up in Georgia and Kentucky; Alabama chartered the Tuscaloosa Scientific and Art Association which offered prizes for the best essay on science, for the most useful invention in mechanics, and for the best work of art; the Mississippi Educational and Manufacturing Aid Society lottery paid the state $5,000 for the benefit of the University; there was a National Charity Lottery in Hot Springs; the Monumental Association con-

[35] Augusta *Weekly Chronicle & Sentinel*, quoted in Elberton *Gazette*, July 4, 1877.
[36] Alexander K. McClure, *The South: Its Industrial, Financial, and Political Condition* (Philadelphia, 1886), 135.

ducted a $500,000 lottery in Georgia to erect a Confederate monument; and the ladies of Columbus, Georgia, set up a lottery to aid Jefferson Davis.[37]

Radical Reconstruction ruined the financial credit of the South and depressed its securities,[38] though it is possibly true that one of the reasons underlying it was to produce the opposite effect, to enhance Northern investments in the South. The increase of state debts became fantastic. Records were so carelessly kept and maliciously destroyed that restored Democratic governments were never able to determine exact amounts, and many later commentators have been unscientific in their appraisals. South Carolina's debt has been estimated from $15,700,000 to $29,100,000; North Carolina's and Alabama's as high as $30,000,000; and Louisiana's at $50,597,000, one fourth for the benefit of the state and the rest "squandered, or done worse with." Many bond issues were sold at a small fraction of their face value. Confusion has arisen because writers have not indicated what part of the debts was secured by railroads and other valuable property and the part that represented values evaporated and gone forever. The amount of debts piled up by local divisions, such as counties and cities, is past finding out, with many records gone and others widely scattered. Irrespective of amounts, it cannot be doubted that the South underwent fearful financial punishment under Radical rule.[39]

Another source of money, either to spend or to steal, was taxation. Since taxing is used more than bond issuing for the ordinary expenses of government, it was to be expected that taxes should be higher after the Civil War than before. This is so on account of

[37] Natchez *Democrat*, August 15, 1867; Little Rock *Weekly Arkansas Gazette*, February 14, 1876; Montgomery *Weekly Advertiser*, June 23, 1868, April 27, 1869; Atlanta *Christian Index*, February 28, 1867; Rome *Weekly Courier*, March 18, 1874; Greenville *Enterprise*, June 7, 1871; Elberton *Gazette*, March 2, 1870; Augusta *Weekly Chronicle & Sentinel*, July 5, 1871; January 31, 1872.

[38] *The Commercial and Financial Chronicle* (New York), IV–VII (1867–1868), *passim*; *De Bow's Review*, IV (1867), 154.

[39] Nordhoff, *Cotton States*, 29, 57, 95; Coulter, *William G. Brownlow*, 375–77; Fleming, *Civil War and Reconstruction in Alabama*, 571–86; Davis, *Civil War and Reconstruction in Florida*, 679; Simkins and Woody, *South Carolina during Reconstruction*, 45, 148–85; Beale, "On Rewriting Reconstruction History," *loc. cit.*, 816. Vicksburg's debt rose from $13,000 in 1869 to $1,400,000 in 1874. Garner, *Reconstruction in Mississippi*, 328 ff.

the many additional services governments undertook to perform for the people. Education was now provided free for all people; more institutions such as insane asylums and poorhouses were set up; and the cost of administering justice was vastly increased. Formerly, if a slave committed a serious crime he received thirty-nine lashes, at no expense to the planter or the state; now, when Negroes committed crimes their arrest, trial, and punishment brought on expenses which the state must pay.

In ante-bellum times Southerners had never been subjected to burdensome taxes, and little of their revenue had been secured from land. In South Carolina in 1859 all agricultural lands were assessed for taxation at slightly more than $10,000,000, whereas lots and buildings in Charleston alone were listed at $22,000,000. With the coming of the Radicals, land was made to bear a greatly increased amount of the tax burden—and not on account of the ease in levying the tax or by simple accident. It was by special design, for those who set the taxes had little land, or, indeed, little property of any sort; but, as they wanted land, they saw that high taxes would depress its value and probably lead to its confiscation by the state for unpaid taxes. Here the Negroes and poor whites would find an easy road to landownership. Joseph H. Rainey, a South Carolina colored Congressman, said, "Land in South Carolina is cheap. We like to put on the taxes, so as to make it cheap!" [40] The amount of land advertised for taxes increased with the carrying out of this program, until whole sections of some states were for sale. In Mississippi about a fifth of the state was advertised for taxes; in St. Landry Parish, Louisiana, there were 821 sales of land for taxes from 1871 to 1873; in Arkansas a book of 228 pages, reprinted from an advertisement taking up sixteen sheets in a large-sized newspaper and costing for one insertion $12,312, was required to list the delinquent lands there.[41]

In some places the tax rate, state, county, and city, ran as high as 50 mills, equivalent to 5 per cent of the assessed value of the property. Though property values in the eleven states which had composed the Confederacy were in 1870 less than one half what

[40] New Orleans *Weekly Times*, June 6, 1874.

[41] Raymond *Hinds County Gazette*, June 7, 1867; August 17, 1870; December 27, 1871; Little Rock *Weekly Arkansas Gazette*, January 16, 1872.

they were in 1860, the amount of taxes paid was more than four times the total in 1860. A South Carolinian who had paid a tax of fifty cents on his lands before the war, now paid $15; another complained that he was forced to sell his last cow to provide money for his taxes. And one of the most discouraging features of Radical taxes was that much of the money was stolen by the collectors. More than a half million dollars of taxes collected in 1872 in Florida were never turned into the treasury.[42] This situation led outraged landholders in many sections of the South to call taxpayers' conventions, one in Louisiana adopting the name of the Tax Resisting Association, which begged its tormentors for relief and sought more practical methods of obtaining it. When Negroes secured land they began to take the white man's point of view on high taxes. The worst tax atrocities came in the South after 1870, but even with its highest taxes it paid little higher rates than were levied in some of the Northern states. In 1870 Illinois had a rate of 45 mills, when the average for the eleven former Confederate States at that time was only 15 mills. The poverty of the South as compared with the North is strikingly shown in this fact: in 1870 the state of New York with a rate of 24.6 mills collected $48,550,000, whereas the whole former Confederate states collected only $32,227,529, state, county, and municipal.[43]

Assuredly, then, Radical government had not given the South that protection of property promised in the first Military Reconstruction Act; did it do any better in protecting life? In a war-ridden region like the South there was destined to be violence irrespective of the efforts of governing authorities to prevent it— whether they be Johnson Conservatives or Grant Radicals. After the Radicals took hold, violence instead of subsiding increased, and for reasons not foreign to provocative actions by the new rulers. Negro militia, which were organized in many of the states, incited violence as much as they promoted law and order; Loyal Leagues incited Negroes into incendiarism and racial clashes. Pistol toting became a custom, and it was said that Colt's arms factory was kept busy supplying the Southern trade. Former Governor

---

[42] Compendium of the Ninth Census, 1870 (Washington, 1872), 640; Compendium of the Tenth Census, 1880, II, 1509; Ku Klux Conspiracy, I, 439.
[43] Ku Klux Conspiracy, I, 228–29.

Perry of South Carolina wrote the Radical Governor Robert K. Scott, "Every week and every day we hear of houses, barns, gin-houses and stores being destroyed and robbed by the midnight incendiary." [44] In one issue of an Upper South Carolina newspaper appeared rewards for the burners of the stables of eight different men, and the machine shop of another. "There seems to be no limit to the insolence of the Carolina negroes," declared a Georgia editor. "They have been taught to regard the whites as their enemies and, having the power, let pass no opportunity to inflict annoyance or insult." [45]

Called into existence by violence, the Ku Klux Klan added to it; riots of serious proportions broke out widely over the South, some provoked by the Klan and others not. Rufus B. Bullock, Radical governor of Georgia, admitted that crimes against Negroes increased from an average of seventeen a month before his administration to forty-six after he took hold.[46] One issue of a state paper carried proclamations of the Governor offering rewards of $15,000 or more for lawbreakers.[47] Early in his administration, 300 armed Negroes "led on by the vermin, black and white, native and imported," incited a riot by attempting to enter Camilla. It was estimated that 150 people were killed at various times in Jackson County, Florida, alone; and Negroes started the most serious riot in Alabama's history when at Eufaula they tried to prevent a member of their race from voting the Democratic ticket. Negroes in Vicksburg provoked a race riot in which a hundred former Federal soldiers and other whites took part, and in which three dozen Negroes were killed. In Louisiana under its miserable travesty on government there was no end of riots and lesser violence—the Colfax riot in which fifty-nine Negroes and two whites were killed, the Coushatta violence in which five Radical officeholders were murdered, and the famous New Orleans uprising of 1874 which was not unlike a Parisian revolution. So bad were conditions that General Sheridan who was sent to preserve law and order, to the amaze-

[44] Greenville *Enterprise,* April 12, 1871; April 3, 1872.

[45] Augusta *Weekly Chronicle & Sentinel,* January 7, 1874.

[46] Thompson, *Reconstruction in Georgia,* 257. W. H. McWhorter, Greensboro, Ga., to Sumner, May 14, 1869, in Sumner Papers, Box 92, No. 176; Tunis G. Campbell, Atlanta, to Sumner, April 19, 1869, *ibid.,* Box 94, No. 45.

[47] Marietta *Journal,* February 10, 1871.

157

ment of sane people everywhere, asked for permission to declare banditti those Louisianians whom he cared to dispose of without further ado. In North Carolina a unique band of lawbreakers known as the Lowrie Gang seem to have suffered little hindrance probably because of their Radical leanings.[48]

Though it might appear that Radicals would be discredited by arguing violence in the South under their own rule, yet they did so with a great show of statistics to prove it. Their purpose was to induce the Federal government to send in troops to uphold their tottering regimes, or to "wave the bloody shirt" in the North to influence elections there. Governor Warmoth asserted that 3,000 Democrats killed 200 Radicals in the St. Landry riot of 1868; and for the Congressional elections of 1874 Representative Joseph R. Hawley of Connecticut got a list of Alabama atrocities from Charles Hays, an Alabama Radical Representative, which he used to great effect until the New York *Tribune* proved them to be myths. A meeting of Radicals from nearly all the Southern states came together this same year in Chattanooga to compile a stunning list of atrocities for the same election campaign.[49] Lucius Q. C. Lamar, Democratic Representative from Mississippi, asked these embarrassing questions: "When you point me to acts of violence, I acknowledge and deplore them; but I ask you, who has governed the States where this violence occurs, for the last ten years? Have we? Who have taxed us, controlled our legislatures, filled our courts, received the patronage of the Federal Government, ruled over us at home, and represented us here?"[50]

[48] Rhodes, *History of the United States*, VII, 112–22; Nordhoff, *Cotton States*, 48, 54, 79; James J. Farris, "The Lowrie Gang—An Episode in the History of Robeson County, N.C., 1864–1874," in Trinity College Historical Society *Papers* (Durham, 1897–), Ser. XV (1925), 55–93.

[49] Henry C. Warmoth, *War, Politics and Reconstruction: Stormy Days in Louisiana* (New York, 1930), 67. See also, Montgomery *Weekly Advertiser*, January 20, 1875; Macon *American Union*, September 25, 1868; Columbus (Miss.) *Press*, September 26, October 13, 17, 24, 1874; Nordhoff, *Cotton States*, 18. Henry B. Denman, New Orleans, wrote Zachariah Chandler from New Orleans, March 11, 1872, that four fifths of the whites there "hate the National Government with a bitterness that can hardly be realized and not possibly expressed or described." Zachariah Chandler Papers, V, Nos. 1072–73.

[50] Edwin A. Alderman *et al.* (eds.), *Library of Southern Literature* (New Orleans, Atlanta, Dallas, 1907–1923), VII, 2973.

Radical Reconstruction had failed in every particular in which the Radical Congress had accused the Johnson governments. Radical rule in Louisiana had produced effects "which in ten years have sunk this fertile and once prosperous State into a condition of decay which it has taken Turkish misgovernment some centuries to bring about in the East." [51] And the people of New Orleans were described by a Northern traveler: "Ah! these faces, these faces; —expressing deeper pain, profounder discontent than were caused by the iron fate of the few years of the war! One sees them everywhere; on the street, at the theatre, in the *salon,* in the cars; and pauses for a moment, struck with the expression of entire despair —of complete helplessness, which has possessed their features." [52] Alluding to the New Orleans uprising of 1874, the *Nation* said there was no instance in modern times "in which the insurgents had more plainly the right on their side," and when the Federal troops were sent to put it down, this journal declared that the Austrians in their seventy years of tyranny in Italy had never "marched on so bad and despicable an errand." [53] An observer saw in Alabamans a despair "more dreadful and depressing than the negro ignorance." [54]

The more intelligent Negroes were beginning to see that their own fate lay buried with that of their Conservative white neighbors, and some of them began to avoid the Radicals and eschew politics entirely. Richard Harvey Cain, a Negro editor in Charleston, said, "When the smoke and fighting is over, the negroes have nothing gained and the whites have nothing left, while the jackals have all the booty." [55]

Also, it should not be assumed that there was no stern opposition and righteous indignation in the North against this Radical withering up of the South. The Democratic party platform in 1868 was strong in its denunciation, and Horatio Seymour, its candidate for President, condemned the barbarous rule of the Radicals. Frank Blair, the vice-presidential nominee, repenting that he had marched

[51] *Southern Magazine,* XVI (1875), 430.   [52] King, *Great South,* 34.
[53] *Nation,* XIX (1874), 199.   [54] King, *Great South,* 333.
[55] Charleston *Missionary Record,* quoted in Augusta *Weekly Chronicle & Sentinel,* November 22, 1871.

through Georgia with Sherman, threatened violence against Radical Reconstructionists. As for Federal commanders, Rosecrans, Sherman, George H. Thomas, George G. Meade, Winfield S. Hancock, George B. McClellan, Don Carlos Buell, Henry W. Slocum, John A. McClernand, William S. Franklin, and others either were silently ashamed or expressed their abhorrence of what was going on.[56] The editor of *Scribner's Monthly* saw Southerners in despair and he blamed the Federal government: "They feel that they were wronged, that they have no future, that they cannot protect themselves, and that nothing but death or voluntary exile will give them relief."[57] The editor of the *Nation* by 1870 had come to view the South with a light different from that of 1865. In the South the people had almost forgotten "that in free countries men live for more objects than the simple one of keeping robbers' hands off the earnings of the citizen."[58] There people were worse off than they were in any South American republic; for in the latter place tyrants could be turned out through the right of revolution, but the South with the army on its back could no longer resort to this ancient remedy. Southerners must continue to suffer enormities "which the Czar would not venture toward Poland, or the British Empire toward the Sautals of the Indian jungle."[59] The North with all its charities to the South had done less good than the Carpetbaggers had done harm.[60] Schurz had learned much since his first visit to the South in 1865. He saw fearful acts perpetrated

[56] Randall, *Civil War and Reconstruction*, 797–98.

[57] *Scribner's Monthly*, VIII (1874), 368.

[58] *Nation*, XIX (1874), 132. South Carolina had produced "not one, but a swarm of little Tweeds and little Butlers, some white and some black." *Ibid.*, XVIII (1874), 247.

[59] *Ibid.*, 326. "They are 'ex-rebels,' but they are not thieves. They have owned slaves, and revolted in defense of slavery; but they are influential, economical, and trustworthy in the management of State affairs, and it was of the first importance not only to the negro, but to the whole Union, that, during the transitional or reconstructive period following the war, they should neither be driven into hostility to the local government nor prevented from giving it the benefit of their experience and ability." *Ibid.*, XII (1871), 212.

[60] Said the *Nation*, XIV (1872), 197: "Seven years have gone over us since the close of the war, and, instead of occupying this precious season with endeavors to re-establish prosperity and to sow the seeds of peace which, in another generation, would ripen into good-will and forgetfulness, we have averted our eyes from the whole problem, refused to listen to the complaints of men whose hands we have tied, and have fallen back upon the lazy belief that in some way this great country is bound to go through."

against the South, all in the name of patriotism, and particularly in Louisiana, "a usurpation such as this country has never seen, and probably no citizen of the United States has ever dreamed of." [61]

[61] King, *Great South,* 93.

CHAPTER VIII

IN DEFENSE OF RACE AND CREED

RADICAL Reconstruction was doomed to fail. With a crass, materialistic design, it was cloaked in a garb of high idealistic justice, but its rulers were inexperienced, ignorant, and corrupt. They forgot what the world had learned and experienced during the preceding two thousand years. Millenniums and Utopias might be written about, but intelligent people knew that they were never to be realized in this life.

Nothing that anyone could have known at this time would indicate that economic equality would fuse a people into a class consciousness, irrespective of race. All history bore testimony to the contrary. Peoples—white, black, brown, red, and yellow, Caucasian, Negro, Malay, American Indian, or Chinese—all had varying antipathies toward one another, though the Caucasian as a dominant race asserted them most. In America the Negro was the disturbing element; racial antipathy toward him was as fundamental in the North as in the South. In fact, McClure, the Philadelphia publisher, asserted that it was "fivefold stronger in the North than in the South,"[1] and the twentieth-century Negro leader, W. E. Burghardt Du Bois, declared that the antipathy of white and black workers depended "not simply on economic exploitation but on a racial folk-lore grounded on centuries of instinct, habit and thought and implemented by the conditioned reflex

---

[1] McClure, *South*, 222. "This prejudice is not confined to the United States; it exists in a greater or less degree all over the Western world. It exists in almost as great a degree in aristocratic circles in England as in Southern circles in this country." *Nation*, V (1867), 90. See also, *Southern Magazine*, XIV (1874), 373–76; Howard K. Beale, *The Critical Year: A Study of Andrew Johnson and Reconstruction* (New York, 1930), 181–82.

of visible color." [2] This Negro, who grew up in the North during the Reconstruction when the Radicals were arguing their leveling doctrines for the South, found a color line in his western Massachusetts surroundings across which he might not step. New York hotels were not open to people even "slightly colored" and the cadets at West Point Military Academy, "Northern boys, Republican boys," treated a Negro cadet "shamefully—because he . . . [was] black." [3]

Added to the Negro's racial difference was the stigma of slavery, "the widest abyss known among men" yawning "for generations after the repelling force" ceased. Also, there was this further impediment: the grotesque act of making the ex-slave the ruler over his disfranchised former master. Indeed would a return of the age of miracles have been required here for success in ironing out race consciousness. Brute force would not be enough, though some Negroes and Radical leaders believed it sufficient.[4] In fact, this supposedly great power turned out to be a fatal weakness.

The Southern nonslaveholder, in truth, had a more intense racial prejudice than the former master, and naturally so. As long as the Negro was a slave his standing was fixed, and there was no problem of race. Logically, then, had the nonslaveholder fought in the Confederate army by the side of the slaveowner, and the nearer he found himself on the level with the slave economically the harder he should have fought. Certainly after the war the nearer a former nonslaveholder came to the status of a poor white, the more intolerant of the Negro he became. This intolerance characterized Americans generally; Frederick Douglass, in the North, declared that it was easier for his son to get a job in a law office than in a shipyard, and a Northern editor said, with as much application to his own section as to the South, "The jealousy which the poor whites felt for a class from which they were separated only by caste became hatred when caste disappeared." [5]

[2] W. E. Burghardt Du Bois, *Dusk of Dawn: An Essay toward an Autobiography of a Race Concept* (New York, 1940), 205. Quoted by permission of the author and the publishers, Harcourt, Brace and Company.

[3] Montgomery *Alabama State Journal,* July 15, 1870.

[4] William H. Ruffner, "The Co-Education of the White and Colored Races," in *Scribner's Monthly,* VIII (1874), 86; New Orleans *Tribune,* May 30, 1865.

[5] Montgomery *Alabama State Journal,* May 29, 1869; *Harper's Weekly,* XV (1871),

It became axiomatic that the poor whites in the South were "at the bottom of nearly every assault and battery on the freedmen." [6] Objecting to Negro education they burned Negro schoolhouses, and fearing the competition of Negro landowners they threatened planters who would sell or rent land to them. A Louisiana planter received this warning: "Now, sir, your gin-house is burnt for renting niggers' land. If this is not sufficient warning, we will burn everything on your place. If that don't break it up, we will break your neck." [7] Poor whites liked to join militias to bedevil the Negroes. In Tennessee those who hated the Negroes most were the former nonslaveholding Radicals in the eastern part of the state; and a Georgian, willing to obey the law against violence, believed there was no prohibition "ag'in cussin' 'em, and I believe it does 'em a heap o' good." [8]

The Negroes themselves realized that their best friends were in the old planter class, for a former slaveowner had a better understanding of Negroes and could sympathize more with their weaknesses. A planter declared in 1866 that his freedmen worked well "when we can keep the poor trash from annoying them," [9] and it was frequently observed that there was less violence against Negroes in the old plantation regions than where the whites were in a bigger majority.

But rich men or poor men, the whites of the South came to see in Radical Reconstruction more and more a question of the survival of the integrity and dignity of the Caucasian race. If these were to survive, the Negro must not be the ruler. "What right hath Dahomey to give laws to Runnymede," asked an Alabaman, "or Bosworth Field to take a lesson from Congo-Ashan?" [10] It was sinning against light to enforce such a system. In the name of two thousand years of history, the South asked its Radical overlords for simple justice: "What do we ask? That the nest of the eagles be not surrendered to . . . ravens and to the vultures; . . . that

---

1194. An Alabama planter declared that the opposition to the Negro came from "those who never owned a slave." *Daily Columbus Enquirer*, July 1, 1866.

[6] *Nation*, III (1866), 2. [7] Kennaway, *On Sherman's Track*, 128.
[8] Andrews, *South since the War*, 362. [9] *Daily Columbus Enquirer*, June 5, 1866.
[10] Quoted in Fleming, *Civil War and Reconstruction in Alabama*, 780.

the purity of the white race be not adulterated and lost; that ten proud and intelligent states be not converted into ten African provinces. This we ask, not as a favor, and on bended knees, but as a right." [11]

Negro rule and suffrage were important elements in this dark picture, but not all. These were means to other calamities, to the rule by Carpetbaggers and Scalawags, to the plundering of the public treasury, and to the debauchery of government. Radical rulers whether in Washington or in the South were in no frame of mind to listen to Southern complaints or pleas. And, so, there instinctively arose the final defense before annihilation—a remedy not unknown in the histories of other peoples in dire distress, in England, in Germany, in Italy—violence hatched in secrecy and springing out of the unseen.

The instrument of this resurgence was the Ku Klux Klan, though the South would have asserted itself through other covert violence if there had never grown up this grandiose order. In fact, the Klan was merely a suggestion which was seized by an outraged people and made into the far-flung order which it appeared to be in the minds of its contemporaries. It had been organized before the end of 1865 by Confederate veterans for amusement and prank-playing, but not until 1868 did it spread and become generally known. By this time the evils of Reconstruction were evident and the Loyal Leagues had set their pattern of operating.

Secrecy, loyalty to a principle, grandiloquence, ceremony, denial of existence, mystery, humor, and violence—these were some of the characteristics of this age-old method now called the Ku Klux Klan. Secrecy was an absolute requirement for evading the power of Radical rulers and Federal troops; secrecy also had the advantage of confusing the enemy and leading him to exaggerate the number of Klansmen. It is the unseen that the human race has learned throughout its existence to fear most. Because it was secret no one could deny such news items as this: "We have been informed that this Klan will soon have a foothold in every town and village in the South, and sooner or later they must burst forth in all their fury, and the horrors of their doing will be too fearful

[11] Fleming (ed.), *Documentary History of Reconstruction*, II, 346.

to contemplate." [12] Or who could deny that the poet was telling the truth when he said,

Thrice hath the lone owl hooted,
And thrice the panther cried,
And swifter through the darkness
The Pale Brigade shall ride.
No trumpet sounds its coming,
And no drum beat stirs the air,
But noiseless in their vengeance
They wreak it everywhere.[13]

Its origin was bound up in mystery. Had it been imported from China, or was it brought back from south of the Rio Grande by soldiers returning from the Mexican War? Those who knew would rather heighten the mystery. And how did the name Ku Klux Klan originate? Was it in imitation of the gun as it was cocked, "click, cluck, clack?" Later it was to be learned that Ku Klux was an adaptation of the Greek word meaning "circle." What was seen or known was grandiloquent and awe-inspiring. Its ruler, the Grand Wizard, presided over the Invisible Empire, which was divided and subdivided into Realms with Grand Dragons, Dominions with Grand Titans, Provinces with Grand Giants, and Dens with Grand Cyclopes. Other officers were Genii, Hydras, Furies, Night Hawks, Magis, Monks, Scribes, Sentinels, and Turks; its members were Ghouls. Their costumes varied with the regions where they operated, but flowing robes and high hats seemed necessary.[14]

It issued warnings in horrendous style and at times it affected in them extreme illiteracy, and it posted notices of its meetings and sent its warnings in language of dire forebodings—in a code using for the names of months, days of weeks, and hours of the day

[12] Montgomery *Advertiser*, quoted in Augusta *Weekly Constitutionalist*, April 1, 1868. "Something New—'Ku Klux Klan' " "This is the name of a secret organization, which is said to be extending rapidly throughout the North and West, and is striking terror into the Loyal Leaguers.—Its object is announced to be Conservative, and hostile to extreme Radicalism. . . . We would not be surprised if the 'Kuklux Klan' has a great run." Greenville *Southern Enterprise*, March 18, 1868.

[13] This is one of five stanzas. *Weekly Austin* (Tex.) *Republican*, April 8, 1868.

[14] Horn, *Invisible Empire*, is the most recent study of the Klan.

such words as Dismal, Dark, Furious, White, Black, Fearful, Awful. Each letter of the word CUMBERLAND stood for one of the ten digits. In its early existence newspapers made bold to announce its meetings, but editors would always absolve themselves from membership by announcing that the notice had been found under their doors. This warning was sent to Thaddeus Stevens: "Thou hast eaten the bread of wickedness, and drank the wines of violence. Thou hast sown to the wind, thou shall reap the whirlwind in the *moon's last quarter.* Thy end is nigh. The last warning." [15] Besides being written in shocking language most warnings were decorated with such reminders as coffins, skulls and crossbones, and a new moon and the seven stars.

At first the Klan's method was to frighten not only by warnings but by putting in an appearance, almost invariably on horseback. Claiming to be the ghosts of Confederate soldiers, generally killed at Shiloh, Klansmen with phosphorous trimmings visited troublesome Negroes and frightened them out of their wits as well as out of the community by appearing to drink many buckets of water apiece, taking themselves apart, and making unearthly noises. Negroes spread reports of seeing Klansmen coming out of wells on muleback and descending into the ground through crayfish holes. A dozen or two Klansmen by skillfully executed maneuvering might appear to scared Negroes to be a thousand; and in 1868 actually fifteen hundred did parade through Huntsville, Alabama. According to a Georgia editor, a victim might receive this treatment: "He is instantly hurled, headlong into a huge box, where sharp knives, poisoned at the points with the deadly venom of the rattlesnake's tooth, pierce and lacerate his quivering flesh, and the box is then closed to exclude the breath of life." [16] This poetic description of what awaited Negroes and Leaguers appeared in South Carolina:

> *Thodika Stevika! Radical plan*
> *Must yield to the coming of the Ku Klux Klan!*
> *Niggers and leaguers, get out of the way,*
> *We're born of the night and we vanish by day.*

[15] Dated New Orleans, 4th month, 10th day, and postmarked Washington, D.C., in Stevens Papers, XI, No. 54793.
[16] Americus *Tri-Weekly Sumter Republican,* April 2, 1868.

No rations have we, but the flesh of man—
And love niggers best—the Ku Klux Klan;
We catch 'em alive and roast 'em whole,
Then hand 'em around with a sharpened pole.
Whole Leagues have been eaten, not leaving a man,
And went away hungry—The Ku Klux Klan;
Born of the night, and vanish by day;
Leaguers and niggers, get out of the way! [17]

Klansmen made special effort to promote the humorous side of their activities, such as this play on their mystic K: "The Ku-Klux Klan are kalled upon to kustigate or kill any kullered kusses who may approve the konstitution being koncocted by the kontemptible karpetbaggers at the kapitol," [18] or the initiation of a neophyte such as this: "3ice the scorpion's tongue has hissed . . . 3ice the bloody grave has gaped." A mangled corpse stood upon a pyramid of skulls holding a coffin in each hand and saying, "Mortal—I am the Bloody Butcher of the Bogus Blunderers of Babylon. Swear to keep our secrets or dye." He was then stabbed, drugged, boiled in a caldron, put on a hot gridiron, tattooed, and scalped. He "was dragged through tubular boilers to the tune of the Rogues' March, stripped to the suit of clothes in which . . . [he] was born, powdered to atoms, and told that . . . [he] had a mission to perform to all outside barbarians—which it was to annihilate every living thing, and to kill every decade member of society." He "act-seeded." He was then cast into a den of worms and given "only 1 bottle of Mrs. Winslow's soothing syrup, and told to await the action of the impeachment committee." [19]

K.K.K. became the most exciting device of the times; it was capitalized throughout the South. There was the "Ku Klux Klan Smoking Tobacco" containing the "spirits of a hundred faithful K. K. K.'s with an accurate and attractive full-length portrait of the 'Great Grand Cyclops' on the outside." [20] K.K.K. was used instead of "Notice"; there was a theatrical show called the "Ku

17 Greenville *Southern Enterprise*, April 29, 1868.
18 Augusta *Weekly Constitutionalist*, May 13, 1868.
19 Montgomery *Weekly Advertiser*, April 28, 1868.
20 Vicksburg *Daily Times*, November 5, 1868.

Klux Klan"; an act in a circus was called the K.K.K.; and there were K.K.K. music, knives, paint, and pills.

Klansmen did not content themselves with humorous sallies in the newspapers, with posting warnings, with frightening Negroes, and even with ghostly parades. These methods eventually became ineffective, especially after Negroes fired into Klansmen and by killing them proved they were not supermen. Then the Klansmen began their serious work. They shot, hanged, burned, and drowned Negroes, Carpetbaggers, and Scalawags. Some they drove out of the country. They came to the rescue of a Mississippi court by executing three Negroes who had burned Meridian and who had then killed the judge who was trying them. Seven hundred Klansmen in black robes and masks stormed the Greenville, South Carolina, jail, loosed two of their comrades, and hanged six of their enemies. Less violent, but equally effective, was the work of the Klan in subduing the spirits of violent troublemakers, inducing Negroes to abide by their contracts to work, and scaring them away from elections.

The Klan was most active in Tennessee, Alabama, and North Carolina. It was almost unknown in Virginia and Texas, and in Louisiana it was the Knights of the White Camelia who took the place of the Klan. In fact, there were many lesser organizations, the Red Jackets, Native Sons of the South, Society of the White Rose, Knights of the Black Cross, the White Brotherhood, and others, which operated in many parts of the South and which were lumped together in the popular imagination as the Klan. And, in addition, there was a normal violence, unorganized but generally attributed to the Klan.

The periods of greatest activity of the Klan were in 1868, when it was organized by Nathan Bedford Forrest into the Invisible Empire, and again in 1870. In the interim Grand Wizard Forrest attempted to disband the Klan, and the respectable element of Southerners who had widely joined the order, now withdrew; but a whirlwind had been started which was not easily stopped. The Klan organization continued in the hands of cutthroats and riffraff, for private gain and vengeance. In fact, the power of the former members was invoked to put down its spurious offspring. Said

Ryland Randolph, the Klan editor of the Tuscaloosa *Independent Monitor,* "The power that created and promoted this laudable Klan until its disbandment is and will be invoked to crush out and destroy its spurious and bogus off-spring." It left a heritage which was to bedevil and disgrace the South thereafter, as mobs took the law into their own hands and engaged in barbarous lynchings —unjustified under any code of civilized rule.

The political activities of the Klan, especially in the Presidential election of 1868, struck terror into Northern Radicals, for here was a direct threat to the Southern support which they had built up by their whole Reconstruction program. The Fourteenth Amendment had not conferred upon the Negro the right to vote, though it was supposed to have guaranteed him all other rights of Americans; but the Fifteenth Amendment, ratified in 1870, was designed to give the Negro the suffrage in effect, by forbidding any state or the nation to deny the vote to anyone on account of his race. Violence and intimidation of Negroes continued, as was seen especially in North Carolina in the summer of 1870 when Governor Holden declared martial law in the central part of the state and called into being a reign of terror in which Colonel George W. Kirk and his ragamuffin army ran wild. To enforce the rights of Negroes, particularly their right to vote, Congress passed its three Enforcement Acts (May 31, 1870, February 28, April 20, 1871), and appointed a joint committee to investigate Klan activities throughout the South.[21] By throwing the control of elections into the hands of Federal officials and by guaranteeing civil and political rights through the Federal courts, these acts overstepped the Constitution and were in their essence a few years later declared unconstitutional. Under the Third Enforcement Act, more often called the Ku-Klux Act, President Grant declared martial law in nine counties in upper South Carolina and sent in troops who terrorized the population and arrested many suspects.[22] Arrests were made in other parts of the South and trials

21 The report of this committee was published in 1872 in thirteen volumes. See *Ku Klux Conspiracy,* I, 1–2.

22 Great confusion prevailed in upper South Carolina. Farmers plowed with their horses saddled and ready to be mounted for a quick escape. In Laurens County over 500 people fled to avoid arrest. "The wholesale arresting of citizens, just at the time of planting of crops, is obliged to have a most disasterous [*sic*] effect upon the interests

which attracted much attention were held in Raleigh, Columbia, Charleston, and Oxford, Mississippi. Reverdy Johnson and Henry Stanbery, eminent lawyers of the North, came to Columbia to defend those charged with Ku-Klux activities. In all the trials throughout the South for the next few years, only about 10 per cent of the defendants were convicted—in fact, in the Oxford trials no one was convicted—though ordinarily about half of the people tried in Federal courts were declared guilty. This fact indicated that arrests were made more to terrorize the people and to promote the Radical party than to secure actual justice. Many of those convicted were sent to the state penitentiary in Albany, New York, but all were released by 1873.[23]

In the meantime, various Southern states under Radical control had passed laws of great severity against the Ku Klux Klan. They placed high penalties against anyone wearing a mask or engaging in any violence while disguised, or even being a member of the Klan. The Alabama law assessed a fine of $5,000 against any county in which a person should be killed by an outlaw, mob, or by anyone in disguise. Tennessee, under the heel of Governor Brownlow, outlawed all Klansmen and declared parts of the state under martial law.

The Klan as originally promoted received the support of the best element in the South, and was given credit for its good intentions by a considerable number of people in the North. General Sherman felt that the violence of the Klan was "greatly overestimated" and that if the "Ku Klux bills were kept out of Congress, and the army kept at their legitimate duties," there were "enough good and true men in all the Southern States to put down all Ku Klux or other bands of marauders." [24] To bring the sub-

of those counties. . . . There cannot be much prosperity for a State where a pandemonium is ever and anon made of its communities. Not only will the people become discouraged and reckless, but they must of necessity find a quiet in other States which is denied them at home." Greenville *Enterprise*, April 17, 1872.

[23] New York *Evening Post*, January 17, 1872; Dunning, *Reconstruction*, 270–71; William W. Davis, "The Federal Enforcement Acts," in *Studies in Southern History and Politics*, 205–28; Edwin C. Wooley, "Grant's Southern Policy," *ibid.*, 183; J. G. de Roulhac Hamilton (ed.), *The Papers of Randolph Abbott Shotwell* (Raleigh, 1929–1936), III, *passim*. The Ku-Klux Act had much to do with turning Alabama back to the Radicals in 1872. Fleming, *Civil War and Reconstruction in Alabama*, 707.

[24] *Weekly Columbus Enquirer*, May 9, 1871.

ject home, the *Nation* declared that if the intelligent people of New York were disfranchised, and they thought that "Ku-kluxing would work reform, they would be busy at it day and night, and many a hardened ruffian would be yelling for Federal troops to save him from the consequence of his villainy." [25]

The Ku Klux Klan helped to save the outward forms of Southern life, but to guard and preserve the inner spirit, the Southern conception of what should be got out of living, other forces were called up. First, the South was determined to make plain that it had not surrendered everything—certainly not honor nor a manly spirit. "The sword has never, nor will it ever, decide a principle or establish a truth," said Wade Hampton.[26] An understanding minority in Congress asked, "Are intelligent and high-spirited men expected to be transformed all at once into abject and senseless clods, and to submit, without complaint or remonstrance, to a course of polity which not only strips them of their rights, but degrades their very manhood?" [27] Five years after the Surrender the editor of the *Nation* felt sure that it "would be easy to count on one's fingers the number of 'repentant rebels' south of Mason and Dixon's line—that is, of men who are not simply sorry on grounds of expediency for having revolted against the Government of the United States, but who look on their conduct with horror as sinful and immoral, and therefore needing to be expiated by some process of atonement or purification," and he did not blame them. He blamed the Radicals for not reading history to see what miserable failures along the same lines the English, the Austrians, and the Spaniards had made with their subject peoples.[28]

The South knew immediately after the war that it now had its civilization to defend as surely as it had attempted for the past four years to defend its political independence. The victors seemed to assume "that because the dynamic question was decided against us we have become a mere lump of clay in the hands of the potter, that we are to be ground up politically, socially and morally in the Northern mill, tempered anew with the waters of New England,

[25] *Nation*, XII (1871), 213.   [26] Elberton *Gazette*, June 29, 1870.
[27] *Ku Klux Conspiracy*, I, 539.
[28] *Nation*, X (1870), 36. See also, Little Rock *Weekly Arkansas Gazette*, October 13, 1868.

and shaped into vessels of honor or dishonor at the sovereign pleasure of our conquerors." [29] The South must not permit the North to set the pattern for Southern thought on the war, though it might set it for the rest of the world for a time. The South would not permit itself to be erected into a horrible example to be used to deter people from doing evil—to be told that "if they kept on lying and stealing, they might be as bad at last as we are." Southerners had had "no inglorious past; woe to them, if, in the day of their humiliation they . . . [strove] to forget it." [30]

The South was not supinely cringing in the dust of shattered hopes. It was still manly and could hate lustily, as Ennes Randolph, a Baltimore lawyer, half humorously showed in the classic hate poem of the English tongue:

> Oh, I'm a good old Rebel,
>   Now that's just what I am;
> For this "fair Land of Freedom"
>   I do not care a dam.
> I'm glad I fit against it—
>   I only wish we'd won
> And I don't want no pardon
>   For anything I've done.
>
> . . . .
>
> I hate the Yankee Nation
>   And everything they do;
> I hate the Declaration
>   Of Independence too.
> I hates the glorious Union,
>   'Tis dripping with our blood;
> I hates the striped banner—
>   I fit it all I could.
>
> . . . .
>
> I can't take up my musket
>   And fight 'em now no more,
> But I ain't agoin' to love 'em,

[29] Southern Magazine, XIII (1873), 177–83, 181–82.
[30] Land We Love, II (1866–1867), 281.

173

Now that is sertin sure.
And I don't want no pardon
For what I was and am;
I won't be reconstructed,
And I don't care a dam.[31]

The South would not for some years after the war celebrate the Fourth of July "for we cannot forget the present, and we dare not mock the past." [32]

Though Northern soldiers and most Northern generals were looked upon as honorable enemies, Southerners, forgetful of Sherman's good will after the war, early singled him out for their withering hate. He was a "child of hell" and even "Beast" Butler was an angel compared to him. The world would declare "that the fame of a great soldier was stained by acts of cruelty and brutality which would have disgraced the chieftain of a tribe of Indians or the leader of a band of brigands." [33] To be more specific, a Georgia editor compiled this tale of infamy: "—a man who deserves no mention in civilized war, except to reprobate him as the flagrant violator of its well defined rules—a man who fought not with shot and shell, but with flames and with the torch—a man who dared not to attack men, but was sufficiently bold in assailing women and children—a man to whom mercy was a stranger and cruelty was natural—a man who, knowing that he should only meet noncombatants, glories in his march to the sea, as the wolf vaunts his prowess when he carries terror into the sheepfold—a man to whom history, as the meed of justice, will assign infamy." [34]

In the early 1870's both Boston and Chicago suffered disastrous fires; and they called for pity and help from every direction. Though some aid was given by an impoverished South, there was more satisfaction taken in the fact that Northerners now knew

[31] *The Week-End Book* (London, 1931), 188–89. As quoted here, this poem differs slightly from the copy appearing in the Augusta *Weekly Constitutionalist*, July 10, 1867. In the latter place, it is entitled "O! I'm a Good Old Rebel" "A Chant to the Wild Western Melody, 'Joe Bowers.' " "Respectfully Dedicated to Thad. Stevens." There are six stanzas.

[32] Nashville *Republican Banner*, June 27, 1866.

[33] Augusta *Weekly Chronicle & Sentinel*, May 26, 1875.

[34] *Plantation*, II (1871), 184–85.

how hot and destructive were the fires that burned Atlanta, Columbia, and many lesser towns in the South. When had the North
taken up a collection to rebuild Atlanta or Columbia? Religious
Southerners believed that these fires were the "visitations of Providence." The tradition long lasted in the South that unreconstructed Robert Toombs reported on the Chicago fire by saying
that every means was being used to put it out, but "The wind is
in our favor."

The South could show its devotion to its better self by loving
rather than hating, and whom could Southerners think of quicker
for their devotion than Lee? A few months after his Surrender,
Lee was elected president of Washington College in his native
Virginia, a choice that seemed happy, natural, and inevitable to
Southerners—but rebellious, disgusting, and unthinkable to many
Northerners. *Harper's Weekly* declared that he was "one of the
weakest of men, . . . whose treachery to the Government was not
less contemptible than odious," and that he ought to be hanged.[35]
This journal never changed its opinion throughout Lee's life. The
Nation, now in the midst of its fire and brimstone period, protested against Lee's election and declared that he was "not fit to be
put at the head of a college"; and Wendell Phillips, outraged at
the act, said that if Lee was fit to be a college president "then
for heaven's sake pardon Wirz and make him professor of what
the Scotch call 'the humanities.' " [36] But Lee to Southerners was so
complete an embodiment of the good South that some suggested a
society to be called the "Lee Association" whose duty it would
be to preserve that South in every way possible. When he died in
1870 the South creped itself in mourning and held memorial exercises in all the principal cities.[37] The Augusta meeting resolved
that "This day, disfranchised by stupid power, as he was; branded,
as he was, in the perverted vocabulary of usurpers as rebel and
traitor, his death has even in distant lands, moved more tongues
and stirred more hearts than the siege of a mighty city and the

[35] *Harper's Weekly*, IX (1865), 243; XII (1868), 595.   [36] *Nation,* I (1865), 329, 546.
[37] Few Scalawags sank so low as not to mourn Lee's death. For being one of these
few, R. W. Flournoy received from James L. Alcorn, Scalawag governor of Mississippi,
a stinging rebuke. Augusta *Weekly Chronicle & Sentinel*, January 18, 1871.

triumphs of a great king." [38] His birthday was set apart to be observed annually, and the North soon forgot its ill will and claimed him as an American.

"Sweet are the uses of adversity" for otherwise Jefferson Davis might never have become a Southern hero. As the war neared its close he had few admirers even in his own land. Edward A. Pollard, the Richmond editor, bitterly hated him and blamed him for losing the war. In fact, it became common in the South to say that the Confederacy had "died of Davis." Joseph E. Johnston and many other military men did not like him. Then, in May, 1865, Davis was arrested and maligned as having tried to escape in his wife's clothing; he was imprisoned in Fortress Monroe and shackled. Though charged with complicity in the assassination of Lincoln and $100,000 was paid for his arrest on the ground that he was a murderer, he was never indicted for murder; instead, he was kept in prison. The heart of Southerners softened toward the man, sick though proud, who was bearing their cross for them. Said a Georgia editor, "And now that man is dying for our sakes.—As these lines are being written wolfish eyes are on him—eyes that have watched his daily crucifixion, and will watch him until that stubborn head shall bow." [39] Petitions went up for his release, signed by people throughout the South, and legislatures passed resolutions demanding his freedom. Albert T. Bledsoe wrote his book, *Is Davis a Traitor*, a force in his ultimate release,[40] and Dr. John J. Craven wrote *The Prison Life of Jefferson Davis* and "earned the lasting gratitude of all good men, North and South, by his noble, generous, and self-sacrificing course toward the illustrious State prisoner." [41] Finally Davis was set free without ever having been tried.

His release was brought about by the strangest of the many strange uses to which the Fourteenth Amendment has been put. In 1867 he was indicted for treason and then admitted to bail. The next year when he was about to be tried it was argued in his defense that the Fourteenth Amendment, which in the meantime

---

[38] *Ibid.*, October 19, 1870. [39] Augusta *Weekly Constitutionalist*, August 15, 1866.
[40] *Southern Review* (Baltimore), XIX (1876), 252.
[41] *Scott's Monthly Magazine*, VI (1868), 891–92; *Land We Love*, I (1866), 406–409; *De Bow's Review*, II (1866), 334.

had been ratified, provided as a penalty for the Southern leaders no greater punishment than disqualification for holding an office. And so, in 1869, Jefferson Davis went free, to grow higher in the estimation of Southerners and become a symbol of their Lost Cause.[42]

Lee and Davis were objects of devotion in their own names, but the great nameless Confederate soldiers, living and dead, must not be forgotten. The flags of the Confederacy had scarcely been lowered before there burst forth that resounding Southern oratory praising the valorous deeds of Confederate soldiers, so familiar to succeeding generations. General Henry A. Wise early raised his voice, for at first, "There were those who feared to welcome back to their homes and their firesides the men who had gone forth at their behest to peril life and limb, and all that the heart of man holds dear." Less than a year after the war was over Wise was saying, "The noblest band of men who ever fought or who ever fell in the annals of war, whose glorious deeds history ever took pen to record, were, I exultingly claim, the private soldiers in the armies of the great Confederate cause." [43] The style was thus early set for Southerners; but Senator Henry Wilson of Massachusetts was sure that the memory of the Confederacy would "blacken and blacken to the 'last syllable of recorded time.' This is punishment enough." [44] Thaddeus Stevens' anger was whetted sharper when he was told that all the feelings of Virginians were "Confederate—Confederate Generals are their heroes —Confederate bravery, and endurance under difficulties, their pride and boast—Confederate dead their martyrs." [45]

It was safer and more politic for Southerners first to concentrate their glorification upon the Confederate dead, for associations of

[42] Randall, *Civil War and Reconstruction*, 806–808; Roy F. Nichols, "United States vs. Jefferson Davis, 1865–1869," in *American Historical Review*, XXXI (1925–1926), 266–84; Dorris, "Pardoning the Leaders of the Confederacy," *loc. cit.*, 17–21.

[43] *Land We Love*, I (1866), 14, 20. "There can be no surer mark of national degeneracy and public corruption than indifference to the great deeds of the good, the noble, and the true. Rome ceased to be the mistress of the world when she began to neglect her illustrious living and to forget her mighty dead." Editorial comment on Wise's address, *ibid.*, 15.

[44] Raleigh *Tri-Weekly Standard*, May 4, 1867.

[45] Sharp, Petersburg, Va., to Stevens, January 17, 1866, in Stevens Papers, VI, Nos. 53746–48.

the living might well be looked upon in the North as preparation to renew the struggle. Women were the most uncompromising part of Southern creation and their power was great. The war had put them in a considerable majority in many communities, and by setting the tone of society they came near establishing a matriarchy. Eight years after the Surrender, Davis said he had never seen a reconstructed Southern woman.[46] Some of them formed societies pledged never to speak to a Federal soldier. Joseph E. Brown of Georgia firmly asserted in 1867 that there "could be 25,000 women selected in the South to-day who could reconstruct this Government in twelve months, and cause tens of thousands of people to come to the South and bring tens of millions of dollars to aid and build up and develop it." They could do so by ceasing to ostracize everyone who was not a Confederate.[47]

It was the women who tried hardest to get Davis out of prison, and it was they who first began to gather the remains of the Confederate dead from the battlefields and give them proper burial, to decorate their graves with flowers, and to erect monuments to them. A group of women in Columbus, Georgia, originated the idea of Southern Memorial Day or Decoration Day early in 1866, and out of this activity grew the many Southern memorial associations. As at this time it probably would have been forbidden by Federal authority to erect monuments to the Confederate dead, the women decided to dedicate "one day in each year to embellishing their humble graves with flowers." The Stars and Bars had been furled forever, "but the veriest Radical that ever traced his genealogy back to the deck of the May Flower, could not deny us the simple privilege of paying honor to those who died, defending the life, honor and happiness of the SOUTHERN WOMEN." [48] April 26, when the blossom season was at its height in the South, was the day chosen, and with pageantry, oratory, and flowers the memory of the Lost Cause was kept alive throughout the old Confederacy.

Interred in shallow graves and disturbed by rooting swine or

[46] *Nation*, XVII (1873), 126.

[47] *Speech of Ex-Gov. Joseph E. Brown, of Georgia,* . . . *in Milledgeville* . . . *1867,* p. 2.

[48] Augusta *Weekly Constitutionalist*, March 21, 1866.

left unburied and bleaching on the battlefields of the South lay the remains of Confederate soldiers. These memorial associations raised money to provide for their proper burial. As for faraway Gettysburg, agencies there had to be depended upon to return Confederate remains, and sometimes impostors, "wretched hyenas in the form of human beings," preying alike on Confederate and Federal, trafficked in the spurious "remains of the dead." [49] The remains of few Confederate soldiers were ever returned.

The erection of monuments waited for a while, but not for long. With a few exceptions the first markers in the South were erected by the Federals to their own dead—on Stone's River battlefield in 1863, and later at Bull Run and Vicksburg—and by 1866 national cemeteries for Federal soldiers were being planned for many of the great battlefields of the South. In 1867 Radicals, for political gain, unwisely agitated the erection in Atlanta of a monument to Lincoln. A segment of Southern reaction was epitomized by one editor who bitterly suggested that it be made of the bleaching bones of Confederate soldiers cemented with their blood, "a fitting monument of Southern devotion to the memory of him who will pass into history as the greatest and most wicked murderer of his or any other time." [50]

Unafraid of expense or of Federal displeasure the ladies of Cheraw, South Carolina, unveiled the first monument to Confederate dead in 1867, and started a movement all over the South to erect memorials to the soldiers, to Lee, to Jackson, and with the passing of time to many lesser leaders. They were chaste in design and true to the region in their emblematic figures such as plants and leaves. Simple, tragic inscriptions were chiseled, as this one

> *To the Confederate Dead*
> *Come from the four winds, O Breath,*
> *And breathe upon these slain that they may live.*[51]

[49] *Daily Richmond Enquirer*, June 20, 1866; Atlanta *Christian Index and South-Western Baptist*, July 26, 1866; *Daily Columbus Enquirer*, May 30, 1866; Sandersville *Central Georgian*, January 10, 1866; Elberton *Gazette*, July 31, 1872; Trowbridge, *South*, 266, 324.

[50] Augusta *Weekly Chronicle & Sentinel*, August 21, 1867.

[51] Leigh, *Ten Years on a Georgia Plantation*, vi.

The University of Virginia and the Virginia Military Institute published memorial volumes made up of sketches of the lives of their slain alumni.

The dead could wait; what of the living, widows, orphans, veterans? Benevolent associations were organized to educate orphans, provide necessities for the widows, and artificial limbs for soldiers. The Grand Army of the Republic flourished for Federal soldiers long before Confederate veterans dared to organize associations. General Daniel Sickles in 1866 specifically forbade any organization for "the commemoration of any of the acts of the insurgents prior to the fatal surrender." [52] "No reunion, no shaking of hands, no campfire reminiscences, no social gatherings of the boys in gray," ruefully observed "One of the Boys" in 1878.[53] But in some parts of the South veterans had begun to organize much earlier. They called themselves Confederate Survivor Associations, held reunions, listened to grand oratory, and as time went on came to be a power in making and unmaking political leaders. When the South returned to its original rulers, there were few places where a candidate who was not a Confederate veteran could be elected to an important office.

The Confederate tradition soon cast its resplendent light throughout the South—the Lost Cause had been regained, if not taken too literally. "Dixie" and other war songs were the favorites; war poetry filled the leftover space in the newspapers; lithographs of famous Confederates adorned the offices and walls of business houses; medallions and neat prints of Lee, Jackson, and Davis had a place in the home, and in 1866 editor De Bow hoped to see them before long "adorning all the parlors of the South"; schoolboys declaimed on "The Downfall of the Confederacy"; and even here and there the term "rebel" was used with proud distinction—especially when it was remembered that Washington was the first great "rebel."

With Yankee shrewdness Southern businesses began to capitalize on the Confederate tradition. There were Bull Run saloons, Bob Lee cigars, Queen of the South pipe tobacco, Georgia Rebel snuff, "Our Own Southern Bitters" carrying the picture of Stone-

[52] Fleming (ed.), *Documentary History of Reconstruction*, I, 211.
[53] Marietta *Journal*, June 20, 1878.

wall Jackson "and used throughout the Southern armies with magic effect," and Dr. Tutt's Hair Dye dedicated to the "Boys in Grey" but guaranteed to change grey hair and whiskers to any color desired. Impostors claiming to be Belle Boyd, the great Confederate spy, wandered over the South living off the credulous charity of her admirers, while beggars soon hit upon the technique of beginning their approach to their victims with, "Would you speak to a poor Confederate soldier?" Even lowly Confederate paper money was erected into a memorial to the nation it once served, now outlawed by the Federal government:

> *Representing nothing on God's earth now,*
> *And naught in the water below it;*
> *As a pledge of a nation that's dead and gone,*
> *Keep it, dear friend, and show it.*
> *Show it to those who will lend an ear*
> *To the tale that this paper can tell;*
> *Of liberty born, of the patriot's dream,*
> *Of a storm-cradled nation that fell.*[54]

Thus did the South answer those who would attempt to cheat her out of her soul as part of their price of victory—those "buzzing insects of the hour," the "spawn of spies and spinsters," who would attempt to remake the South in their own image.[55]

As an answer more permanent and dignified, the South early made preparations to rest her case before the Bar of History. She had lost on the fields of carnage, but she was determined to win in the Battle of the Records. All who played a part in this work, said Pollard, would "perform a last, but most important office of faithful love, and do a noble work in rescuing the name of a lost cause from the slanders of those who," having been the South's accusers and executioners, would now become its future judges.[56] Benjamin H. Hill was consoled in the feeling that the greatest re-

[54] *Land We Love*, I (1866), 160. This is the first of four stanzas.

[55] *De Bow's Review*, II (1866), 122; Augusta *Weekly Constitutionalist*, October 24, 1866.

[56] Edward A. Pollard, *The Last Year of the War* (New York, 1866), 4. See also, E. Merton Coulter, "What the South Has Done About Its History," in *Journal of Southern History*, II (1936), 17–18.

source the South had left was History—"impartial, and unpassioned, un-office-seeking history." [57] R. Randolph Stephenson said the South would be recreant to its duty if it permitted "the false allegations of the Northern historians to be accepted as true without attempting a refutation and vindication." [58] To disprove the most potent and persistent atrocity mendacities, long peddled in the North for political purposes, the Andersonville prison horrors, he wrote the book, *The Southern Side; or, Andersonville Prison.* When the war was over, Lee thought of writing an account of his campaigns as a tribute to his soldiers. He soon gave up the idea, but he recommended to other commanders that they set down for the record the military exploits of their armies. Many of them did so. In defense of the civil and political fronts Alexander H. Stephens wrote *A Constitutional View of the Late War Between the States* and Jefferson Davis wrote *The Rise and Fall of the Confederate Government.*

For a sustained campaign of Southern defense, something more than individual and unrelated efforts was needed. The idea of historical societies occurred to Benjamin G. Humphreys of Mississippi in 1866. He thought they should be organized in every county in his state, to preserve the records of "minute details of battles, skirmishes, robberies, conflagrations and vandalism—together with the heroic part acted by our brave people." [59] The idea grew and soon there were plans for a historical society for the whole South, which should not only collect every kind of record of the South's heroic past but also publish a historical journal to tell of its greatness and to brain any "error whenever it lifts its ugly head within range of our shillelahs." [60] On May 1, 1869, such a society was born in New Orleans, fathered by General Dabney H. Maury and attended at its birth by such Confederate generals as Bragg, Simon Bolivar Buckner, and Beauregard. The Presbyterian preacher-orator Benjamin M. Palmer became the first president. It was named the Southern Historical Society, but it was inevitable that its chief work would be to record the history of the Con-

[57] Hill, *Senator Benjamin H. Hill*, 405.

[58] R. Randolph Stevenson, *The Southern Side; or, Andersonville Prison* (Baltimore, 1876), 6.

[59] *De Bow's Review*, I (1866), 664–65.   [60] *Southern Magazine*, XIII (1873), 509–10.

federacy, and it might more properly have been called the Confederate Historical Society.

This Society became a power in collecting and preserving the records of the Confederacy, newspapers, soldiers' letters, books, handbills, official orders, and everything which bore the impress of war years. It carried on its first publishing activities in the *Southern Magazine,* but in 1876 it felt strong enough to issue its own publication, which it called the *Southern Historical Society Papers.* It cherished and defended the Confederate tradition and heritage, and with becoming dignity was seldom forced to use the shillelagh. The South had answered. North might or might not be North, as it pleased; but the South would be South.

CHAPTER IX

NEW ECONOMIC HORIZONS

TO MANY Southerners the South was no more attractive economically and socially than politically. They would leave the land of desolation to those who had made it. At the end of the rainbow lay a pot of gold—they would go and find it. The war had scarcely ended before they began their hegira to Brazil, Venezuela, Honduras, and Mexico. All of these countries welcomed their newcomers, but Brazil ruled by Dom Pedro II and Mexico still under her short-lived Emperor Maximilian offered the greatest attractions. Land was cheap and payments might be long deferred. In Brazil slavery still existed, an inducement for those Southerners who could not tolerate or understand a free Negro population.

In many parts of the South colonization societies grew up which appointed agents to spy out new lands of Canaan and make arrangements for migrations. Ballard S. Dunn, rector of St. Philip's in New Orleans, and Lunsford Warren Hastings, filibuster and gentleman of fortune, were leaders in the Brazilian movement; Matthew F. Maury, oceanographer, and William M. Gwin, antebellum California Senator, schemed in Mexico. Between 8,000 and 10,000 Southerners expatriated themselves and emigrated to Brazil, but not so many went to the other countries.[1] The movement was more spectacular and imaginative than efficacious as a remedy for Southern ills. Most of the expatriates ultimately returned, some being forced to ask aid of the hated government they had disowned.

[1] Lawrence F. Hill, *The Confederate Exodus to Latin America* (Austin, 1936), 1–94. A great deal of information is scattered through the newspapers; for examples, see Montgomery *Weekly Advertiser*, April 28, 1868; Augusta *Weekly Constitutionalist*, January 24, March 14, 21, May 9, 1866. See also, Jaquelin A. Caskie, *Life and Letters of Matthew Fontaine Maury* (Richmond, 1928), 148–61.

The movement never could have become general on account of the expense necessary for making the trip. The South's greatest leaders, such as Lee, Hampton, and Lamar, frowned upon the migration as ill-advised and impractical and upon the *émigrés* as deserters. Now was the time when the South needed even greatei devotion than during the days of the Confederacy. John H. Reagan said it would take "time, and patience, and wisdom, and justice" [2] to build a new South and it would take all her people to do it. A Texas editor thought the speculators who had grown rich during the war might leave to escape the frowns of their outraged fellow citizens and the chief actors in the war might go to seek safety, but the ordinary Southerner should best stay at home. [3] A Louisianian asked pointedly whether Southerners "had breathed out all their devotion" to the South on the battlefields. "Do they owe her no future duty?" Farm leaders could see no sense in moving to "Brazil, Mexico, and other 'outlandish' and half-civilized regions," and they could not discover a "single advantage possessed by these countries, which we of the South have not in a greater degree." If discontented Southerners wanted to buy experience in farming and stock raising, they could "buy it cheaper here than in Brazil or British Honduras." Expatriation provided "no 'royal road' to competence and ease, for the poverty that 'cannot dig.' " [4] Though many newspapers published extensive accounts of the migration, a few adopted the policy of refusing to mention it.

Holding the normal feeling that there is a pot of gold a little farther on, a great many more Southerners, not resorting to expatriation, set out for more attractive parts of their own country. Some, believing that the Lower South was destined to be overrun by Negroes, argued that the whites should concentrate in the Upper South, but such a movement never developed. Westward the course of empire spread and many Southerners decided to go with it—to Texas, to Arkansas, even to the Far West. The Middle West was too much in the grasp of strange Germans and of the recent

2 Fort Warren Letter, August 11, 1865, in Reagan Papers.
3 Galveston *Tri-Weekly News,* June 16, 1865.
4 These citations appear in the order of the quotations to which they refer: *De Bow's Review,* I (1866), 660–61; *Southern Cultivator,* XXIII (1865), 153; *De Bow's Review,* V (1868), 371; Atlanta *Christian Index,* February 20, 1868.

enemy, but the Pacific Coast attractions drew a few. John and Joseph LeConte, inseparable brothers and scientists, left South Carolina and arrived in California in time to stamp their lasting influence on the university of that state. Staying within their own South, many went to Arkansas, but Texas received the great outpouring.

Of the eleven states which made up the Confederacy, Texas was third from the bottom in population in 1860; in 1880 it was the most populous state in the South. It was claimed that a half million people arrived within the two years preceding 1876. Many of the 50,000 people who left Georgia in 1875 went to Texas. Migrants were attracted because it was an empire within itself; land was fertile and cheap, and it had never been invaded far during the war. There many Southerners hoped to escape the enormities of Radical Reconstruction besetting states of the older South, and so many went that, although they did not escape these evils, they hastened Radical downfall there. At least one Alabaman went to Texas because he expected to find few Negroes there: "I hain't nothin' agin a free nigger, but I don't want him to say a word to me. The world's big enough for us both, I reckon. We ain't made to live together under this new style o' things." [5] But the main reason for this migration, "this great silent exodus, this rooting up from home and kindred, . . . [producing] the anguish . . . which so many hearts have felt," [6] this crowding of trains and whitening roads with covered wagons,[7] was the eternal quest for a better living. Southerners were told in 1865 that with $500 one could buy 200 sheep in Texas which within ten years by their natural increase would be worth $20,000. Raising horses and cattle was advertised as equally profitable.[8]

To stay the loss of their population, the older parts of the South told of the drouths, sudden floods, and crop failures that inevitably hit the Texan at some time or other. They admitted that there were some parts of the state which were good, but Texas was made up mostly of wild country, "the meanest the least secure, the most burdensome, most tyrannical, and altogether the worst

5 King, *Great South*, 291.   6 *Ibid.*, 133.
7 *De Bow's Review*, VIII (1870), 420; Somers, *Southern States since the War*, 110.
8 New Orleans *Times*, quoted in Galveston *Tri-Weekly News*, October 6, 1865.

to be found in any civilized country in the World." [9] Even some Texans were impressed with the evils of their state and decided to move on. "Don't go to California or anywhere else," pleaded a Texas editor. "Stay where you are, or, if you are anxious for a change, make the change *in* Texas, not *out* of it." [10]

That Southerners would migrate northward, to the heart of the enemy country, might seem improbable and unnatural; but as the economic urge can easily overstep sentiment, it was so with many Southerners after the war. They knew that much of the North had never been hostile to the South before the war, that it had been lukewarm during the struggle, and that afterwards it had become downright friendly. New York City, whose merchants had been closely allied with the South in ante-bellum days and whose mayor at the outbreak of war had threatened to keep the city out of the struggle if not, indeed, to join it to the Confederacy, now became a mecca for many Southerners. Within a year and a half after the Surrender it was estimated that 20,000 were living there. [11] "They are found at the bar, on the press, practicing medicine, in educational institutions, engaged in mercantile pursuits, in banks and insurance offices, employed as clerks in wholesale stores, and, in fact, following every business on the long list of avocations in New York." [12] Soon emerged such names as Roger A. Pryor and Charles C. Jones, Jr., in law, John H. Inman in the cotton trade, John R. Thompson in journalism, and George Cary Eggleston in letters. The New York *Journal of Commerce* declared that as "soon as a young man finishes his education down South, and, in many instances, before the completion of his studies at school, he fancies that he is cut out for a salesman, and that New York is the divinely-appointed theatre in which to play his part in life." [13] New York welcomed Southerners, for they made it easier for the city to recapture its old-time Southern business.

[9] Montgomery *Weekly Advertiser*, January 11, 1870. See also, Dalton *North Georgia Citizen*, December 9, 1869.

[10] Austin (Tex.) *Tri-Weekly State Gazette*, May 1, 1868.

[11] Nashville *Republican Banner*, November 28, 1866; *De Bow's Review*, III (1867), 215; Trowbridge, *South*, 293.

[12] Mobile *Register*, quoted in *Scott's Monthly Magazine*, VI (1868), 892. See advertisement of Southern Hotel, in *Land We Love*, I (1866).

[13] Quoted in Atlanta *Weekly Sun*, March 13, 1872.

The great mass of the people remained in the land of their birth, both through necessity and choice—there to make their living and to rebuild their section. Four years of warmaking and of destruction had left much to be done. There were railroads to be constructed and repaired, agriculture to be reorganized, minerals to be mined, forests to be cut, factories to be set up, and cities to be built and rebuilt. This was enough to engage the efforts and attention of all, and though politics afforded the news that filled most of the newspapers and made it appear that Southerners were more political than economic beings, yet the everyday concern of the people was making a living. Voices were often raised against futile political activity, for it resulted ultimately in the "liberty of doing as we are told." "Were it not that we have to *pay* heavily for the poor privilege of being harshly governed without a voice in the Government, we do not know that we would be materially worsted," thought a Southern editor. Indeed, the South had a power "more potent than any and all political combinations." Dollars had won the war for the North and dollars after all would win the peace for the South—"As this world goes," said a Southerner, "the Dollar rules, and just in proportion to the number of these potent influences we can command, will be our possession of the great and inestimable right of political freewill." The South should forget politics, go forward with her industries, and "leave Butler and his Congress to rear and snort until they get tired." When the South should cease to be a colony of the North, "Depend upon it, Pharaoh never made greater haste to send for Moses in the periods of his several 'plagues,' than the calculating Yankees would make to negotiate with us for a return of our trade and a restoration of our political rights!" [14]

The South was just as necessary for national economic sufficiency after the war as before, and it is illogical to assume that Reconstruction did not have as an important element the rebuilding of the South within the old pattern—a continuation of its old colonial status. Stevens' promise that his reconstructed Southern govern-

---

[14] These citations appear in the order of the quotations to which they refer: Augusta *Weekly Constitutionalist,* September 5, 1866; *Daily Columbus Enquirer,* January 21, 1866; *De Bow's Review,* III (1867), 111; Augusta *Weekly Constitutionalist,* September 5, 1866; March 3, 1869; *Daily Columbus Enquirer,* June 21, 1866.

ments were displacing their predecessors to protect life and property, had convinced the Northern economic lords of his sincerity, irrespective of whatever other motives he might have had in mind. The failure of the South to raise cotton would affect the North almost as much as the South. Northern factories would be forced to shut down, Southern exports which kept the international trade balance favorable to the North would cease, and the consequent decline of foreign gold importation would hit the Northern rulers in a most vital spot—the holders of Federal bonds could no longer receive their interest and principal in that yellow metal. In fact, the exports of Southern products for the year ending June 30, 1867, made up about seven tenths of the total.[15]

A prosperous South was just as necessary for the West also as for the North. In ante-bellum times the West had sold the South mules, farm machinery, food, and feed, and with its income had bought Northern manufactures just as the South had done. The South and the West, then, were both tributary to the North, and they were logically allies, economically as well as politically. For a time they had had an alliance, actually and consciously, but slavery had ultimately upset it. The West's surplus could still be drained down the Mississippi, and as the stumbling block had been removed the South was now ready to woo her. "Let us propitiate the West," said a Southerner. "Naturally, geographically and commercially she is our best confederate, and, while on terms of amity with the East, in so far as she is just or generous, we must march to victory side to side with the West." [16] "The West and the South join hands," "The South extends to the Northwest a cordial welcome," were expressions heard at Southern commercial meetings.[17] Most Federal economic legislation hurt the West as much as the South. The tariff was equally obnoxious

[15] *American Annual Cyclopaedia . . . 1867*, pp. 127–28.

[16] Augusta *Weekly Constitutionalist*, June 17, 1868. See also, Charleston *Courier*, May 31, 1865.

[17] Dalton *North Georgia Citizen*, May 27, 1869; Richmond *Daily Dispatch*, April 11, 1877. In attempting to induce the West to join the South again, a Southerner argued that Northerners were exploiting each equally. "Is not all their wealth the result of the mere tricks of trade?" he asked. "Like the Faro Banker, they cut, shuffle, and deal the cards, and rob everybody's pocket, and nobody can understand how." *De Bow's Review*, II (1866), 464–65.

to Westerners and to Southerners. The same one-sided legislation if used against Pennsylvania or Massachusetts, according to an Englishman, "would in twenty-four hours convert these hives of Northern patriots into nests of rebels, ready to break up the Union and the Universe, rather than submit." [18] That the West saw faintly this side of the picture was shown in the Cincinnati newspaper called *West and South,* with the device of the clasped hands and the motto "The West and the South United."

Undoubtedly an outburst of economic buoyancy accompanied the despair that followed Lee's surrender. The first legislatures following the war, and succeeding ones, granted charters in amazing numbers to mine, to manufacture, to build railroads, to do anything that was being done in the North. Almost a third of the public acts of the first Georgia legislature were charters, making up more than half of the text of the statutes. It was easy to get charters but difficult to translate them into going businesses. Roving freedmen were soon tamed into workers again, but no miracle could quickly transform anything in the South into capital. The Southern commercial and governmental debt at the end of the war was staggering. It was over $200,000,000 more than the national debt at its maximum; it was more than all the eleven states which made up the Confederacy could have been sold for, according to their assessed value in 1865. The debts of Southern business to the North, counting interest to the end of 1865, amounted to $408,000,000.[19] How impossible, then, it was for Southern business to rise in this vast void!

Little credit could be expected until Southerners had settled with their Northern creditors. Some never made an effort to meet their prewar obligations, but old concerns tried valiantly to come to terms; and many Northern creditors met them in a helpful way by compromising for as little as 25 per cent. It has been estimated that the South paid about half of this debt.[20] At least, all Southern businessmen did not lose their ante-bellum integrity, which had often led Northern merchants to prefer Southern honor to a flimsy legal paper, though some postwar Southerners

18 Somers, *Southern States since the War,* 206.   19 *Ku Klux Conspiracy,* I, 216.
20 *Ibid.* See also, Americus *Tri-Weekly Sumter Republican,* December 13, 1866; Andrews, *South since the War,* 6.

considered it getting even with a Yankee to cheat him out of a debt.

Most Southern states began meeting interest on their public debt by 1867. The Federal government was less obliging than Northern businessmen; it insisted on collecting from those who had been postmasters and collectors of custom in 1861 the government funds which the Confederacy had confiscated. It was not to be expected that a government under Radical control would provide a loan fund for the South, but in Gerrit Smith's suggestion that the United States lend $50,000,000 to the South, as it was no more responsible for slavery than the North, Stevens saw only "sickly humanity." [21] At one time Jay Cooke, the mightiest of Northern financiers, thought an industrial credit arrangement should be set up to aid the South, and he was reported to have promised that $150,000,000 of Northern capital would be invested in the South if the Fourteenth Amendment were ratified. By 1867 Cooke had changed his mind; now he would not invest a penny in "a land of whisky and bowie knives." [22]

Southern banks, never in ante-bellum days sufficient for the South's needs, had practically disappeared by the end of the war. Charleston's banking capital, which had been $13,000,000 before the war, was in 1870 only $1,892,000, and the whole state of Georgia, with an equal amount in 1860, reached only $2,000,000 in 1872. George W. Williams, an ante-bellum Charleston merchant prince, fortunately investing his money during the war in English sterling exchange, was able to establish a bank in Charleston with a capital of $500,000. In 1870 there were only thirty-six national banks in the states of Virginia, North Carolina, South Carolina, Georgia, Alabama, and Louisiana, with a capital of only $7,000,000. There were a few state banks. Duff Green, long a dreamer of many impractical ideas, talked of hazy plans to establish credit agencies, but they never materialized. With few banks there was little capital to lend, and what money there was in the South was scattered out among its people. This fact led to widely circulated statements that the South was hoarding its

[21] Tallahassee *Sentinel,* July 29, 1867.
[22] Oberholtzer, *Jay Cooke,* II, 23, 85; Augusta *Weekly Constitutionalist,* February 27, 1867.

money and not spending it in the North, as it should do. Where, it was asked in 1870, was the money the South got from its sale of the cotton crops since the end of the war? It might be answered that in 1865 Southerners' pockets were empty of all money except the valueless Confederate variety, and that to stock the pockets of 9,000,000 Southerners, for now the freedmen must have some change, too, would take both time and currency. It was estimated that the South absorbed $20,000,000 annually during the first five years following the Surrender. Even so, this supply was not

PER CAPITA WEALTH OF FORMER SLAVE STATES COMPARED WITH THAT OF NORTHERN AND MIDDLE WESTERN STATES, 1860–1880

State *	Rank according to per capita wealth 1860	1880
Connecticut	1	5
Louisiana	2	37
South Carolina	3	45
Rhode Island	4	3
Mississippi	5	46
New Jersey	6	6
Massachusetts	7	2
Georgia	8	40
Texas	9	36
Kentucky	10	31
Maryland	12	15
Florida	15	41
Alabama	16	44
Ohio	17	10
Illinois	18	11
Arkansas	19	43
Virginia	20	35
Pennsylvania	21	7
New Hampshire	23	13
New York	24	4
Tennessee	25	38
Missouri	26	26
Delaware	27	14

* Southern states are in boldface type.

State	Rank according to per capita wealth	
	1860	1880
Indiana	28	22
Vermont	29	17
Iowa	30	16
North Carolina	31	42
Wisconsin	32	24
Michigan	33	18
Nebraska	34	27
Minnesota	35	19
Maine	36	20
Kansas	37	29

In assessing the decline of per capita wealth in the former slave states, it should not be forgotten that the change in the status of the Negroes produced an important part of that decline. It not only destroyed over a billion dollars worth of personal property in slaves, but also added the poverty-stricken Negroes to the population on which per capita wealth was reckoned. This table was adapted from Plate 71 in F. W. Hewes and H. Gannett, *Scribner's Statistical Atlas of the United States* (New York, 1883).

sufficient; and to make up the deficiency, states, counties, and cities issued paper notes, and many business firms issued shinplasters and tokens—all unconstitutional according to the United States Comptroller of the Currency.[23]

In the panicky flurry of 1867 the South traversed no great distance in reaching the bottom of its returning prosperity, but that little was felt as keenly as a much greater drop in the North. Prices went down and business withered. A factor in New Orleans wrote, "Commercial matters here are in a sad state—almost everybody ruined—planters factors and merchants." [24] In the eyes of

[23] Somers, *Southern States since the War*, 45; E. Merton Coulter, *A Short History of Georgia* (Chapel Hill, 1933), 333; Simkins and Woody, *South Carolina during Reconstruction*, 269; Augusta *Weekly Chronicle & Sentinel*, March 2, April 6, 1870; Fletcher M. Green, "Duff Green: Industrial Promoter," in *Journal of Southern History*, II (1936), 29–42; *Ku Klux Conspiracy*, I, 217; Benjamin P. Poore (ed.), *Message from the President of the United States to the Two Houses of Congress . . . Third Session of the Forty-Second Congress, with the Reports of Heads of Departments and Selections from Accompanying Documents* (Washington, 1872), 132–33.

[24] Barnsley, New Orleans, to Edward Parsons, December 2, 1867, in Barnsley Papers.

the New York financial district, the South was "utterly prostrate, politically and commercially." [25] New York financiers might well have seen a connection between Radical political corruption and commercial bankruptcy. The crushing Panic of 1873 had less effect on the South than on the North for it had fewer institutions susceptible to panics; nevertheless it was reflected in a harder existence for millions of people seeking to catch up with the falling prices paid for their products. It was long-drawn-out in both sections; in the first six months of 1875 failures in the South amounted to $11,000,000.

Under such a financial situation, and in the absence of usury laws, interest rates became fantastic. In South Carolina the rates usually ran from 25 per cent to 30 per cent; and 18 per cent to 24 per cent were normal over the South. Little wonder that such epitaphs as this could be humorously though truthfully written:

> *Here lies Thirty-six per cent.,*
> *The more he got, the more he lent;*
> *The more he got, the more he craved—*
> *Good God! Can such a soul be saved!* [26]

The scarcity of money and excessive interest rates led to the system of crop liens adopted widely over the South immediately following the war. A tenant, habitually having no money and being unable to secure credit, was allowed by the lien laws to pledge his crop for food and other necessities which he might obtain from his landlord or merchant. More often than not the landlord, having no money, would pledge the crop to the merchant for needed supplies, part of which he would use and the remainder he would pass on to the tenant. But, as a rule, the merchant was doing business on capital borrowed from the bank; and so at the end of the vicious chain were the banker and other moneylenders reaping their high rates of interest. It was only the independent merchant or landlord who profited, and they were not in the majority. The tenant and landlord did not pay interest on money, but they paid for what they received a credit price

[25] *De Bow's Review*, III (1867), 487.
[26] Montgomery *Weekly Advertiser*, August 31, 1869.

twice as high as the cash price. The merchant who sold nine-cent bacon for eighteen cents had little profit left after he had paid the moneylenders 25 per cent interest, or particularly if through crop failures or other misfortunes he was unable to collect from those he had credited.

Business needed money, which it could not get; business also needed mail facilities, which it was denied in varying degrees. Not until two full years after the end of the war was the South given service equivalent to what it had enjoyed in 1860. This situation was, of course, not due entirely to design, for it was difficult to remedy Southern disorders and disorganization immediately; but it appeared to be worse than petty spite when two hundred post offices were discontinued in North Carolina because the postmasters of 1861 did not repay the receipts confiscated by the Confederacy. Six months after the war ended there were not more than a dozen post offices in the whole state of Georgia. A year after the war, of the 8,902 post offices in the state in 1860, only 2,152 had been restored, and towns which claimed the facilities often went for ten days without the arrival of mail. Southern newspapers had great difficulty in reaching their subscribers; for months the Southern Express Company was the only vehicle of distribution. A difficulty which the government purposely made for itself was to require the ironclad oath of all postmasters and mail carriers. This effectively closed many post offices which otherwise might have continued. It was assumed that women could take this oath; many of them did so, and then frequently hired men to perform the labor. A clever scheme to carry this idea into the big business field was hatched by one Bryan Tyson, who, being able to take the oath, planned to get many contracts and then sublet them to others.[27]

In the story of the rebuilding of the South, it became a tradition that the Confederate soldier unhitched his artillery horse and, joining the cavalryman, rode home to hitch up again to a plow. If not so fortunate as to own a horse in the army, he walked

[27] Atlanta *Christian Index*, July 11, 1867; *De Bow's Review*, III (1867), 607; *Daily Richmond Enquirer*, December 18, 1866; July 3, 1867; *Southern Cultivator*, XXIII (1865), 169; Sandersville *Central Georgian*, April 18, 1866; Garner, *Reconstruction in Mississippi*, 140; Americus *Tri-Weekly Sumter Republican*, August 30, 1866.

back, to hitch to the inevitable plow a straggling discarded war horse. But what happened to the officers? Like the private soldiers, their paroles protected them from the necessity of flight. If they had not already known how to dig for a living, they soon became acquainted with the process, whether it was literally digging in the fields or making a living in some other equally laborious fashion. Beauregard rigged up a wagon in North Carolina, loaded it with knickknacks, and peddled his way back to New Orleans. There he became president of a railroad only to lose his position through the consolidation of his road into a system; then he nearly entered the service of the Argentine Confederation; next he was deprived of a commission in the army of the Khedive of Egypt through the spite of a kinsman of Ben Butler; finally he ended up with a $10,000 a year position lending respectability to the Louisiana Lottery. Simon Bolivar Buckner, finding himself in Louisiana at the end of the war, went to New Orleans and became in turn a cotton factor, an editorial writer, and an insurance director, but ultimately reaped wealth from Chicago real estate, went back to his Kentucky, and became governor. Admiral Raphael Semmes became a member of the faculty of Louisiana State Seminary of Learning. Forced out by political pressure, he became editor of the Memphis *Daily Bulletin*, but pursued by his reputation as pirate Semmes and compelled to move again he lectured widely over the South on the "Cruises of the Alabama." Tiring of the road he returned to law practice in Mobile where he died in 1877. John B. Hood, unfortunate in war, became a merchant in New Orleans, failed, and died, and his family became an object of pity and charity. Richard S. Ewell became a farmer and stockman in East Tennessee. Lee became president of Washington College at $1,500 a year; William Preston Johnston taught history and English under Lee; Matthew F. Maury, returning from Mexico, became professor of physics at Virginia Military Institute; Admiral Franklin Buchanan, of "Virginia-Monitor" fame, was elected president of the Maryland Agricultural College; and William M. Browne, native of Ireland and a member of Jefferson Davis' staff, became professor of history in the University of Georgia. Though many Confederate officers joined educational institutions, they entered practically

196

every occupation. New Orleans early became a nest of ex-Confederate officers; by 1866 there were twenty-eight in business in the Crescent City.

Confederate officers shone resplendently in the educational world, where sentiment could be closely connected with service; they also became active in what was expected to be more gainful employment, life insurance, where they speculated on that same sentiment highly tinged with sectionalism and unsound business principles. Tributary to the North in life insurance as in so many other fields, Southerners were prevented by the laws of war from paying their premiums during that struggle, and by a strict application of the rules their policies lapsed. Northern insurance companies, intent on making the most of their opportunities, refused to reinstate policies held by those who had aided the Confederacy, and required physical examinations of others at their own expense and payment of all back premiums with interest at 7 per cent compounded. In some cases the companies offered to settle for $75 with policyholders who had been paying for as long as fourteen years. In one instance a company offered $140 for a policy on which the owner had paid, including interest, $3,600.[28]

Well might Southerners have eschewed doing further business with Northern insurance companies. Even had they received just treatment, they had excellent reasons for establishing their own insurance business, for Northern companies drained money from the South and invested it elsewhere. It was estimated that in 1868 New Orleans was paying to Northern or foreign companies $500,000 annually, and that for the whole South the amount was $6,000,000.[29] The South had sought to change this situation immediately after the coming of peace. Insurance fever infected the land and led to the chartering of dozens of companies; eleven were authorized in Georgia alone in February and March of 1866.

[28] *Plantation*, I (1870), 346–47. See also, *ibid.*, 314–15; Arndt M. Stickles, *Simon Bolivar Buckner, Borderland Knight* (Chapel Hill, 1940), 308–12. To combat Southern propaganda some of the Northern companies published in Southern newspapers the names of policyholders whose policies had been reinstated. See, for instance, Augusta *Daily Chronicle & Sentinel*, June 3, 1869.

[29] *De Bow's Review*, V (1868), 448; *Land We Love*, VI (1869), 350–51.

Here was an excellent opportunity to capitalize Confederate sentiment by placing at the heads of these companies and on their boards of directors war heroes—civil as well as military. Lee declined to lend his influence but many others with fewer scruples and less financial ability sold their names. Still others very legitimately entered the business as a career, and gave all they had, which, unfortunately too often, was not enough. Davis was elected president and Hampton one of the vice-presidents of the Carolina Life Insurance Company. General Gordon became president of the Southern Life Insurance Company, with which were associated many other Confederate officers. This company became outstanding in the South, selling in 1869 over $11,000,000 of insurance. It promoted a farm journal called *Plantation*, which served life insurance and agriculture with equal zeal, and employed all the appeals that have become customary with insurance agents. The magazine used with special effect the argument that here was an opportunity for those who had lost their fortune in the war to re-establish their family standing when they should pass on. It exposed the villainies of Northern insurance companies and warned Southerners against doing business with them, and, thereby, brought down on all Southern insurance attacks from the North. Attempts to wreck Southern companies, General Gordon said, had been "persistent and *most cowardly.*" The South also employed the honest argument that the money received was kept at home and made to work for the South. Using this reasoning to the fullest extent, some of the companies organized branches in various states according to state lines and announced that all premiums received within the state would be kept there.[30]

Life insurance was pushed beyond its legitimate limits, approaching a fad in one direction and a racket in the other. It was claimed that ten times as much was being sold after the war as before. In this contest for business, both among themselves and with the North, Southern companies departed far from sound practices. Some advertised rates of only half what Northern companies charged; they made loans on improper security; and in the absence of regulatory laws they did with their business as

[30] *Plantation*, I (1870), 8, 15, 122, 266; II (1871), 89; III (1872), 576; Augusta *Daily Chronicle & Sentinel,* June 3, 1869; Greenville *Enterprise*, April 3, 1872.

they pleased. The Co-Operative Life Insurance Company divided its policyholders into classes of 1,000, and on the death of anyone in the class, every remaining member paid the beneficiary a dollar. This was called "Insurance for the Rich and Poor." There was a movement in Virginia to have the state enter the fire insurance business. Aided by the Panic of 1873, bankruptcy soon hit many of the Southern companies and ruined them together with their policyholders and officials. In this manner Davis lost most of what he had been able to accumulate after the war. The low tone of business morality in the North, assisted by the same panic, brought about many failures in that section.[31]

No more eloquent proof of the revolutionary effects of the Civil War could be found than the impress it left upon Southern women and upon that gentle society of which they were a part. Southern hospitality in the grand manner was now on the defensive, and there emerged ultimately a hospitality no less insistent and sincere, but more simple. There emerged also the emancipation of women no less than of slaves, but it was farewell, mistakenly thought one disconsolate Southerner, to "all gracefulness of social life which comes of leisure and command. A long adieu to that confident, dignified hospitality which spoke of plenty for the guest, and the rarer and richer treat of quiet entertainment and the flow of soul."[32]

The war left tens of thousands of widows and made of them and of other women breadwinners or paupers. The former they had never been; the latter they were resolved not to be. Heretofore women without losing caste might have worked their lives out in charitable enterprises or in helping the church to save the heathen beyond the seas, "but the moment money . . . [was] received, then it . . . [became] disgraceful."[33] It now became respectable for a woman to engage in any work to make a living which did not unsex her according to the standards of her contemporaries. Rough work in the fields, peasant-like, was near the

[31] Americus Tri-Weekly Sumter Republican, May 14, 1868; Raymond Hinds County Gazette, January 3, 1868; Columbus (Miss.) Press, June 27, 1874; Greensboro Herald, March 18, 1869; Daily Richmond Enquirer, December 17, 1866; Carthage Panola Watchman, March 15, 1876; New Orleans Weekly Times, December 12, 1874; Montgomery Weekly Advertiser, April 26, 1876; Nation, XXIV (1877), 157.
[32] Plantation, I (1870), 569.   [33] Marietta Journal, February 23, 1872.

border line in the eyes of many, and in the eyes of some it went across into the forbidden zone. But all were agreed that manual labor was eminently respectable when compared to the antics of some Northern women—"We want no 'strong-minded women,' no female lecturers, no female voters, no office holders. We have no wish to see our wives and daughters unsex themselves." [34]

What could women do, and what did they do? In *The Employments of Women. A Cyclopedia of Woman's Work,* Virginia Penny told of the many little things a woman might do in her own home to earn money. She might plait straw hats, engage in willowware work such as basketmaking, keep bees, run a dairy, can fruit, raise flowers for sale, and engage in many other pleasant and lucrative activities. For those women who would make a career rather than merely supplement housewifery with gainful work, there was the opportunity to become an author, a musician, an artist, a clerk in a store, a typesetter in a print shop, a postmistress, a cobbler, a teacher, a plantation manager.[35] According to a Richmond editor, "We know some women who could drive a locomotive or run a saw mill, but we do not advise them to engage in these pursuits." [36] A young Georgia widow, who grew up in affluence, now managed her plantation; a Mississippi editor praised young women within his acquaintanceship who in antebellum times had belonged to the wealthiest families, "who can now chop wood, drive a two-horse wagon, go to market, and do all the housework." [37] Apart from the great number of women who felt called upon to write, but most of whom made no money out of it, the most becoming pursuit for women was teaching school. Here were good style and patriotism combined. Satisfied Southerners could now say, "It is a subject of congratulation that Southern children are now taught by Southern women." [38] To make it easier for women to enter their new fields of labor, good breeding forbade uncomplimentary and belittling comments, especially where the labor was manual. "All cannot be school teach-

[34] *Plantation,* I (1870), 625.

[35] James W. Davidson, *The Living Writers of the South* (New York, 1869), 412; *Scott's Monthly Magazine,* VII (1869), 307–309; *Land We Love,* III (1867), 364; V (1868), 285–86.

[36] Richmond *Times,* quoted in *Southern Cultivator,* XXIV (1866), 104.

[37] Quoted in Tallahassee *Sentinel,* March 8, 1867.   [38] *Plantation,* I (1870), 625.

ers," observed an Alabaman, "all cannot become authors and poets; some must labor. Pave the way, then, we beg you, by smiling upon and kindly taking by the hand those of your less fortunate sisters." [39]

What of the generation of young men, those who had fortunately returned from the war and those who were coming along after the war? According to tradition, Southern men were no more supposed to be manual laborers than Southern women, but this taboo had always been magnified far beyond the reality. Southern men had always engaged in manual labor when they could not command the labor of slaves. In every land there were people of social standing who considered themselves above manual labor; it may have been that in ante-bellum times the South had no bigger proportion of this class, but that it merely talked about it more. A Southerner declared in 1872 that he did "not think that manual labor was looked upon as degrading in the South any more than it . . . [was] in Europe or in the North." [40] But then as always it was a human characteristic to look for the work that was the least laborious. Hence, half-humorously, "Dilsy Ann" could banter her brothers by saying, "The majority are afraid of manual labor, and prefer standing behind the counter with a few boxes of cigars, a few bottles of liquor, or a few dry goods, filling some petty office or setting up to teach a few children, rather than taking hold of the plow handles or the hoe." [41] Yet the residents of Columbia, South Carolina, might have noticed almost any day the son of a former rich aristocrat driving a dray on the streets of that city. The whites of the South, now through necessity, set to work in greater numbers and with more zeal than ever before.

"Dilsy Ann" was more nearly correct than humorous when she charged young Southern gentlemen with wanting to become clerks in stores or to set up for themselves. They flocked into this new departure, for the old plantation supply house was now transformed into a store, where the freedmen who had money or "time" traded. Also, with the breakup of the old plantation economy, purchasing power was scattered and led to the estab-

[39] Montgomery *Alabama State Journal,* August 4, 1871.
[40] *Southern Magazine,* XI (1872), 126.   [41] Greensboro *Herald,* August 31, 1867.

lishment of many stores in the small towns and cities, to the evolution of small convenient crossroads stores around which country settlements grew up, and to the "dead fall" establishments in out-of-way places, catering to the purveyors of stolen cotton and other farm products.[42] Now arose the Northern drummer who came South to scatter his wares over the country, first to introduce widely a thousand knickknacks and exotic products like bananas, to bring into the common parlance and to set apart the distinction between "ho'-made" (homemade) and "Northern." Interested only in business, these drummers brought down upon themselves charges of outdoing "rebels themselves in their expression of rebel sentiment." [43]

The plantation stores fixed upon the South that unique system set up by the lien law, which, for credit advanced, gave the planter or merchant a lien on the growing crop of the tenant and, therefore, gave him the right to dictate what the tenant should raise. Inevitably it was cotton, which was always readily marketable. The law produced the same effect where the planter who was not a merchant was forced to seek credit.[44] Cotton now became king again and more—it became a ruthless dictator.

The end of the war saw an invasion of Jews to reap a harvest in trade; the ante-bellum Jewish peddlers with their packs on their backs or in rumbling hacks now settled down and opened stores. Sticking to their business and treating the freedman as an important businessman, not eschewing to call him "Mister," they secured, "with their tumble-down shanties and Cheap Jack goods," a great amount of the Negro's trade.[45] A Connecticut Yankee on a trip South to spy out business possibilities remarked of a number of Jews, "They'll make more money in the Southern country in this next year than you or I will." [46] The fact that Southerners never developed anti-Semitism led to the great prosperity the

---

[42] Nordhoff, *Cotton States*, 38, 106; Andrews, *South since the War*, 375; Raymond Hinds County *Gazette*, December 21, 1870; Montgomery *Weekly Advertiser*, December 7, 1869; *Southern Cultivator*, XXXI (1873), 286–87; Fleming, *Civil War and Reconstruction in Alabama*, 769–70.

[43] Gainesville (Ga.) *Eagle*, October 11, 1878; Marietta *Journal*, April 22, 1880; *Harper's Weekly*, X (1866), 631; Thompson, *Reconstruction in Georgia*, 327.

[44] King, *Great South*, 271.   [45] Leigh, *Ten Years on a Georgia Plantation*, 302.

[46] *Nation*, I (1865), 76.

Jews found in the South. "Where there are no Jews there is no money to be made," said a Georgia editor. "We hail their presence in such numbers in the Southern States as an auspicious sign." [47] In Richmond, where whole streets were given over to their business, "a soberer, steadier, and more industrious and law abiding class of population . . . [did] not exist." [48] Jewish merchants used the lien law to great advantage, crediting Negro tenants and often getting the cotton remaining after the landlord had secured his share. It was the sharp practices of Jewish merchants and moneylenders in dealing with the Negroes that led John F. Slater to become interested in the Negroes' plight and to set up a fund of $1,000,000 for their advancement. [49]

The end of the war seemed suddenly to wake not only the South, but also the whole country to the immense natural wealth of the late Confederacy—its land, its climate, its timber, its minerals, its water power. If ever a people had been sleeping in and on the edge of a land of opportunity, here it was. The South was almost as undeveloped and as much a frontier as the West. The Commissioner of Agriculture declared "that little more than five per cent. of the area . . . [was] annually cultivated"— 300,000,000 acres awaiting the plow. [50] Away with the idea that the white man could not work in the Southern climate! Scientist Josiah C. Nott brushed aside speculation and declared facts were abundant "to prove that whites can live, labor and make cotton in our climate, and the bait is too tempting to be resisted." [51] Here was the poor man's paradise as well as the capitalist's, crying out mightily for both. A few years after the war *Scribner's Monthly* spent $30,000 in its project of sending author Edward King and artist J. Wells Champney through the South to gain firsthand information for enlightening the nation on the wonder-

[47] Sandersville *Central Georgian,* November 7, 1866.

[48] Richmond *Whig,* quoted in Sandersville *Central Georgian,* November 7, 1866.

[49] "Jew money lenders living in the South as store-keepers, cheated the negroes out of their lands by taking mortgages upon their holdings which they afterwards foreclosed." Robert P. Sleep, Norwich, Conn., to Jabez L. M. Curry, December 7, 1899, in Jabez L. M. Curry Papers (Alabama Department of Archives and History).

[50] *Report of the Commissioner of Agriculture,* 1867, p. xi; *Weekly Columbus Enquirer,* February 1, 1870; *De Bow's Review,* I (1866), 553–54; V (1868), 81; King, *Great South,* 335.

[51] *De Bow's Review,* I (1866), 172.

ful resources of that region. They traveled 25,000 miles, were received everywhere with "courtesy and serviceable kindness," and sent back their findings which were published by *Scribner's* in its "Great South" series of articles and later brought out as a book.[52]

The South stood ready to welcome labor and capital from the North, because the Northerner who came to invest his life and his money could never be considered a political adventurer. He would "neither have the time or inclination to engage in a 'wild hunt after office,'" and moreover men of this character were not Carpetbaggers, "however small their luggage or empty their purses."[53] The New York *Journal of Commerce* came to the rescue by declaring that anyone who went "down there with money, a willingness to work and a disposition to mind his own business, may find and occupy spots as near like Paradise as exist anywhere on this globe."[54]

That the South was engaging in more than wordy promotion and empty invitation was seen in its eagerness to sell land to all who would buy and at prices that were fantastically low. If a stranger appeared and did not want to buy land he was likely begged to write to his Northern friends and tell them of the bargains that could be had. An Englishman appearing on the streets of Richmond had not been there three minutes before an Irishman was trying to sell him a cow and a calf. Land companies both Northern and Southern advertised farm land and plantations for sale everywhere, in the newspapers, by notices posted in hotels and in other public places. Eighty thousand acres of Mississippi bottom land at $5.00 an acre; 100,000 acres of Alabama land at prices "unprecedentedly low"; a 2,690-acre plantation with a mansion on it completed in 1859 at a cost of $22,500, all for sale at $10.00 an acre; land worth $25.00 to $50.00 an acre offered at from $5.00 to $8.00 an acre by the American Land Company of New York City; organization of the Southern Land Emigration and Produce Company to introduce "capital, mechanical skill, emigration, and labor-saving machinery into the Southern States";

[52] *Scribner's Monthly*, IX (1874), 248.
[53] Augusta *Daily Press*, January 9, 1869; Elberton *Gazette*, February 26, 1873.
[54] Quoted in Augusta *Weekly Constitutionalist*, May 19, 1869.

the United States Land Agency with farm lands, water power, and mines to sell; a land company showing how, with a plantation of 1,250 acres, 1,000 in cotton and 250 in corn, a person could clear $84,600—who could want for information or opportunities!

For many Northern soldiers the blare of advertisements was not necessary; they had seen the South and had picked out their opportunities as they marched along. At the end of the war a private in Tennessee begged John Sherman to get him out of the army immediately for there was "a large number of prizes now lying idle in this state" and he wanted to get his share.[55] The first speculative wave was in cotton raising:

> We go to plant the working-man
> In freedom's Southern clime,
> And press from without the cotton-tree
> The polished Northern dime.[56]

Thousands of soldiers immediately turned planters without returning home, and thousands of other Northerners came south to buy or rent cotton lands. The Mississippi River was lined with Northern cotton planters; it was claimed that there were 5,000 Northerners in Alabama soon after the war ended; and with much greater exaggeration it was asserted that there were 50,000 in Louisiana and that it was actually becoming a Northern province.[57]

Not all of these first investors in the South were unknown common men. Whitelaw Reid, journalist, tried farming in Louisiana, and failed; Henry Lee Higginson, of the Massachusetts family, lost $65,000 farming in Georgia; John Hay, one of Lincoln's secretaries, lost money on his orange grove in Florida; Governor John A. Andrews of Massachusetts spent $30,000 in Mississippi,

---

[55] Sherman Papers, LXXXIII, No. 19460.

[56] Stearns, *Black Man of the South*, 542.

[57] Trowbridge, *South*, 411, 448, 580; Campbell, *White and Black*, 343; Reid, *Southern Tour*, 579; Andrews, *South since the War*, 375; Warmoth, *War, Politics and Reconstruction*, 30; James A. Padgett (ed.), "Some Letters of George Stanton Denison, 1854–1866: Observations of a Yankee on Conditions in Louisiana and Texas," in *Louisiana Historical Quarterly* (New Orleans), XXIII (1940), 1132–1240. For a life history of a specific Northern cotton planter, see Stearns, *Black Man of the South, passim.*

and failed. Politicians Benjamin Wade, James R. Doolittle, and Simon Cameron tried farming in South Carolina and did little better. Some Northerners sought out manufacturing and mining opportunities. Most of the Northern cotton farmers failed; many returned to the North, while others turned to politics and became detested as Carpetbaggers.

With the claim of having freed the slaves, the aid of the Freedmen's Bureau, and a modicum of ready cash, the Northern cotton farmers had advantages over Southerners in capturing a labor supply; but they soon dissipated them when they tried to apply their fixed Northern notions of farming. Expecting the lackadaisical freedman to work like Northern hired help and refusing to take advice from experienced cotton growers, they soon turned the Negroes against themselves. Laughing to scorn the "experiences of the old planters," they brought forth from Southerners remarks like this: "Well, all things are to become new perhaps, but it might be upon the safe side to hasten a little slowly." [58] In their failures they were "reaping the fruits of their skill and superior intelligence at the 'little end of the horn.' " [59] There was the further cause for which they were not to blame—falling cotton prices.

Those who succeeded were generally the ones who entered into partnerships with Southerners or who worked in harmony with their Southern experience, took on Southern ways, and embraced Southern ideas, racial and political. These situations were true often enough to lead the *Nation* to complain: "The spectacle of those Northern men whom the South engulphed and completely assimilated to itself, has been but too frequent and painful." [60]

After the failures of the first cotton farmers, Northern capitalists were more wary in seeking the South in the capacity of planters. They turned to storekeeping; they promoted schemes, such as the rival town which was to sap the life out of Pensacola; they engaged in railroad speculations and political corruptions; they attempted capitalistic farming; they bought up tracts of state-owned land as did Hamilton Disston in Florida, who obtained

[58] *De Bow's Review*, I (1866), 219.   [59] *Southern Cultivator*, XXIV (1866), 226.
[60] *Nation*, II (1866), 102.

4,000,000 acres; they sought out mining lands as did James Ford Rhodes, later a historian, and William D. (Pig Iron) Kelley, a politician; and they invested in cotton factories as did Senator William Sprague of Rhode Island. The South courted English capital, and some came, but not enough to be of much help.

The South was becoming a playground and health resort for Northern tourists, especially South Carolina and Florida for the winter and North Carolina for the summer. *Appletons' Hand-Book of American Travel,* the Baedeker for America, claimed in 1874 that 25,000 Northerners, mostly invalids, visited Florida every winter. Many of them stayed in Fernandino, and 50,000 tourists visited Silver Springs every year. Even Harriet Beecher Stowe in her home on the St. Johns was also an attraction, worried much by too many prying, ill-mannered Northern tourists. Solon Robinson, agricultural expert of many years standing, went to live in Jacksonville and say good words about his new home. All one needed in Florida "to start in life on these lands," according to another promoter, were an "axe, a hoe, a gun and fishing tackle." [61] An envious South Carolinian said in 1875 that 33,000 "health and pleasure seekers" were leaving $3,000,000 annually in Florida.[62] Orange growing was appealing to many Northern capitalists, who began investing their money in groves on the St. Johns from Jacksonville to Palatka. Aiken, in South Carolina, was beginning to attract Northern winter tourists.

There were few places east of the Rockies "where Nature has piled up her fantastic shapes, or poured out her loveliest waterfalls, with a more lavish hand than" in western North Carolina;[63] and many summer tourists were going there to see. In fact, the whole South became tourist-conscious and claimed to be an epitome of the whole world—the flowers of Eden, in Florida; the mountain scenery of Europe, in the Southern Appalachians; the jungles of India, in Arkansas; the pampas of Argentina, in Texas; and the fertility of the Nile, in the Mississippi River Valley.

Northern investments in the South fell far short of Southern expectations. It was difficult to understand why Northerners would

[61] Greenville *Enterprise and Mountaineer,* April 7, 1875.
[62] *Ibid.,* May 12, 1875.
[63] Jones (ed.), *Appletons' Hand-Book of American Travel, Southern Tour,* 116.

waste their money in fraudulent railroad stocks in their own section rather than buy Southern land or invest in Southern factories. De Bow declared in 1866 that he could see little evidence of Northern investments,[64] and another observer averred that "twenty times as many Northern men and women came to the South to settle or to engage in business before the war as come now." [65] The *Nation* answered in 1866 that it was the "rebel" governments that kept capital away—"Men will face wild beasts, swollen rivers, trackless forests, disease, hunger, and even the attacks of savages, but they will not face bad government." [66] But a year later when Radical government came in, the South knew the answer—"negro government will not encourage capital and business to embark in profitable pursuits." [67]

Northerners often complained of social ostracism if not worse from Southerners, but such complaints generally came from Carpetbaggers who should have expected nothing better. "If a Northern rowdy gets drunk in a Southern hotel, becomes riotous and receives deserved punishment, it is generally published in the North as an instance of Southern ill-treatment of Northern travellers," explained a Southerner.[68] People in the South constantly reiterated that they had ever a welcome for the "industrious, honest emigrant, who minds his own business, . . . and cultivates friendly relations with his neighbors," [69] and a Macon editor pointedly remarked that no "gentleman would offer premeditated insult" to a respectable Northerner, and there was "no use in accepting one from a blackguard." [70] Northern settlers frequently testified to the friendliness of their neighbors. William Warner, a prominent Ohioan who settled in Alabama, wrote John

[64] *De Bow's Review*, I (1866), 220.   [65] *Ibid.*, III (1867), 352.
[66] *Nation*, III (1866), 370.

[67] Greenville *Southern Enterprise*, January 1, 1868. See also, Shugg, *Origins of Class Struggle in Louisiana*, 258–60.

[68] *De Bow's Review*, III (1867), 485–87.

[69] *Southern Cultivator*, XXIV (1866), 119.

[70] Macon (Ga.) *Citizen*, quoted in *Southern Cultivator*, XXIV (1866), 119. The editor of the Augusta *Daily Press*, February 5, 1869, said, "But our business men are the parties that can render most important service to their section. Let them make it a rule in all their correspondence with Northern houses to iterate and reiterate the amiable disposition of our people. This will be no sacrifice of dignity."

Sherman in 1866: "My partner who has been here on the planta-tion *alone* all winter, has met with only the kindest treatment and the *heartiest encouragement* from all our neighbors. I have yet to hear, (and I inquired of the Bureau in Montgomery), of the first instance, in this state, of injury to Northern men. A North-ern man, who is not a natural fool, or foolish fanatic, may live pleasantly any where in Alabama, without abating one jot of his self-respect, or independence." [71]

Yet there was some hostility against Northern investments in the South, which was based on a deeper philosophy and under-standing of ultimate value than that which actuated some foolish Southerners. It was a protest against the same dependence on the North which had long plagued the South, but which now was appearing in a more intimate and more malignant form. It could not apply to the Northerner who settled permanently in the South; it was directed against the Northerner who sent his dollars but remained in the North to reap his harvest and spend his profits there. Moreover it was a humiliating admission to make if it were true "that the eight millions of Southern people can not revive their prosperity, or build a railroad, or a manufactur-ing establishment, without the money and the personal presence of some man of the Northern Radical type." [72] The South had a heritage which it was honor bound to transmit to the succeeding generations. Would it sell it to the North for a mess of pottage? A Southerner expressed opposition to Northern capital coming down and fattening upon the land. "We have children growing up," said he, "and they will be our new settlers, if we have room for them, and they our men of enterprise and capital if we do not barter away their inheritance and their privileges." [73] Southerners should not look with equanimity upon the North's buying up their most lucrative and valuable possessions. In announcing the purchase by Northern capitalists of a burrstone quarry, *De Bow's Review* declared, "As usual, this valuable quarry has fallen into the hands of northern capitalists and the profits derived from one of the most valuable discoveries yet made in the South will flow

[71] Warner, Prattville, Ala., to Sherman, April 15, 1866, in Sherman Papers, XCIX.
[72] Montgomery *Weekly Advertiser,* March 3, 1869.   [73] *Ibid.,* August 31, 1869.

into the pockets of those whose enmity has for over two years outlived the suspension of hostilities." [74]

Though the South had a great surplus of land and anxiously advertised much for sale, there were outcries against parting with the old homestead or even with any land whatsoever. Land was something that would endure forever; it could not burn up or otherwise disappear; and a living could always be secured from it. There was something sacred about the land one owned: "Cling to the homestead. Whether it be the humble cottage or the stately mansion that has sheltered you and your fathers, let it continue to shelter you and your children and your children's children." [75] Some felt that the most malignant and sinister part of Radical Reconstruction was the effort "to make life and property so insecure at the South that our rich cotton, rice, sugar and tobacco lands, would become so depreciated in value, that loyal men might come in and get them for a trifle." [76] Robert Toombs, unreconstructed to the last, never ceased to cry out against anything and everything Northern, but few other men of standing in the South joined in. The main surge in the South was to beg for Northern investments so that the South might sometime, too, become rich like the North.

[74] *De Bow's Review,* IV (1867), 266.   [75] *American Farmer,* I (1867), 216.
[76] *Land We Love,* VI (1868–1869), 427.

CHAPTER X

AGRICULTURAL REORGANIZATION

CLIMATE, soil, and an experience of two and one-half centuries had made the South predominantly agricultural, and there was little chance after the Surrender that Southerners would be able, if they willed, to overstep these forces. Agriculture had afforded the good life in ante-bellum times; to disown it now would be a breach with the past and an abandonment of a heritage, little less than sacrilegious. Within this good life there were many changes and rearrangements that might be advocated and made. Such programs had been characteristic of the South since the days of Thomas Jefferson and John Taylor of Caroline. The war had forced the South to reorganize its agriculture and now peace with its new problems was calling as insistently for change.

With the passing of the ownership of labor the old plantation organization disappeared. Money heretofore used in buying slaves was now freed for a thousand necessary improvements as only a part of it was needed for wages. Southerners were beginning to see that it was better to hire the Negro than to own him. Now that it was cheaper to engage in agriculture, more people, especially young men who must find a place in life, could turn to this honorable occupation. Planters' sons who had returned from war could now no longer look forward to West Point and the army, to easy political preferment, or to useless lives of ease. Agricultural leaders decried an incipient "great *mania* of Southern planters for transforming their sons into lawyers, doctors and merchants."[1] Farming was an honorable occupation, and Southerners must see it in this light more than ever before. The many operations and

---

[1] *Southern Cultivator*, XXV (1867), 172.

decisions in successful farming called for the highest intelligence and should challenge any young Southern man. Farming was "a profession, and not a mere trade; a profession in which new developments . . . [were] daily taking place, and being seized upon by the ready and intelligent and turned to profitable account, while the dull sluggard, who . . . [degraded] his calling by his indifference, . . . [let] them slip by and . . . [ran] in the same old rut."[2] Young white men as well as freedmen had flocked to the towns and people might well ask what the one could do more than the other. If young men replied that they had no money for setting up as farmers, they could be confronted with the examples of those who, like them, were trying it and were succeeding.

The new day looked away from the wastage of the large plantation to the small farm with its intensive and varied agriculture. In this new order lay a new society and a new prosperity, made up of and enjoyed by proprietors, not peasants. "The day of large farms in the South is at an end," said a Mississippian, and a Georgian believed that it required "just as much force of character . . . to regulate matters on a modest farm," as on a plantation. "In short, our *planters* will become *farmers,* and improvement will take the place of waste." One Southerner of thirty years' standing, once a Northerner, would take a leaf from the Northern farmer's book: "Do this, and the everlasting Yankee will stand confounded; for, if you pursue the same course he does, you will have no wants for him to supply; and the citizens of Lowell and other manufacturing towns will soon find their spacious factories to be habitations for bats and owls, if they depend on us or our cotton to keep them up." The South would lose none of its ante-bellum character if it tried this new departure. Sensing what his section was about to get, a Southerner called for this program: "smaller farms, more villages, less pride, more industry, fewer stores and clerks, and more laborers. We need not be any less gentlemen, any less hospitable, intelligent, refined or chivalrous." Francis O. Ticknor pictured "Sergeant Wadd, of the 'Cincinnati,' " returning not to the plantation but to the small farm:

2 Augusta *Weekly Constitutionalist,* December 23, 1868.

He has doffed his dusty armor;
I see him moving slow
In his furrowed field, a farmer
Of the single horse and hoe;
And the sun is something warmer
Than a battle-trench, I know.[3]

Farms of less than 100 acres greatly increased following the war. The number of holdings of from twenty to fifty acres increased tremendously. In South Carolina farms of less than 100 acres jumped from 352 in 1860 to 10,286 in 1870. The number of farms more than doubled from 1860 to 1880 in Alabama, Arkansas, Georgia, Mississippi, North Carolina, and Tennessee. During the same time they trebled, or nearly so, in Florida, Louisiana, and South Carolina. In Texas they increased more than four times. The only state of the old Confederacy with little growth was Virginia.[4] But this increase does not mean that the complete dream of the Southerners was coming true; the number of small farms was increasing, but the ownership of the land did not go with it. That hoped-for proprietor population was instead becoming peasant, white and black. An interesting example of what happened to the old plantation appears vividly in developments on the Barrow plantation in Georgia. Most of the Negroes who had been slaves on this ante-bellum plantation of 2,000 acres remained when peace came or, having left, soon drifted back and became tenants, cutting it up into about two dozen farms.[5]

[3] The sources of the quotations in their order are: Raymond *Hinds County Gazette,* quoted in Memphis *Daily Bulletin,* December 12, 1866; Augusta *Weekly Constitutionalist,* December 5, 1866; December 4, 1867; *Southern Cultivator,* XXIV (1866), 6, 81; *Scott's Monthly Magazine,* VIII (1869), 646.

[4] Some examples of the increase in number of farms follow:

	1860	*1870*	*1880*
Alabama	55,000	67,000	136,000
Florida	7,000	10,000	23,000
Mississippi	43,000	68,000	102,000
Texas	43,000	61,000	174,000
Virginia	93,000	74,000	119,000

Compendium of the Tenth Census, 1880, I, 650.

[5] David C. Barrow, Jr., "A Georgia Plantation," in *Scribner's Monthly Magazine,* XXI (1881), 830–36. The United States Census has confused many people by listing as a farm "what is owned or leased by one man and cultivated under his care." Thus

This tendency toward small farming was countered by both sentiment and economic arguments. Not only did large landowners dislike selling their land, but also many disliked breaking it up into tenant farms. They believed that there were economies in large-scale farming which could not be practiced on small farms. Though they might control their tenants to some degree, and, indeed, to a tyrannical degree in forcing them to raise cotton, yet there was with tenantry no centralized management. There were some who advocated setting up corporations to engage in large-scale farming. Though the number of farms under 100 acres increased tremendously from 1860 to 1880, thus causing the average size of farms to decrease, yet it must not be forgotten that there was a large increase in the number of farms over 100, over 500, and over 1,000 acres. An example of a large-scale planter was Colonel B. G. Lockett of Albany, Georgia, who employed 350 freedmen and raised a yearly average of 3,000 bales of cotton.[6] A better-known large planter was David Dickson of Sparta, Georgia, who ran a farm of 20,000 acres. His success was so remarkable and excited so much interest throughout the South that he was constrained frequently to disclose its secrets in articles to farm journals. His large-scale operations made it possible for him to diversify his activities and utilize all sources of gain. He was able to afford his own cotton gins and to develop water power for his machinery. He agreed with the dictum that "to be a farmer, a man must almost necessarily, be every thing else."[7]

Whether farms were large or small, all intelligent tillers of the soil knew that they themselves should be more careful in the management of their land, their labor, and their capital. It was coming to be recognized that greater profits could be had by using methods which would give a greater yield from fewer acres, for labor was now an item which represented a definite and recognizable drain on the farmer's resources. It cost as much to plow and till an acre from which a third of a bale of cotton was taken as the acre which produced a whole bale.

---

the Barrow plantation, though owned by one man, would be listed as two dozen farms. See Carroll D. Wright, *The History and Growth of the United States Census* (Washington, 1900), 161.

[6] *Plantation*, III (1872), 213.

[7] *Southern Cultivator*, XXV (1867), 195; XXVI (1868), 3; XXXVII (1879), 3-4.

Many farmers came to see that the greatest promoter of the whole bale was commercial fertilizer. "Labor Question Settled. Cultivate Much Less Land. Use One-Third the Labor. Raise Three Times the Crop," advertised a superphosphate company in a Macon, Georgia, newspaper; and the editor added his agreement: "The hire of one negro invested in phosphate of lime and judiciously applied, would return double the amount of corn or cotton that the best hand could produce." [8] Commercial fertilizers, especially Peruvian guano, had begun to make their appearance in ante-bellum times, but not until after the war did they take the South by storm. Farm journals were loaded with fertilizer advertisements: Orchilla Guano, Navassa Guano, Chesapeake Guano, Phospho-Peruvian or Manipulated Guano, Redonda Guano, Ammoniated Soluble Phosphate, Berger & Butz's Excelsior Superphosphate of Lime, Baugh's Raw Bone Phosphate, Maryland Powder of Bone, Calumet Mills Bone Dust, Nitro-Phosphate of Lime, Double-Refined Poudrette—all these and more were advertised in one issue of a farm magazine.[9]

Baltimore became a center of fertilizer manufacture and distribution, but the source of much of the phosphates used in the South was a strip of territory in the vicinity of Charleston, under which lay vast quantities of phospate rock. Edmund Ruffin, who had come down from Virginia in ante-bellum times to make a survey of South Carolina's natural resources, had first noted these rock beds, but no efforts were made at that time to utilize them. Immediately following the war chemists suggested their great value and promoters attempted to organize mining and manufacturing companies. Lack of capital delayed success until two Philadelphians were induced to invest in the project in 1867. When once started, this business developed rapidly; other companies were set up; and within a half-dozen years the annual output amounted to about $2,000,000. In 1880 there were twenty-one companies manufacturing phosphates in Charleston or its vicinity, and for the first time since 1861 this war-ridden city learned again the taste of prosperity.[10]

[8] Macon (Ga.) *Daily Journal & Messenger,* February 13, 1866.
[9] See *American Farmer,* III (1868).
[10] *Southern Magazine,* XIV (1874), 585; Jones (ed.), *Appletons' Hand-Book of American Travel, Southern Tour,* 130–31; Capers, *Memminger,* 385–86.

The fertilizer craze was soon tinged with humbuggery. With no governmental inspection service yet dreamed of, faked fertilizers made their appearance, and farmers were soon growing suspicious of all brands. "The Southern people have been drunk upon guano," complained a Georgian; "they must wake up, *reform*, sign the pledge; and hereafter, use it only *medicinally*, if they wish to make it a blessing." [11] Those who thought that the South was raising too much cotton complained that all ready money was being used to buy fertilizer to raise more cotton— "Gone where the guano smelleth, that the cotton plant may bloom and flourish, and the people perish." [12] In 1871 an Augusta dealer was pushing his sales by agreeing to give a ton of fertilizer for a bale of cotton. Farmers were soon complaining about the high prices exacted by the fertilizer companies, who by agreement used every opportunity to increase their profits. Commercial fertilizers increased the yield of farm products, extended the frontiers of agriculture into poor and worn-out lands, and helped the South to recover its prosperity; but commercial fertilizers also deadened the farmer's interest and ingenuity in building up his soil by proper crop rotation and by using soil restorers which he could make at home.

Increasing the yield led to farm prosperity, but reducing the costs of a smaller yield would have had the same effect. Here was an opportunity for laborsaving machinery to make its appearance, and here a craze spread as quickly. According to promoters, steam plows would do the work of twenty horses, and when not being used to plow the ground the engines could be harnessed for sawing lumber, and even stationary engines with cables to pull plows were serviceable. The first steam plows were imported from Leeds, England, and used in Louisiana. After a few years of the craze, the steam plow was forgotten, but fortune awaited the inventor of a successful cotton picker. Every year someone patented such a machine. [13] Howe's Cotton Picker was a two-

11 *Southern Cultivator*, XXXIII (1875), 375.

12 Augusta *Weekly Chronicle & Sentinel*, May 25, 1870; Sandersville (Ga.) *Herald*, January 30, 1879.

13 *American Farmer*, I (1867), 294; *Plantation*, II (1871), 328; Americus *Tri-Weekly Sumter Republican*, November 20, 1868; Augusta *Weekly Constitutionalist*, February 6, 1867; King, *Great South*, 81.

pound contraption carried over the shoulder; its suction power was produced by a hand crank; and it was guaranteed to do the work of five or six people.[14] It soon turned out to be a fake; but finally in 1870 it was announced that the millennium had arrived: "Hundreds of inventors have puzzled their brains to invent a substitute for the fingers of Sambo—to perfect a machine that did not vote, go to circuses, barbecues, &c., just when it was needed in the field." [15] This newly advertised picker turned out to be worse than Sambo; it would not pick at any time.

In slave days the plantations had used little farm machinery besides simple tools which a slave could not easily break. After the war the South was given its first acquaintance, though slight, with the standard farm equipment which Northern farmers had long been using—cultivators, straw and hay cutters, corn shellers, reapers, self-discharging hay and grain rakes, corn planters, threshers and separators, force pumps, cider mills, churns, grain drills, mowers, and the like. Hydraulic rams were making small streams doubly valuable as sources of water supply.[16]

The South still revolved around cotton. Though often dethroned and disowned in conversation and in public print, cotton to Southerners as well as to Northerners was of the essence of the South. Those who talked about abandoning cotton were cautioned to remember that they had "neither the money nor the time to be *experimenting* upon *hops* and other foreign crops" of which they knew "just nothing." [17] Cotton was particularly a sharp weapon which could be used against the North. A threat to limit the crop or give it up altogether might well cause the North-

14 Wiley, "Salient Changes in Southern Agriculture," *loc. cit.,* 71; *Southern Cultivator,* XXIV (1866), 212–13, 230.

15 Louisville *Courier-Journal,* quoted in Raymond *Hinds County Gazette,* October 5, 1870.

16 Nevertheless, the value of farm machinery was much less in 1880 than in 1860, a situation produced by war destructions and the Southerners' inability to replace worn-out machinery during the years following the war. *Compendium of the Tenth Census, 1880,* I, 659.

17 Americus *Tri-Weekly Sumter Republican,* October 13, 1866. For an extensive study of cotton production, see Eugene W. Hilgard, *Report on Cotton Production in the United States: also Embracing Agricultural and Physico-Geographical Descriptions of the Several Cotton States and of California,* in *Tenth Census of the United States, 1880,* V–VI, *Cotton Production.*

ern mills uncomfortable moments, make exporting and importing merchants uneasy, and cause the national government, which must have gold, to pause.

But at best cotton was an uncertain crop, uncertain in amount and uncertain in price. Eighteen-hundred-sixty-six was a lean year, producing 200,000 bales fewer than grew in 1865 and 1,000,000 fewer than in 1869. Not until 1878 did the number of bales equal the crop in 1860, but even in 1880 Alabama, Florida, Louisiana, and Mississippi did not raise as much as they had produced twenty years before. Sea-island cotton, which grew in the coastlands and sold for about twice as much as upland cotton, gradually disappeared after the war, driven out by unsettled labor conditions among the coastal Negroes and by the competition of Egyptian cotton.[18]

The price fluctuated equally widely and not always in proportion to the amount raised. In 1865, with a greater yield than the following year, the price was much higher. Farmers were never satisfied with the price they received, always considering themselves at a disadvantage. The cotton they sold on the plantation brought in Liverpool three and four cents more a pound, and the articles they bought from Liverpool cost them 200 to 300 per cent more because of the tariff—so a sympathizing Englishman believed.[19] How could the farmer help himself? He might store his cotton until prices suited him; he might demand gold and refuse to accept the "waste paper" which some considered greenbacks to be; he might even take the advice of Edward Atkinson, Boston cotton manufacturer, and be more careful in ginning, baling, and protecting his cotton bales against the weather. Atkinson declared that the South lost from 2 to 5 per cent of the value of its cotton crop by offering for sale "dirty, wet, muddy bales of cotton fibre, badly ginned, badly covered, and badly packed." [20]

Dealing in cotton futures became the custom after the war. This led to manipulation of prices and added the uncertainty of

[18] *Compendium of the Tenth Census, 1880,* I, 666; *Report of the Commissioner of Agriculture,* 1869 (Washington, 1870), 8; *Southern Cultivator,* XXV (1867), 198.

[19] Somers, *Southern States since the War,* 133.

[20] *Address of Edward Atkinson, . . . 1880 . . .* (Boston, 1881), 17.

the price to the uncertainty of the cotton crop itself, as speculators sought advantage without reference to the amount of the crop. It was downright gambling in the eyes of the old cotton factors, for which, according to a New Orleans dealer, "I have neither inclination or talent and believe I am now too old for business as now conducted." [21] Even so, the inexorable law of supply and demand must ultimately assert itself, and Southerners had good reason to believe that many of their ills lay in a lack of information as to the size of the cotton crop until they had sold it—then it was too late. No one had a reasonable idea of what the amount was when the farmer was selling it in the fall; in the late spring when the farmer no longer owned the cotton, the amount could be reasonably fixed, and if it was not as large as supposed, then the middleman made the profits. The situation in 1866–1867 showed eloquently the outrageous plight of the cotton farmer. The price in December when the farmer was selling his cotton was based on a large crop and was, therefore, low; in the following May, when the crop had been sold and the amount was known, the price almost doubled, for the crop was far below expectations. In 1872 a farm editor estimated that in this manner the South had lost $200,000,000 since the war.[22] Yet the cotton farmer could be the winner in this system, and he was, in 1865–1866. Atkinson estimated the amount at considerably less than it actually was, not realizing that there was much cotton in hiding that would come out. Prices based on a small crop were high and the Southerners made $50,000,000 more than they would have received had the amount of cotton been known. Atkinson later declared that he was glad his mistake had helped the Southern planters.[23]

Southerners early began a movement to collect information on which to base an estimate of the cotton crop. In 1866 they organized the Central Cotton Growing Association whose purpose was to develop branches in all the cotton-producing states and

[21] Barnsley, Woodlands, Ga., to unstated person, September 15, 1869, in Barnsley Papers.

[22] *Southern Farm and Home: A Magazine of Agriculture, Manufactures and Domestic Economy* (Macon, Ga., Memphis), III (1872), 246–48.

[23] Harold F. Williamson, *Edward Atkinson, The Biography of an American Liberal, 1827–1905* (Boston, 1934), 27–29.

send out questionnaires calling for information on cotton acreage and crop prospects. Two years later the Southern planters and the Northern manufacturers organized for the same purpose the National Association of Cotton Manufacturers and Planters with Amos A. Lawrence of Massachusetts as president and Daniel Pratt of Alabama as one of the vice-presidents. Its main purpose was to collect information on the cotton crop and make estimates.[24] Ultimately the United States government developed the crop estimate service into an efficient institution.

The other two most characteristically Southern crops were rice and sugar. After the war rice gradually disappeared from its old habitat, the Carolinas and Georgia, ruined by the uncertainties of labor in the new dispensation and by the more economic methods of cultivation which could be used in Louisiana and Texas. A South Carolina rice plantation worth $500,000 in 1860 was considered worth half that much in 1865, but ten years later was sold for $6,000. Yet, in 1880 South Carolina and Georgia were still the first and second rice-producing states, with Louisiana a fast-rising third. Sugar was a much more uncertain crop than cotton and came closer to suffering extinction than rice. The Louisiana sugar plantations were valued at $200,000,000 in 1861; in 1865 they could have been bought for $7,000,000. A sugar plantation was a capitalistic undertaking which combined both farming and manufacturing, and not until the end of the 1870's, when the two processes began to separate, could small sugar plantations be started.[25]

Uncertain yield and manipulated prices were not the only complaints against cotton; it was reproached even more loudly because it crowded out all other crops and prevented diversified farming. Too many people forgot that though cotton would

[24] De Bow's Review, II (1866), 83; Southern Cultivator, XXIV (1866), 155–56; Montgomery Weekly Advertiser, May 5, June 23, 1868; Weekly Columbus Enquirer, March 6, 1869.

[25] Campbell, White and Black, 338; Leigh, Ten Years on a Georgia Plantation, 116; Compendium of the Tenth Census, 1880, I, 670; New Orleans Weekly Times, February 7, 1874; Montgomery Weekly Advertiser, December 15, 1875; Somers, Southern States since the War, 200; Walter Prichard, "The Effects of the Civil War on the Louisiana Sugar Industry," in Journal of Southern History, V (1939), 321–32.

bring money, it would not save money: "I do not know of any business in which our people may engage that will so certainly result in loss as that of planting cotton," said a Georgian.[26] Diversified farming, a program as old as the South itself, was advocated after the war with greater vehemence than ever before. Now Southern economy should center around the "spindle, the anvil and the loom, the vineyard, orchard, hay meadow, stock and grazing, and grain fields." [27] A farm in St. James Parish, Louisiana, was held up as a model of diversification; on thirty acres with the help of only his son, the farmer raised two bales of cotton, two hogsheads of sugar, and considerable amounts of rice, corn, sweet potatoes, Irish potatoes, onions, pecans, peaches, beans, lettuce and other vegetables—and perique tobacco.[28]

The South was amazingly slow in regaining its ante-bellum agricultural prosperity, eloquent proof of how grievously it had been wounded by war and Reconstruction, in economics, in society, and in government. Excluding Tennessee, Florida, Arkansas, and Texas, the South had not caught up in 1880 with its production in 1860 in any principal crop, except cotton and oats. The latter crop swept the South after the war and made remarkable progress in every state except Virginia, which was so frightfully used up that a decrease was registered there in almost every line of economic activity. In the production of rye every state showed a loss; in sweet potatoes, all except Florida; in Irish potatoes, all except Florida, Tennessee, and Texas; in wheat, all except Alabama, Arkansas, Georgia, Tennessee, and Texas; and in hay and corn, all except Arkansas, Tennessee, and Texas.[29] Farm editors made a vigorous campaign for corn, often using such appeals as this: "Will the South ever learn anything? . . . Let all editors in our land raise the corn song, and let the people join the chorus, 'raise corn!' Let us do it quick, before Uncle Sam has a chance to tax us. . . . It's time for us to speak out and

[26] Augusta Weekly Constitutionalist, December 4, 1867.

[27] Galveston Tri-Weekly News, June 11, 1865; Carrollton Times, November 17, 1866; Atlanta Georgia Weekly Opinion, December 10, 1867; Augusta Daily Press, January 8, 1869.

[28] De Bow's Review, V (1868), 363–72.

[29] Compendium of the Tenth Census, 1880, I, 662–73.

warn the people, plant corn! May God bless us next season with a cornucopia of corn!" [30]

The old Southern custom of grasping at every new crop that anyone could suggest, exotic or native, was revived after the war with redoubled force. Some were fakes, humbugs, and crazes, which soon played out; others led to developments which in time added new agricultural wealth to the South. The lowly peanut, which only Negroes and small boys might be caught eating without losing social standing, had roused the taste of marching armies, which lingered after the war. Southeastern Virginia, around Norfolk and Suffolk, became the cradle of this industry, its production jumping from 75,000 bushels in 1867, to 1,000,000 in 1879. Soon the peanut vendor set up his stand in the small towns and cities, and the bandanna-bedecked Negro mammies infested the small railroad stations and peddled their peanuts to passengers on stopping trains.[31] Thus was born a new industry.

Small hints of truck gardening and fruitgrowing were made in ante-bellum times, but the former got little beyond supplying limited and local needs and it was almost unheard of for a gentleman to sell his fruit. Now along the Atlantic seaboard from Maryland to Florida the production of early vegetables and fruits for markets as far away as New York City began to appear. "It is no prophecy to say that Florida is destined to be the future garden for semi-tropical fruits and vegetables for the supply of Northern cities," said a boosting Floridian in 1869.[32] The Florida orange crop was noted by visitors. Dr. Clayton A. Cogwill of Dover, Delaware, was widely credited with pioneering in raising oranges for the market as early as 1865. Strawberries and watermelons, also, were important crops which found their way to Northern markets. One Georgia planter in 1870 set out 5,000 hills of watermelons and sold many melons weighing thirty-five and forty pounds. In 1869 a North Carolina fruit farmer sent 1,000 bushels of peaches to New York and sold them for $7.00 a bushel. Orchards expanded rapidly over the South. P. C. Berk-

[30] Greenville *Southern Enterprise,* March 7, 1867.

[31] *De Bow's Review,* VI (1869), 346; *Harper's Weekly,* XIV (1870), 449; Thomas J. Wertenbaker, *Norfolk, Historic Southern Port* (Durham, 1931), 313. Peanuts were not recognized by the United States Census until 1890.

[32] Jacksonville *Florida Union,* quoted in *De Bow's Review,* VI (1869), 348.

mans of Augusta, Georgia, set out large peach, apple, and pear orchards, but peaches were the fruit which best found an early market in the North.[33] An Englishman traveling through Georgia in 1870 was impressed with the number of peaches he saw there: "The people scarcely know what to do with them. They dry them, pickle them, preserve them, and distil them; and after all, the hogs, I daresay, eat a great many." [34]

After the war there was a resurgence of the wine-making movement. Though it was claimed that orange juice would make "a sparkling wine as nearly resembling the champagne of Rheims as do any of our American grape wines," [35] orange groves did not supplant vineyards in developing this industry. A Mississippi farmer reported that he had realized from $800 to $1,600 an acre in wines from his vineyard. The scuppernong was the favorite grape with many farmers. There was one scuppernong vine in Columbus County, North Carolina, which produced annually 120 bushels of grapes.[36]

Hopes of great wealth from a variety of old, new, and outlandish crops arose, flourished a short day, and withered. Only a few developed any economic importance, and then only in limited regions. Ramie, a plant resembling the sunflower or the Jerusalem artichoke, was soon on all tongues. A native of Java, but imported directly from Mexico, it was planted like sugar cane and cultivated like tobacco, and developed not only more fiber than any other plant known but also one which could be spun as fine as flax and 50 per cent stronger. It would grow wherever cotton could be raised, would yield from three to five crops annually, and would sell for sixty cents a pound in London—so ramie growers claimed. China tea would grow from North Carolina to Florida. William Jones, one of the editors of the *Southern Cultivator,* had from 12,000 to 15,000 plants growing in Liberty

[33] M. B. Hillyard, *The New South* (Baltimore, 1887), 15, 16; *Plantation,* I (1870), 293; Atlanta *Christian Index,* August 19, 1875; *Report of the Commissioner of Agriculture,* 1871 (Washington, 1872), 143–59; *Southern Cultivator,* XXXVI 1878), 275; *Daily Richmond Enquirer,* July 4, 1866; Sandersville *Herald,* July 31, 1879.

[34] Somers, *Southern States since the War,* 100.

[35] Fernandina *Florida Mirror,* January 18, 1879.

[36] *Southern Cultivator,* XXXII (1874), 238; XXXIII (1875), 115; Austin *Tri-Weekly State Gazette,* October 28, 1868.

County, Georgia, in 1870, and was producing tea which brought forth praise from ladies attending parties incident to the Horticultural and Floral Fair recently held in Augusta. Sumach could be made into a money crop, for the leaves could be dried and sold for dyeing and tanning. One poor family was known to have sold $600 worth in one season. Cinchona trees would grow on the slopes of the Southern mountains, and to prove it the United States Commissioner of Agriculture was urged to import the shrubs. The Esparto grass of Spain and Algeria would grow just as well in the South; and as the rag supply for papermaking was not sufficient, here was the solution. Okra, also, was just as serviceable for papermaking, it was more lucrative than cotton, and besides, it would produce two crops a year. Jute would grow in the abandoned rice fields of the coast; flax could easily supplant cotton; and palma Christi or castor beans only awaited a trial to prove their worth.[37] Such were the stories dinned into the ears of farmers.

Lespedeza, a strange cloverlike plant mysteriously appearing in various localities through the South, seemed to be the answer to the region's prayer for a grass, and helped to make up many a conversation among Southerners. It made a valuable hay and was a good soil builder. Botanists finally concluded that it came from Japan and was probably scattered by the invading armies—one good gift from the enemy. This plant was to gain a foothold and ultimately a respectable standing in Southern agriculture. Perique tobacco, defying all explanations, refused to produce its fine qualities in any other quarter of the globe but St. James Parish, Louisiana. Producers squeezed it into a cigar-shaped chunk by pulling on each end of a rope wrapped around a mass of it. "It unfolds within its easy, good-natured grasp, all the soothing excellence of the incense yet burning in the fabled East; its rich, brown leaves, unmatched by the dark hazel of the beautiful Creole eyes." Perique as a special flavoring for tobacco developed its place in world trade. Also it was discovered that a plant, called

[37] Scott's Monthly Magazine, VII (1869), 156–57; American Farmer, I (1867), 360; III (1869), 221; Plantation, I (1870), 280, 401–402; New Orleans Weekly Times, May 2, 1874; Montgomery Alabama State Journal, March 20, May 20, 1869; Augusta Weekly Constitutionalist, December 23, 1868; Fernandina Florida Mirror, February 22, 1879; Rome Tri-Weekly Courier, February 20, 1873.

RUINS IN THE HEART OF CHARLESTON—VIEW FROM KING STREET

From *Harper's Weekly*, July 8, 1865

A DROVE OF TEXAS CATTLE CROSSING A STREAM

From *Harper's Weekly*, October 19, 1867

PRIMARY SCHOOL FOR FREEDMEN, IN CHARGE OF
MRS. GREEN—VICKSBURG, MISSISSIPPI

NOON AT THE PRIMARY SCHOOL FOR FREEDMEN—
VICKSBURG, MISSISSIPPI From *Harper's Weekly*, June 23, 1866

PEANUT SELLERS IN SAVANNAH
From *Harper's Weekly*, July 16, 1870

A MODERN TOURNAMENT From *Harper's Weekly*, December 4, 1869

Above: THE ROCKWOOD IRON FURNACE—EASTERN TENNESSEE. From Edward King, *The Great South*, (Hartford, Conn., 1875). p. 533. *Upper right:* THE GALLEGO FLOUR MILL—RICHMOND, VIRGINIA. From Edward King, *The Great South*, p. 373. *Lower right:* THE EAGLE AND PHOENIX COTTON MILLS—COLUMBUS, GEORGIA. From Edward King, *The Great South*, p. 373

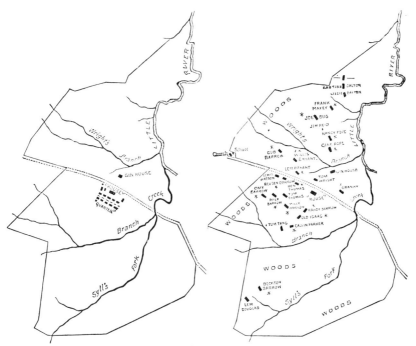

Left: A GEORGIA PLANTATION AS IT WAS IN 1860
Right: A GEORGIA PLANTATION AS IT WAS IN 1881
Negroes who lived on this plantation when slaves are indicated by an asterisk (*).
From *Scribner's Monthly*, XXI (1881), pp. 832, 833

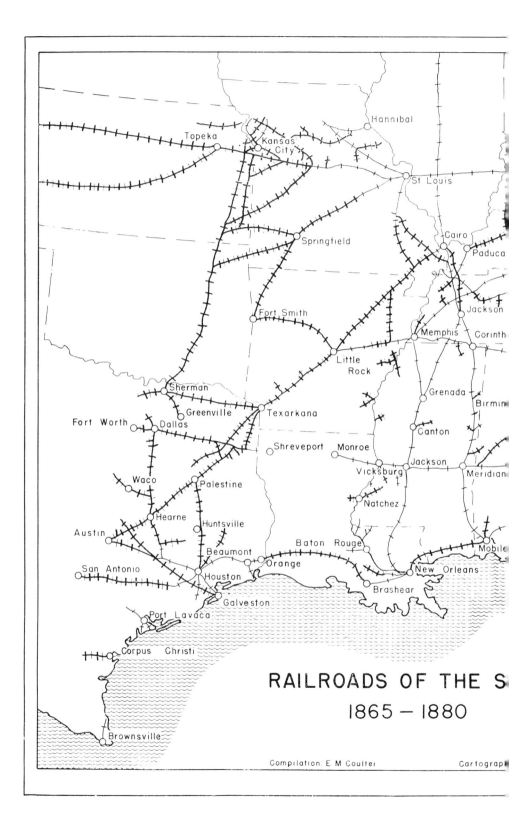

RAILROADS OF THE S

1865 – 1880

Compilation E M Coulter   Cartograph

LEGEND

In Existence
1865

Built
1865—1880

0   100   200

Miles

"Dam Your Soul. The Horrible *Sepulchre* and Bloody Moon has at last arrived. Some live to-day to-morrow "*Die.*" We the undersigned understand through our Grand "*Cyclops*" that you have recommended a big Black Nigger for Male agent on our nu rode; wel, sir, Jest you understand in time if he gets on the rode you can make up your mind to pull roape. If you have anything to say in regard to the Matter, meet the Grand Cyclops and Conclave at Den No. 4 at 12 o'clock mid-night, Oct. 1st, 1871. When you were in Calera we warned you to hold your tounge and not speak so much with your mouth or otherwise you will be taken on supprise and led out by the Klan and learnt to stretch hemp. Beware. Beware. Beware. Beware. (Signed) " PHILLIP ISENBAUM, *Grand Cyclops.*
" JOHN BANKSTOWN.
" ESAU DAVES.
" MARCUS THOMAS.
"You know who And all others of the Klan." " BLOODY BONES.

SPECIMEN OF A KU-KLUX NOTICE

deer tongue, which grew widely over the Lower South, added a special aroma to smoking tobacco and cigars. Families in out-of-way places added to their meager income by gathering these leaves. It was also found that a market existed for the Spanish moss that hung so gracefully from the trees in the Lower South. It was good for filling various kinds of mattresses.[38] Gathering this moss became an industry, especially for the Negroes of the low country.

Streams on many farms could be easily dammed for fishponds. The South was entering a fish-craze era, and as always there was the usual great-wealth example. At his country seat in Spring Villa in Alabama, Colonel W. P. C. Yonge had a six-acre pond fed by springs and surrounded by weeping willows, with a few rustic seats scattered here and there along the banks—there was beauty on the outside, but in the lake was the wealth. Schools of trout and bream thrived there, from which Colonel Yonge was making hundreds of dollars. A visitor who saw all these things "would rather own those six acres of water, with its herd of trout and bream, than any hundred acres of meadow in Alabama with a herd of cattle capable of being supported thereon." [39] There was wealth in pisciculture: Catholics had to eat fish every Friday, and they and other people might well eat them at any time. The United States government supported the fishpond idea to the extent of distributing many German carp widely over the country. Yet pisciculture came to be more of a short-lived craze than a substantiality. This was the experience of a Georgian who was able to emancipate himself from the fad: "Now, aside from the pleasure of having my ponds and believing that I have a great many fish, they are of no benefit or value whatever to me. I have tried many ways to catch them, and utterly failed." [40] When the craze died out, a few fishponds continued here and there over the South, more for pleasure than for profit.

No farm could be considered well ordered without some live-

[38] *Land We Love,* IV (1867–1868), 409; Augusta *Weekly Chronicle & Sentinel,* October 9, 1867; November 11, 1868; *De Bow's Review,* II (1866), 85; *Tenth Census, 1880,* XIX, *Cities,* Pt. II, 271; *Southern Farm and Home,* III (1872), 418; Trowbridge, *South,* 449.

[39] *Plantation,* I (1870), 292; *Southern Cultivator* XXVIII (1870), 76–77.

[40] *Southern Cultivator,* XXXV (1877), 46.

stock—work animals, of course, but also cattle for milk and butter, and, perhaps, beef, as well as swine and sheep if the farmer would make the most of his opportunities. The war was especially destructive of such wealth, but the South also suffered from the depredations of freedmen. In 1880 most of the South was poorer in livestock than in 1860, both in numbers and in value. In Texas alone of the former Confederacy was livestock worth more. Only Florida, Louisiana, and Texas had more horses; Arkansas, Florida, Georgia, and Texas, more sheep; Arkansas, Florida, and Texas, more swine; and Arkansas, Florida, Tennessee, and Texas, more beef cattle. Only in milch cows, mules, and asses had a majority of the Southern states recovered.[41]

Raising livestock as a business attained importance only in Texas, though there lingered the fine-horse tradition in Tennessee and Virginia, of the old Confederacy, and, of course, in Kentucky and Maryland. In 1880 Texas had almost twice as many cattle as any other state in the Union; she had more than twice as many sheep as any other Southern state, increasing her number three times over what she had in 1860; and she had more than three times as many horses as any other Southern state, more than doubling the 1860 number. Her great cattle ranches had their beginning directly after the war. Before 1870 Colonel Richard King had over 84,000 acres on which he grazed 65,000 cattle, 10,000 horses, and 7,000 sheep, attended by 300 Mexican herdsmen. But there was no money in cattle if they must remain in Texas. Cows in Texas could be sold for no more than $4.00 a head; in the North they would bring $40.00. As Texas had no railway connections with other parts of the nation until some years after the war, there was no easy way to market. A few cattle were shipped out of Galveston over the Morgan Steamship Line, but the main outlet came to be the long drive, famous for the cowboys who directed them and for their songs. Between 1866 and 1880 almost four and a quarter million cattle were driven northward to Abilene, Kansas, and to other cow towns on rail-

[41] *Compendium of the Tenth Census, 1880,* I, 674–81. Brahmin cattle were now being introduced into the South. They were considered good dependable work animals, and when crossed with other strains were held to be good milch cows. *Southern Cultivator,* XXIX (1871), 372.

roads where they were shipped to markets in Kansas City, Chicago, and other cattle centers. Some were driven to California and sold for Western gold. In 1868 sixty cowboys drove a herd of 5,000 cattle to the Pacific coast.[42]

Many cattle were slaughtered in Texas when methods of handling beef were devised. By 1869 refrigerator ships were beginning to carry it to New York, and in 1871 a cargo of 170,000 pounds of fresh Texas beef was received in Philadelphia. Texas beef cured and packed in barrels made its appearance and led many Southern farmers to expect it to supplant salt pork as a food for Negro workmen.[43]

Though the rest of the South could never develop a ranching business like that in Texas, persistent arguments were used to induce farmers to supplement their farming with sheep raising. Daniel Lee, an agricultural reformer of long standing, ran a sheep farm in East Tennessee and argued that freedmen would make good shepherds. There had been a long-standing prejudice against sheep because of their ravenous appetites. One planter had remarked, "If I had a flock of two hundred sheep, I should count myself broke; they would eat up my whole plantation." Besides this prejudice against sheep, there was the hazard of depredations on the flocks by dogs. The effort to legislate dogs and their masters into conformity with sheep raising by taxing all dog owners ran afoul of political entanglements, for the dog was the poor man's friend, and a freedman would as readily lose his liberty as his dog. One friend of sheep remarked, "The dogs consume more food than would pay for the education of all the children of the country. So that the children's bread of life is actually given to the dogs." [44] And yet the loyalty of the masses to their dogs was no greater than the dog's loyalty to his master.

[42] *Compendium of the Tenth Census, 1880,* I, 674–81; *Report of the Commissioner of Agriculture,* 1870 (Washington, 1871), 347–50; Montgomery *Alabama State Journal,* April 12, 1872; Walter P. Webb, *The Great Plains* (Boston, 1931), 216, 223; *Railroad Gazette,* VI (1874), 294–95; Austin (Tex.) *Daily State Journal,* February 19, 1874; King, *Great South,* 167–74; Austin *Tri-Weekly State Gazette,* April 15, 1868.

[43] *Weekly Austin Republican,* April 7, 1869; Augusta *Tri-Weekly Chronicle & Sentinel,* August 26, 1871; Barnsley, New Orleans, to Parsons, February 11, 1869, in Barnsley Papers; Montgomery *Weekly Advertiser,* April 13, 1869.

[44] *American Farmer,* I (1867), 301; *Plantation,* II (1871), 50; Richmond *Daily Dispatch,* January 25, 1877; *Southern Cultivator,* XXXII (1874), 302.

The Old South made little profit out of cattle raising, apart from a living for the neighborhood butcher and a small income for those who sold him a cow now and then to slaughter. Nevertheless, it clung tenaciously to the old custom of letting livestock browse wherever their instincts or appetites might take them. The South was still frontier. Immediately after the war a movement grew up to force owners to fence their pastures instead of the farmer his fields. The farmer's problem was pressing, because the war had destroyed the fences wherever armies marched; in many communities the timber supply was scant—and freedmen, unlike Lincoln, could never be induced to split rails. Some farmers concluded the fence would cost as much as their fields were worth. Furthermore, cattle should not be allowed to run loose for they soon became scrubby and, also, presented a constant temptation to the freedmen. What right had a person owning five acres of land and 500 cattle to turn them loose to roam on other people's land? "Might not the timber annually cut up and wasted to build defenses against Jones' steers and hogs, be used for some better and more reasonable purpose?" asked "John Plowshares." A voice now and then arose against passing stock laws. A Mississippian argued in 1867 that farming was dying out, that Mississippi was going back into fallow land, and that land could be used for nothing better than grazing. Alabama in 1866 passed a stock law for a few of her counties, and thereafter sundry other states passed such laws, always on the basis of local option. It was suggested in Texas that a line be drawn separating East Texas, a farming country, from the rest of the state, which might remain as open range. By 1879 the appearance of barbed wire in the South made possible a mile of fence for $200 and also speeded up the stock-law movement.[45]

To promote agriculture and allied activities, the South had in ante-bellum times organized many agricultural societies, which later became casualties of war. With the coming of peace, they were revived in some places and in others new organizations were set up. They were promoted by counties, groups of counties, states,

[45] *Southern Cultivator*, XXXIV (1876), 178–79; XXXVII (1879), 335; *Plantation*, II (1871), 755; III (1872), 99; Raymond *Hinds County Gazette*, May 10, June 28, 1867; Atlanta *Christian Index*, April 13, 1876; *American Farmer*, I (1867), 285; *Daily Columbus Enquirer*, February 18, 1866; Carthage *Panola Watchman*, July 14, 1875.

and by the whole South. The Agricultural and Mechanical Association in Louisiana, organized in 1860 and headed off by war, was among the first to be revived after the Surrender; the Arkansas State Agricultural and Mechanical Association was organized in 1867 in Little Rock; two years later South Carolina revived her Agricultural and Mechanical Society, and Georgia, her Agricultural Society. The Georgia society was a federation of county organizations, which received state aid at the hands of a Radical government, and whose delegates enjoyed free transportation over Radical-controlled railroads.[46]

The main work of these societies was to hold annual county, state, and regional fairs. The Louisiana fair, held in New Orleans in 1866, was among the first to meet after the war. In 1870 Augusta began holding annually what it called the Cotton States Fair, and out of this institution grew the Southern Agricultural Congress, representing an attempt to combine all Southern agricultural interests to promote diversified agriculture, improved methods of farming, foreign immigration, and other farm interests. The state fairs drew great crowds of people who forgot for the time their political ills and revived their old spirit of levity and play. They were attracted by displays of farm machinery, the handiwork of the household, livestock, horse racing, tournament displays, balloon ascensions, fireworks, trained hog and mule acts, and the devious doings of chuck-a-luck artists and thimbleriggers.[47] The state fair came to be as much an institution to promote the city where it was held as to help the farmers, and as for the attendants, "some will come to see their friends because travelling is cheap; some for a holiday; some for a spree; some for sporting purposes; some to steal, and a few, a very few, to LEARN something." [48]

State fairs partook too much of the circus to suit serious farmers.

[46] *American Farmer*, II (1868), 282, 297; *De Bow's Review*, II (1866), 666; III (1867), 169–72; VI (1869), 339–44; Little Rock *Weekly Arkansas Gazette*, September 22, 1868; Rome *Weekly Courier*, June 28, 1876; Somers, *Southern States since the War*, 25; Simkins and Woody, *South Carolina during Reconstruction*, 259; *Plantation*, I (1870), 516; II (1871), 600.

[47] Augusta *Weekly Chronicle & Sentinel*, July 13, 20, October 26, November 2, 1870; *Weekly Columbus Enquirer*, August 2, 1870; *Plantation*, I (1870), 665; *Southern Farm and Home*, III (1871), 42–43; Greenville *Enterprise*, September 14, 1870.

[48] Macon *Daily Citizen*, quoted in Macon *American Union*, September 7, 1871.

In the county fairs they found their practical information and their inspiration. Here were displayed the products of the farm at their best, competing for prizes—the best pound of butter, basket of vegetables, pair of spring chickens, brood mare, colt, milch cow, calf, pair of pigs, needlework, bouquet of flowers, homemade bread, guinea fowls, bottle of domestic wine, and so on.[49]

Specialized fairs like horticultural and floral shows began to peep up by 1870, to give the ladies an opportunity to display their flowers and their social graces. And not to be left behind or shunted to the side at the white man's fairs, Negroes held their fairs here and there, where mixed with much loud hilarity incident to greased-pig races, pole climbings, wheelbarrow races, and blaring brass bands, they showed creditable agricultural progress of their race.[50]

Governmental aid to agriculture, state and national, was often asked for by farmers and infrequently received in a halting fashion. In this age of governmental abandon in aiding railroads the farmers might well have wondered why agriculture should be left to languish. In the opinion of a Georgian, "If the Legislature, instead of aiding railroads to Kamchatka, or the moon, or some other out of the way places, would aid the soil to make something for the railroads to transport, that would be beginning at the right end—laying the foundation, and then building the house." [51] Why could not schools be set up to teach practical agriculture and experimental farms established to prove what was best for farmers to do and how to do it? Most of the states answered by organizing departments of agriculture. The United States government appropriated $50,000 to provide free seeds for the South in the hard year of 1867, established the policy of free garden seeds, and extended to the Southern states the benefits of the Morrill Act, which promoted agricultural and mechanical colleges.

Remembering the old adage that the Lord helps those who help themselves, Southern farmers by 1872 were beginning to join the Patrons of Husbandry, popularly known as the Grangers. This

---

[49] *Southern Farm and Home,* III (1872), 283–84; Marietta *Journal,* April 21, 1871.
[50] *Plantation,* I (1870), 280; New Orleans *Tribune,* September 15, 1865; Greensboro *Herald,* December 10, 1874.
[51] *Plantation,* I (1870), 194.

was a farm organization promoted by Oliver H. Kelley, a clerk in the United States Bureau of Agriculture, whom President Johnson in 1867 had sent to the South to study the plight of the Southern farmers. It was secret, nonpolitical, and was open to women as well as men. Southern farmers had been agitating almost since the end of the war for an organization more closely tied together than the agricultural societies. Kelley's order seemed to be the answer. Though it became strongest in the Middle West and Northwest, in 1875 there were 6,400 granges in the seceded states, embracing 210,000 members, a proportion of farmers probably as large as in any other section of the country.[52] Border states of the South supported an additional 4,000 local groups, with a membership of approximately 145,000.

Besides the social and benevolent activities of the Grangers, they advocated the cash system of farming, self-sufficiency of the farms, the promotion of immigration by advertising the resources of the South, the collection of information for crop estimates, and reduction of prices by co-operative buying. The granges in South Carolina saved their members five cents a yard on cotton bagging, $2.00 to $3.00 a barrel on flour, and secured reductions in the prices of other farm necessities. "Granger prices" were often demanded of the merchants. There was talk of setting up Granger cotton mills, and in 1876 there was organized the Grangers' Life and Health Insurance Company, which was to be a federation of state companies. Southern Grangers were careful to keep clear of all political activities; they would not endanger Southern political solidarity; and unlike their Western colleagues they had at this time no severe quarrel with the railroads.[53] "Let them beware of the politicians, who are sure to try to get a fast hold in the order and run it in their interest," warned an Arkansas editor.[54]

[52] *Southern Cultivator*, XXVII (1869), 88; XXXI (1873), 251; Holland Thompson, *The New South* (New Haven, 1919), 31–33.

[53] *Southern Cultivator*, XXXI (1873), 208–209, 249; Little Rock *Weekly Arkansas Gazette*, March 24, 1874; January 31, 1876; Montgomery *Weekly Advertiser*, May 5, 1875; Sandersville *Herald*, March 20, May 22, 1874; Rome *Weekly Courier*, March 20, December 3, 1873; July 26, August 30, 1876; Carthage *Panola Watchman*, September 29, 1875. Yet there were beginning to be heard in the South protests against railroad rates and monopolies. Columbus (Miss.) *Press*, December 6, 1873.

[54] Little Rock *Weekly Arkansas Gazette*, October 21, 1873; Dardanelle *Arkansas Independent*, March 10, 1876.

It was not without many difficulties that the granges were organized in the South. The natural conservatism and inertia of farmers had to be overcome—those qualities alluded to by the Southerner who said, "Sir, the farmers, for the sense and wealth they possess, are the biggest fools on the top side of the earth— even the negroes can beat them in discipline and unity of action." [55] This organization was held by sundry farm editors and others to be hostile to the merchants; and though called forth by conditions Kelley had seen among Southern farmers, it was branded a Yankee institution, coming from the same habitat as the Credit Mobilier. It was being used chiefly as a weapon in the fight between the Western farmers and the railroads, and according to George W. Gift of Memphis, "So far as we are concerned, it is eminently a skunk and rattlesnake fight, and I trust that no Southern man will be so decidedly verdant as to contribute to it, or give mite to the organizing patriots who go about getting up Granges. . . ." [56] The Southern Grangers disappeared within a few years, later with other farmer recruits to rise up as Alliance men and Populists.

[55] *Southern Cultivator*, XXXI (1873), 208–209.   [56] *Ibid.*, 252.

CHAPTER XI

TRANSPORTATION

THE war had many revolutionary effects on the South, but it did not break up the old Southern custom of holding conventions. For a few years afterwards there was no purpose to be served in meeting in great political assemblages; politics had long been too much with the South, and some leaders were now calling for an adjournment of such interests. The old commercial conventions were, however, still in as good standing as ever; they were revived to formulate the South's programs and to popularize them, if they could do nothing more practical. These groups were soon making their rounds of the Southern cities, Norfolk, Memphis, New Orleans, Louisville, and so on, dipping now and then out of the South into the Middle West, to Cincinnati, St. Louis, even to Keokuk. These newer commercial conventions had fewer of the old politicians who had made the ante-bellum meetings somewhat ridiculous by their narrow and provincial programs. Being now desirous of securing the aid and good will of the North, they invited such capitalistic politicians as Senator Sprague; and in 1869 they resolved themselves into a great Peace Convention, which met in Louisville, presided over by former President Millard Fillmore, and which, it was claimed, was attended by delegates from every state in the Union.

There were some Southerners who, not having forgotten the old bombast of the ante-bellum conventions, looked with misgivings upon this revival. An editor in expressing his opinion of the Louisville convention, said he doubted not that the delegates were respectable people but the convention's proceedings exhibited "the same batch of high-sounding reports and unmeaning resolutions

233

which have characterized the activities of all similar conventions." [1]
Yet these meetings charted and promoted a few ideas which were
to materialize, as well as some, such as those for attracting immigrants, which were to fade out. Southern wants were many, but
they tended to crystallize around manufacturing, commerce, and
especially transportation. The South should trade direct from her
own ports to Europe, exporting and importing; she should promote nature's great highway, the Mississippi River, by demanding
that levees be repaired and new ones constructed along its banks
and that its mouth be deepened; and she should have a network of
railroads built, and especially should she demand that the United
States give aid to the Southern Pacific Railroad as it had done to
the Union Pacific and other railroads serving the North.[2]

During the war the United States had seized whatever Southern
railroads there were in the invaded regions, and at the end it took
control of all of them for a few months; but in August, 1865, President Johnson ordered the military authorities to restore them to
their owners. As the Radicals were not in control at this time, the
government adopted a railroad policy based on principles of honorable treatment. Had these principles been carried out in other
fields they would have immeasurably aided the South in re-
establishing quickly its proper place in the Union. The railroads
should be recompensed for all military use that had been made
of them, but they must pay for improvements and for new equipment which the government had brought in. Realizing their impoverished condition, the government gave them two years in
which to make payment, charging on the debt an interest rate of
7½ per cent. In July, 1866, the United States retired entirely from
the Southern railroad business by selling the Brazos Railroad in
Texas, which it had built. Most of the railroads in the Southeast
promptly paid their obligations; others, however, objected to the
prices set for the equipment and complained that the United States
had not allowed them a fair return for the use that had been made
of the roads during the war. Cases arose in the courts, and in 1871

1 *Scott's Monthly Magazine*, VIII (1869), 881–82.

2 *Nation*, XXIV (1877), 82–83; Montgomery *Weekly Advertiser*, May 18, 1869; *American Annual Cyclopaedia . . . 1869* (New York, 1871), 114–18; Somers, *Southern States
since the War*, 183.

Congress passed a relief act, scaling down the debt. In 1888 there were still three companies which had not made a settlement.[3]

The railroads thus fared much better than did plantations, factories, state governments, and other casualties of war. Some of the roads made quick recoveries, aided by good luck and foresight. Within six months after the end of the war the Mobile and Ohio Railroad bought $679,000 worth of equipment consisting in part of 21 locomotives and 263 cars; the Central of Georgia was able to rebuild its torn-up tracks by using rails made in England, which it bought with credit built up there during the war; by 1867 the New Orleans, Jackson, and Great Northern had resumed interest payments on its bonds; and railroads began joining up their tracks in cities, or special companies were organized to do so. The South, always having had a brisk enthusiasm for railroads, took up the subject after the war with a vigor born of the feeling that along this line lay its surest road to recovery. Railroad conventions, small and large, were frequently held, calling for the construction of new roads, begging Northerners to bring their capital and invest it in Southern railroads, and asking legislatures to aid with the credit of the state.[4] Said one editor in 1869, "The principal subject, and by far the most important one, that is now agitating the minds of the people of the South, . . . is Railroad Communications." Said another the next year, "The most numerous and most needed class of improvements now on foot are railway enterprises." [5] Edward King, who traveled more than 25,000 miles over the South in 1873 and 1874, declared that next to agriculture railroads provided the greatest occupation in Georgia.[6]

Apart from the desire of each community to have its own interests served, Southerners sensed the great trends of trade, and to grasp the larger opportunities offered by them they projected

[3] Carl R. Fish, *The Restoration of the Southern Railroads* (Madison, Wis., 1919), 11, 14, 18; Edward G. Campbell, "Indebted Railroads—A Problem of Reconstruction," in *Journal of Southern History*, VI (1940), 167–88.

[4] *De Bow's Review*, II (1866), 209–10; Somers, *Southern States since the War*, 72; Howard D. Dozier, *A History of the Atlantic Coast Line Railroad* (Boston, 1920), 117; Aberdeen *Daily Sunny South*, January 4, 1867; *Weekly Columbus Enquirer*, August 2, 1870; Dalton *North Georgia Citizen*, February 18, 1869.

[5] Elberton *Gazette*, October 22, 1869; Augusta *Weekly Chronicle & Sentinel*, January 12, 1870.

[6] King, *Great South*, 364.

long lines and systems. The oldest and the most important of all the grand schemes of Southern railroad development was the one first advocated and fondly dreamed of by Calhoun and Hayne— to connect the Middle West with a South Atlantic port and drain its wealth and interest, economic and political, into the South. Both of these men died without seeing their dream come true; the Civil War came, hastened by this failure; and now that great gap between the Southeast and the Middle West still existed, more glaring than ever. For seven hundred miles, from the Baltimore and Ohio in the east to the Louisville and Nashville in the west, not a railroad cut across this great barrier to Southern trade with the Middle West. Every Atlantic city or port from Richmond and Norfolk to Savannah and Brunswick planned to be the terminus for such a railroad.

Virginia afforded one of the most active fields in which efforts were made to bridge the gap, by consolidating existing lines and constructing new ones; and General William Mahone, of Confederate fame, became the leader. Immediately after the war he began to consolidate the Norfolk and Petersburg with the South Side, which led on to Lynchburg, and to these he added the Virginia and Tennessee, which carried his line to Bristol. From here he planned to build the Virginia and Kentucky to Cumberland Gap, whence he hoped a railroad would be constructed to Cincinnati and Louisville to give him connections with the Ohio River. Also, he would build and consolidate lines which would send out a Southwestern prong through Nashville to Memphis on the Mississippi. In 1870 he secured a charter for the Atlantic, Mississippi, and Ohio Railroad, which embraced these plans. The Panic of 1873 gave him a setback and added to his troubles made by machinations of John Garrett of the Baltimore and Ohio and of Thomas Scott of the Pennsylvania Railroad who were contesting for the control of Virginia railroads. English interests secured large holdings in Mahone's road and brought the scheme to its doom. In 1881 the Atlantic, Mississippi, and Ohio was sold and the purchasers renamed their holdings the Norfolk and Western.[7] The first successful spanning of the mountains south of the Baltimore and Ohio Rail-

[7] *De Bow's Review,* IV (1867), 117–19; Nelson M. Blake, *William Mahone of Virginia, Soldier and Political Insurgent* (Richmond, 1935), 110–34; King, *Great South,* 559.

road was made by the Chesapeake and Ohio in 1873, which was a consolidation of the old Virginia Central and the recently completed Covington and Ohio. This road ran from Richmond through Gordonsville and Covington, Virginia, through White Sulphur Springs and Charleston to Huntington, West Virginia, on the Ohio. Successful in her western connections, Richmond sought also to tie to herself eastern North Carolina. Here she collided with the ambitions of Norfolk and ultimately lost to this rival when the Norfolk and Southern was completed to Edenton, North Carolina, in 1881.[8]

To the southward, the Western North Carolina Railroad reached Asheville in 1880 in its westward course, but there were no plans to continue it or consolidate it with others to go beyond the valleys of East Tennessee. The old Calhoun dream of breaking through the mountains of Upper South Carolina and of joining with a road down the French Broad Valley in North Carolina and on to Cincinnati by one of various routes had reached as far as Walhalla in South Carolina by 1859; the revival of the idea after the war still got the road no farther than Walhalla. A modification shifted this route westward across the Savannah River, where an ambitious movement grew up to build a road from Augusta northward through Elberton and Rabun Gap to Knoxville. Thence it would continue across the mountains to Lexington, Kentucky, where there would be easy connections with the Ohio River. Attempts were made to interest Northern capital in this undertaking, but the road was never built.[9] Georgia had begun the movement to connect her seaports with the Ohio by completing in 1851 the Western and Atlantic from Atlanta to Chattanooga, there to form connections with roads which ran to Nashville and then on to Louisville, spanning the last distance over the Louisville and Nashville, finished in 1859.

One of the most interesting railroad developments in American history was produced by the bitter rivalry between two cities, Louis-

---

[8] Henry V. Poor, *Manual of the Railroads of the United States for 1880* (New York, 1880), 439; *ibid., 1883*, pp. 404–405; Wertenbaker, *Norfolk*, 305; *De Bow's Review*, IV (1867), 117–19.

[9] Somers, *Southern States since the War*, 34, 58; Elberton *Gazette*, February 26, 1873; Athens (Ga.) *Southern Watchman*, December 17, 1873.

ville and Cincinnati, and was largely a belated fulfillment of Calhoun's dream. Much of Cincinnati's ante-bellum prosperity had come from her Southern trade, carried on largely down the Ohio River. With the end of the war, most of the river trade was seized by the railways and Cincinnati now found her rival Louisville in control of the only railroad which ran into the heart of the South, the Louisville and Nashville, and which Louisville was not disposed to let her rival use. As a last resort in her effort to reach the South, Cincinnati decided to construct on her own account a railroad to Chattanooga. She secured a charter from the Ohio legislature in 1869, but she must get the right of way from Kentucky and Tennessee. Tennessee immediately complied (1870), but the Kentucky legislature, dominated by Louisville, twice refused (1870 and 1871). A threat by Congress to grant the right of way led Kentucky to comply in 1872. The next year Cincinnati began constructing the road and finished it in 1880 at a cost of $28,000,000. The city not being prepared to operate its railroad leased it to the Cincinnati, New Orleans, and Texas Pacific Company. Now for the first time the heart of the great Appalachian barrier had been pierced. This road not only gave Cincinnati a great share of the Southern trade, but it also reduced freight rates to the Middle West as much as 20 per cent.[10]

At the same time that the South was trying to cross the mountain ramparts into the Middle West, it had another equally important trade trend to serve and promote—to connect by direct lines New Orleans and the South Atlantic with New York and the East. In ante-bellum times Southeast Virginia, North Carolina, and South Carolina had been by-passed by the railway lines running from Richmond and Lynchburg through East Tennessee to Chattanooga and Atlanta, or left aside on the other extreme by the roundabout route through Wilmington or Charlotte to Columbia and Augusta and on to Atlanta. The heart of this great region should now be pierced, and this was done in 1873 by the Atlanta and Richmond Air Line connecting Atlanta and Charlotte and by a consolidation of existing roads. At Atlanta, "a perfect crow's foot of railroads," connections could be made with all important South-

10 E. Merton Coulter, *The Cincinnati Southern Railroad and the Struggle for Southern Commerce, 1865–1872* (Chicago, 1922), 40–64.

ern cities, including a direct line to New Orleans in 1870 when the New Orleans and Mobile Railroad was opened.[11]

Texas was long an oasis of railroad development, an empire within herself, unconnected with any outside systems. Houston was the Texas hub, with lines reaching out to Galveston on the south, to Orange on the Sabine River eastward, and to no apparent stopping places to the west and north. The logical outlet for Texas was eastward to New Orleans, but her first rail connections with the outside led her to St. Louis. Not until 1880 was the gap to New Orleans closed by the completion of the Louisiana Western Railroad. In 1880 Texas had more miles of railroad than any other Southern state, and Georgia was a close second. They had respectively 2,700 and 2,500 miles with no other Southern state having as many as 2,000 miles.[12]

This railroad fever was largely a Southern product. It grew up here and was promoted by good and bad means, with Southern capital and Southern men building all the railroads that lay within their power. The political corruption which became so much a part of the railroad story during the period of Radical control merely crept in through the venality of the politicians, and Southerners were no less interested in striking good bargains with them than were Northerners. No Southerner, however, went to the lengths of the speculators who came down from the North, first because Radicals were partial to Northerners and again because Southerners had a keener conscience than did the Northerners who came south for railroad speculations.

Immediately after the war Southern trains with dilapidated equipment dared not try to run faster than a dozen miles an hour, and for their poor accommodations they charged passengers from six to eleven cents a mile. A typical train, a month after the Surrender, consisted of a baggage car, a passenger car, a Negro car,

11 *Railway Monitor* (New York), II (1874), 72, 153; Jones (ed.), *Appletons' Hand-Book of American Travel, Southern Tour*, 156; Montgomery *Alabama State Journal*, December 23, 1870; Trowbridge, *South*, 458–59.

12 Charles S. Potts, *Railroad Transportation in Texas* (Austin, 1909), 22, 38–40; Jones (ed.), *Appletons' Hand-Book of American Travel, Southern Tour*, 208; *Tenth Census, 1880*, IV, *Transportation*, 307; *Railroad Gazette*, IV (1872), 74–75; Galveston *Tri-Weekly News*, August 11, 1865; Carthage *Panola Watchman*, August 18, 1875; Houston *Daily Telegraph*, January 6, 1872.

and a freight car or two. The Negro car was attached next to the engine and was likely a freight car supplied with plank benches. Any white passengers who cared to smoke must retire to this Negro car. The locomotives were wood burners, and whenever the supply of fuel ran low they stopped at woodyards, which grew up anywhere along the track, and waited for slow Negro workmen to supply a new load. Negroes might act as brakemen on the trains, and the custom grew up for them also to serve as firemen. The conductor was the most important man, and his correct title was "captain." For the convenience of passengers, trains stopped at mealtimes at designated stations where food was served. Measured by modern standards railway travel was exceedingly inconvenient; but for the Negroes, even with the poorer accommodations they received, it was an experience greatly enjoyed, for never before had they been allowed to ride on the cars at will. Only after Radical tutelage in equal rights for the races, and after Negroes had become rulers, were complaints heard from them. Negroes of importance demanded the right to ride in sleeping cars, and some railroads acceded to the point of allowing them in one end of a car. They also objected to being excluded from the railway restaurants, for when traveling they were "often made sick from hunger." [13]

The gauges of railway tracks, though they were hit upon without any scientific investigation, were long a subject of discussion. In England they had varied from 7 feet to 4 feet 8½ inches, but the latter came to be the standard there, and it was generally adopted in the North. In the South there was great variety, with 5 feet coming to be the Southern standard so far as one existed. In 1880, 77 per cent of Southern railway mileage was of this gauge.[14] For a few years following the war many Southerners advocated a narrow gauge of 3 feet, basing their argument on the cheapness. It was claimed that this gauge could be built for $4,000 a mile whereas the wider gauge cost $15,000. Also, some Southerners who were attracted by the English compartment style of passenger cars,

13 Kennaway, *On Sherman's Track*, 18, 105; Somers, *Southern States since the War*, 82, 83; King, *Great South*, 377, 580; Andrews, *South since the War*, 108, 201; Atlanta *Christian Index*, May 20, 1875; Macon *American Union*, January 11, 1872.
14 *Tenth Census, 1880*, IV, *Transportation*, 300.

and who believed that American railroads should adopt that arrangement, argued that the 3-foot gauge would best serve this change.

Most American railroads were originally constructed as local enterprises, to serve primarily local interests. Only occasionally did there appear farsighted men like Calhoun, with visions of the important part railroads would play in sectional and national developments, commercial as well as political and social. Southern railroads at the end of the war were still local in their interests and organization, but immediately ideas of making them serve larger purposes gained strength. Duff Green had hazy schemes of consolidations which he never followed to any practical conclusion, and most people who were forced to travel far in the South saw, amidst the inconveniences involved in the constant changing of trains and the buying of new tickets, the great advantages that could be served by combining the railways. Of course, as long as there was no uniform gauge there would always be inconvenience to the traveler, and much more important disadvantages to freight traffic.

Ultimately the South adopted the Northern gauge of 4 feet 8½ inches, but in the meantime freight was either loaded from one car to another, or the whole car was lifted from one truck to another, when freight must be carried over roads of different gauges. The first scheme short of actual consolidation through ownership or lease, designed to hasten freight along its route, was the development of agreements among railroads to allow specially marked cars to pass over their lines. The Green Line was the first such organization to make its appearance. The cars were painted green and all lines over which these cars ran owned some of them. For pulling cars not their own, railways charged a fixed rate. A variation of the Green Line system led to the organization of a separate company which owned the cars and paid the railroads for pulling them. As early as 1868 Green Line cars were running from the Middle Western cities as far as Montgomery, and soon thereafter they were to be seen throughout the South. Before this system had been developed a shipment of freight from St. Louis to Augusta was transferred from one car to another four times; now, by merely lifting the car from one set of trucks to another where there was a change in gauge, there was no transfer required. To serve the fruit and vegetable shippers who were beginning to supply the Northern markets, either the railways or separate companies ran refrigerator and ventilated cars. The best-known of these lines was the Atlantic Coast Dispatch, organized in 1887.[15]

At the outbreak of the Civil War the Adams Express Company retired from the Southern field, leaving all such business south of the Potomac River to the Southern Express Company, which was chartered at that time. This company continued through and after the war, and held a virtual monopoly on hauling small packages and highly valuable articles. In Texas it operated under the name of the Texas Express Company. Henry B. Plant, later to become interested in railroads in Florida, became its president and established headquarters in Augusta. Railroads made contracts with this company whereby they furnished car space and took their recompense by various methods. The Mobile and Ohio provided a car for $150 a day; the Selma and Greensboro rented part of a baggage car for $150 a month; the Nashville, Chattanooga, and St. Louis charged fifty cents per 100 pounds per 100 miles; the Savannah, Florida, and Western took half the net earnings; and so on.[16]

To speed the traveler in comfort George Pullman invented in 1864 a sleeping car, which soon made its way into the South. Before the end of the decade Pullman cars were running over the principal Southern railroads, all owned by the Pullman Palace Car Company, which paid the railroads three cents a mile for pulling each car. This company enjoyed a monopoly of the business. Like the Green Line cars the Pullmans were so constructed that they could be lifted from one set of trucks to another, when gauge variation made it necessary. In 1871 a passenger could board a

15 Green, "Duff Green," *loc. cit.*, 41–42; Trowbridge, *South*, 234; *De Bow's Review*, V (1868), 610; *Plantation*, III (1872), 503; Dozier, *Atlantic Coast Line Railroad*, 124.

16 George H. Smyth, *The Life of Henry Bradley Plant, Founder and President of the Plant System of Railroads and Steamships and Also of the Southern Express Company* (New York, 1898), 233–34; Alexander L. Stimson, *History of the Express Business; Including the Origin of the Railway System in America, and the Relation of Both to the Increase of New Settlements and the Prosperity of Cities in the United States* (New York, 1881), 169–78; *Tenth Census, 1880*, IV, *Transportation*, 391–93.

Pullman in New Orleans and continue in the same car to New York.[17] The sleeping car was a great attraction and object of wonderment, with its mirrors and curtains and other ornate furnishings. One Southern editor having made his first trip on a sleeper advised his readers that if they had never taken "a 'snooze' on a Sleeping Car you ought by all means to go somewhere some night just to 'get to try it on,' " and another said that he was contemplating seeking permanent board and lodging on one.[18]

The financial weakness of Southern railroads offered an inviting field to Northern railroad capitalists to continue in the South the work of combining railroads which they had been carrying forward elsewhere. In 1871 a group representing capitalistic interests in Baltimore, New York, Philadelphia, and Liverpool secured from Pennsylvania a charter incorporating the Southern Railroad and Securities Company, for the purpose of buying control of Southern railroads. Buying up securities at about half face value, before the end of the year they had achieved a far-flung combination of these railroads, controlling 1,425 miles through purchase and 363 miles through lease. The fingers of this system with Richmond as a center reached far into the South. They controlled the route down the Atlantic seaboard to Weldon, Wilmington, Charleston, and on to Columbia and Augusta; to the westward their power extended all the way to Mobile, running down through Danville, Greensboro, Charlotte, Atlanta, and Montgomery; and they brought under their domination an interior route leading to Bristol, Knoxville, Chattanooga, and Memphis. By securing in 1872 the Memphis and Charleston, running from Chattanooga to Memphis, they became rivals of Mahone's Atlantic, Mississippi, and Ohio Railroad in its efforts to reach the Mississippi, and they also developed hostilities with the Baltimore and Ohio. In 1872 this Securities Company, in order to reach the South Atlantic, laid its plans to capture the Central of Georgia and the Georgia Railroad as well as to extend its tentacles into other quarters. Through simplifying schedules and connections it brought Atlanta and Baltimore within twenty-four hours of each other and helped many other lines of

17 Andrews, *South since the War*, 109; *Railroad Gazette*, III (1871), 39.
18 Dalton *North Georgia Citizen*, May 6, 1869; Greensboro *Herald*, March 25, 1869.

travel, but in so doing it roused up suspicions and hatreds.[19] It was a "cormorant monopoly," which would ruin whatever it touched, complained a Georgian.[20] Another Southerner warned, "There is a grand scheme now on foot at the North to destroy the present commercial centers of the South and to make the Southern Railroads tributary to the commercial cities of the North." [21] The Panic of 1873 came to the rescue of the enemies of this combination by smashing it. In disentangling itself from its obligations, the Securities Company ceded to the Pennsylvania Railroad Company, which was heavily interested, the Richmond and Danville Railroad and the Atlanta and Richmond Air Line, keeping for itself the Atlantic seaboard route. The Pennsylvania Railroad held to its Southern spoils until 1880 when it sold out to the Southern Railway Company.[22]

Panics jar railroad systems to pieces as well as throw individual railroads into bankruptcy and make it easy for new combinations to form. The Panic of 1873 helped the Louisville and Nashville to extend its dominions and incidentally it led to the organization of the Southern Railway Company some years later. Also, it opened the way for Northern railroad interests to secure control of many Southern lines. In another field of railway development the Panic of 1873 had an immediate effect on the South opposite to that on the North. Instead of leading to rate wars and cutthroat competition as in the North, it brought about a unique development, later to be adopted by the whole country and continued until ultimately suppressed by laws and prosecutions. This was the freight pool. In 1873 the principal Southern railroads formed what they called the Southern Railway and Steamship Association to guard its members against ruinous competition. This association was strengthened two years later, and Albert Fink, a railroad wizard of Louisville and Nashville background, was made its central agent. With headquar-

[19] Howard W. Schotter, *The Growth and Development of the Pennsylvania Railroad Company* (Philadelphia, 1927), 110–11; *Railroad Gazette*, III (1871), 387; *ibid.*, IV (1872), 41; Elberton *Gazette*, November 29, 1871; Marietta *Journal*, January 19, 1872.
[20] Augusta *Weekly Chronicle & Sentinel*, January 10, 1872.
[21] Marietta *Journal*, February 9, 1872.
[22] Schotter, *Pennsylvania Railroad Company*, 110–11.

ters in Atlanta he conducted the pool and prorated all through traffic among the competing railroads.[23]

The operations of this pool soon became common knowledge and led to a hostile reaction against railroads, forcibly directing the attention of the people to the question of high freight rates. For some years Southerners had been complaining about high rates as well as discriminatory rates. In 1866 it cost more to send freight from Memphis to Richmond than to New York City, 300 miles farther away, and Marietta, about twenty-five miles north of Atlanta, paid more for freight from St. Louis than did Atlanta though the freight passed through Marietta in reaching Atlanta. A flour mill moved from Rome, more than fifty miles north of Atlanta, to Atlanta, for the rate on Western wheat was the same to each place, though the wheat might pass through Rome in reaching Atlanta. This move was dictated by the fact that the milling company's chief market was in Atlanta and beyond, and that the rate on a barrel of flour between the two places was fifty-five cents. The effect of this system of rates was to build up some cities at the expense of others, under the justification that certain places had to be established as basing points for rate making. Water competition also played havoc with what inland cities considered just rates. In addition to suffering discriminatory rates between various cities within her own limits or between Southern and Northern cities, the South was forced to pay rates averaging 50 per cent higher than in the North. It cost as much to send a pair of pigs from Kentucky to Georgia as from Nebraska to Pennsylvania. As rates must be based largely on the amount of business offered, the South was suffering the penalty of high rates because it had less freight to offer.[24]

Passenger rates were excessively high in the South—just about twice what they were in the North. The ordinary rate was five cents a mile. The Southern railroads drew a Pullman car for two cents

[23] Dozier, *Atlantic Coast Line Railroad,* 139; Slason Thompson, *A Short History of American Railways* (Chicago, 1925), 196; Martin D. Stevers, *Steel Trails: The Epic of the Railroads* (New York, 1933), 340; *Railroad Gazette,* VIII (1876), 151, 152–53; Augusta *Weekly Chronicle & Sentinel,* February 10, 1875.

[24] Rome *Weekly Courier,* August 30, 1876; *Daily Richmond Enquirer,* September 22, 1866; Marietta *Journal,* April 28, 1871; *Plantation,* II (1871), 402, 650.

less per mile than they carried an individual passenger, but it should be remembered that the passenger in a Pullman car paid the railroad for a ticket for car space which the railroad did not own. The Pullman company made its profits from an additional ticket which called for its space at rates of from $2.00 to $3.00 a day.[25] Just as the South had a dearth of freight, she also had a smaller amount of passenger traffic than the North.

Complaining Southerners believed that if the railroads would charge less for freight and for passengers, more of each would develop. People would form the habit of making short trips to towns to trade, a movement that would aid the merchants as well as the railroads. In 1869 the Central of Georgia to give this idea a test reduced its passenger fares one half, if a return ticket were purchased. Hostility to railroads was beginning to find expression by 1870. The opinion was that they should remember that their prosperity and growth depended on what the public had to offer them and "get out of the notion that they are above and beyond the necessity of popular conciliation." In some places railroads cleverly took advantage of their opportunities to conciliate the most powerful and, therefore, the most dangerous element among the discontented: they gave the farmers free transportation to agricultural conventions and made a special rate on fertilizers. This move had its effect in preventing the Southern Grangers from making railroad regulation a political issue, as was done by the Northern Grangers. Nevertheless, by the end of the 1870's Southern legislatures were debating the regulation of railroads.[26]

The improvement of country highways played little part in the Southerner's program of progress; he seemed to be contented with his makeshift roads, cut deep with ruts and almost impassable in the winter for all except light traffic. Yet a few reformers raised their cries: in Arkansas people complained that the roads were so bad that the mails could hardly get through; Virginians in Richmond declared that Henrico County must have the worst roads in the world; and some Georgians wondered why the state govern-

[25] Jones (ed.), *Appletons' Hand-Book of American Travel, Southern Tour,* iv; Macon *Daily Telegraph,* May 16, 1868.

[26] Montgomery *Weekly Advertiser,* September 21, 1869; Macon *Telegraph,* quoted in Montgomery *Weekly Advertiser,* September 21, 1869; *Semi-Annual Bulletin of the Georgia State Agricultural Society* (Atlanta, 1874).

ment might not come to the aid of the country roads as it had done for the railroads. Farmers began to realize that they would save millions of dollars if they had better roads over which to travel to markets. The use of convicts to supplement the scanty work on roads legally required of near-by residents was suggested in the 1870's.[27] This generation was never to know that it would take a motor age to produce good roads.

Nature had done much to promote transportation in the South by providing many navigable rivers which were used extensively in ante-bellum times. This fact, together with the coming of railroads, was the principal reason why the South had never built many canals. There was one canal project, however, which had been agitated for many years and which was carried over into the period after the war, to continue even down into the twentieth century—a ship canal across the northern part of Florida, running either from the St. Marys River or the St. Johns to the Gulf of Mexico. During this period the project never got beyond the agitation stage. Another project, almost as old but less practical, was joining the Tennessee River with the Gulf and the South Atlantic by building a canal from the Big Bend of the Tennessee across Alabama to the Coosa in Georgia, thence to the Chattahoochee above Atlanta, and then across to the Ocmulgee which flows by Macon ultimately forming the Altamaha and debouching into the Atlantic at Darien. The Chattahoochee would lead by Columbus and on to Appalachicola on the Gulf. This was a water version of the Calhoun dream, which engaged some interest in the West as well as in the South. A meeting of the governors of various states was held in Atlanta in 1873 to promote this scheme, but it resulted in nothing more than speeches.

After the war a few steamboats, used principally for taking cotton to market, continued to ply the Southern rivers, but, except on the Mississippi, the day of the river boats was fast passing, both in the South and in the North. With thousands of miles of coastline and some good harbors, the South had long had an inviting

[27] Little Rock Weekly Arkansas Gazette, August 13, 1867; Southern Cultivator, XXXVII (1879), 43–44; Richmond Daily Dispatch, November 18, 1876; Report of the Commissioner of Agriculture, 1867, p. 428; Crawford (Ga.) Oglethorpe Echo, December 10, 1875.

field of marine activities for the investment of its capital as well as for the development of the careers of its people; but following Jefferson's philosophy of the good life which excluded trading and manufacturing, the South devoted both its enthusiasm and its capital to agriculture. Now, with the new day dawning, people began to advocate the abandonment of Jefferson. Why could not Southerners set up steamship lines and become seafaring people like New Englanders? They had shown great skill on the waters in the recent war; they had the tradition of the *Alabama* and of Southern maritime inventive genius shown in ironclad ships and submarines. But having meager capital after the war, the South itself could do little toward setting up new lines or re-establishing old ones; and furthermore Southerners never learned to like the sea. Northern lines and capital were soon serving the South again. William P. Clyde of New York, believing that it was more logical to join the South Atlantic to Cuba directly rather than through New York City, in the early 1870's established a line of steamers from Cedar Keys on the Florida Gulf Coast to Havana, which brought Cuban products into the United States, to be distributed thereafter by rail. Charles Morgan, another New York capitalist, became a significant economic force in the development of the transportation facilities in Louisiana and Texas. He it was who provided for a decade and more before the railroad came the connecting link between the two states. From New Orleans to Brashear City on the Atchafalaya River ran the only railroad which before 1880 helped people or freight to reach Texas. As it was more than 150 miles across trackless swamps and prairies to Orange, the first railway point on the Texas border, Morgan set up a line of steamers from Brashear City to Galveston and made that the main highway between Texas and the rest of the South. In 1877 this steamship line was merged with railroad interests into Morgan's Louisiana and Texas Railroad and Steamship Company, chartered by the Louisiana legislature and capitalized at $10,000,000. In 1880 it owned four steamships plying between New Orleans and New York and fourteen steamers running from Morgan City (old Brashear City) to various Texas ports. In 1872 the Central of Georgia Railroad bought six steamships to be run between Savannah and New York by the Ocean Steamship Company, which the railroad controlled.[28]

The United States government, in the hands of Radical leadership, was much used as an instrument for carrying out the exploitations of Northern capitalists. The South, since it was not sufficiently within the preview of their undertakings, got few of those attentions for which government is instituted among men. This was conspicuously true in harbor improvements in the South, which would draw to the South better steamship service and connections. A half dozen years and more after the war ended there were still wartime obstructions in the mouth of the Savannah River, which greatly retarded the growth of the port of Savannah. The port of Mobile was likewise suffering from the ravages of war, with a situation existing there which led an Englishman to suppose that "the Federal Government, so zealous hitherto in reconstructing the South, would long since [have] effaced these marks of rebellion." [29]

Whether the refusal to improve Southern harbors was designed to delay the development of Southern ocean-going commerce or not, it had that effect, and helped to destroy the resurrected Southern plans of instituting direct trade with Europe. Before the war direct trade had been much discussed with little practical result; now most commercial conventions began a new agitation. Direct commercial connections with European ports would build up importing houses in the South, reduce the cargo rates as the seasonal cotton-exporting vessels would ply regularly and carry cargoes in both directions instead of coming over in ballast, lower railroad rates as the railroads would have a larger and more constant bulk of freight, and lessen the prices of imported goods. New Orleans afforded a striking example of the situation. In 1869–1870 the value of its exports amounted to $107,658,000 while its imports were only $14,992,000. Even such commodities as coffee, sugar, and molasses which should normally enter the United States at New

[28] Little Rock *Arkansas State Gazette*, June 2, 1866; Somers, *Southern States since the War*, 262; *De Bow's Review*, VI (1869), 498–505; Poor, *Railroad Manual, 1880*, pp. 518, 521, 568; Galveston *Commercial Bulletin*, November 23, 1867; King, *Great South*, 101; *Railway Monitor*, I (1873), 120.

[29] Somers, *Southern States since the War*, 181–82.

Orleans now went around to be received at New York, Philadelphia, Boston, and other Northeastern ports.[30]

The neglect by the Federal government of the improvement of the Mississippi River was equally impressive. In ante-bellum times the river had been kept within its proper bounds by levees constructed by the states along or through which it flowed or by individual planters. The neglect of levees during the war or their destruction for military purposes left the Lower Mississippi Valley open to every flood which came rolling down from Pennsylvania to Montana. The states which suffered most were Mississippi, Louisiana, and Arkansas. In Louisiana alone there were 28,800,000 acres subject to overflow, the richest plantation area in the state and the region from which most of the state's revenues came. Every spring there was distress, but in some years the floods became calamities. In 1874 there occurred one of the greatest floods in the history of the lower valley. It inundated many plantations in Arkansas, Tennessee, and Mississippi; in Louisiana it left 25,000 people homeless. Much livestock was drowned throughout the flooded regions.

Immediately after the war people began memorializing Congress to aid in controlling the river, but this body of lawmakers seemed interested only in the political development of the South. It was not an impartial body; it was neither national in its composition nor in its outlook. It passed two kinds of laws, one set for the South and another set for the North. "Why are there bounties for the shipping interest of the East, while the broken levees of the West make a marsh and a wilderness of the finest sugar and cotton lands in the world?" asked the editor of Land We Love.[31] Manifestly it was a national obligation to control the Mississippi. Its floods gathered in a dozen and more states, and it was not to be expected that the lower valley states could act in any unison in levee work (and no other arrangement would be effective); furthermore, the states were so impoverished by war and Radical rule that they could never pay for such a great undertaking. Finally in 1879, when Radicalism had largely faded out, Congress established a Missis-

---

[30] Plantation, III (1872), 153; Somers, Southern States since the War, 75, 201; Elberton Gazette, September 24, 1869; Blake, Mahone, 89.

[31] Land We Love, IV (1867–1868), 358.

sippi River Commission to survey the needs and to set up plans for levees. Federal control of the Mississippi floods was assumed at this time and from now on became a major interest of the government in Washington.

Flood control not only helped agriculture but it also aided the navigation of the river. A greater impediment, however, to Mississippi River navigation than floods was the formation of mud bars off the mouths of the river, to such an extent that entrance by large ships became impossible. Constant dredging was necessary to keep a channel open and the expense was great. As a solution engineers had considered cutting a canal beginning near Fort St. Philip and leading southeastward to deep water in the Gulf. Before the war Louisiana had sought without success the aid of Congress in carrying out such a project, the cost of which was estimated to be $8,000,000. With unobstructed navigation to the Gulf the trade of New Orleans would be quadrupled. In 1874 Captain James B. Eads of Indiana, who knew the river from war days when he had constructed ironclad river boats and who had recently completed an iron bridge across the river at St. Louis, laid before Congress a scheme which would keep the mouth of the Mississippi open. He would build jetties out into the Gulf to confine the river current to a narrow channel whose force would cut through the mud banks made by the crosscurrents of the Gulf. In 1875 Congress accepted his plan, agreeing to pay him $500,000 for opening a channel twenty feet deep and promising an equal amount for every additional two feet up to a maximum depth of thirty feet. In 1879 Eads succeeded in opening up a thirty-foot channel to deep water in the Gulf. By bridging the Mississippi he had removed its hazards to land transportation, and by building his jetties he had made it better serve water traffic.[32]

[32] *Tenth Census, 1880*, XIX, *Cities*, Pt. II, 270; King, *Great South*, 77.

CHAPTER XII

CITIES AND FACTORIES

THE breakup of the plantation and the consequent disruption of country life; emancipation, which freed the Negro from the country no less than from his slavery; the resurrection of the ante-bellum movement for manufactories; the building of railroads—all had their effect in turning people from the country into the towns and cities. The South, rural before the war, was to continue so afterwards in comparison with the North, but in comparison with its former self, it was to go far toward urbanization.

For the decade between 1860 and 1870 the population of the whole country increased about 22 per cent and the urban population rose about 50 per cent; but in the South, the urban population increased from about 17 per cent in Louisiana, which represented the smallest gain, to 235 per cent in Arkansas, the greatest. Only in Virginia, North Carolina, South Carolina, Georgia, and Louisiana was the increase less than the national average.[1] In 1880 the number of people living in towns of 4,000 and over (such places being defined by the census as urban) varied from Arkansas with 13,000 to Louisiana with 231,000. The only other states with over 100,000 urban population were Virginia (178,000), Georgia (119,-000), Texas (115,000), and Tennessee (105,000). The number of such towns varied from one in Arkansas to eleven each in Virginia and Texas. Yet Massachusetts had more towns than all the South combined, and its urban population was almost 300,000 more.[2] The percentage of urban population in the South was still very

---

[1] *Southern Magazine,* XV (1874), 109–28. The border states are not included in this study of cities and factories unless specifically mentioned.
[2] *Tenth Census, 1880,* I, *Population,* xxx–xxxi.

252

small, ranging from 1.6 in Arkansas to 25 in Louisiana, where New Orleans threw the picture out of focus. Each of the other states of the Confederacy had less than 11 per cent urban population. The tendency in the South was for small communities to grow up around railroad stations, cotton gins, and crossroads country stores, but not having enough people to entitle them to be considered urban by the census takers. This movement is well illustrated in South Carolina where in 1860 there were 16 towns and trading places, according to Southern standards, 33 in 1870, and 493 in 1880; but only three of these places in the last-named year had as many as 4,000 people.[3]

Many Southern towns had a character and personality that set them apart not only from Northern cities but also from one another. New Orleans was the largest, most famous, and most colorful in its history and composition. It increased in population from 168,600 in 1860 to 216,000 in 1880. Though suffering much from the transfer of commerce from rivers to railroads and the diversion of freight from the interior to Eastern ports instead of down the Mississippi, New Orleans continued to have after the war an annual commerce amounting to about $500,000,000 in the 1870's. In 1880 a third of all Southern cotton exports went through this port, and here was the largest customhouse in the country which was also the second-largest building in the United States. New Orleans was not only the greatest port in the South, but was also the largest manufacturing city. It had 915 establishments with a capital investment of $8,500,000, an annual pay roll of $3,717,000, and an annual output of products valued at $18,808,000. Its greatest industries in the order of the value of their output were crushing cottonseed, cleaning and polishing rice, refining sugar and molasses, turning out the products of foundries and machine shops, and manufacturing men's clothing—each one amounting to more than $1,000,000 annually. In comparison with Middle Western rivals like St. Louis, Louisville, Cincinnati, and Chicago, or with her own ante-bellum promise, New Orleans was suffering hard times. Plagued by war and its aftermath of corruption and by obstructions to the navigation of the Mississippi, New Orleans lost to the upriver cities much of its wholesale trade. In its fight to turn the

3 Simkins and Woody, *South Carolina during Reconstruction*, 277–79.

outlet of Middle Western grain down the river, the Crescent City built a grain elevator with a capacity of 750,000 bushels, but it succeeded in doing little more than rousing the fighting spirit of its rival, Chicago.[4] There was a charm about New Orleans, however, which could not be wrested from it: it had its historic buildings and architecture, its cities of the dead with their white mausoleums, its opera houses and hotels, and the "best restaurants in America" where still lingered "the last remains of the famous creole *cuisine* of ante-war times." [5]

Two other Southern towns, wreathed in the nostalgic past but with widely differing backgrounds, were San Antonio and Charleston. San Antonio, founded two centuries before the pushing Americans came, had its old missions, its Alamo, "the Thermopylae of Texas," its plaza still dominated by Roman Catholic processions, and was "the only town in the United States," according to a Northern traveler, with "a thoroughly European aspect," with its older quarters "like some remote and obscure town in Spain." [6] The population of San Antonio was 8,000 in 1860, increasing to 12,000 by 1870; but it jumped far ahead in the latter part of the 1870's, when the Galveston, Harrisburg, and San Antonio Railroad reached it. By 1880 the population was 20,550. In danger of losing its soul, still it was able to continue "full of interest to the tourist, but to the sons of Texas" it was "almost a shrine; for in its streets" had flowed "again and again the blood of heroes, fighting for home, for liberty, and for independence." [7] San Antonio's greatest industries were flour mills and meal and saddle and harness shops.

"Alas! dear old CHARLESTON! The blight is still upon her. At every step the marks of cruel war. The streets are still unpaved. The wharves are comparatively deserted. There is no life or activity visible." So mused editor De Bow in 1867 when he visited his native state.[8] In the eyes of a resident editor, who saw it every day, "Grim, black, crumbling chimneys, bending and broken walls, shapeless piles of former splendor, are the silent sentinels, the

[4] *Tenth Census, 1880,* XIX, *Cities,* Pt. II, 213, 294–95; *De Bow's Review,* VI (1869), 21–29, 136–38, 355–56; Somers, *Southern States since the War,* 197; King, *Great South,* 51, 58.

[5] Jones (ed.), *Appletons' Hand-Book of American Travel, Southern Tour,* 193.

[6] King, *Great South,* 148.   [7] *Tenth Census, 1880,* XIX, *Cities,* Pt. II, 329.

[8] *De Bow's Review,* III (1867), 216.

speechless witnesses of both glory and ruin." [9] To tourists it left an impression of "retiring respectability" with its noble mansions in "a sort of dingy stateliness." [10] Largely robbed of its wholesale business by the upcountry towns and debased by political corruption, Charleston got its first glimmers of returning prosperity when the near-by phosphate beds began to turn out their rocks to be made into fertilizer. Then its port began to take on life with the exportation of these products, cotton, and naval stores. Carpentering, the lumber industry, and printing afforded its most valuable output. In 1860 it had 40,500 people; by the uncertain Federal census of 1870 it was given 48,900; ten years later it had gained only a thousand people.[11]

Richmond, Atlanta, and Nashville came through the furnace of war to be rejuvenated and made prosperous in the new day. The "burnt district" of Richmond stared at all who came that way in 1865; the next year it was fast disappearing as impressive structures took its place, built with Southern capital. Richmond was in 1880 the second-largest manufacturing city in the South with its 598 establishments, almost $7,000,000 capital investment, and almost $21,000,000 annual output, paying over $3,000,000 in annual wages. Tobacco manufactures were its greatest business, plug and pipe products, snuff, cigars, and cigarettes. Ninety-two establishments with an annual output worth almost $8,000,000 were busily supplying satisfaction for these human tastes. The next greatest industry was flour and grist milling, whose products amounted annually to almost $2,500,000, and whose reputation was world-wide. Brazilians and Australians ate bread made with Gallego flour from Richmond. The third of the three big businesses that made Richmond famous was iron and steel. Of the companies engaged in this undertaking the best known was the Tredegar Iron Works, which made over 2,000 freight cars annually in addition to its many other products. Richmond had a steady growth, from 38,000 in 1860 to 51,000 in 1870 and to 63,600 in 1880. Fifteen years after Appomattox it knew greater prosperity than it had

9 *XIX Century*, I (1869), 65.

10 Jones (ed.), *Appletons' Hand-Book of American Travel, Southern Tour*, 121.

11 *Tenth Census, 1880*, XIX, *Cities*, Pt. II, 95; Jones (ed.), *Appletons' Hand-Book of American Travel, Southern Tour*, 122; Somers, *Southern States since the War*, 46–47.

ever known before.[12] Virginia gentlemen of the old school looked upon this upstart Richmond with sadness; it had sold its old self for a mess of prosperity.

Atlanta had no birthright to lose. Never having been a typically Southern city before the war, it would not become so afterwards, though from the ashes in which Sherman left it, it had an opportunity to start out in any direction. Atlanta leaped out of its ruins as quickly as Richmond, but the force behind it was Northern instead of Southern. It was one of the most talked-about cities in the South and least liked by Georgians. Travelers found nothing Southern in it. It was "modern and unromantic"; brash, brick-built, muddy, and money-mad; "nervous and palpitating"; "an architectural chaos" from center to circumference; with streets that began nowhere and ended everywhere; and with property selling for $40 a front foot.[13] "Chicago in her busiest days could scarcely show such a sight as clamors for observation here," thought one visitor; and a Georgia editor observed of his newly acquired fellow Georgians, "They live fast and they die fast. They make money fast and they spend it fast. They build houses fast and they burn them down fast." Another Georgian felt "Yankee doodle has come to town certain." Even if Atlanta were not Southern, still it had its good points: "Social ostracism or persecution for opinion's sake is almost unknown—a fact that stands out in bold relief against the cloudy social horizon still visible in other sections of our country." A Federal census expert in making the Atlanta report declared, "The growth of the city was marvellous." In 1860 it had 9,500 people; in 1870 there were 21,700; and in 1880 Atlanta had 37,400 people. The city had less than $2,500,000 invested in 196 industrial establishments. Flour and grist mills came first, followed in the order of the value of their output by carpentering, slaughtering and meat packing, lumber working, candymaking, and foundry and machine shop. To a resident such activities apparently did not seem sufficient explanation for the city's growth, for he remarked,

---

12 *Tenth Census, 1880,* XIX, *Cities,* Pt. II, 79, 80, 85; *Scribner's Monthly,* XIV (1877), 303–12; *De Bow's Review,* II (1866), 53.

13 King, *Great South,* 350; Campbell, *White and Black,* 369; Andrews, *South since the War,* 310; Somers, *Southern States since the War,* 93; Charles W. Hubner, "Atlanta," in *Appletons' Journal* (New York, 1872), 378; Kennaway, *On Sherman's Track,* 116.

"What makes Atlanta nobody can tell. Yet Atlanta is made." Really, what made Atlanta was the railroads, which were drawn into a knot here at the southern ramparts of the Appalachian Mountains.[14]

More than twice as old as Atlanta in 1880, Nashville was only slightly more populous; but after the war it had a rapid growth. In 1860 it had 17,000 people; in 1870 its population had increased to 25,800; and in 1880 it reached 43,300. Next to Atlanta it was the most rapidly growing town in the South. Its chief products in the order of their value were flour and meal, carriages and wagons, lumber, furniture, the manufactures of foundry and machine shops, and of printing and publishing houses. Nashville was distinctive as a cultural center and a guidebook declared that its social attractions were "not excelled by those of any city in the South." [15]

Four cities, two large and two small and all of respectable age, which lost in the struggle for population and prosperity, though not permanently, were Mobile, Memphis, Vicksburg, and Beaufort. Surrendering three days after Appomattox, Mobile the next month was devastated over more than a dozen city blocks by a tremendous explosion of ammunition. With its retail trade taken by smaller towns and its wholesale trade captured by larger ones, and with its harbor long blocked by war obstructions, it settled down to a precarious existence. In 1880 it had fewer people than in 1860, dropping from 29,258 to 29,132. Its first port prosperity was reflected in its importation of Brazilian coffee, which increased in the early 1870's from 8,000 to 75,000 bags.[16] Memphis had a career which by 1880 had become as somber as that of Mobile. With a rapidly developing prosperity following the war, this river town had almost doubled its population in 1870 over 1860, increasing from 22,600 to 40,200. It became the greatest inland market for

14 Andrews, *South since the War*, 340; Thompson, *Reconstruction in Georgia*, 333; Sandersville *Central Georgian*, November 21, 1866; Somers, *Southern States since the War*, 96; *Tenth Census, 1880*, XIX, *Cities*, Pt. II, 157; *Plantation*, II (1871) , 265.

15 *Tenth Census, 1880*, XIX, *Cities*, Pt. II, 151; McClure, *South*, 136; Jones (ed.), *Appletons' Hand-Book of American Travel, Southern Tour*, 217.

16 *Southern Magazine*, XIV (1874), 385; *Tenth Census, 1880*, XIX, *Cities*, Pt. II, 191; Jones (ed.), *Appletons' Hand-Book of American Travel, Southern Tour*, 177–79; Somers, *Southern States since the War*, 184; Trowbridge, *South*, 421; King, *Great South*, 325.

cotton in the United States, exporting much of it through Norfolk instead of down the river through New Orleans, and enjoying the advantages of being a port of entry. Then in the 1870's it was visited by a series of yellow fever epidemics, the worst being in 1878 when 5,150 people died, a calamity which scattered its population and scared away its business. Feeling the situation to be hopeless, it induced the Tennessee legislature to strike it out of corporate existence to save itself from being sold for debt, and its legal name now became the "Taxing District" of Shelby County. St. Louis and Atlanta reaped business profits from Memphis' fall.[17] Vicksburg on the high bluffs of the Mississippi, besieged and captured in war and plundered by Radical government in peace, showed a rapid growth in population in the decade of 1860–1870, from 4,500 to 12,400, but declined to 11,800 by 1880.[18] Beaufort, the seat of South Carolina lowland aristocracy before the war, was captured at the outset of the struggle and handed over to the Negroes, who seized its government and occupied its mansions, huddling together "in gorgeous parlors, once decorated with elegant furniture." The beauty of nature was still around, but a visitor in the 1870's declared that "a silence as of the grave reigned everywhere. . . . The whole aspect of the place was that which I afterwards found pervading other South Carolina towns—that of complete prostration, dejection, stagnation." There and thereabouts the Negroes were "cumberers of the soil; their ignorance impedes, their obstinacy throttles." [19]

A group of towns, ranging in population from 7,000 to 31,000—respectable in size according to Southern standards—and regarded as social and trading centers for regions more extensive than those served by country towns, were Wilmington, North Carolina's largest city and chief port; Fayetteville with its woolen mills consuming 3,000 pounds a week; Columbia, gradually rising from its ashes; Macon in the heart of Georgia; Augusta, partaking of some pros-

17 Tenth Census, 1880, XIX, Cities, Pt. II, 140, 142–43; Fernandina Florida Mirror, August 2, 1879; Gerald M. Capers, Jr., "Yellow Fever in Memphis in the 1870's," in Mississippi Valley Historical Review, XXIV (1937–1938), 483–502; Dennis A. Quinn, Heroes and Heroines of Memphis, or Reminiscences of the Yellow Fever Epidemics that Afflicted the City of Memphis during the Autumn Months of 1873, 1878, and 1879 (Providence, 1887), passim.

18 Tenth Census, 1880, XIX, Cities, Pt. II, 209.   19 King, Great South, 425–28.

perity brought by its cotton mills and tobacco factories; Savannah, steadily expanding as a port; Pensacola, consumed by fire in 1880; and Montgomery, of historical fame. All had a steady growth after the war.[20]

Towns west of the Mississippi, especially in Texas, grew fast. Shreveport, though in Louisiana, had close relations with Texas, promoted by wagon trains before the coming of railroads and enjoying its first railroad experiences when the road to Marshall, Texas, was completed. Retarded by a yellow fever epidemic in 1873, still Shreveport in 1880 was almost four times its size in 1860, increasing from 2,100 to 8,000. Little Rock, the only town in Arkansas in 1880 according to census standards, grew from 2,700 in 1860 to 13,100 in 1880. Texas developed towns rapidly. In 1880 the largest town in the state was Galveston with its 22,200 people, the gateway to the world beyond and the chief port of entry. Houston with its 16,500 people was the railroad center of the state; Austin, the capital, was growing fast with many newcomers from the older parts of the South; and Dallas was fast becoming the metropolis of North Texas. In 1872 Dallas was a village of about 1,500 people, too small to have been noticed by the census in 1870; in 1880 it had 10,300 people, "passing from a quiet village to a thriving city." It grew "like an enchanted castle in a fairy tale." It was made by the railroads, just as was Denison near the Red River, one year a wilderness and the next, after the arrival of the Houston and Texas Central Railroad, a town of 4,500.[21]

A dozen other Southern towns became significant for their quick growth and for their special industrial activities. First among those that tobacco made was Durham which in turn made the Bull the symbol of pipe and cigarette tobacco all over the world. Previous to this time no trademark had ever been pushed as far or as fast. It was peppered over America, it was plastered on the rocks of the South Pacific, it desecrated the pyramids of Egypt. Bull Durham tobacco was recommended by Alexander H. Stephens, who

20 *Tenth Census, 1880*, XIX, *Cities*, Pt. II, 93, 105, 163, 169, 173, 185-86, 199; *American Farmer*, I (1867), 247; *Plantation*, I (1870), 280–81; King, *Great South*, 472.

21 *Tenth Census, 1880*, XIX, *Cities*, Pt. II, 211, 296, 298, 301, 311, 312, 315, 317, 323; King, *Great South*, 125; Jones (ed.) *Appletons' Hand-Book of American Travel, Southern Tour*, 208.

probably never knew the taste of tobacco throughout his life; visitors of Lord Tennyson and of Thomas Carlyle reported finding them enjoying the aromas of Bull Durham; the Philadelphia Centennial gave it a gold medal. William T. Blackwell, a North Carolina country boy, started the business and devised the trademark; but Washington Duke, another country boy who came to the village of Durham Station after the Surrender with fifty cents which he had got from a Yankee for a $5.00 Confederate note, soon gained control of the Durham tobacco business. Durham tobacco was first advertised for pipes, but with cigarettes coming into style shortly after the war, it was soon recommended as equally fine for that type of smoking, though a rhymster in 1865 doubted that there was much satisfaction to be got out of them:

> "Oh, little tantalizing twists—
> Unsatisfying things!
> Six whifs and one no more exists—
> Oft five this ending brings."

"No town in North Carolina was ever known to spring up so quickly and grow so rapidly" as Durham, said a proud Tarheel. In addition to Richmond two Virginia towns, rivals in the tobacco business, were Lynchburg with 35 factories manufacturing almost 11,000,000 pounds in 1872, and Petersburg with not only its tobacco factories and Negro laborers but also its cotton mills in which no Negro ever worked. Norfolk, which promoted its railroad connections southward to dominate eastern North Carolina and westward as far as the Mississippi to bring in cotton, was Virginia's chief port.[22]

Towns with "Yankee" stamped on them as boldly as on Atlanta were Chattanooga, Birmingham, Anniston, Jacksonville, and Key West. Chattanooga, which grew from a village of 2,500 in 1860 to 12,800 in 1880, was largely promoted by the Federal soldiers who fought around it, subdued it, liked it, and either remained or returned after the war. With its iron and steel business it claimed to be the Pittsburgh of the South. Birmingham, destined to become

22 William K. Boyd, *The Story of Durham, City of the New South* (Durham, 1925), 59, 67, 68, 87; Raleigh *Daily Sentinel*, July 3, 1874; *Tenth Census, 1880*, XIX, *Cities*, Pt. II, 60; King, *Great South*, 556, 582, 591; Wertenbaker, *Norfolk*, 299-304.

a greater Pittsburgh than Chattanooga, was developed largely by land companies interested in the underlying coal and iron. Eighteen months after the first house was erected, Birmingham claimed 4,000 people. Anniston, near by, a model town made to order in 1875, with churches, schools, factories, business houses, and residences, was owned by the Woodstock Iron Company. Jacksonville was Yankee not in origin but by adoption after the war; in addition to ocean trade, it was interested in the lumber business and cigar making. Exotic Key West, southernmost of American cities, reared its reefs in the paths of ocean steamers and profited $200,000 a year from salvaging their wreckage. It made 40,000 "choice Havana cigars per day," evaporated 30,000 bushels of salt annually, and dealt in sea turtles, sponges, and tropical fruits.[23]

Of Mississippi's three chief cities, on almost the same parallel of latitude, Vicksburg, Jackson, and Meridian, the last-named gave promise of quicker recovery after the war, surviving fires and yellow fever, and nursed along by the railroads which crossed there. In Georgia, Columbus, in about the same latitude as the Mississippi cities, gave promise of becoming the greatest cotton manufacturing city in the state and impressed a traveler "more favorably than any other manufacturing town" he had seen in the South. Asheville began to grow and prosper with the coming of railroads and summer visitors.[24]

An important element aiding the growth of Southern cities and contributing to their problems was the Negroes. Many who first went to the towns after their freedom later drifted back to the country, but a large number remained permanently. According to the undependable Census of 1870, thirty-five Virginia towns showed an increase over 1860, with the Negroes making up 25,834 and the whites 705 of that increase. By 1880 among the towns having a majority of colored people were Wilmington, Charleston, Columbia, Macon, Savannah, Montgomery, Selma, and Shreveport. The Negroes were segregated on the edges, in back alleys, along railroad tracks, and in hollows, forming communities which were given such

23 Tenth Census, 1880, XIX, Cities, Pt. II, 135; King, Great South, 336–37, 530, 534; Hillyard, New South, 252–71; Tenth Census, 1880, XIX, Cities, Pt. II, 181–82; Jones (ed.), Appletons' Hand-Book of American Travel, Southern Tour, 174.
24 King, Great South, 312, 373, 505.

names as "Black Smoky," "Black Centre," and "Dark Town." In some cities a street might fall wholly into their possession, such as Beale Street in Memphis or Cotton Row in Macon. Real estate speculators bought tracts of land on the edges of towns, cut them up into small lots, and sold them to Negroes; or they themselves might build shanties and rent them. Negro tenements were generally crowded, unsanitary, and crime ridden. In Nashville one nine-room house afforded shelter for forty Negroes. An observer declared in 1873 that a majority of the Negroes in South Carolina, in town and country, lived "in huts and hovels, so poor that their total destruction from one end of the State to the other would not diminish the taxable value of the State one-tenth of one per cent" and that they were "worth no more than so many dog kennels or pig sties." Negroes formed towns of their own at Hampton, Virginia, and James City, on the outskirts of Newbern, North Carolina. They greatly increased crime and added much to the cost of administering justice. Their most frequent crimes were murder, fighting, theft, drunkenness, vagrancy, and using obscene language. On certain occasions curfew laws were invoked.[25]

Many of the services required by advancing civilization for people huddled together in cities began first to make their appearance in Southern cities after the war. Measures for promoting public health were among the most pressing needs. Yellow fever, first appearing in America in 1796, became periodically a scourge to the cities of the Lower South. New Orleans was most grievously affected by it, losing, it has been estimated, 100,000 people by 1880. Negroes were almost immune. A Louisianian declared in 1880, "But for this one great drawback to its progress, I think I am warranted in the belief that New Orleans, at this hour, might aspire to be considered the first commercial city of the Union. This is not the language of exaggeration. It is the natural deduction of facts." [26] The great epidemic of 1878, which spread up the Missis-

25 Wesley, *Negro Labor in the United States,* 136; Gerald M. Capers, Jr., *Biography of a River Town; Memphis, its Heroic Age* (Chapel Hill, 1939), 163; Nashville *Republican Banner,* April 25, 1866; Taylor, *Negro in Tennessee,* 32, 159; Nordhoff, *Cotton States,* 71; Columbus (Miss.) *Press,* December 20, 1873; *Daily Columbus Enquirer,* December 21, 1865; May 13, July 13, 1866; Trowbridge, *South,* 219–23; Wertenbaker, *Norfolk,* 254–98; Americus *Tri-Weekly Sumter Republican,* December 23, 1865.
26 *Tenth Census, 1880,* XIX, *Cities,* Pt. II, 286.

sippi Valley as far as Hickman, Kentucky, with towns everywhere setting up their "shotgun quarantines," led New Orleans to organize its Auxiliary Sanitary Association, induced the movement for a national board of health, and caused practically all Southern cities to set up boards of health or strengthen those already in existence. Another disease less deadly than yellow fever, though painful and debilitating, and found only in the South, was dengue fever, called by the Negroes "dandy-fever" and commonly known as "break-bone fever."

In furtherance of good health many cities were beginning by 1880 to put in effective sewers to supplant open gutters and inefficient underground drains. Most populated places which had got beyond the point of being content to be called villages no longer depended on a town pump; practically all cities had waterworks by 1880, with many of them set up since the war. Few cities had many streets paved; a considerable number had none. Savannah streets were long famous for their black sand; Galvestonians called Houstonians mud turtles on account of their muddy streets, and the latter replied by calling their rivals sandlappers. The largest cities immediately after the war built street railways, with the cars drawn by horses—Charleston in 1866, Augusta in 1867, Atlanta in 1869, Norfolk in 1870, and so on.[27]

Voluntary fire departments had existed in all cities in antebellum times, but after the war many cities took over fire control as a function of government, supplying new engines and paying the firemen. Firemen's tournaments now became familiar and spectacular sights, as representatives from many cities met and the company that squirted water farthest and quickest won the prize. All cities had gaslights, most of them having acquired this convenience before the war, and by 1880 they were beginning to consider the possibilities of the electric light. Every city had paid police forces, increasing their number and training them better after the influx of Negroes; improved street lighting made their night work more effective. City governments were run by mayors and councils, who during the period of Radical rule were often interfered with by military commanders, assistant commissioners of the Freedmen's Bureau, and other instruments of the Radical regime. Governor

[27] Atlanta *Constitution*, January 28, 1872; King, *Great South*, 104, 362.

Brownlow of Tennessee got control of the police forces of Memphis, Nashville, and Chattanooga. Negroes never became mayors, but they sat in the councils of various cities; Wilmington ousted them from control of her council by gerrymandering them into one ward containing twice as many people as the two white wards combined.[28]

Innovations coming after the war and receiving much comment were soda water and English sparrows. The new drink, though not entirely unknown before the war, was reputed to be a New York invention and was a hot weather beverage to be taken only from May to October. Drugstores served it.[29] The new bird was brought from England a year or two after the war and turned loose in the parks of New York City to eat the worms on the trees. These sparrows increased to an astonishing degree and spread in an amazingly short time to the cities everywhere—they were not country birds —and became the most evident and blatant residents of the streets and of the eaves and gutters of buildings. At first it was believed that they would rid the nation of its insect pests and afford a considerable part of the food supply, for were they not good to eat? Two pairs of these John Bull immigrants were set loose in Richmond and within a short time, according to a city editor, they "have so multiplied that they are everywhere. In and out, and out and in they go, and over and under, and all around." They built their nests wherever their fancy or instinct directed. The Richmond editor looking at the equestrian statue of George Washington, saw the "poor horse's mouth . . . stopped up and so . . . [were] his nostrils. The fact is curious, and it is funny to see both Washington and Jefferson, like lunatics, carrying hay in their pockets." [30] In fact, it turned out in no great length of time that the English sparrow was a scavenger, like the wise American buzzards which according to tradition sat on the comb of the roof of the Charleston

28 Augusta *Weekly Chronicle & Sentinel*, May 14, 1873; Greenville *Enterprise and Mountaineer*, October 29, 1879; Fleming, *Civil War and Reconstruction in Alabama*, 430, 481–82; James W. Patton, *Unionism and Reconstruction in Tennessee, 1860–1869* (Chapel Hill, 1934), 227; Coulter, *William G. Brownlow*, 342–43; King, *Great South*, 369, 580; William A. Mabry, "The Negro in North Carolina Politics since Reconstruction," in Trinity College Historical Society *Papers* (Durham, 1897–), Ser. XXIII (1940), 18.

29 Nashville *Republican Banner*, July 18, 1866; Reid, *Southern Tour*, 136; Somers, *Southern States since the War*, 246.

30 Richmond *Daily Dispatch*, June 4, 14, 1877.

market [31] every day except Sunday—for there were no scraps on that day.

The growth of manufactories in the cities was in part an answer to the campaign which the South resurrected after the war to diversify its activities. There had been some success in ante-bellum times in setting up factories, but not the fruition of the hopes of men like William Gregg, who spent his life running cotton mills and advocating more of them. Gregg had been unable to jar the South out of its restrictive agricultural philosophy of the good life, but in 1865 there seemed to be good reason to believe that the war had done so. "With the emancipation of the slaves, agriculture ceases to be the all absorbing pursuit," said a Georgia editor. "Manufacturers must take their proper position, and, this fact once thoroughly comprehended, let the grand Anvil Chorus of a thousand sturdy hammers awaken the highway and the by-way with resounding clamor." [32]

Just as cotton had long been synonymous with South, now cotton mills offered the least break with that tradition, and so the South centered its greatest factory efforts on this departure. The new cotton industrialists compiled a thousand and one reasons why the South should manufacture its cotton. An early argument was the relief cotton mills would give the widows and orphans of the war, by affording them jobs. Thus was Southern patriotism joined with relief and prosperity. A Georgian declared that his state would probably spend $300,000 for relief in the year 1866. How much better it would be to appropriate this money to aid in setting up half a dozen cotton mills where the unfortunate could earn a living! Governor Patton of Alabama announced that there were 20,000 widows and 60,000 orphans awaiting jobs in cotton mills in his state. Another humanitarian was sure that the South "must build a poor-house and a prison, or a cotton factory in every county or parish." [33]

Indeed, why should not the state governments aid cotton factories? They had for many years been aiding banks, canals, turn-

[31] Trowbridge, *South,* 513.
[32] Augusta *Weekly Constitutionalist,* December 6, 1865.
[33] Montgomery *Weekly Advertiser,* August 11, 1868; *Daily Columbus Enquirer,* May 25, June 13, 22, 1866; *De Bow's Review,* V (1868), 983.

pikes, and railroads. It was better for the state to supply the capital, unterrified by such terms as state socialism, than to have the South exploited by Northern capital even if it were inclined to come. Though there was no departure from old principles, yet state governments could never be induced to act beyond relieving new cotton mills and other factories from taxation for a period of years, generally ten.

At the time the new industrialists were seeking state aid, they were also carrying on a campaign against impediments set up by the North and the Federal government. During the war it had appeared to Southerners, and to others, also, that Federal armies took special delight in the destruction of cotton mills. An Englishman observed that "one can hardly harmonize the pure antislavery professions of the war party in the North with depredations so systematically directed against establishments employing only free labour." [34] There was a tariff of 40 per cent on cotton-mill machinery which Northern industrials kept up against their would-be Southern rivals —a situation which led a Southerner to think, "This looks very much as if New England were determined to monopolize the manufacture of cotton in the United States, and was determined that the South should do nothing but grow cheap cotton for the benefits of her lords, and pay all the taxes and sustain the credit and finances of the Government, and not be permitted to diversify her pursuits." [35] Some saw in the whole scheme of Radical Reconstruction, Negro suffrage, and other bedevilings of the South, an attempt to make the region so unattractive that no one would go there or send his money. Northerners gave the South advice, kind but unsought, such as this advanced by the Boston *Post:* "Agriculture must be the pursuit of the South for all coming time. Manufactures may prosper to a limited extent, but the men who know her best and have most interest in her future, pin their confidence to her agricultural growth." [36] Edward Atkinson of Boston, industrial statesman, cotton expert, reformer, and a friend of the New South, who did not fear its industrial competition, honestly felt that the South would prosper most if it eschewed cotton mills

[34] Somers, *Southern States since the War,* 136.
[35] Augusta *Weekly Chronicle & Sentinel,* April 13, 1870.
[36] Quoted in Marietta *Journal,* July 31, 1879.

and directed its attentions toward raising better grades of cotton.[37]

Others of the many reasons why Southerners thought they should manufacture their own cotton were: The South had "a greater water power than any similar area in the world"; having its raw material at the very doors of the factories, it would escape the 70 cents a hundred pounds freight rate from the South to New England; it would also escape various nibblings of middlemen and of insurance agencies; the South had an abundance of cheap labor; the climate afforded the required temperature and humidity and could be freely let into Southern mills through open windows while Massachusetts laboriously manufactured her own climate within the mills; and many Southern cotton farmers living near cotton mills could take their cotton directly to the mills and be relieved of the costs of having it ginned and baled.[38]

This last-named reason suggested the close co-operation that could be built up between Southern cotton mills and the cotton farmers. In fact, the two might well be combined: "The planter begins a process which the manufacturer completes, and both are dependent on aids furnished by mechanic arts. . . . The relation between agriculture, mechanics and manufactures is a natural one— they mutually support each other." So thought Enoch Steadman, a New England Yankee now of long Southern standing. In fact, he thought that Southern planters should organize throughout all the cotton counties and, by combining their resources, set up their own cotton factories.[39] Carrying this idea a step further, Lewis T. Clement, a Tennessee cabinetmaker, patented in 1869 a piece of machinery which was designed to be hooked onto cotton gins to spin the cotton as it came out. A mania for the Clement Attachment grew up. A few were used, but they did not prove a success.[40] Another will-o'-the-wisp was Mendenhall's Improved Self-Acting

---

[37] *Address of Edward Atkinson, 1880,* pp. 4–8.

[38] New York *Journal of Commerce,* quoted in *Weekly Columbus Enquirer,* July 25, 1871; *Tenth Census, 1880,* II, *Manufactures,* 952; *Southern Farm and Home,* III (1872), 257–61.

[39] *Southern Cultivator,* XXVIII (1870), 174–76. See also, *ibid.,* XXXI (1873), 173–74; *Plantation,* II (1871), 1–2.

[40] Harriet L. Herring, "The Clement Attachment: An Episode of Reconstruction Industrial History," in *Journal of Southern History,* IV (1938), 185–98; Somers, *Southern States since the War,* 143; Sandersville *Herald,* November 6, 1879.

Hand and Power Loom, which, it was claimed, a person could operate by turning a crank and thereby make from fifteen to eighty yards of cloth a day. This machine seems never to have made into cloth more yarn than the Clement Attachments were able to spin.

The advantages the South had over New England in running cotton mills did not result in Northern mills moving South, nor did they seem to attract much Northern capital. Yet the fact was undeniable that the South had real advantages. Most Southern mills averaged about 20 per cent annual dividend before the hard times following the Panic of 1873 reduced them to about 8 per cent. During these same hard times some New England mills shut down, and others curtailed their business. Southerners made claims that their profits from manufacturing a bale of cotton varied from $22 to $82 more than New England mills got out of a bale, and that they could manufacture cotton, send it to the North, pay a 5 per cent commission for selling it, and make a good profit competing with Northern products. Yet the tendency was for Southerners to confine their activities to making the kind of cloth that had the greatest market in the South, such as the colored check and striped variety, though they also made finer qualities. The Eagle and Phoenix factory in Columbus, Georgia, won high praise from General Lee for its products when it presented him with some cotton blankets and plaids.[41]

Southern cotton mills were the result of Southern initiative and were financed by Southern capital. Though in five states—Virginia, Florida, Alabama, Louisiana, and Texas—the capital invested in cotton mills was less in 1880 than in 1860, in three others—North Carolina, South Carolina, and Georgia—the increase was large. Georgia's investment of $6,348,000 was more than twice as much as any other Southern state had, but in the number of mills North Carolina stood first with 49. Georgia came next, with 40. Florida had only 1, and Arkansas, Louisiana, and Texas, 2 each. The South had a total of 158 mills, with 533,000 spindles, 11,800 looms, and a total investment of $17,000,000. But Massachusetts alone had

41 Augusta *Weekly Chronicle & Sentinel,* June 1, 1870; July 7, 21, September 1, 1875; King, *Great South,* 335, 373, 728; Montgomery *Weekly Advertiser,* May 18, 1869; January 4, 1870; June 23, 1876; Augusta *Weekly Constitutionalist,* October 20, 1875.

175 mills, with 4,230,000 spindles, 95,300 looms, and a total investment of $72,300,000. Southern cotton mills failed to bring much relief to widows and orphans, for only 9,700 females found jobs there, a majority, however, of the 16,300 cotton-mill workers in 1880. This was about the same ratio of female to male workers as in the New England states. A few model mill villages were being set up in the South, such as the Trion factory in Georgia.[42]

The South turned its attention to many other industrial activities—all indicating "a practical reconstruction which even political fraud and folly cannot much longer even delay in its rapid march." Northerners tainted with corrupt political activities were forgiven if they helped in this practical reconstruction. As for Hannibal I. Kimball, one of them of unsavory reputation in Georgia, "We greatly mistake the people of Georgia if the impulse to enterprise which he has given does not grow and increase and expand, whatever may be Kimball's fate, be it saint or felon." [43]

An industry confined wholly to the South was the cottonseed-oil mills, which numbered 40 in 1880. Though of ante-bellum origin the potentialities in crushing cottonseed were only now coming to be realized. The oil had various uses—for illumination, for lubrication, and for seasoning and other table uses. The cake made excellent cattle feed or it might be used directly as fertilizer. This industry was mainly located in the Lower South.

The South took a small part in almost every kind of manufacturing activity to be found in the nation, even to making paper out of cotton stalks and the waste found around cotton gins, and the concocting of "Sweet Southern Bouquet" perfumery, made of fragrant Southern flowers and dedicated to Southern ladies. It was with great satisfaction that the South freed itself from one Northern monopoly and even invaded the land of its former economic exploiter—ice. Being cut off during the war from the New England ice ponds, the Confederacy manufactured a little ice in

42 *Tenth Census, 1880*, II, *Manufactures*, 542–44, 955; Augusta *Weekly Chronicle & Sentinel*, November 9, 1870; *Weekly Columbus Enquirer*, March 6, 1869; *Southern Magazine*, XIV (1874), 569; *Report of the Commissioner of Agriculture*, 1869, p. 9; Hillyard, *New South*, 32; Rome *Weekly Courier*, September 6, 1876; King, *Great South*, 347.

43 *Southern Magazine*, XIV (1874), 587; Columbus (Ga.) *Sun*, quoted in Marietta *Journal*, November 24, 1871.

Augusta. This business was continued and by 1870 all the principal cities had ice factories. New Orleans was long the principal ice-manufacturing center, having factories that made seventy-two tons daily. Northern ice held on for a few years, but it could not compete with artificial ice, for it customarily sold for $60 a ton whereas Southern ice could be had for $15 and still leave 25 per cent profits for the icemen.[44]

In the forests of the South was wealth of great value, hardly touched in ante-bellum times. In the upcountry the hardwoods held sway; in the great coastal plain from Virginia to Texas the yellow pines, the cypresses, and other coniferous trees "waved in the wind making music of a melancholy sort, an almost unbroken solitude." Beneath were grasses varying from the inedible wire-grass to vegetation on which herds of cattle of uncertain breed and ownership grazed. For the benefit of this precarious wealth in cattle Southerners developed the barbaric custom of burning the forests every spring, making the grass spring up on a cleaner ground but depriving the soil of its rightful sustenance, destroying billions of young trees, killing valuable bird life, and burning down trees notched for naval stores. Burned over by fires purposely set or caused by careless hunters in the year 1880 were 569,000 acres in Alabama, 858,000 in Arkansas, 705,000 in Georgia, 546,000 in North Carolina, 985,000 in Tennessee, 599,000 in Texas, and smaller areas in other states.

The naval stores industry rapidly expanded after the war. In 1880 the Southern pine forests produced 17,565,000 gallons of turpentine, 1,542,000 barrels of rosin, and 90,000 barrels of tar. North Carolina stood first with 6,279,000 gallons of turpentine, 663,000 barrels of rosin, and all the tar except 10,000 barrels. At this time the industry was still young in Mississippi and Louisiana.[45]

The greatest source of wealth derived from Southern forests was

[44] *Tenth Census, 1880*, V, *Cotton Production*, Pt. 1, 55–63; *Southern Magazine*, XIV (1874), 573–74, 586; *De Bow's Review*, VIII (1870), 633; Somers, *Southern States since the War*, 184, 185, 235; Hillyard, *New South*, 34; Americus *Tri-Weekly Sumter Republican*, April 18, 1867; *Plantation*, I (1870), 374–75; II (1871), 265; Macon *American Union*, September 7, 1871; *Daily Columbus Enquirer*, July 20, 1866; Sandersville *Herald*, April 10, 1879.

[45] Tallahassee *Semi-Weekly Floridian*, May 19, 1867; *Tenth Census, 1880*, IX, *Forests*, 491, 517–19, 529–30; Somers, *Southern States since the War*, 33.

in lumbering. Cutting lumber with small sawmills offered an easy road to setting up a modest business and appealed widely to returned Confederates, drawing the contemporary observation that it "was the refuge of our Confederate generals." [46] The lumbering business did not long remain entirely in the hands of small capitalists or continue exclusively in the hands of Southerners. Many of the first Northern immigrants after the war set up sawmills, and in the course of a few years Northern capital in large amounts was invested in Southern timberlands and in cutting lumber. Since transportation facilities were of the first importance, the panoramic pattern of the lumbering regions of the South took on the shape of a band along the coast with long fingers reaching inland along the river courses and railroads. One of the greatest centers of activity was in western Florida and southeastern Alabama along the Perdido, Escambia, Choctawhatchee, and Blackwater rivers, with Pensacola as the outlet. During the year ending August 30, 1870, 403 vessels entered this port to carry to New Orleans, Great Britain, and other parts of the world 60,000,000 feet of sawed lumber and almost 7,000,000 cubic feet of sawed timber. Besides, great quantities of cedar boards were sent to New Jersey for pencil making. Another great producing area was along the Gulf coast of Mississippi, centering at Moss Point, and along the Pearl River. The industry in Georgia reached its greatest height in the Altamaha River Valley with the shipping port at Darien where as many as 60 vessels collected at one time awaiting lumber cargoes. In addition to the large mills, thousands of small mills sprang up throughout the coastal plain and every Southern port exported lumber. In 1880 North Carolina had the largest number of mills, 776, but Georgia produced the greatest quantity of sawed lumber, 451,788,000 board feet. The Southern mills also produced great quantities of shingles, laths, and staves.[47] In Arkansas a considerable business grew up in Osage orange timber, which was used as paving blocks and for wagon hubs and wheels.

[46] *Southern Magazine*, XIV (1874), 582–84.

[47] *Tenth Census, 1880*, IX, *Forests*, 523, 531–32, 544; *Compendium of the Tenth Census, 1880*, II, 1162–63; *De Bow's Review*, II (1866), 201–202; VIII (1870), 462; Leigh, *Ten Years on a Georgia Plantation*, 300; Albert T. Morgan, *Yazoo; or, on the Picket Line of Freedom in the South* (Washington, 1884), 29; Trowbridge, *South*, 297; King, *Great South*, 330.

Some Southern states under Radical rule sold to favored purchasers their public lands at fifty cents an acre or less and made possible the accumulation of many holdings of 100,000 acres and more. In addition to state lands, there were millions of acres of Federal lands in the five states of Florida, Alabama, Mississippi, Louisiana, and Arkansas. By the Congressional enactment of 1866 these lands were closed to all purchasers and could be had only by homesteaders. Believing that this law had been passed more to retard Southern lumbering and prevent competition with the Northern lumber industry than to help prospective settlers, Southerners sought to have it repealed and finally succeeded in 1876, when Radical power was waning. But this repeal was not an unmixed advantage, for Franklin H. Head of Chicago and many other Northern speculators soon bought up vast timber holdings, and in another field did the South contribute to Northern prosperity.[48]

The upland forests, holding the heavy Southern rains in the soil, regulated the flow of streams in their rapid progress to the lowlands and made possible the vast wealth of water power in the Atlantic states. In 1880 Virginia, North Carolina, South Carolina, and Georgia got more than half their power for their manufacturing establishments from the streams.[49]

Under the ground lay mineral wealth which formerly had been more suspected than mined. Most important were coal and iron, centering chiefly in northeastern Alabama around Birmingham, in northwestern Georgia and eastern Tennessee around Chattanooga, and in southwestern Virginia. In 1880 Tennessee stood first in coal, producing 494,000 tons, with Alabama next; in iron ore, Alabama came first with 184,000 tons, with Virginia next. The Birmingham area had the rare combination of coal, iron, and limestone, which began to be developed in the early 1870's and had a rapid growth. Since Alabama iron was tenacious and soft, it was especially good for car wheels; much of it was exported to England. General John T. Wilder, who led Federal forces at the battle of Chickamauga, saw the economic possibilities of the region. At the end of

[48] Gates, "Federal Land Policy in the South," *loc. cit.* 310–25. A few people were beginning to raise a cry against the indiscriminate destruction of forests. They declared that forests might be worth as much as agricultural lands. Marietta *Journal*, March 8, 1872.

[49] *Tenth Census, 1880*, II, *Manufactures*, 495.

the war he returned, organized the Roane Iron Works, and began to make pig iron at Rockwood, Tennessee. There he erected the first coke ovens to be established in the South.[50]

Southerners looked with pride on their mining activities and metallic manufactories and boasted that the growth of cities like Birmingham threatened "to make Pennsylvania tremble for the monopoly" she had so long enjoyed. Some believed they were entering a new kind of prosperity which would be worth more than all their cotton fields. Mountaineers and countrymen throughout the uplands became mining-conscious and many of them made collections of unusual fragments of mother earth to show to the "rock-hunters" as they called the mining prospectors. Copper mines around Ducktown, Tennessee, yielded much copper ore; quarries in Alabama provided limestone not only for the blast furnaces but also for reduction into lime, which would free the South from the Maine monopoly; and mica was known to exist in western North Carolina, but little was mined before 1880. North Carolinians and Georgians were never completely cured of that ante-bellum gold fever which had produced the principal gold supply of the nation before California was opened up. In 1880 North Carolina produced about $119,000 in gold, and Georgia $81,000. Saltville, in southwestern Virginia, with a million-dollar investment, continued to boil its saltwater; and the owners of the fabulous rocksalt mines under Petit Anse Island in Louisiana, after twice failing to mine their wealth, shortly after 1879 let them fall into the hands of a group of New York capitalists.[51]

People organized companies and prospected for petroleum all over the South. Signs were evident but no petroleum was produced before 1880, though a petroleum-burning stove was on exhibit at the New Orleans fair in 1866. While boring for oil at the wrong place in Louisiana, a drill turned up a sulphur deposit and started

[50] *Compendium of the Tenth Census, 1880,* II, 1242; *De Bow's Review,* II (1866), 371; Montgomery *Weekly Advertiser,* June 2, 1875; Nordhoff, *Cotton States,* 94; King, *Great South,* 533, 550; Hillyard, *New South,* 28, 31; Bond, *Negro Education in Alabama,* 127.

[51] *Southern Magazine,* XIV (1874), 576, 577, 581; King, *Great South,* 491, 525, 549, 571, 793; *De Bow's Review,* III (1867), 82–83; Somers, *Southern States since the War,* 173; *Compendium of the Tenth Census, 1880,* II, 1170, 1230–31; *Tenth Census, 1880,* II, *Manufactures,* 1019.

a sulphur business in that state in the early 1870's which led to an outstanding industry.[52]

Most industrial workers in the South were white, but Negroes were generally to be found in tobacco factories, where the more skillful received $1.50 a day. Also, Negroes did the cruder work in many flour mills, especially in Richmond. No Negroes worked in cotton mills. "Put a negro in one of those rooms with a hundred looms, and the noise would put him to sleep," remarked a Southern mill superintendent. Women in cotton mills received about fifty cents a day; men were paid from seventy-five cents to $1.00. Skilled workmen such as carpenters, tinsmiths, and printers received from $2.00 to $5.00 a day, varying with time and place. Industrial workers were too few and varied for a labor consciousness to grow up in the South at this time. The nearest approach was among railroad workers. Trainmen and mechanics on the East Tennessee, Virginia & Georgia Railroad struck in 1873 on account of a 20 per cent reduction in their wages, and forcibly prevented the running of all trains except those carrying the mails; and in 1876 the engineers struck on the Georgia Railroad for higher wages.[53] Industries in the South for many years to come were to be free of the labor troubles that were beginning to beset the North.

[52] *De Bow's Review*, III (1867), 466–67; *American Farmer*, II (1868), 283; Little Rock *Weekly Arkansas Gazette*, November 6, 1866; *Southern Magazine*, XIV (1874), 582; Somers, *Southern States since the War*, 234.

[53] Campbell, *White and Black*, 298, 322; King, *Great South*, 373; Somers, *Southern States since the War*, 77, 91; Augusta *Daily Chronicle & Sentinel*, November 6, 1873; Greensboro *Herald*, November 17, 1876.

CHAPTER XIII

CULTURAL DEVELOPMENTS

THERE had been an ante-bellum Southern culture, recognized by both North and South as peculiar, which grew out of the interaction of soil, climate, occupation, and race. The finer feelings and expressions of life built upon these conditions and attuned to them constituted the people's culture. Marked differences between Northern and Southern cultures had helped to bring on the war, and as the South lost, extreme Northerners felt that the South had forfeited its right to be different and that it must be remade in the New England mold. The South resisted these cultural attacks as strongly as it did attempts at political remaking and ultimately won in both.

The development of Southern culture after the war was less antagonistic than defensive, and as has been true of the rest of the world for a thousand years, it expressed itself more clearly and more voluminously in literary activities than in the more restricted and difficult arts of sculpture, painting, dramatics, and music. Before the war much writing had been expended in the sectional dispute; now the North was to be left out of the picture. The nostalgic ante-bellum days might be recalled but Southerners got from their war years most of their inspiration and their will to write. "We have heroes, and battle-fields, and feats in valor to celebrate in song," wrote a Southerner.[1] Like tempestuous Scotland and Ireland, the South had a rich and peculiar heritage to exploit; a Georgian predicted "that the next quarter of a century will be the Augustan age of Southern Literature."[2] Actuated by these feelings Southern writers could not be otherwise than romanticists; the realism of Radical Reconstruction they had sufficiently with them to behold

---

[1] *Scott's Monthly Magazine*, I (1865–1866), 429–30.   [2] *Ibid.*, I (1865–1866), 63.

and suffer every day. They would combat it, but not base their literature upon it. Only as romanticists could they escape it.

They would be poets, novelists, and historians, and the numbers who tried were great. Not many were successful enough to deserve these titles, but the uncritical literary dabbler James W. Davidson, a South Carolina journalist, listed in his *Living Writers of the South,* published in 1869, 241 names, 166 men and 75 women. Of these, most wrote verse principally; fewer wrote fiction; and still fewer wrote history, biography, and memoirs.[3] Though considering all worthy of being called writers, he divided them into three classes, those having "talents and character," "limited ability," and "none."

The historians or biographers were the first in the field; in fact, James D. McCabe, Jr., immediately after the firing on Fort Sumter began to prepare his book on the war which appeared in 1866 and which he called *Life and Campaigns of General Robert E. Lee.* Lee became the inspiration of a flood of biographies, most of them written after his death in 1870 and by Virginians. Prolific and stormy Edward A. Pollard, Richmond newspaper editor, wrote *Lee and his Generals,* published in 1867; and after Lee's death, there shortly followed the volume by John Esten Cooke, Virginia romanticist, *The Life of Gen. Robert E. Lee* (1871); a year later Emily V. Mason, friend of the Lees, published *Popular Life of General Robert Edward Lee* (1872); in 1874 appeared *Personal Reminiscences, Anecdotes, and Letters of Gen. Robert E. Lee,* by J. William Jones, Baptist minister of Lexington; and *Four Years with General Lee,* by his assistant adjutant general Colonel Walter H. Taylor, was published in 1880.

Various biographers set to work to write the lives and campaigns of other Confederate commanders. Robert L. Dabney wrote the *Life and Campaigns of Lieut. Gen. Thomas J. Jackson* (1866); John Esten Cooke made pen sketches of Virginia cavalry officers in his *Wearing of the Gray* (1867); and William Preston Johnston wrote the *Life of Gen. Albert Sidney Johnston* (1878), his father. The lives of civil officials of the Confederacy attracted less attention, though Richard Malcolm Johnston, Georgia sketch writer,

[3] Davidson, *Living Writers of the South,* iii, iv.

and William H. Browne of Johns Hopkins University, wrote a *Life of Alexander H. Stephens* (1878).

Many commanders, themselves, had a story to tell and some of them wrote of their campaigns, sometimes in such a fashion as to open up old quarrels among themselves or to start new ones. With no thought of controversy, Lee early decided to write an account of his campaigns as a tribute to his men. He gave up the idea because of the difficulty of securing documents, but he advised other commanders to proceed. Jubal A. Early as a sort of defense of his hard luck in his retreat before Sheridan in 1864 came out in 1866 with *Memoir of the Last Year of the War for Independence in the Confederate States of America;* Admiral Raphael Semmes wrote his *Memoir of Service Afloat during the War between the States* (1869) and was applauded by many readers; Joseph E. Johnston was vigorous and unsparing in his *Narrative of Military Operations* (1874), adding to his disesteem of Jefferson Davis; Richard Taylor's *Destruction and Reconstruction* appeared in 1879; and unfortunately John B. Hood, who with his wife and eldest daughter died of yellow fever in 1879, did not live to see the publication of his *Advance and Retreat: Personal Experiences in the United States and Confederate Armies* (1880).[4]

Having lost the war against the Federals, some Confederate commanders and other Southerners who had not been in the army continued hostilities among themselves. Edward A. Pollard was obsessed with the idea that Davis had lost the war, and despite the doubtful honor Pollard gave him in displaying the former President as the frontispiece in his *Lost Cause* (1866), he did not relent in the text. Frank H. Alfriend, of *Southern Literary Messenger* fame, came to Davis' rescue in his *Life of Jefferson Davis* (1868). Pollard was thoroughly hated and despised by many Confederates and by none more than by Daniel H. Hill, who characterized Pollard's *Lost Cause* as "a rare amalgam of venom and ignorance," and added, "There was not a drummer boy or colored servant in Lee's army, who had not more accurate knowledge of the battles of the late war than the bomb-proof, penny-a-liner, who set himself

[4] For a valuable summary of Confederate writings immediately after the war, see Douglas S. Freeman, *The South to Posterity* (New York, 1939).

up as their chronicler." [5] What happened at the Hampton Roads Conference in 1865 got Davis, Robert M. T. Hunter, and others into a controversy; and the contest over Gettysburg, involving James Longstreet, Fitzhugh Lee, Early, and others, was being fought out in the printed page in 1876 as bitterly as the two armies fought on the field of battle in 1863.

To tell their stories and set the world aright on secession and the Confederacy, both President and Vice-President wrote ponderous works, each divided into two volumes. Stephens' *Constitutional View of the Late War between the States* appeared in 1868–1870, written on the unusual pattern of a colloquy between himself and three fictitious persons representing three other points of view. Davis after a long labor produced *The Rise and Fall of the Confederate Government* and miraculously made it almost devoid of interest, little then and even less now.

Wartime diaries, many of them kept by women without thought of publication, did not as a rule reach the printed page until many years after the Surrender. *Diary of a Southern Refugee, During the War*, by "A Lady of Virginia" (Mrs. Judith B. McGuire), appeared in 1867; but the best-known Civil War diary to appear during the Reconstruction times was written by John B. Jones and published in 1866, *A Rebel War Clerk's Diary at the Confederate States Capital*.

Two historians who were able to resist the Civil War as a subject were Charles Étienne Gayarré, proud Louisiana Frenchman, who brought out in 1866 the last volume of his history of Louisiana, *The American Domination*, and Charles C. Jones, Jr., a young Georgia lawyer, who was beginning an impressive list of books and monographs relating to Georgia and ranging from the Indians and the Revolution to the Civil War. Jones became also a favorite orator for Confederate memorial days and reunions.

None of the war books was of sufficient distinction to live long beyond its day or generation or outside the limits of the South. Little more may be said for the writers of fiction. William Gilmore Simms belonged more to the age that was past though he lived

[5] *Land We Love*, VI (1868–1869), 175. Hill bitterly attacked Pollard for his discussion of the famous "lost order" in the Antietam campaign. *Ibid.*, IV (1867–1868), 270-84.

until 1870, and Joel Chandler Harris, Thomas Nelson Page, and George W. Cable were just beginning careers of national importance by 1880. Cable, exploiting the French Creoles before a Northern clientele, wrote his *Grandissimes* in 1880 and succeeded in rousing a loathing disgust and contempt in Gayarré and Paul Hamilton Hayne, who charged him with being a cheap money getter who would belittle the South and degrade himself to please the Yankees.[6] John Esten Cooke through his romantic and sentimental works of fiction gained himself a permanent place in the esteem of the Southerners of his day and thereafter. Among the works he wrote between 1866 and 1880 were *Surry of Eagle's Nest, Fairfax; or, The Master of Greenway Court, Hilt to Hilt,* and *Mohun; or The Last Days of Lee and his Paladins.* In 1871 Richard Malcolm Johnston brought out his *Dukesborough Tales,* sketches relating to the ante-bellum village in Georgia where he was brought up, of such continuing popularity as to be reprinted almost a quarter century later.

In the field of poetry appeared the Southerners who came nearest to greatness. Sidney Lanier and Henry Timrod stand high in the estimation of the judges of good poetry, without reference to geographical limits; and Paul Hamilton Hayne, who always placed his abilities below Timrod's, was far above the level set to distinguish poetry from rhyming lines. Lanier, beginning in Macon and ending in Baltimore, fought a little, taught a little, practiced law a little, fiddled a little, and reached great heights in his poetry. He could not resist his war experiences in "Tiger Lilies," but he got other inspiration in his "Song of the Chattahoochee," and "Marshes of Glynn." In "Corn" he decried cotton and commerce and joined the agricultural reformers. Drawing together the poetry of sound and of words, he wrote, by request, the "Centennial Cantata" for the Philadelphia Centennial of 1876. Tuberculosis ended his career in 1881. Born in Charleston, Timrod died in Columbia in 1867, a casualty of tuberculosis and starvation. War was too rigorous for his weak body and gentle nature, yet he engaged in it for a while.

6 William P. Trent, *Southern Writers: Selections in Prose and Verse* (New York, 1910), 396, 417. See also, Charles R. Anderson, "Charles Gayarré and Paul Hayne: The Last Literary Cavaliers," in Jackson (ed.), *American Studies in Honor of William Kenneth Boyd,* 221–81.

His war background inspired most of his poetry thereafter. His best after the war was his "Ode Sung on the Occasion of Decorating the Graves of the Confederate Dead, at Magnolia Cemetery." Though sneered at by those in the North who could not distinguish between poetry and prejudice, Timrod received high praise from Whittier, Longfellow, Emerson, and other Northern writers.[7] Another South Carolina poet was Paul Hamilton Hayne, also born in Charleston, who moved to a piny-woods cabin in Georgia, almost as rude and secluded as Thoreau's on Walden Pond. Here he eked out a living from his poetry and became an apostle of good will between the sections. Having lost his library in the flames of Sherman's march through South Carolina, William Gilmore Simms contributed little to the impressive list of poems, as well as novels and histories, which he had written in ante-bellum times. He collected an anthology of war poems which appeared in 1866, and which was considered by some critics as not including some of the best and as being inaccurate as to authors in some cases.[8]

In addition to Lanier, Hayne, and Simms a few other Southern poets worthy of the name were Father Abram J. Ryan, cosmopolite but claimed most insistently by Georgia, Francis O. Ticknor of Georgia, Irwin Russell of Mississippi, and Armistead C. Gordon of Virginia. Father Ryan greatly touched the heart of the Confederate South in his "Conquered Banner" and "The Sword of Robert E. Lee"; Ticknor won lasting fame in the South in his "Little Giffen of Tennessee" and was claimed by his contemporary Georgia as the outstanding Southern poet;[9] and Gordon, helping to build up the tradition later carried on by Thomas Nelson Page, wrote poetry and prose in keeping with that point of view. Russell was the poet of promise and considerable performance, cut short when only twenty-five years old, whom the South could least afford to lose. He first brought distinction to Negro dialect poetry and found a ready outlet in *Scribner's Monthly*. His best-known poem is "Christmas-Night in the Quarters." Two other dialect

[7] Rome *Weekly Courier*, April 30, 1873; Jay B. Hubbell (ed.), *The Last Years of Henry Timrod, 1864–1867* (Durham, 1941), 5–6, 111–78.
[8] *Land We Love*, II (1866–1867), 309.
[9] *Scott's Monthly Magazine*, V (1868), 14–17.

poems not as long but just as good are "Nebuchadnezzah" and "Mahsr John."

The number of people who tried to write poetry was great, just as it had been in ante-bellum times. Newspapers and magazines always found a supply of verse on hand waiting to fill a fugitive bit of waste space or to land in the poet's corner. Editor Hill of the *Land We Love* was plagued into keen impatience by importunate versifiers. He announced to them, "We have poetry (?) enough on hand to last us seven years and five months. If, at the end of that period, we are alive and well, we will lift the floodgates and let the deluge in." Receiving too many poems such as "Ode to the Moon," "Lines to Sarah Ann," and "Monody on the death of my favorite tom-tit," he declared "The glad days are those in which no poetry comes to the office. Well do we remember two such days in our two years of editorial life." [10]

The ante-bellum South had had a flair for earthy humorous writing and had done well at it; now in defeat more than at any other time it needed to maintain a sense of humor. A humorist could observe and criticize where a serious writer or editor would get himself suppressed or jailed by the Radicals. It required a more philosophical and detached point of view to do this than most Southerners could lay hold of. Editor Hill thought that Reconstruction had "broken the backbone of fun throughout the Confederacy, so-called"; [11] yet Charles H. Smith, who called himself Bill Arp in his writings, succeeded in amusing his fellow citizens. In 1866 appeared his *Bill Arp, So Called. A Side Show of the Southern Side of the War* with the slogan, "I'm a good Union man, so-called; but I'll bet on Dixie as long as I've got a dollar." Later he wrote many humorous sketches for the newspapers.

Women writers attained prominence among their contemporaries but none became famous enough to be remembered or read long after her death. Too many took the advice often given that women might supplement the family income by becoming authors. Most who wrote for money tried fiction, but many more tried poetry as an outlet for their feelings. Enough got their names

[10] *Land We Love*, IV (1867–1868), 449; VI (1868–1869), 178.
[11] *Ibid.*, IV (1867–1868), 250.

in print to enable Mrs. Mary T. Tardy, who used the pen name Ida Raymond, to compile in two volumes *Southland Writers, Biographical and Critical Sketches of the Living Female Writers of the South, with Extracts from their Writings* (1870). Belying its title, it was uncritical and filled with foolish praise. Emily V. Mason got the urge to collect war poetry even before Simms did, and doing it no better, produced in 1867 *Southern Poems of the War.* She promised to use any profits in educating the orphans of Confederate soldiers. Sallie A. Brock also collected Southern war poetry and made a great jumble of it in *The Southern Amaranth,* sometimes transposing whole stanzas.[12]

A practice frequently resorted to by women was to write under a pen name, sometimes through modesty and sometimes by taking a man's name to hide their sex and escape the discount that went with being a woman. Frances Christine Tiernan, who called herself Christian Reid, wrote novels and in her *Daughter of Bohemia* won Hayne's praise. Being a North Carolinian she wrote in 1876 a travel book which she called *The Land of the Sky,* dealing with the western part of the state; this became a popular expression and stuck to the Asheville region. Elizabeth Jane Poitevant was born on the Pearl River in Mississippi, and being of a pensive nature and loving the outdoors she began to write poetry when she was fourteen. She took the name Pearl Rivers. Attracted by her talent Colonel Alva M. Holbrook, owner of the New Orleans *Picayune,* made her literary editor and married her. On his death in 1876 she became owner of the paper and later married her business manager, George Nicholson. Mary Noailles Murfree grew up in Middle Tennessee, got interested in the mountaineers to the eastward, took the name Charles Egbert Craddock, and began selling stories to Northern magazines under that name.[13]

Cornelia Phillips Spencer became well known, especially in North Carolina, for her poetry, sometimes set to music, and for her *Last Ninety Days of the War in North Carolina* (1866). Mary E. Bryan, born in Florida, educated in Georgia, where she wrote

12 *Southern Magazine,* VIII (1871), 241–50; *Land We Love,* II (1866–1867), 309; VI (1868–1869), 433; *De Bow's Review,* III (1867), 222.

13 *Southern Magazine,* XIV (1874), 653–55; Alderman *et al.* (eds.), *Library of Southern Literature,* IX, 3767–69; XII, 5369–74; Edd W. Parks, *Charles Egbert Craddock (Mary Noailles Murfree)* (Chapel Hill, 1941), 56–111.

a novel when she was fifteen, married a Louisiana planter and after his death edited a newspaper for a short time in Natchitoches. She returned to Florida in 1868 and led some people uncritically to say that she was the most gifted female writer in the South. The poet who won the most solid appreciation of contemporary critics was Margaret J. Preston, Northern born but long wedded to John T. L. Preston, a professor in the Virginia Military Institute. The first collection of her poems was published in 1870 under the title *Old Songs and New*. Five years later *Cartoons* appeared, which critics declared contained some of her best work. The woman of this period to be remembered longest and most widely was Augusta Jane Evans, born in Georgia but associated more with Mobile, marrying in 1868 Colonel Lorenzo M. Wilson. She wrote her first novel when fifteen; in 1866 appeared *St. Elmo*, " 'the most praised, best abused novel ever written,' " read by most of the reading public then and by many people later, leading to a wide use of the term as a name for inns and homes.[14]

It is logical and natural for a people to develop a local patriotism, which may be called provincialism and which constantly tends to lead them into an unreasoning desire to promote their own interests in opposition to those of other people. Being so long an unwilling tributary to the North, Southerners were excessively susceptible to this influence, and they were led by their loyalty to their region to defend anything Southern against anything Northern. Transferred to literary criticism, this habit led to the destruction of valid standards of excellence and to piling up foolish praise upon any production because it was Southern. It was well enough to say, "Our strength is in our pen. Let us then build up a literature that the civilized world will bow in deference to and recognize as the axiom of our greatness," but it was just as well to say, "It is a covert insult to the good sense and literary taste of our people to attempt to foist on them an inferior article, and then, as an extenuation of its inferiority, claim that it belongs to one's section, and must, therefore, be supported."[15] Hayne was outstanding among those Southern critics who did not fear to point out the

14 *Land We Love*, II (1866–1867), 308–309; *Scott's Monthly Magazine*, VI (1868), 717–18; VIII (1869), 590–94; King, *Great South*, 327.
15 Elberton *Gazette*, July 27, 1870; Crawford *Oglethorpe Echo*, February 4, 1875.

inferiority of a literary work, whether Southern or not. He declared that every "half-educated person who has composed and read aloud some crude essay upon nothing in particular before a local literary club or library association, straightway rushes into print" and is proclaimed the originator of a new school of thought. Nothing could stop this growing evil "until our own scholars and thinkers have the manliness and honesty to discourage instead of applauding such manifestations of artistic weakness and artistic platitude as have hitherto been foisted upon us by persons uncalled and unchosen of the muses." [16] In 1873 he thought that there existed "in the entire South, but a single periodical of such reputation for scholarship, judgment and talent, as to entitle its literary and aesthetic views to respect." [17] This periodical, he said, was the *Southern Magazine,* edited in Baltimore by William H. Browne. Hayne was unduly severe in this criticism; the *Southern Review,* edited by Albert T. Bledsoe, upheld as high a standard of excellence.

The severity of Southern criticism had some effect on Southern literature, for one editor recorded it as "a matter of regret that some of our best writers have been assailed with an unsparing, savage criticism that would be often discouraging to the stoutest hearts." [18] Chastened by Southern critics and made strong in adversity by an indomitable will, the South began producing writers and literature as good as any in the country. So thought the editor of *Scribner's Monthly* in 1881, and he added, "It is to the everlasting credit of the Southern people that they so received this terrific discipline that they have emerged from it purified, exalted, catholic, and armed with noble purposes." [19]

In the fight to uphold literary standards some magazines played an active part. The periodical press now, as in ante-bellum times, led an uncertain life. Magazines were born fast and they died fast. Few had come across the great chasm of war. In 1880 the number of monthly magazines ranged from none in Florida to thirty-three in Virginia.[20] James D. B. De Bow, able to bring out only

---

[16] *Southern Magazine,* XIV (1874), 651–55.
[17] Rome *Weekly Courier,* April 30, 1873.
[18] Atlanta *Weekly Sun,* April 29, 1873.   [19] *Scribner's Monthly,* XXII (1881), 786.
[20] *Tenth Census, 1880,* VIII, *Newspaper and Periodical Press,* 170.

two issues of his famous *Review* after the fall of New Orleans, resurrected it in Nashville after the war and issued his first number in January, 1866, now "Devoted to the Restoration of the Southern States and the Development of the Wealth and Resources of the Country." De Bow died in 1867 but the magazine continued under various editors, with a gap between 1870 and 1879, and it finally ended its existence in 1880.[21] Journals born since the war and dead before 1880, attaining a fame that spread beyond their locality, were: *Scott's Monthly Magazine,* set up in Atlanta in December, 1865;[22] the *Land We Love,* which Daniel H. Hill began in Charlotte, in May, 1866, and which he made into a sort of Confederate veterans' mouthpiece though he also advocated a new day for the South brought on by a new kind of education; the *Southern Review,* which Bledsoe set up in Baltimore, in 1867 and made as learned and philosophical as any in the country, though reverentially Southern; the *XIX Century,* set up in Charleston in 1869; and the *Southern Magazine,* beginning in Baltimore in 1871 under Browne's editorship, and declared by *Scott's Monthly Magazine,* agreeing with Hayne, to be "decidedly the most learned, independent, suggestive and original *Quarterly* in the United States."[23] The *Sunny South,* a literary weekly, began in Atlanta in 1874 and immediately became popular with Southerners.

Newspapers from their very nature could uphold no literary standards; that was not their purpose. Their function was to give the news and convert and hold people to political dogmas and parties. For these reasons they had more vitality than magazines and lived to riper old ages. In 1880 there were 1,500 newspapers in the South, many of them originating in ante-bellum times, including 41 that were fifty years old or more. Most of them were weeklies, and the number per state ranged from 45 in Florida to 264 in Texas. As should be expected there was a much larger increase in the decade 1870–1880 than in the preceding one. Statistics for representative states follow:

21 James A. McMillen, *The Works of James D. B. De Bow* (Hattiesburg, Miss., 1940), 15–21.
22 In 1869 the editor of this magazine claimed it was "the OLDEST, LARGEST, and CHEAPEST magazine in the South." *Scott's Monthly Magazine,* VIII (1869), 957–59.
23 Augusta *Weekly Constitutionalist,* December 23, 1868.

Number of newspapers established in

	1860–1870	1870–1880
Alabama	16	53
Georgia	21	118
Texas	31	168
Virginia	35	85 [24]

Practically all newspapers, unlike periodicals, were political and most of them were Democratic. Some Republican papers were established during the war and others immediately on its conclusion by the seizure of newspaper plants by Federal armies and the installation of Northern sympathizers as editors. Sherman when he reached Savannah in 1864 set up a New York *Tribune* correspondent as editor of the Savannah *Republican,* who made it the outstanding Republican paper in the state until his death in 1868. On February 21, 1865, the Federal military authorities seized the Charleston *Courier,* and converted it into a "loyal Union newspaper"; they first made the dateline read "Charleston, S.C., United States of America," and on April 14 used these unbecoming headlines:

THE END OF THE REBELLION

LAUS DEO!

SURRENDER OF GENERAL ROBERT

E. LEE AND THE ENTIRE

ARMY OF NORTHERN

VIRGINIA

Not until the seizure of the Southern state governments by the Radicals did the Republican press begin to thrive, for most white people refused to subscribe for or place advertisements in Republican papers, and most Negroes being unable to read and having nothing to sell were of little help. Now Republican papers came to be subsidized by the Federal government as well as by the Radical state governments, to promote the party as well as to enrich the editors and proprietors. The national authorities farmed out to Radical papers selected laws and resolutions and paid these papers for printing them for many months after they ceased to be

[24] *Tenth Census, 1880,* VIII, *Newspaper and Periodical Press,* 63–64, 170, 182.

news or of any interest. Holden's Raleigh *Tri-Weekly Standard* was still publishing the March 2 Reconstruction Act at the end of the year 1867. Where there was no Radical paper in a county, the officials gave their legal advertising to one in some other county, with the result that some papers carried legal advertisements and notices for a half dozen or more counties. It often happened that a paper would be established and well endowed in this manner. General John Pope, commander of the Third Military District, forbade legal advertisements being given to other than Radical papers.[25] Governors had their proclamations published for many issues to aid these newspapers, some of which they themselves owned. Rufus B. Bullock, Radical governor of Georgia, paid $98,300 for advertising his proclamations during three years in office, whereas for the period 1855 to 1860 the state had spent only $5,000 for such services.[26] Specially favored newspapers received contracts for state printing and reaped rich harvests.

Some of these papers were as well edited and made up as well as their Democratic rivals, while others were firebrands. Practically all of them were edited or owned by Carpetbaggers.[27] One of the most offensive was the *American Union,* edited first in Griffin, Georgia, and then in Macon, by J. Clarke Swayze, who became stranded in the South at the outbreak of the war. By his outrageous attacks on prominent citizens he invited assassination many times, but this remedy was not applied until he used the same style of journalism in Topeka, Kansas, where he moved after the Radicals had been ousted in Georgia. One of his Georgia contemporaries called his paper "an insignificant and contemptible little sheet" and regretted "that we have to kick this skunk as we pass along." [28] Another rabid paper was the Augusta *Loyal Georgian,* edited by J. E. Bryant, a Carpetbagger from Maine. A few papers were run

[25] Atlanta *Daily New Era,* August 18, 1867; Montgomery *Alabama State Journal,* January 16, 1869. Administrators, executors, and guardians, not being public officials, could publish their notices wherever they pleased; Democratic newspapers generally got these notices.

[26] Thompson, *Reconstruction in Georgia,* 227.

[27] Robert H. Woody, *Republican Newspapers of South Carolina,* in *Southern Sketches,* No. 10 (Charlottesville, 1936).

[28] Americus *Tri-Weekly Sumter Republican,* December 1, 1866; Macon *American Union,* April 9, 1869.

by Negroes, as the *Weekly Planet* in Memphis; the *Weekly Pilot* in Nashville; the *Missionary Record*, the most influential Negro paper in South Carolina, edited by Richard Harvey Cain; and the incendiary New Orleans *Tribune*, run by three Santo Domingan Negroes in the interest of making Louisiana a Negro state.[29]

As the Radicals lost their hold on the South, their newspapers began to vanish with them. A North Carolina Radical in answering the question of why he was giving up his paper asked another: "Do you think I'm a d——d fool, to print a paper for a party that can't read?"[30] Now Radical party leaders in the South sought to induce the Republican National Committee to give them money to enter the newspaper field to carry national elections. R. S. Saunders of Nashville wrote William E. Chandler in 1872 that a half dozen key papers controlled public opinion in the South and if he had some money he could buy them away from supporting the Democrats. A Georgia Radical said that with $10,000 he could buy from fifteen to twenty Georgia papers. Even Democratic newspapers were not above toning down their opposition to Radicalism if they were favored with printing contracts.[31]

Radicals hoped to influence the Democratic press, not only with bribery, but also with intimidation. Military authorities arrested William H. McCardle of the Vicksburg *Times* for the vigorous language he used in his paper against Reconstruction, and a judge of a Memphis court, "formerly a common loufer [*sic*] about Cairo," Illinois, imprisoned J. M. Campbell, editor of the *Avalanche*. Democratic editors charged Radical mail clerks with such meanness as purposely misdirecting their papers or throwing them away. Now and then editors got involved in encounters among themselves which resulted in murders, or infrequently in duels, a more refined method of murder which had not entirely disappeared.[32]

The Radical press was of short duration in the South; the Demo-

[29] Sandersville *Central Georgian*, May 16, 1866; Savannah *Journal*, November 14, 1872; Thompson, *Reconstruction in Georgia*, 346; Taylor, *Negro in Tennessee*, 156; Warmoth, *War, Politics and Reconstruction*, 32.

[30] Nordhoff, *Cotton States*, 97.

[31] William E. Chandler Papers, XXIII, Nos. 4614-15, June 28, 1872; Volney Spalding, Atlanta, to J. W. Edmunds, July 12, 1872, *ibid.*, XXIV, Nos. 4748-49; Pike, *Prostrate State*, 30.

[32] Little Rock *Weekly Arkansas Gazette*, March 10, 17, 1868; Columbus (Miss.) *Press*, June 6, 13, 1874; April 10, 1875; Alderman *et al.* (eds.), *Library of Southern Literature*, IX, 4147-50.

cratic newspapers were always to be there. At the end of the war many newspapers, realizing the important part they had played in bringing on the conflict, now addressed themselves to the South's rebuilding. When this rebuilding they had in mind was departed from by the Radicals, they were a decisive force in undoing this kind of reconstruction. The mightiest power in the land, which even the military authorities could not control, was exercised by the newspaper editors. No man was more fearless than Josiah Turner, editor of the Raleigh *Sentinel*, and none had a greater influence on any state than Francis W. Dawson, Englishman and editor of the Charleston *News and Courier*. Other well-known postwar editors were James R. Randall, author of "Maryland, My Maryland" and editor of the Augusta *Constitutionalist;* John Forsyth of the Mobile *Register;* Albert Pike of the Memphis *Appeal,* also poet and high Mason; Henry Watterson of the Louisville *Courier-Journal;* and Alexander H. Stephens of the Atlanta *Sun,* better known for his political activities. Admiral Semmes was editor of the Memphis *Bulletin* long enough to win the praise of his contemporary editors.[33] Joel Chandler Harris and Henry W. Grady, though making a start now, were to win most of their fame after 1880.

Of the country editors there were a few of originality, who exercised an outstanding influence in their communities, but the mass of them were inconsequential in their ideas and their leadership. They followed the larger papers and contented themselves with being looked up to by their neighbors as the local editor who had a right to about as many gratuities in his vicinity as the preacher. Visions of being an editor inspired these lines:

> *If I was a lokel editor,*
> *Wouldn't I have a time?*
> *I wouldn't print a cussed word*
> *For less'n a $ a line.*

> *I'd git my grub and licker free,*
> *& tickets to the show.*

---

[33] Hamilton, *Reconstruction in North Carolina,* 388; Woody, *Republican Newspapers of South Carolina,* 52; Davidson, *Living Writers of the South,* 448; Atlanta *Weekly Sun,* March 6, June 24, 1872; Raymond *Hinds County Gazette,* March 15, 1867.

I wouldn't pay for buggy hier,
& wouldn't I wear good close? [34]

Setting up a newspaper was open to anyone who had the required money or who could get the credit. There were no examinations to pass, no standards that had to be met short of avoiding libel. Yet signs were beginning to appear that some people and especially educators thought that editors should be trained for their work. Washington College, soon to become Washington and Lee University, set up twenty-five scholarships to be awarded each year to students preparing for newspaper work. There were also signs that the newspapers were abandoning their old staid chivalrous feeling that young ladies' names might not be brought into public print without the possibility of a duel.[35] This new departure did not set well with some editors, as appears in this expression of indignation by a Georgian: "We insist that a lady or a gentleman, has the right to leave town or enter it, think, speak, act, to visit or stay at home, to dress in blue, red or white garments, to eat, drink or sleep, without having these particulars heralded to the public through the columns of a newspaper, and without being oppressed with the feeling that the Argus eyes of a 'Jenkins' reporter is upon him or her, and his notebook ready for an item of this sort of 'personal mention.' "[36]

The question of what was news was beginning to receive some attention. Editors had been accustomed to publish without much consideration anything that came to their hands, and if this practice be persisted in, thought a Georgia editor, such news would "soon be as little noticed as the proof, that Plantation Bitters cure all diseases."[37] Newspapers were too prone to cater to the worst traits of their readers rather than to build up better tastes. According to a Louisiana editor, "A large number of readers demand sensational stuff, revel in abuse of opponents, smack their lips over palpable, big, nasty, lies, and are ravenous for a big supply of victims."[38] Southern newspapers swallowed down all the petty local

[34] Dalton *North Georgia Citizen*, December 9, 1869.
[35] *De Bow's Review*, VIII (1870), 573–74; Sandersville *Herald*, June 20, 1878.
[36] Atlanta *Christian Index*, January 9, 1879.
[37] Greensboro *Herald*, August 5, 1869.
[38] New Orleans *Weekly Times*, May 29, 1875.

sensationalism and trivialities sent to them by the Northern news-gathering agency, the Associated Press, items that were in no wise related to Southerners or of interest to them. "Matters, such as murders, suicides, thieving Revenue officers, village conflagrations, &c., &c.," declared an Alabama editor, "are of no more concern to us when occurring in New England or in Kansas or Iowa, than if they occurred in China." Furthermore, who cared whether Grant's mare Ida was dead or not? [39]

Manifestly there were many problems calling for the attention of editors and the best way to approach them would be through an association of their newspapers. The Southern Press Association grew up as a sort of business organization to direct the collection and distribution of news and to tap the Associated Press for items. It maintained an agent in Washington to select news that seemed pertinent to Southern interests, and it met annually in one city or another as much for social recreation as for business. In most states press associations were organized, but they served little purpose beyond acquainting editors with one another at their annual meetings, where social activities predominated.[40] A code of editorial ethics and standards of news values still remained a hope.

Southerners liked music, but they composed or wrote little, even though they had a rich background of romantic imagery which had inspired others to action. They sang Stephen C. Foster's songs and appropriated and securely held as their own Dan Emmett's "Dixie." They also sang and played war songs like "The Wearing of the Grey" and "The Stonewall Jackson March." The colored South-erners in their days of slavery had converted camp-meeting songs into spirituals, but in the days of freedom they were too busy exercising their rights of citizenship to add to their ante-bellum contributions. Blind Tom, however, continued to amaze audi-ences with his performances at the piano, adding to his ante-bellum accomplishments his "Battle of Manassas," which was "a musical high-strike (or hysteric) intended to imitate on a piano the clamors

[39] Montgomery *Weekly Advertiser*, September 21, 1869.

[40] The Radical press took little part in these state associations. W. B. Moore, editor of the San Antonio *Express*, wrote Horace Greeley, September 9, 1868, that there were nine Republican papers in Texas and that they wanted to protect themselves "against the infamy of a lying and dishonest associated press, and other rebel infamy." "Letters to him, 1866–1872," in Greeley Papers.

of a battle," and Emma, another colored prodigy, was beginning to acquire a reputation at the piano, which some critics claimed would go beyond Blind Tom's.[41]

Music helped Southerners to forget their defeat and their continuing troubles during the Reconstruction, and many a household and community found this forgetfulness around the organ or piano and the village brass band. To promote music, shops appeared and journals were set up, such as the Savannah *Southern Musical Journal* in 1871 and the Richmond *Baton* in 1877. A Georgia music house advertised: "There are thousands of homes to-day in our sunny Southland that would be rendered happier by the presence of a fine new Piano or an Organ. We want to fill such homes with instruments, and we mean to do it if we live long enough." [42] The Knabe piano was manufactured in Baltimore "with special view to the trying changes of Southern climate." Music lovers organized their Mozart Clubs within their social circles, and many country villages as well as the larger cities organized brass bands. Contests for musical supremacy were sometimes held at which, according to some critics, more noise than music was made. Houston afforded music lovers a free band concert every evening in the summertime. Traveling musicians, especially opera companies, visited the larger and more accessible cities, and New Orleans had her own opera season famous from antebellum times, which inspired a local editor to say, "We certainly recommend to all readers who visit New Orleans in the season not to omit a visit to the French Opera House. To those who do not care for music, the audience and spectacle will be pleasant to look upon." [43]

Traveling theatrical companies returned to the South immediately after the Surrender, generally giving Shakespeare's plays, which had for many years been favorites. One of the best-known

---

[41] *Daily Columbus Enquirer*, July 6, 1866; Montgomery *Weekly Advertiser*, January 12, 1869.

[42] Sandersville *Herald*, March 27, 1879.

[43] *De Bow's Review*, II (1866), 71–73; VIII (1870), 310; Dalton *North Georgia Citizen*, November 10, 1870; Columbus (Miss.) *Press*, March 27, 1875; Macon *American Union*, August 16, 1867; Sandersville *Central Georgian*, September 12, 1866; Sandersville *Herald*, June 13, 1878; Galveston *Tri-Weekly News*, July 26, 1865; *Weekly Austin Republican*, April 15, 1868; King, *Great South*, 35.

Southern companies was the W. H. Crisp players, who in ante-
bellum days had established themselves in the Shakespearean tradition. Local talent organized itself in towns and gave performances,
sometimes as dramatic corps and sometimes as *tableaux vivants*.
The tableau boys of Rome, Georgia, gave "The Officer's Funeral"
in 1867 in which a Confederate flag was displayed as a necessary
part of the scene. The Federal commander immediately had them
arrested and only after the pleas of Bill Arp, then mayor of the
town, did he release them, but with the warning that hereafter
they should remember that it was treason "to glory in their shame,
and flaunt the symbol of their crime in the face of the country."
Another tableau of the Confederate tradition, which, however,
escaped Federal military suppression, and which traveled over the
South, represented the bombardment of Fort Sumter and the
seige of Charleston. It was produced by two Confederates veterans,
each of whom had lost a limb. Other tableaux or panoramas which
entertained spectators portrayed Niagara Falls, Mammoth Cave, a
naval battle, and other exciting or interesting scenes.[44]

To instruct as well as to entertain, lecturers made their appearance. The most successful and most welcomed were Confederate
officers or other Southerners. Admiral Semmes thrilled audiences
with his account of the "Cruise of the Alabama"; General John
C. Pemberton told how Longstreet lost the battle of Gettysburg,
exploded the tale of Grant refusing Lee's sword at Appomattox,
and of the Surrender having taken place under the apple tree, long
since carried away root and branch by souvenir hunters; and Bill
Arp dispensed humor and pathos in his lecture on Dixie. The
pseudo science of phrenology having not yet died out, lecturers
in this field told of its wonders, felt heads, and sold their charts
and booklets.[45]

Matching wits in literary clubs and in debating societies still
appealed to the young, male and female, and sometimes to their
elders. Country school communities organized their debating so-

[44] *Weekly Austin Republican*, April 1, 15, 1868; Columbus (Miss.) *Press*, November
28, 1874; Natchez *Democrat*, January 24, 1867; Americus *Tri-Weekly Sumter Republican*, November 24, 1866; February 21, 1867; October 1, 1868; Sandersville *Central
Georgian*, May 16, 1866; February 13, 1867.

[45] Elberton *Gazette*, April 30, 1872; Thompson (Ga.) *McDuffie Weekly Journal*,
December 1, 1880; Austin *Tri-Weekly State Gazette*, September 7, 1868.

cieties; and towns, with more varied outlets, sometimes did likewise. As it was not fashionable for young ladies to harangue in public debate, they organized literary clubs for poetry reading and reports on fiction, and they gave their clubs such mystic names as Mnemosynean or Platonic.[46]

Just as the South sought and found literary inspiration in its heroic past, it dreamed of finding its artistic inspiration there also. Why should the South not spread its heroes on canvas or chisel them in marble? To attempt these difficult arts required more than the will, which seemed to be sufficient for those who would soar in literature. The only artist of this period who won lasting fame was the sculptor Edward Virginius Valentine. Born in Richmond, he went to Europe to study with great artists, returning in 1865 in good time to catch the Confederate tradition and chisel its heroes, Beauregard, John S. Mosby, Stuart, Jackson, Maury, and others. His fame rests mainly on his Lee. He took Lee's measurements and modeled a bust of him from life. Then, on Lee's death, Valentine made his remarkable recumbent statue, discarding "both the conventional stiffness of the medieval and the superficial elaboration of modern sarcophagi." This contemporary description and appreciation of the recumbent Lee has been almost universally accepted by subsequent generations: "The expression of the face is neither sleep nor death—but contentment—a calm, dreamy, conscious repose, irradiated by that nobility of soul that characterized the living man and endeared him to the Southern heart. But the artist's greatest triumph is in the train of thought his work suggests and the feelings that steal over us when in its presence." [47]

Museums, where works of art might be housed, protected, and displayed, were not common American institutions at this time, but awakening desires for them followed the war, North and South. The North, situated in the main currents of world thought and better endowed financially, developed its museums on the basis of art alone, while the South at this time still looked to its own past. Lee in marble, however, was to sleep not in a museum but in the

[46] San Antonio *Daily Herald*, October 25, 1871; Thompson *McDuffie Weekly Journal*, July 24, 1878; Griffin *American Union*, September 20, 1867; Greensboro *Herald* October 3, 1872.

[47] *Scott's Monthly Magazine*, II (1866), 541–44; *Southern Magazine*, XI (1872), 224–27

chapel on the campus of his own college. But when Southern museums did arise they were first to grow up around the Southern tradition—as the Confederate Museum in Richmond. This development was in keeping with what Valentine wanted. He suggested in 1873 that some Southern city should promote a museum there to preserve all that was best in Southern art, science, literature, and historical objects, to attest to the past greatness of the South, and to light up the present.

CHAPTER XIV

FASHIONS AND RECREATION

IF SOUTHERNERS had been only political beings and had got their daily emotional excitement only from newspapers and political speeches, they probably would have succumbed to the pestilence of the times and developed widespread abnormalities. Salvation lay in their being able to forget and ignore as well as to remember and rebel. They acquired some characteristics from their Reconstruction experiences, such as the poverty concept with its good and bad implications, but as a people they emerged with their fundamental characteristics unimpaired, later to be held in the light of envy by other sections of the country which had been engulfed in technocracy. During the Reconstruction they continued to play, laugh, and waste their time on things not too ponderable, remembered that Rome was not built in a day and that some projected Romes could never be built, and momentarily forgot politics.

The South soon got back to her normal social activities and forms of entertainment, and as a Tennessee observer said, the people were everywhere viewing life "with a commendable spirit of philosophy dispelling gloomy memories in successive merry-makings and literally strewing our forward path with flowers." [1] In the autumn following Lee's Surrender the circuses reappeared with their outlandish animals and tightrope walkers, and soon "P. T. Barnum's Great Traveling Museum" emerged from its New York quarters to show its wonders to gaping thousands. Smaller outfits, such as ventriloquists, conjurers, trained dogs and cats, or humorous lecturers appeared in the country villages. An entertainer turned up in the Georgia country town of Lincolnton, who after

[1] Nashville *Republican Banner,* May 22, 1866.

regaling his audience with Mark Twain, Artemus Ward, and phrenology, concluded by awarding a tin cup to the ugliest man in the audience and a silver dollar to the prettiest girl.[2]

Although Confederate as well as Federal cavalrymen had raided the South of its best horses, the racing tastes of Southerners were not so high but that they could be reasonably satisfied by nags that were left. In some towns jockey clubs were organized or reorganized, and cities like Memphis, Louisville, Nashville, Montgomery, and Little Rock held races regularly. In the last-named city "crowds of ladies . . . fashionably attired, with smiling faces," attended in 1866. The old plantation races came back in some places, but the place where most of the people had opportunity to enjoy this sport was the agricultural fair, and any new departure was as acceptable as the old Kentucky or Virginia fashion. At the San Antonio fair in 1871, the race continued for 100 miles and carried a prize of $100 in gold. The distance had to be run within a period of five hours, but as many horses might be used in the relay as the entrant might desire.[3]

Suggestive of horse racing but the product of quite a different emotional background was the remarkable manifestation of tournaments. Revived widely over the South immediately after the war, they were a survival of that spirit in the ante-bellum Southerners that made the novels of Sir Walter Scott favorite reading. They represented a sentimental attachment to the past and a salute to the heroic days of the war. Serving as an escape from the realities of the present, they gave participants and spectators an outlet for their social longings. They were held as events within themselves as well as important attractions for agricultural fairs. The idea originated in medieval times, and naturally there had to be fair ladies and brave knights, maids of honor, queens, and ladies in waiting. The participants took such titles as "Knight of the Lost Cause," "Leopard," "Lone Star," or "Count Robert of Paris." Mounting their horses they rode at full speed with leveled lances

2 *Daily Columbus Enquirer*, November 10, 1865; Atlanta *Weekly Sun*, September 27, 1872; Thompson *McDuffie Weekly Journal*, April 24, 1878.

3 Little Rock *Weekly Arkansas Gazette*, August 11, 1866; *Weekly Austin Republican*, July 6, 1870; Montgomery *Weekly Advertiser*, April 28, 1868; Thompson *McDuffie Weekly Journal*, September 12, 1877; San Antonio *Daily Herald*, September 5, 1871.

seeking to pierce and carry away suspended rings, about six inches in diameter; or with flashing swords they tried to behead wooden figures. The successful knight received from the queen a crown or some other royal insignia. When the riding of the day was over, there followed a banquet with dancing late into the night.

In a defeated land there was still life and finery as is indicated by this description of a crowd attending a tournament: "There were any quantity of sparkling faces, fair young girls and blooming matrons, like crown roses on a stem, encircled with their wee budding children, and there were folds of lace and velvet and ermine, that made one wonder if there was such a thing as want in the land. There were stately and handsome men, beautiful horses and jubilant freedmen." [4] Some Southerners who did not care to amuse themselves or to forget their troubles in this way thought the tournaments ludicrous and in bad taste. A New Orleans cotton factor, struggling for existence, thought a tournament must have been quite interesting, yet it seemed "to be out of place in the present state of the country." He admitted, however, that "the effervescence of life must show itself in some way." [5] Another critic thought it was a survival of the dark ages, senseless and dangerous, for sometimes participants were maimed for life if not killed.[6]

The most savage criticism of the tournament came from Northerners, who chided the South for such provincialism and lack of a sense of humor. While Northerners were having healthy outdoor exercises, Southerners were engaging in the mockery of tournaments. A New York editor declared that "any country, in which it is the custom, in our day, to assemble in great crowds to watch men doing these things in broad daylight, in the midst of great public distress, dressed up in fantastic costumes, and calling themselves 'disinherited knights,' 'knights of the sword,' 'knights of the lone star,' and pretending to worship a young woman from a modest wooden house in the neighborhood as the 'queen of love and beauty,' and to regard the bestowal of a shabby theatrical coronet by her as the summit of earthly felicity, we need not have the

---

[4] Augusta *Weekly Constitutionalist*, January 16, 1867.
[5] Barnsley, New Orleans, to Mrs. Berrien, March 14, 1870, in Barnsley Papers.
[6] Dalton *North Georgia Citizen*, November 17, 1870.

least hesitation in pronouncing semi-civilized." As for these Southerners, he found that one must have "a tolerable supply of humor to endure them at all without extreme exasperation." [7]

The Mardi Gras, long domiciled in the South, with a more colorful display and even more ancient lineage in its imagery than the tournament, drew no frowns from anyone, anywhere. It was the particular glory of New Orleans and was revived immediately after the war, to continue annually except in 1875 when it was given up on account of the political situation. The mythical figures and the glittering pageantry varied from year to year, but the many private parties and exclusive dances regularly took place. Louisiana in the midst of her worst Radical humiliations took special pride that her Mardi Gras could not be reconstructed by her unwelcomed tormentors, nor could its social activities be participated in by them. An observer of the scene in 1869 proudly recorded that "There was not a negro, nor scallawag present, at this assemblage of the elite of domestic and foreign society in the city. There were numbers of Northern people, gentlemen and ladies. There were numerous Federal officers. There was no distinction whatever of section, or of past opinion, but the lines were scrupulously drawn against those who came south to plunder, to slander, or to incite the colored people against the whites." [8]

The Mardi Gras festivals though peculiarly New Orleans' own were not confined to that city. Many of the Southern cities and larger towns put on small imitations, and Memphis adapted it to her carnival. Playing upon her Egyptian name, she had her mysterious Memphi and the pageantry of the Nile.

Dancing need not have the background of Mardi Gras and carnivals; it broke out spontaneously among people anywhere. The proof that Charleston was coming out of its social and economic desolation was the revival in 1869 of the famous St. Cecilia Society. All over the South dancing societies were organized or reorganized. In 1865 the Young Men's Social Club in New Orleans made preparations to give a series of balls during the winter; tickets for a grand masquerade and dress ball in Natchez cost $5.00; calico balls grew up out of Southern poverty and made it financially easy for

[7] *Nation*, III (1866), 371; VII (1868), 456.   [8] *De Bow's Review*, VI (1869), 221.

all to dance.[9] Social gatherings as well as dancing were resumed in the home circles.

In those smaller villages where society was governed by the churches, social activities could not center around dancing. To draw the groups together and to entertain them, oyster suppers, fish fries, and candy pullings were held, and now and then some honoree would suddenly find herself in the midst of a surprise party. For the bigger outdoor community meetings the people still held their barbecues. Smaller outdoor parties took the form of picnics in the woodlands or hills. The picnic was often used as a special device for building up and holding together Sunday School classes. Railway companies began running excursion trains to places of unusual attraction such as seaports where good beaches had been developed, or to resorts in the mountains. In Texas, Galveston became a favorite terminus for excursion trains; in Georgia, Tybee, on the sea, became an attraction. Excursion steamers ran up the St. Johns River in Florida, from Jacksonville to Palatka or farther and offered sportsmen the opportunity to test their marksmanship on sleeping alligators.

For general public amusement skating rinks were making their appearance in the larger cities by the early 1870's. San Antonio was looking forward to developing this whirling sport as the first gift of the new year 1872. In the Southeast, skating rinks had already grown up in sufficient numbers to call forth the frowns of some of the religious denominations, who feared that skating might develop into as great a moral hazard for the young people as dancing.[10]

The greatest outdoor attraction which might be enjoyed by all without cost was the public hanging. It gave the people an emotional orgy, surpassed only by the guillotine of the French Revolution or the gladiators in the Roman arena. News of a prospective hanging spread fast and far, and for weeks ahead people made their plans for attending. A hanging in Mississippi was attended by 5,000 spectators.[11] The colored population made a hanging into a grand

[9] Carrollton *Times*, November 18, December 13, 1865; Natchez *Democrat*, January 24, 1867.

[10] San Antonio *Daily Herald*, December 31, 1871; Atlanta *Christian Index*, November 24, 1870.

[11] Columbus (Miss.), *Press*, January 16, July 31, 1875.

jubilee. The execution of a Negro in a small Georgia town drew Negro spectators from all the surrounding counties and from South Carolina. The local editor in announcing the date as the inevitable "Friday" said there was a good prospect "for a 'large and enthusiastic' turn-out to witness the hanging." On the day of another hanging an observer, in describing the converging of the multitudes making their way to the county seat for the spectacle, saw "Men riding and men walking, men drunk and men sober, grave and gay, aged and young—all seemed to think the occasion one for a general holiday and jubilee." [12]

It was a far cry from a hanging to a baseball game, but both served to give people an outdoor diversion, and the more opportunities they had to see baseball games the less likely they would care to see hangings, and the less likely they might engage in crimes for which they might themselves be hanged. Baseball made its appearance immediately after the Surrender and it was participated in by all classes of people from clerks in the stores to gentlemen of leisure. Since the teams did not represent cities, as they were later to do when they became professional, a city might have half a dozen or more clubs, all bearing names to suit their fancy. In Mobile in 1868 there were five well-known clubs, the Mobile Democratic Base Ball Club, the St. Elmo, the Mobile, the Pacific, and the Gulf City. The science of the game was only in its infancy, and contests generally lasted the whole afternoon, frequently resulting in such scores as 67 to 15. The two clubs in Thompson, Georgia, called the Up and At Em Club and the Up and Skump Em Club, played a game in 1877 in which the former defeated the latter 57 to 27. The captain and pitcher of the Up and At Em Club was the future storm center of Georgia politics, Thomas E. Watson. It was to be a long time yet before newspapers would set apart a column or a page to report baseball contests, but stray eyewitnesses were beginning to describe games in language which had none of the picturesque terms and technical jargon known to a later generation. An Alabama game in 1869 was reported thus: "Without particularizing, or dwelling upon special plays made by different members of the Clubs, it is considered only necessary to state that the result was in favor of

[12] Elberton *Gazette*, April 23, 30, 1873.

301

the Wetumpka Club by as many as thirty runs." The game appeared to some spectators as too dangerous to be engaged in lightly. A Florida reporter observed, "There is danger in those balls, but we trust we shall not have to chronicle the death of any of our young men from accidents while engaged in this game." [13] Fatalities in sports were to await the arrival of football.

In the beginning some baseball clubs had a social tinge, and it was considered entirely genteel for ladies to attend games. It sometimes happened that the losing club would be given a consolation dance in the evening. Individual clubs drew up constitutions for their organization and management, and soon associations of clubs were formed with a constitution adopted for the federation. In 1868 the Alabama Association of Base Ball Players was organized in Montgomery, with five cities represented.[14]

A game as inexpensive and as easy to play as baseball naturally appealed to Negroes. They organized their teams and held their contests, sometimes traveling a hundred or more miles to meet their opponents in another city. They dressed in gaudy uniforms, bordering on the burlesque.

Interest in the outcome of what is considered an uncertainty, and betting on it, is as widespread as the human race. It has, therefore, always been easy to promote a race or a contest. Though prize fights later were to attract much interest, the greatest contest in the South of Reconstruction times, appealing most to the imagination of the people, was a steamboat race, which later became so much a part of the folklore of the people as to lead to a song about it. This was the race of the two Mississippi steamers, the *Robert E. Lee* and the *Natchez,* made in 1870 between New Orleans and St. Louis. Though these two steamers ostensibly represented two rival Southern steamship lines, the *Robert E. Lee* was in fact owned by that Massachusetts Yankee, Oakes Ames, of Credit Mobilier infamy, and on its decks for the first part of the race stood

13 Montgomery *Weekly Advertiser,* April 21, 1868; September 21, 1869; Tallahassee *Weekly Floridian,* May 5, 1874; Little Rock *Weekly Arkansas Gazette,* May 14, 1867; Thompson *McDuffie Weekly Journal,* August 15, 1877; Tallahassee *Semi-Weekly Floridian,* February 8, 1867.

14 Montgomery *Weekly Advertiser,* April 21, 28, 1868; Natchez *Democrat,* January 24, 1867.

Henry Clay Warmoth, the Illinois Carpetbagger governor of Louisiana, who made a fortune out of Pelican politics.[15]

The steamboats left New Orleans without cargo or passengers except the few adventurers who were willing to undergo the risk of being snagged, drowned, blown up, or otherwise skyrocketed into the next world. News of the race was well known long before the start, and people flecked the riverbanks throughout the length of the course, firing cannon in the day and lighting bonfires by night, cheering their favorite. The progress of the contest produced the greatest excitement. The *Robert E. Lee* won, arriving in St. Louis in three days, eighteen hours, and fourteen minutes. The *Natchez* was probably an inferior boat and was less skillfully managed, but it also had the bad luck to get caught in a fog and to break a pump. It took four days and one hour. A crowd estimated at 75,000 greeted the winner. "Salutes were fired, and immense enthusiasm prevailed. Nothing like it was ever known in the history of St. Louis." Betting had been widespread and much money was lost and won. The editor of *De Bow's Review* moralized in this fashion: that since both captains were Southern men there could be no sectional significance but in this race there was the double argument that Southerners were good navigators and the South should, therefore, set up a merchant marine.[16]

Soon after the war Southerners living in coast cities revived their boat clubs and held regattas. Contests between cities, ancient rivals like Charleston and Savannah or New Orleans and Mobile, led to the revival of some of the old social splendors connected with entertaining visiting crews with banquets and dances.

Betting added something to the interest of the spectators in regattas, although many enjoyed boat races without any pecuniary interest in the winner; but there crept into the South in the latter 1870's a sort of contest that appeared to have little in it for the watchers unless they had a wager. This was the walking match, in which a group set out around a track of half a mile or more and continued to walk until only one participant was left. The fad first appeared in the North and led a Southern editor to remark

15 Warmoth, *War, Politics and Reconstruction*, 157–59.
16 *De Bow's Review*, VIII (1870), 586–603; *Weekly Columbus Enquirer*, July 12, 1870.

of one such contest. "It seems almost incredible to us people here in the south that so much money could be wasted by people, merely to gratify the curiosity of looking at four men walk around a half mile track, for a whole week, but such was the fact." However much Southerners might congratulate themselves on being more sensible than Northerners, they generally succumbed to Yankee tricks and fashions. Soon in a hall in Savannah a walking contest was started and the moralizing Southerner was forced to remark, "The introduction and engrafting of such Northern gambling and demoralizing amusements in southern soil is to be deplored." A variation of the walking mania was thought up by a "walking lady" in Philadelphia who accepted a wager of $10,000 that she could walk from that city to New Orleans and return within a period of five months. She would carry only a cane and a revolver.[17]

Appreciation of style and fashion is as great a common denominator as the urge to take a chance on an uncertainty, and in order to cater to these tastes and display their clothes and fine manners people must move in circles wider than the home parlor. In addition to great occasional gatherings like fairs and Mardi Gras, there must be a more constant resort for such display. Every city deserving the name had at least one staid hotel which served these needs the year round, and for the summer season there were the old watering places, the seaside resorts, and the mountain hotels just beginning to gain popularity. Some city hotels came to be known almost as well as the name of the city itself. The St. Charles and the St. Louis hotels immediately suggested New Orleans and a visit to that city might well be considered a failure which did not include either a short residence in one of these "palaces of fashion and fun" or at least a social occasion there. The St. Louis Hotel was declared by a widely traveled Northerner to be "one of the finest hotels in the United States." In Mobile it was the Battle House; in Montgomery, the Exchange Hotel; in Savannah, the Pulaski House; in Charleston, the Charleston Hotel, "famous for its great stone pillared piazzas reaching from pavement to roof"; in Nashville, the Maxwell House; and in Atlanta, the Kimball House, new and Northern like the rest of the city. Hannibal I. Kimball of Boston spent $660,000 building and fur-

[17] Sandersville *Herald*, May 27, June 19, October 23, 1879.

nishing the Kimball House into "the finest and most elaborately-appointed hotel in the Southern States." It had steam elevators, a vast lobby, rooms enough to accommodate a thousand guests, and dining and banquet halls sufficient to take care of any number of diners who were likely to come.[18]

Southern hotels, which had been most miserable in all their appointments for some time after the Surrender, were within a few years becoming fashionable. Their managers begged Southerners to stay at home and enjoy their own hotels. To heighten their standing with the elite and confuse the masses many of them began to use the French names for certain dishes, making it impossible for nine out of ten diners in ordering a particular food to "tell whether it is a mutton chop or a cabbage." At this time not enough Americans had yet exposed themselves to European customs to bring back the degrading practice of tipping.

In most people's minds it was illogical to consider a vacation worth while unless it were spent away from the home locality. As Southerners took their recreation in the summer months, their own Florida offered them no attractions. Indeed, Northerners seeking health and pleasure were beginning to appropriate Florida as their winter sanitorium and playground, and Jacksonville and St. Augustine drew most of them. Sometimes they stopped short of Florida in such a place as Savannah where one might hear in the hotels "the cheery laugh of the tall and handsome planter, as well as the cough of the Northern invalid." Aiken, South Carolina, was also beginning to become a center for wealthy Northerners who wanted to escape the rigors of their winter climate.

Southerners sometimes found themselves in a quandary as to whether they would go to the seashore for their vacation or to the mountains. Tallulah Falls in Georgia, Caesar's Head in South Carolina, and North Carolina's "Land of the Sky" attracted an increasing number of sight-seers.[19] South Carolinians, especially Charlestonians, never gave up their preference for the western North Carolina mountains. The Lookout Mountain region of

[18] King, *Great South*, 37; Jones (ed.), *Appletons' Hand-Book of American Travel, Southern Tour*, 127, 150; *Plantation*, II (1871), 264; Somers, *Southern States since the War*, 97–98.

[19] King, *Great South*, 368; Jones (ed.), *Appletons' Hand-Book of American Travel, Southern Tour*, 137, 157–58.

Tennessee became more attractive with the years, adding the mellowing traditions of Civil War battlefields to its natural beauty.[20]

On the Louisiana Gulf coast Grand Isle, famous in ante-bellum times for its gay throngs but unfortunate in fires and hurricanes, was now advertised as the best seaside resort in the South. It still had its pleasant beach, and immediately after the war its hotel was hopefully prepared for many more summer seasons. Planters and others who had formerly enjoyed the Mississippi coast from Bay St. Louis to Pascagoula did not forget it after the war. Jefferson Davis spent his last years at his Beauvoir home near Biloxi on the shores of the glittering waters of the Gulf.

Still the greatest social distinction was attached to those who could go to the springs of Virginia. Soon after the war they broke out in all their ante-bellum splendor and in 1869 reached a peak of brilliancy and sustained social whirl never equaled in ante-bellum days. The most famous of these watering places was Greenbrier White Sulphur Springs, now in West Virginia since the disruption of the Old Dominion; but within the "spring region" of this Virginia and West Virginia country were the Old Sweet Springs, Red Sweet Springs, Red Sulphur Springs, Blue Springs, Warm Springs, Hot Springs, Bath Alum Springs, Healing Springs, Rockbridge Alum Springs, Alleghany Springs, Montgomery White Sulphur Springs, Yellow Sulphur Springs, and others almost as well known. These springs burst out in small beautiful valleys, and around them grew up the large guest houses surrounded by many cabins and cottages, pavilions, and other buildings. In the 1870's the rates were uniformly $3.00 a day or $70.00 a month, except at Greenbrier White Sulphur where the rate was $4.00 a day. Guests who felt able to afford it always went to the Greenbrier until this place was saturated, and those who were then turned away scattered to the other places. Some people chose to make the rounds of all the principal springs, spending only a few days at each place.

Guests amused themselves according to their social dispositions and their health. Those who came only for the cure drank much water, strolled into the near-by woods, or sat on the verandas or the lawns. The more vigorous hiked with their guns into the

[20] Atlanta *Christian Index*, July 11, 1878; Buck, *Road to Reunion*, 160–61; Mrs. A. M. Meeker. *Eliza Ross: or, Illustrated Guide of Lookout Mountain* (Atlanta, 1871).

mountains to hunt deer or pheasants, went horseback riding or swimming, or rolled at ninepins. The greater number came for social opportunities. Dancing was almost continuous, beginning even in the morning. After meals the guests went to the great ball-room where they did the treadmill, a walking exercise. Whether promoted by the treadmill or the dance, there were fewer matches to be made now than in ante-bellum times, for the young gentle-men were in a smaller minority than formerly.

Southern society dominated the springs. The best of the Lower South came up, driven from their homes by the heat and the dangers of yellow fever. There were "Judges, generals, colonels, senators, governors, leading journalists, presidents of railways, and 'prominent people' generally." Every summer the Southern Con-federacy was reborn at the Virginia springs. In 1867 Lee rode over to the Greenbrier with his family, especially to see if the waters would help Mrs. Lee's arthritis. Retiring as his gentility made him, he was, nevertheless, soon the center of admiring groups.

There was not the flashy tassel and tinsel and the gaming in-stinct running wild, as might be found at Saratoga Springs or at other Northern watering places where the guests had larger amounts of money to spend. Instead, as a Northern observer noted, these Southerners were "the worst dressed but the best mannered men in America." Or as another said, after praising the cultured society he saw at the Virginia springs, "At the North, on the other hand, manners, even as taught to children, are apt to concede nothing except that you have an immortal soul and a middling chance of salvation."

The Virginia springs not only promoted the revival of Southern society; they helped to knit the sections together again. Northerners came in increasing numbers, putting to the test the South's an-nouncement: "So far from apprehending any unpleasantness or any coldness of reception in the summer resorts of Virginia, they may be assured of a welcome much more lively than what pe-cuniary interest habitually extends to its customers." One day General Lee, noticing a group from the North sitting alone with Governor Andrew G. Curtin of Pennsylvania, went over and in-troduced himself and others to make smooth their social path. The greatest gesture of friendship the South ever made toward the

North at the springs was the Peabody Ball in 1869, to honor George Peabody who had recently set up the Peabody Foundation to aid Southern education. In fact, the Virginia springs with their warm social amenities melted down the barriers throughout the land. There the "West and the East, the South and the North seem to have forgotten their sectional bickerings and to have come together in friendliest mood." [21]

The Virginia springs far outshone the other watering places of the South, but the others should not be regarded as of no importance in social recreation. Most of the Southern states had their less pretentious springs where the minor gentry, who could not afford to go far from home, had their experiences no less real and enjoyable. Among them were the Montvale Springs in East Tennessee, of more than local importance, described in 1868 as fast becoming "the Saratoga of the South"; Piedmont Springs near Morganton, North Carolina, and Wilson's Springs near Shelby in the same state; Indian Springs and Warm Springs in Georgia; Blount Springs and Bladen Springs in Alabama; and far to the westward in Arkansas the Hot Springs, "in a wild and almost inaccessible mountain region," where a "cool and delicious" atmosphere and many health-flowing hot springs attracted the hardier invalids and pleasure-seekers, and where health and recreation were delightfully combined.[22]

The socially-minded must know the fashions and keep true to them. No war could ever strike deep enough to destroy woman's taste for styles of dress. The Civil War turned Southern women away from all things Northern except the fashion plate. Here they needed no reconstruction as they had not seceded further than stern necessity required. Yet there was hope among some Southern men that the women would no longer remain the slaves of Yankee

---

[21] Sources of information on the Virginia springs: Perceval Reniers, *The Springs of Virginia* (Chapel Hill, 1941), 205–29; Jones (ed.), *Appletons' Hand-Book of American Travel, Southern Tour*, 90–107; Richmond *Daily Dispatch*, July 1, 1876; Augusta *Weekly Chronicle & Sentinel*, August 30, September 6, 1871; King, *Great South*, 567–68, 674; Douglas S. Freeman, *R. E. Lee: A Biography* (New York, 1934–1935), IV, 320–32; *Nation*, XXV (1877), 179.

[22] *Scott's Monthly Magazine*, V (1868), 409; Augusta *Weekly Chronicle & Sentinel*, September 20, 1871; Jones (ed.), *Appletons' Hand-Book of American Travel, Southern Tour*, 213; King, *Great South*, 286.

fashions, which were largely importations from Paris, but that they would develop Southern fashions.

A Georgia farm editor recommended to the state fair that it offer premiums for the best styles designed by Southern women, and that the winners be published in fashion plates. "Parisian and Yankee fashions are all the rage among Southern ladies," he lamented. Alluding to Napoleon III's Eugénie, he declared the Parisian styles had been suggested by an empress "whose character before her marriage would have excluded her from genteel society at the South." And as for the Yankee fashions, they had their origin "among the cyprians and *demi mondes* of New York, distorting those fair proportions which God pronounced perfect into a mass of heterogeneous absurdities." [23]

To rail against woman's fashions is a custom as old as dress itself, though at times it be done half-humorously. The sharpest weapons have been the morality and health arguments. "Fashion kills more women than toil and sorrow" was an expression often heard, followed with a moral like this: "The washerwoman with scarcely a ray of hope to cheer her in her toil will live to see her fashionable sisters die all around her." Fashionable women were mere doll-forms in the hands of milliners: "If they rear children, servants and nurses do all, save to conceive and give them birth." [24] Now and then women themselves rebelled, at least in print, against the tortures that styles inflicted upon them. One of them prayed: "Oh! that good Christian Southern women would inaugurate a war against the abuses of that most detestable tyrant, Fashion . . . by entering their protest against, and by showing their disregard for, the silly, health-destroying, extravagant demands of fashionable folly." [25] But women must be in fashion, and a second Southern woman was pictured as offsetting this prayer with another: "Bless, O Fortune! my crimps, rats and frizzles, and let thy glory shine on my paint and powder." [26] It was to be expected that someone would call a halt to the silly styles in the name of economy. "Women of the South! I pray you, burst these fetters of folly and fashion,

23 *Plantation*, I (1870), 265.
24 Marietta *Journal*, February 8, 1878; Greensboro *Herald*, August 12, 1869.
25 *Plantation*, I (1870), 229.
26 Thompson *McDuffie Weekly Journal*, April 24, 1878.

and stand forth noble and independent. Study fashion plates less and science more, and retrieve the decaying fortunes of your husbands." [27] Women kept their knowledge of the latest fashions up to date by following the pages and plates in *Godey's Lady's Book* and to a lesser extent in *Peterson's Magazine*.

Fashions were constantly changing, swinging the whole arc of the pendulum in the course of a few years. Directly after the war the hoop skirt was stylish. The "Empress Trail Duplex Elliptic" was advertised as the easiest to handle in church, theater, the railroad cars, or wherever a lady should go. Spreading out downward in undetermined dimensions, the hoop skirt must in its slope upward almost vanish in a wasp-waist held so by "French and glove-fitting corsets." If properly worn it hung "gracefully over a hoop of respectable dimensions," but not one that described "an orbit equal to a planet." The feminine figure terminated skyward in a bundle of hair resembling a Japanese pagoda. The fact that hoops could not be dragged on the ground led to the shortening of the skirt and the exposing of the feet and with the abandonment of hoops, shorter skirts became stylish. Some purists considered the feet immodest, but others thought well of them: "With the pretty, tight-lacing high heeled boots, most any foot looks well encased in them." "Of course these short-walking skirts," observed a stylist, "would not be suitable to ladies advanced in years, but we hope those who are in their sunny days, especially the lassies, will continue to use them, and leave street sweeping to others." [28] One authority, in estimating how short a skirt might be, allowed "to any lady whose years and physical development render the process a decent one, the privilege of raising her skirts to a height not exceeding one-fifth of her entire person from the ground." [29] By 1869 the skirt had been metamorphosed sufficiently to lead to this editorial comment: "This hook-em-up and rumple-em fashion of skirts makes some women look like a frizzled chicken on pontoons." [30]

In the latter 1860's the Grecian bend made its appearance, of

[27] *Weekly Columbus Enquirer,* April 27, 1869.

[28] Americus *Tri-Weekly Sumter Republican,* August 16, 1866; Raymond *Hinds County Gazette,* April 7, 1869; Natchez *Democrat,* October 26, 1867.

[29] Nashville *Republican Banner,* October 10, 1866.

[30] Dalton *North Georgia Citizen,* May 27, 1869.

which the Greeks were blameless, but which was said to have grown up to ape a crippled old Duchess who walked that way. This bend was most aptly described as a tortured position in which a young lady, encased in a tightly laced corset, threw "her body forward and head back, as though she were trying to catch a soap bubble on the end of her nose," while she was "compelled to walk almost on the tips of her toes" because of "gaiter-heels from three to four inches high." [31]

Within a few years the hoop skirt entirely folded up, and by 1875 ladies began to look "like sheathed umbrellas." One observer remarked, "Skirts are long, and cling so closely that one is fain to wonder how the wearer can walk." [32]

Men, if they were to be dudes and dandies, must also bow to fashion. They were made to look spindle-legged, and no fashionably dressed man should appear without a mustache. Good news was widely published for those who were unable to produce this adornment by natural growth: "Whiskers and Mustaches! Forced to grow upon the smoothest face in from three to five weeks by using Servigue's Restaurateur Capillaire." [33] The typical Southerner who carried forward the tradition of the Old South, unswerved by fashion, wore a long-tailed coat and a broad-brimmed hat, just as the typical Northerner went hatted in a stovepipe.

Besides the fantastic styles in dress there were other fashions and customs. Boys and girls sent one another sentimental and comic Valentines for the Fourteenth of February; [34] and they were beginning to adopt the abominable manners of chewing gum, from which their elders tried to break them. For the purpose of nauseating gumchewers, reports were spread that much of the content of gum was fats "expressed from the bodies of hogs, cats, dogs, and other animals found dead in the streets of cities. Nice, isn't it?" [35] In some communities the familiar name for it was dog tallow, as it was sold in white tallow-looking sticks, not the flat slices of chicle gum of a later time. When the girls learned what was in

[31] Montgomery *Weekly Advertiser*, October 27, 1868.

[32] Augusta *Weekly Chronicle & Sentinel*, August 18, 1875.

[33] *Scott's Monthly Magazine*, III (1867), advertisement; Griffin *American Union*, August 16, 1867.

[34] *Daily Columbus Enquirer*, February 18, 1866.

[35] Greensboro *Herald*, August 12, 1869.

their gum, they would still "have a perfect right to chew gum if they want," remarked an editor.[36]

Radicalism, Southerners believed, embraced a system not only of politics but also of the whole gamut of human conduct. It seemed to be an attack on the *status quo* all along the line. Hence the woman's movement throve in the North, led by such notorious characters as Victoria Woodhull and her sister Tennessee Claflin, and the more respectable Elizabeth Cady Stanton and Susan B. Anthony. They stood not only for woman's right to vote and for the complete emancipation of woman, but some of them would carry it to the extent of free love. The South would have none of this unsexing of woman or none of this degrading of her sex, for these were the unmistakable signs of a decaying civilization. "We can proudly say that no Southern woman has yet asked for the ballot," said a Southern woman in 1871.[37] Two years later a woman's congress met in New York City, which advocated waking up Southern women to the larger vision. Prominent in the proceedings was a Mrs. Maria Jourdan Westmoreland, claiming to be until recently a Georgian from Atlanta, who advocated setting loose on the South a horde of female lecturers. Southerners disowned her, and a Georgia editor declared that the South's last advantage over the North would fall "never again to stand, when a female lecturer shall draw within sound of her voice an audience of decent Southern women." [38] By 1879 one Southern woman, who refused to flee her section, began to take an interest in the questions of the day and to impress herself on the consciousness of the South to such an extent that she became an epitome of the new woman of the South. She was Rebecca Latimer Felton, who in 1922 finally received her reward through a two-day appointment to the United States Senate, the first of her sex to sit there.

There were three traditionally Southern aspects of life and living which seemed to be so deeply embedded in fact or fiction that no Radical program could upset them—Southern beauty, Southern cooking, and Southern speech. The tradition of the beauty of Southern girls continued to thrive through war and Reconstruc-

[36] Dalton *North Georgia Citizen*, June 2, 1870.
[37] *Weekly Columbus Enquirer*, September 5, 1871.
[38] Augusta *Weekly Chronicle & Sentinel*, March 4, 1874.

tion. It was a beauty that was not entirely induced by what they wore, as a Northern traveler was to discover in Alabama. Writing of this state he declared: "It is a land of beautiful women; one even now and then sees among the degraded poor whites, who 'dip snuff' and talk the most outrageous dialect, some lovely creature, who looks as poetic as a heathen goddess, until one hears her speak, or she pulls from her pocket a pine stick, with an old rag saturated in snuff wrapped around it, and inserts it between her dainty lips." [39]

Southern cooking did not appeal to all Northern palates, but even the most determined schoolteacher, Freedmen's Bureau agent, or Carpetbagger politician never attempted to change it, either by reducing its grease content or by outlawing corn pones, "hushpuppies," or hominy. The more fancy cooking which adorned the tables of the well-to-do or which was served in the celebrated restaurants added a special charm to the South which no one would want to destroy. Both to guarantee that tried recipes should not be lost and that new discoveries should be widely known, people in all times have written cookbooks. Mrs. E. J. Verstille of Louisiana wrote *Southern Cookery* in 1866 and the next year Mrs. Maria Massey Barringer of North Carolina wrote *Dixie Cookery, or How I Managed My Table for Twelve Years. A Practical Cook Book for Southern Housekeepers.*

Even all the bitterness in Southerners' minds and words could not change their soft inflections and make their talk as harsh as Yankee speech. They still dropped their "r's" and said "you all" to emphasize their politeness in including more than one. They spoke a language less affected by outside influences than the speech in any other part of the nation, and, therefore, more in its pristine purity. According to a Mobile editor, writing in 1875, "The English language is spoken with greater purity by the educated classes, and more correctly by the peasantry of the Southern States, than in any other section of the Union." [40] Thus it was that Southerners used words which became more and more unfamiliar to other Americans. Few Yankees would understand what a Southerner meant when he used "feist" for a small dog and "tote" for carry. But Southerners like other people developed speech habits, jarring

[39] King, *Great South*, 340.
[40] Mobile *Register*, quoted in Greensboro *Herald*, June 17, 1875.

and happily transitory, such as interspersing "you know" through-out their conversations.

The South passed through Reconstruction, resisting social change with as much tenacity as political remaking. Not until the twentieth century came down upon it with all the leveling instruments of science did Southerners begin to lose their sectional individuality and tend to become as other people.

CHAPTER XV

SCHOOLS AND CHURCHES

THE hard reality was that the South had lost the war. Why she lost it was generally explained in various ways without much thought or reason—she had been overpowered by foreign hordes; she had been strangled by the blockade; the blunders of Jefferson Davis had brought about defeat; she had worn herself out whipping the North; she never admitted that the morale of the people had broken down. Few could be found who were brave enough or wise enough to say that she had lost because her civilization had not prepared for her the sinews of war, that she had not been educated in the right direction, in fine, that there were some parts of her old civilization that she must give up. Yet there were a few who early began to argue that the South must adopt a new conception of the education that the people must now have.

First among those who called for a new kind of education was General Daniel H. Hill of North Carolina, who used his *Land We Love* from its first issue, in May, 1866, to spread his ideas. He was followed by Benjamin H. Hill, who, in 1871, stated the problem in his celebrated New South address to the alumni of the University of Georgia. A few years later Henry W. Grady, an apostle of the latter Hill, carried the message of the new day throughout the country by newspaper articles and oratory. The South in its ante-bellum education had not been practical enough, argued General Hill: "The old plan of education in the palmy days of the South gave us orators and statesmen, but did nothing to enrich us, nothing to promote material greatness." Now too much subdued by defeat, he contended, the South "must abandon the aesthetic and the ornamental for the practical and the useful." Thus

315

did he see in the South's defeat a great good. Even the disfranchisement and disqualification of Southerners to hold office might be an advantage, at least for a time. Deprived of the chance for a political career, Southerners would be forced into practical occupations, and trade, commerce, and labor would thereby be dignified. General Hill asked, "Is not a practical acquaintance with the ax, the plane, the saw, the anvil, the loom, the plow and the mattock, vastly more useful to an impoverished people than familiarity with the laws of nations and the science of government?" [1]

Benjamin H. Hill declared to his University of Georgia audience that the South was blessed with everything that a bountiful nature could bestow, but it had supinely slept on this wealth. Slavery in degrading labor had made Southerners turn away from developing their natural resources, and the education which the South had early adopted had not given that training which must be had if the people were to dig and smelt their ore, harness their water power, utilize their timber wealth, manufacture their raw products, and thereby become rich like the North. To develop these resources, said Hill, "we must honor, elevate, and educate labor, and to this end we must establish schools of science, and train our children to businesses and callings other than law, medicine, and theology." In reorganizing Southern universities for the new education, Hill would begin with his own alma mater, the University of Georgia. He would not abandon the "strictly classical and literary education," but he would have in addition "independent polytechnic schools, [with] courses of study, abstract and applied, scientific, regular, and elective." "I would provide every facility," he declared, "to make and accomplish the universal scholar and the special expert." [2]

Others raised the cry for diversification in education as well as

---

[1] *Land We Love,* I (1866), 3, 9, 11. Commenting further on the old kind of education promoted by Southerners, he said, "Their scholastic training, as well as their system of labor, turned their thoughts away from the study of science, and its application to discovery and invention." Their education was "an accomplishment, or at most a preparation for the legislative hall, and not for the development of our resources; with whom mental training was whetting the sword for gladiatorial contest in the political arena, and not the sharpening of ax and plow for subduing the powers of nature." The South was now beginning to see its mistake; the "everlasting twaddle about politics is giving place to important facts in history, in the mechanic arts, in agriculture, in morals, in philosophy, etc." *Ibid.,* 237–38.

[2] *Ku Klux Conspiracy,* VII, 804, 806.

316

in industry. The two went together. The South must have geologists, chemists, mineralogists, engineers, machinists, superintendents of railroads, and captains of ships; but the ante-bellum universities had attempted to melt all its students down into classical scholars. The diploma was in fact only "a receipt for money, and a certificate for character." The whole South should now adopt the elective system which Thomas Jefferson had established at the University of Virginia, and to make it effective Southern universities should develop new courses and schools. The new education should embrace the girls, too. "Fashion for the last twenty years," declared George Fitzhugh in 1866, "has had more to do with the education of girls than the cut of their bonnet, the fitting of their dresses, or the color of their ribbons." [3] Now this situation should be changed and it could be done without much cost—all, the result of a bright side to the dark picture of defeat. Girls would for some time have to get most of their education within the family circle, where it could be made as practical as life itself.

This sudden zeal of the South to become scientific represented a compromise with the victorious North, which in politics Southerners would not tolerate for a moment. If the South had only known it, the scientific age was to be much more dangerous to the old Southern way of life than all the political reconstruction that was being attempted from the Potomac to the Rio Grande. In fact, all Southerners as well as all Northerners had not yet learned that the panacea of human ills was a pellet out of the scientific pillbox. Mark Twain could not refrain from ridiculing the pompous pretensions of some scientific findings. Taking the established fact that the Mississippi River in cutting through some of its bends was steadily shortening its lower stretches, he deduced from that truth the startling conclusion that in exactly 742 years the lower Mississippi would have reduced its length to one and three-fourths miles and that the streets of New Orleans and Cairo, Illinois, would join. After this wonderful scientific deduction he observed, "There is something fascinating about science. One gets such wholesale returns of conjecture out of such a trifling investment of fact." [4]

Southern colleges and universities changed radically their old

[3] De Bow's Review, II (1866), 51.
[4] Mark Twain, "Old Times on the Mississippi, VII," in Atlantic Monthly (Boston), XXXVI (1875), 193.

curricula, by following the lines laid down by the Hills, Grady, and other educational reformers. Though General Lee was the essence of the chivalry of the Old South in the eyes of his contemporaries and of subsequent generations, yet he was a bold educational iconoclast. In his Washington College he promoted departments of practical chemistry, experimental philosophy, practical mechanics, applied mathematics, modern languages, history and literature, and journalism.[5] Vanderbilt University, beginning in 1873 when it got its first half million dollars from Cornelius Vanderbilt, entered the world untrammeled by any previous educational practice. Though restricted by Methodist control for a third of a century and more, it immediately assumed a leadership in Southern education. But the institution to whose birth many Southerners looked forward with greatest eagerness and impatience, as the blazer of a new trail for the whole country, was the Johns Hopkins University. Looking forward to the new institution, a reformer, pitching his desires on a plane higher than that wanted by the practical developers of natural resources, exclaimed, "We are dying of demagogues and sciolists; we are falling to pieces with ignorance and its besotting sins. Let us have some institution once more among us capable of promoting and imparting rational thought and generous culture." The Johns Hopkins University under the leadership of Daniel Coit Gilman opened its doors in 1876 and soon set the standards for graduate work in America.[6] People were not yet so oblivious to standards of value as to draw no distinctions between practical training and education. It was possible, therefore, for the so-called business colleges to rise up and flourish in the South, attesting in addition the fact that trade and industry were pushing back ante-bellum inertia and positive opposition.

That the South could not enter into a highly specialized and widespread educational advancement was evident enough. That Southern colleges and universities could open at all for some years after the war, or that when opened they could continue through Radical Reconstruction, was not to be counted on too heavily. Though most of the schools suffered great losses during the war, in their faculties, students, endowments, and some in the destruc-

[5] Freeman, *Lee,* IV, 232–33. See also, *De Bow's Review,* II (1866), 536.
[6] *Southern Magazine,* XVI (1875), 86.

tion of their buildings by Federal armies, a majority opened their doors again in the fall of 1865. The University of Virginia was the outstanding state university during the years following the war. In the fall of 1866 its students numbered more than 500, and its faculty included the South's best scholars. Basil L. Gildersleeve instructed in Greek there for twenty years, leaving in 1876 to carry prestige to the new Johns Hopkins; and British-born George Frederick Holmes impressed himself upon ten generations of students at Charlottesville and spread his name throughout the South with his series of "Holmes Readers."

Radical Reconstructionists dealt variously with the educational institutions which fell under their control; either they laid their withering hands on them or with their shadows darkened the prospect. The Radicals seized the University of North Carolina in 1868, overthrew the old board of trustees, and brought in a faculty of politicians. Outraged by this pollution the students melted away until the institution closed its doors in 1870, to remain so for the next five years—until a reviving state revived its university. The University of South Carolina, having changed its name in 1865 from South Carolina College, was despoiled even more completely. Reopening in January, 1866, it languished until 1873 when the Radicals, having had control of the state for half a dozen years, decided to remake the institution. They reconstituted the board of trustees, appointed some Negro members, and threw the school open to Negroes. They set up a preparatory department where most of the Negro students registered. As Negro politicians from the near-by statehouse and others flocked in, the white students withdrew and the faculty resigned. Teachers from the North were imported and a Negro student body grew up, with a small sprinkling of despised whites. When the white South Carolinians secured control of their state in 1877 they closed the school for the next three years and then reopened it under the name of The College of Agricultural and Mechanical Arts, later to be changed back to the University of South Carolina. The University of Alabama emerged from the war with most of its buildings burnt by Federal armies, but attempted to reopen in the fall of 1865. As only one student appeared, it closed its doors. In 1868 the Radicals sought to revive the institution and elected a president who refused to serve; whereupon they elected another, one A. S. Larkin, a Carpetbagging Methodist preacher of the worst motives, who was warned away by the Ku Klux Klan. The next year they succeeded in assembling a faculty, made up mostly of Northern adventurers, who attracted a student body varying from ten to thirty. Being highly repugnant to the native white Alabamans, the University dipped lower, and finally in 1871 it was closed by the Democrats, reorganized, and reopened the same year.[7]

The universities of Georgia, Mississippi, and Louisiana, the first reopening in January, 1866, and the other two in the fall of 1865, were not mismanaged by the Radicals. A student oration at the University of Georgia displeased the commander of Military District Number III, but the difficulty was settled without closing the institution. The University of Mississippi, though given a new board of trustees by the Radicals, was not thrown open to Negro students, who instead were given a college and two normal schools all their own. Louisiana State Seminary (changing its name to University in 1870) reopened unterrified with four students in 1865, and continued at its old Alexandria location until 1869 when its buildings were burnt, it was claimed, by Negroes. This calamity led to its removal to Baton Rouge. Its president, David French Boyd, was able to maintain the good will of Governor Warmoth, who continued state appropriations; but in opposing Governor Kellogg's efforts to open the institution to Negroes, he lost the state support from 1873 to 1877. Arkansas, never having had a state university before the war, received one at the hands of the Radicals in 1872, open alike to both races. Only one Negro student applied for entrance, however, and he was taught privately by the president off the campus.[8]

---

[7] Hamilton, *Reconstruction in North Carolina*, 619–30; Farish, *Circuit Rider Dismounts*, 256–58; Edgar W. Knight, *The Influence of Reconstruction on Education in the South* (New York, 1913), 82; Edwin L. Green, *A History of the University of South Carolina* (Columbia, 1916), 87, 93, 94, 409–15; King, *Great South*, 460–63; Simkins and Woody, *South Carolina during Reconstruction*, 417–20, 440–42; Fleming, *Civil War and Reconstruction in Alabama*, 611–17; Horn, *Invisible Empire*, 128.

[8] Augusta *Daily Constitutionalist*, August 23, 1867; E. Merton Coulter, *College Life in the Old South* (New York, 1928), 339–43; Garner, *Reconstruction in Mississippi*, 367–71; Walter L. Fleming, *Louisiana State University, 1860–1896* (Baton Rouge, 1936), 249–77; Farish, *Circuit Rider Dismounts*, 257; Staples, *Reconstruction in Arkansas*, 328, 331; Gustavus J. Orr, *The Education of the Negro, Its Rise, Progress and*

The founding of the University of Arkansas represented no special zeal on the part of the Radicals for higher education. It was part of a bequest which the South had not been able to take advantage of until after the war and the readmission of the former Confederate states. In 1862 Congress had passed the Morrill Act, which allowed every state to share in the bounty of the public domain to the extent of 30,000 acres for each member of Congress, provided the proceeds were used to set up schools which should teach the agricultural and mechanical arts. Most Southern states added such departments to their existing universities; but Arkansas now used her proceeds to supplement the funds for beginning her university.

The private and denominational colleges, being free from Radical molestation, were relatively more important during the Reconstruction times than they were ever to be again. Most of these schools reopened in the fall of 1865 and continued uninterruptedly through Reconstruction. Wofford College, in Spartanburg, South Carolina, remained open through war and Reconstruction. While the University of North Carolina was sleeping in her Radical disgrace, Trinity College was thriving with over 200 students. The University of the South, which had long been in the minds of many Southerners as a special citadel for Southern culture, was finally opened in 1868. Washington and Lee University, so named after Lee's death, offered the South the opportunity to make this institution into a great memorial to its general-president by starting a campaign to induce each Southern state to raise an endowment of $50,000.[9] The old municipally aided College of Charleston was able to reassemble its scattered treasures of books and museum specimens and begin its new lease on life in February, 1866.

Education was to continue to suffer in the South by the division of a scanty income among a great number of institutions. This folly, not yet much used by the state governments, was now being practiced by the religious denominations. In 1884 six Southern states had sixty-seven colleges for men, struggling for existence,

Present Status; Being an Address Delivered before the National Educational Association at its Late Meeting at Chautauqua, N.Y. (Atlanta, 1880).

[9] Farish, *Circuit Rider Dismounts,* 259–60; *Southern Magazine,* XII (1873), 330–39; Augusta *Weekly Chronicle & Sentinel,* January 21, 1874.

while the six New England states had a total of only seventeen.[10]

The Radicals did little to promote higher education in the South; indeed, their activities carried on in the name of helping were, in fact, hindering. Their attempts at coeducation of the races had helped neither white nor black in the field of learning nor in a better understanding of race relations. Throughout the period of Reconstruction higher education made little progress except in the development of a new conception of what should be included.

Common schools, which had been variously dealt with in ante-bellum times, came out of the Reconstruction, established in every state. Both the Radicals and the native white regimes played a part, and neither was wholly responsible for what had been accomplished by 1880. It was neither Radical inspiration nor legislation which made the common schools a practical accomplishment; yet the Radicals by their lip service and laws elevated education into a position of first importance. They provided on paper for elaborate school systems calling for appropriations shocking to Southerners; they established the principle of an obligation to levy taxes for education; and they set up the right of the Negroes to be educated. In these respects the Radicals made genuine contributions.

There was a wide contrast between Radicals' promise and their performance. In no state did they actually set into full operation the systems of education they outlined in law. They withheld the money actually set aside by their laws for education and squandered it; they set up school boards composed of politicians, who were in part illiterate Negroes and who, as in Alabama, accounted for little of the money they received; they saddled upon the South expenses made in the name of education far beyond the ability of the people to pay; they called for mixed schools which neither the whites nor the mass of Negroes wanted; in fine, they prostituted the good name of education to their base designs for raiding the public treasury and building up political machines. T. W. Cordoza, the black superintendent of education in Mississippi, was "shingled with indictments" and spent much of his time in court answering

10 Farish, *Circuit Rider Dismounts,* 276.

them. "What a lovely and improving sight for the children of the State, white and black!" exclaimed a Northern observer.[11] Another, from England, after surveying the school situation in Alabama, where many Negroes who did not know the alphabet were on school boards, said that "the education question here, with all its solemn sanctions and ennobling associations, seems to have received the last touch of ridicule, and common sense is struck completely dumb."[12] An observer of the scene in Louisiana found that the superintendent of education, a mulatto, was so ignorant and careless of his duties that he did not know how many schools were in his state.[13] But Joseph P. B. Wilmer, Episcopal bishop of Louisiana, knew that in 1876 there were at least in one parish thirteen schools attended by Negroes only and not one which the whites would call their own, though the latter bore the whole tax burden.[14] These are some particulars of Radical dishonesties in their educational activities: The Radicals lacked $1,321,000 of paying to the South Carolina schools what they were entitled to; North Carolina Radicals gave their schools in 1870 only $38,900 of the $136,000 which they collected for that purpose; in Louisiana the Radicals sold $1,000,000 of state bonds belonging to the school fund and used the proceeds to pay the expenses of the legislature in 1872; and under the Brownlow regime in Tennessee only 47 per cent of the school taxes were spent on education.[15]

Equally destructive of sound educational progress in the South was the Radical attempt to force mixed schools on the people. Only in South Carolina, Florida, Mississippi, and Louisiana was the policy applied with determination; the wording of constitutional provisions on education in the other states made it possible to set up separate schools for the two races. Louisiana's constitution was most blatant: "There shall be no separate schools or institutions of learning established exclusively for any race by the State of Louisiana." Mixed education was demanded only by the

11 Nordhoff, *Cotton States,* 74.   12 Somers, *Southern States since the War,* 171.
13 King, *Great South,* 97.

14 J. P. B. Wilmer, New Orleans, to Samuel J. Tilden, July 26, 1876, in Samuel J. Tilden Papers (New York Public Library).

15 Boyd, "Some Phases of Educational History in the South since 1865," *loc. cit.,* 261–63.

323

Carpetbagger politicians who thought this would help their standing with the Negroes, and by the impractical reformers who believed that only in this way could racial lines be beat down. The mass of blacks had no desire to be educated in the same schools with the whites. The New Orleans *Picayune* declared, "There are black people who desire to keep their race unmixed; who do not desire to mix either in blood or association with white people. Are they to be compelled to send their children to mixed schools or go without?"[16] White people in Louisiana refused to attend schools with Negroes, and where the constitution was not openly violated by setting up exclusively white schools, the whites attended no schools or set up private institutions. "All this may be prejudice," remarked a New Orleans editor, "but if so, it is a prejudice which has become a part of our average white human nature, and to change it requires something stronger than law—a willing popular acquiescence."[17] Even the Scalawags opposed mixed schools, as indeed did Northern settlers who came South to make their permanent homes. An Ohioan, who had come to North Carolina to teach in Negro schools and who later decided to stay, protested against mixed schools. In a letter to her former teacher, James A. Garfield, she said, "For my part I protest against an attempt to compel blacks and whites to mingle more together. I would not consent to our children's attending a mixed school; for as the blacks are now, their society would be degrading. . . . I wish they had a country, a pleasant one of their own."[18]

Mixed schools constituted a stumbling block needlessly placed in the way of Southern education. The lukewarm attitude or downright hostility of Southerners to education under the Radical regime was due largely to their fear of mixed schools. The outburst in Mississippi was clearly based on this fear. Yet otherwise intelligent and apparently honest well-wishers of the South sought unsuccessfully to include this pathetically unwise principle in the Civil Rights Bill which was enacted into law in 1875. Southerners

16 Quoted in Atlanta *Daily New Era*, October 3, 1867. See also, Somers, *Southern States since the War*, 228.

17 New Orleans *Weekly Times*, December 19, 1874.

18 Mary A. Neely, Jerusalem, N.C., to James A. Garfield, March 14, 1878, in James A. Garfield Papers (Division of Manuscripts, Library of Congress).

solemnly declared that they would abandon their common-school systems before they would submit to mixed schools—"it is better to have no schools than mixed schools." [19] Barnas Sears, a Northerner who was devoting his life to Southern education, seeing how criminal it was to wreck the growing Southern school systems, declared "that if Congress itself should for a shadowy abstraction entail popular ignorance upon the South, after giving universal suffrage, and after all the States had established a free-school law, somebody would have a terrible responsibility, which the Southern people of all parties would be slow to forget." By advising with Benjamin F. Butler, who was promoting the bill, and also with President Grant, he was able to get the mixed-school provision removed. [20]

By forcing Negro suffrage upon the South the national government became clearly charged with the additional duty of seeing that these newly enfranchised voters be educated; it could not sensibly dismiss the idea with the feeling that the impoverished Southerners should bear the expense. Said a Northern traveler, "The negroes have been called *the wards of the nation;* yet we find the Southern States and a few individuals and societies doing all that is done for them. The nation does little but look on." [21] The national government spent many millions of dollars upon the Indians but nothing upon the Negroes. Even English philanthropy gave over $1,000,000 for their education and general welfare; the United States government gave them the ballot and abandoned them. [22]

The Radicals were not entirely responsible either for educational progress or retrogression during Reconstruction, for they had varying leases of life in the different states. Not gaining a foothold before 1867, they began to lose their control as early as 1870 and they made their complete and final exit in 1877. So it was, then, that the first action on education after the war was taken by the native governments set up by President Johnson. The states,

19 Augusta *Weekly Chronicle & Sentinel,* June 10, 1874.

20 Jabez L. M. Curry, *Peabody Education Fund: A Brief Sketch of George Peabody, and a History of the Peabody Education Fund through Thirty Years* (Cambridge. 1898), 64–65.

21 King, *Great South,* 602. See also, Stearns, *Black Man of the South,* 484.

22 Swint, *Northern Teacher in the South,* 21–22; King, *Great South,* 599.

though in utter financial and economic collapse, set about their educational tasks, some like South Carolina doing very little, some like Georgia organizing for the first time common-school systems, and some like Alabama re-establishing their old systems. Indeed, Alabama's system had paid out more money annually for education in ante-bellum days than in any year under Radical rule.[23] Georgia, to provide teachers as well as to aid Confederate veterans, allowed $300 a year expenses for indigent maimed veterans attending the state colleges, if they would become teachers. Though women teachers greatly predominated in the North, men instructed the youth in the South. Only in Louisiana did women teachers outnumber the men. The movement for women teachers, however, was growing in the Southern states. Proof that native Southerners believed in education supported at public expense and for all races, though not in mixed schools, was seen in the fact that when the Radicals disappeared the schools with many minor adjustments and a few short suspensions grew and flourished more than ever before. Intelligent Southerners wanted the Negroes educated but not by Northern teachers in mixed schools. A Northerner who had traveled extensively in the South when most of the governments there were under native white rule found that the Negroes got a fair share of the school fund. Negro normal schools and colleges were set up widely over the South by the native white governments, a division of the Morrill land-grant fund was made with Negro schools, and other appropriations were made. Georgia gave the Negro college, Atlanta University, as large an appropriation as it gave its own University of Georgia. Private Negro colleges received the good will of the South, if no more. Atlanta and Nashville developed centers of Negro higher education. Fisk University, in the latter city, became well known not only because it started its students with the alphabet and ended them with a diploma, but also for its Jubilee Singers who early began to sing before both Northern and Southern audiences and bring back much-needed money. One Northern trip yielded $62,000; and a voyage to England led the Singers to a performance before the Queen and the

[23] Fleming, *Civil War and Reconstruction in Alabama*, 606, 607. See also, Augusta *Weekly Chronicle & Sentinel*, July 12, 1865; Thompson, *Reconstruction in Georgia*, 121-22; Simkins and Woody, *South Carolina during Reconstruction*, 417.

amassing of an income of £10,000 from the whole season of activities.[24]

The old ante-bellum academies disappeared with the war, both in name and in many cases in fact. The mass of the common schools during Reconstruction were concerned with the first few grades alone. Only in the towns and cities and in a few other favored communities were there high schools. Apart from government-supported high schools, some were set up by religious denominations and some run by private educators. William Gordon McCabe became famous for his University School at Petersburg, a sort of Rugby for young Virginians; a retired New York merchant set up Lookout Mountain School near Chattanooga; and Madame Sosnowski, of European birth, continued in Athens, Georgia, the traditions of the Old South in her Home School for girls.[25]

The greatest act of help and friendship which came to the South during the Reconstruction originated with George Peabody, Massachusetts-born English banker and benefactor. Ever mindful of his native land and especially of the most needy part of it, in 1867 he set up a fund of $1,000,000 in cash and $1,100,000 in Mississippi State bonds of doubtful value, to which he added later another $1,000,000, for the purpose of promoting education in the South, "to be distributed among the entire population, without other distinction than their needs and the opportunities of usefulness to them." [26] The South was deeply moved by this beam of light piercing their blackest darkness. "Did the spirit of GEORGE PEABODY animate the American Congress or the

24 De Bow's Review, III (1867), 492; Thompson, Reconstruction in Georgia, 123, 335, 337; Tenth Census, 1880, I Population, 917; Thompson McDuffie Weekly Journal, January 17, 1877; Campbell, White and Black, 293, 313; Nordhoff, Cotton States, 22; Nation, XXV (1877), 70-71; Augusta Weekly Chronicle & Sentinel, October 7, 1874; Orr, Education of the Negro, 12; Taylor, Negro in Tennessee, 168-204; Coulter, Short History of Georgia, 405; Scribner's Monthly, XIV (1877) 312; King, Great South, 604-606, 613; Simkins and Woody, South Carolina during Reconstruction, 427.

25 Elberton Gazette, January 3, 1872; Farish, Circuit Rider Dismounts, 243; Armistead C. Gordon, Memories and Memorials of William Gordon McCabe (Richmond, 1925), I, 191-252; Macon American Union, September 7, 1871; Southern Magazine, XI (1872), 383-84.

26 Curry, Peabody Fund, 64-65; Phebe A. Hanaford, The Life of George Peabody . . . (Boston, 1870), 155-64.

Northern people, reconstruction would not long remain in a snarl,"
was the appreciative comment of a Georgia editor.[27] A Floridian
said, "Mr. Peabody is justly entitled to all the praise which his admiring countrymen can possible bestow." [28] The nearest approach
Southerners ever came to making a man a king, erecting a court
for him, and doing obeisance to him was in 1869 when Peabody
on a visit to America received at White Sulphur Springs in good
taste and proper dignity the thanks of a grateful South.[29]

To administer this fund, Peabody appointed a board, which
selected Barnas Sears, president of Brown University, as director
of its activities. With great tact and common sense Sears established
his residence in the South and traveled widely over the country,
talking to the people and determining the best way to spend the
fund. Describing the effect of Sears's trip through Texas, a citizen
of that state declared that "never was there such enthusiasm awakened to commence a new and grand educational era." [30] As Sears
found no dearth of claims upon his bounty, the Peabody fund soon
set up these principles: None of the money should be used to
originate schools, and no private or sectarian schools should be
helped. It was felt that the money could be most effectively used
in aiding those schools already in operation and under the stabiliz-
ing and continuing control of governmental agencies. Many city
school systems got their first strength from the Peabody fund. Ad-
hering to the principle of using the money where it was most needed
and where it would do the most good, Sears refused to help the
mixed schools of Louisiana, as well as Freedmen's Aid schools
still in operation. The board expended $35,400 during the first
year of its existence (1868); the greatest amount it expended in
any one year was $136,850 in 1873.[31]

The instruction of thousands of new students called for a large
supply of textbooks and also led to close consideration of the nature of the books. Webster's famous Blueback Spellers and the Mc-
Guffie Readers were in good repute, many having been used during

27 Augusta *Weekly Constitutionalist*, February 20, 1867.
28 Tallahassee *Semi-Weekly Floridian*, February 12, 1867.
29 Curry, *Peabody Fund*, 52.
30 *Ibid.*, 58–59. See also, Edwin A. Alderman and Armistead C. Gordon, *J. L. M. Curry: A Biography* (New York, 1911), 221.
31 Curry, *Peabody Fund*, 147.

the Confederacy. When the war ended in 1865, one San Antonio dealer had 100,000 copies of these books on hand which he had, by circumventing the blockade, brought in through Mexico. The Peabody gift awakened in Northern publishers a generosity, not entirely unselfish, exemplified in a donation to the Peabody Board by D. Appleton & Company and A. S. Barnes & Company of 200,000 copies of their textbooks.[32] A Texas editor in commenting on these gifts warned, "Now we would rather see two hundred thousand vipers uncoil themselves and crawl all over the face of our country than the same number of Messrs. Appleton or Messrs. Barnes text books." [33]

The Peabody gift also suggested to Southerners the opportunity of entering the publishing business and using sectional appeal to increase their business. Even with ulterior motives of increasing their own sales of textbooks, Southerners would have been less than ordinary mortals had they not raised a cry against certain Northern histories which taught that Southern slaveowners had been degraded beings, that Confederate heroes were vile conspirators, and that Sheridan, Sherman, and other Northern generals were delivering angels. John B. Gordon declared he would never allow his children to be subjected to teachings which attempted to make them despise their father, and he believed that no other self-respecting Southerner would permit it.[34]

Various publishers, North and South, vied for Southern business; but the most ambitious and best known was the University Publishing Company of New York City, formerly known as Richardson & Company, which was in fact owned by Southerners, three thousand of them. Gordon was one of the vice-presidents. This company engaged outstanding Southerners to write textbooks in their special fields and advertised that it would publish those which were "Unsectional, Unpartisan, and Unpolitical . . . Prepared by the most Eminent Southern Scholars and entirely acceptable to Southern Teachers and Parents." These books were widely adopted over the South and recommended by state legislatures.

32 Galveston *Tri-Weekly News*, June 9, 1865; *De Bow's Review*, III (1867), 491; Sandersville *Central Georgian*, July 10, 1867.
33 Houston *Telegraph*, quoted in Sandersville *Central Georgian*, July 10, 1867. See also, *De Bow's Review*, IV (1867), 597.
34 *Plantation*, I (1870), 696.

Matthew F. Maury was engaged to write or edit a geographical series; George Frederick Holmes, readers, spellers, and histories; Charles S. Venable, arithmetics; John and Joseph LeConte, a scientific series; Basil L. Gildersleeve, Latin texts; and Richard Malcolm Johnston, English classics.[35] This group of authors produced texts as noteworthy and respectable as any in the country. Generations of Southerners developed a debt of gratitude to these men.

With all the South's zeal for education both for whites and for Negroes, it made slow progress in banishing illiteracy from its population. Despite its undiminished tenacity to the principle of local control of education, the South often tried to induce the Federal government to provide money for this great labor. In 1878 representatives from nine Southern states met in Atlanta in the Southern Educational Convention to promote a bill in Congress which would distribute to the states on the basis of illiteracy the receipts from land sales.[36] The percentages of the population above ten years of age in 1880 unable to write follow:

	White	*Colored*
Virginia	18	74
North Carolina	32	77
South Carolina	22	78
Georgia	23	82
Florida	21	71
Alabama	25	81
Mississippi	17	75
Louisiana	20	79
Texas	14	75
Arkansas	25	75
Tennessee	28	72 [37]

[35] *De Bow's Review*, V (1868), 1108; *Southern Cultivator*, XXIV (1866), 241; *Plantation*, II (1871), 272, 650; *Land We Love*, IV (1867–1868), 448; San Antonio *Daily Herald*, September 28, 1871; Atlanta *Weekly Sun*, May 20, 1873; Buck, *Road to Reunion*, 58.

[36] Greenville *Enterprise and Mountaineer*, February 13, 1878; Atlanta *Christian Index*, February 14, 1878.

[37] Fletcher W. Hewes and Henry Gannett, *Scribner's Statistical Atlas of the United States, Showing by Graphic Methods their Present Condition and their Political, Social and Industrial Development* (New York, 1883), lvii.

Counterparts to educational developments were to be seen in the field of religion. Just as Northern leaders sought to seize the Negro's mind and convert the whites to Northern educational thought and practices, they attempted likewise to deal with Southerners, white and black, in their religion. The end of the war found the chief denominations broken into Northern and Southern divisions, the Methodist and Baptist schisms being of long standing. It might well have been supposed that the churches, actuated as they supposedly were by a Christian forgiving spirit, would have quickly healed their breaches and have offered themselves as examples to the politicians. The only divided denomination which immediately decided to forgive and forget was the Episcopal. The Confederate branch decided in November, 1865, in a meeting of their bishops and deputies at Augusta, to return, and the Northern branch coalesced with it in the spirit of equality. This quick action did not come soon enough to prevent overweening Federal commanders from demanding the return of the name of the President of the United States to the prayers of the Episcopal priests. On the refusal of Bishop Richard H. Wilmer of Alabama to pray for the President before civil government was restored in his state, the Federal commander forbade him and his clergy to preach "or perform divine service." The Bishop complied in January, 1866.

Episcopal reunion was easy because the members of this faith had not embraced the progressivism of the age; they considered their ancient religious principles sufficient. It was not so with the Presbyterians, Baptists, and Methodists. The Presbyterians continued some unfinished ante-bellum quarrels; while the Baptists, who had never been closely bound into a national organization, ignored each other, except for a few stinging expressions like this one from the Georgia Baptists; "There is not the least prospect of a re-union of Northern and Southern Baptists, for many years to come, if *ever*. We think the subject had better be dropped. No good can come from fighting the air." [38]

[38] Atlanta *Christian Index*, January 13, 1866. See also, Columbia (S.C.) *Southern Presbyterian*, September 6, 1866. According to the Richmond *Daily Enquirer*, June 11, 1866, the Northern Methodists, Baptists, and Presbyterians were "far more of political organizations than of religious fraternities, and being such, are already much too strong for the public safety."

The most uncompromising clerical gladiators throughout the nation were the Northern Methodists, whose church polity and practice became so steeped in the new isms of the age as to make it difficult to distinguish them from a wing of the Republican party. A Richmond editor declared that it was "the most powerful organization in this country." [39] As radical and uncompromising as Thaddeus Stevens himself, they believed in Negro suffrage, the confiscation of Southern property, and death to traitors. The most extreme advocated miscegenation. A New Hampshire minister exclaimed, "Instead of giving the rebels place and power again, they ought to be taken by the nape of the neck and held over hell till they squalled like cats." [40] Jefferson Davis was "the bloody dregs and *debris* of the 'lost cause'"; and Carpetbaggers were the "martyrs of today, chosen of God and precious." The New York *Christian Advocate* proudly said, "Born with the Republic, the Methodist Episcopal Church has become the guardian of American liberties"; and the New York Conference resolved "that at least some of the leaders of the rebellion be punished with death." [41]

After the war Methodists flocked into the South to remake the people in the image of Thaddeus Stevens. "The field is large. Society is to be recast in a higher mold," said a Methodist paper.[42] Many Methodist ministers became agents in the Freedmen's Bureau, selected "as being the most devout, zealous, and loyal of that religious sect known as the Northern Methodist Church." [43] They claimed to have at least a hundred missionaries in each Southern state promoting Reconstruction. Said one, "I felt as truly called of God to enter the political arena for the reconstruction of the State government as I ever felt called to my ministerial

[39] Richmond *Daily Enquirer*, August 26, 1876. The New Orleans *Christian Advocate* said, "To obliterate State lines, unite the Churches, and surrender society to the unchallenged dominance of Northern fashions and opinions, would be a disaster to Christendom." Quoted by Farish, *Circuit Rider Dismounts*, 148. The *Southern Christian Advocate* said, "Religion is the pretence; to add to the political power of a sectional party, to which that Church has allied itself, is the real purpose, and all the utterances of their missionaries and perverts, and of their new-fledged religious papers in the South prove it." Quoted by Farish, *Circuit Rider Dismounts*, 156.

[40] Augusta *Weekly Constitutionalist*, November 30, 1867.

[41] Quotations from Farish, *Circuit Rider Dismounts*, 118, 123, 133–34, 135.

[42] *Southwestern Christian Advocate*, quoted *ibid.*, 107.

[43] *Ku Klux Conspiracy*, I, 442. See also, Macon *Daily Telegraph*, May 16, 1868.

office and functions." [44] A Methodist leader approached the Republican party in the campaign of 1868 and promised to get all the New York conferences to endorse Republicanism and thereby influence 3,000,000 people. Most of their preachers "will feel free to preach or pray in accordance with the resolutions adopted by the conference." [45]

The Northern Methodists had no desire to reunite with the Southern wing of the church. In fact, they considered "coalescing with its foul Southern sister" would be "spiritual death." A Methodist paper characterized the Southern congregations in 1872 as "pro-slavery, man-stealing, Negro-whipping, whiskey-drinking, Ku Klux Churches." Their plans were to civilize Southerners into Northern Methodists; and part of their plan, and the most lucrative part, was to seize all Southern Methodist church property possible. They had made a beginning during the war, when the Secretary of War had allowed Bishop Edward R. Ames to assume control of all churches not served by loyal preachers. Now with the war over, they attempted to hold the property permanently. According to a Methodist Federal soldier, "We Federal soldiers regard horse thieves and the Southern Methodist Church as the only two rebel organizations but what surrendered with Lee's army." The Northern Methodists, violating the ante-bellum agreement, in addition to seizing Southern Methodist property, a practice from which they finally desisted in the Cape May agreement in 1876, also set up their congregations, especially in those regions where there had been Union sentiment during the war and among the Negroes. They were determined that there should be no Mason and Dixon's Line through the Methodist Kingdom of God. [46]

At the end of the war the Southern Methodists had varying feelings on the subject of reunion with their Northern brethren, but the official position of the Church was expressed by a conference of bishops which met in Columbus, Georgia, in August, 1865. They

[44] John H. Caldwell, *Reminiscences of the Reconstruction of Church and State in Georgia* (Wilmington, Del., 1895), 10.

[45] H. Dunn, Mooers, N.Y., to Chandler, June 20, 1868, in William E. Chandler Papers, VI, Nos. 1068–69.

[46] Stearns, *Black Man of the South*, 504; Farish, *Circuit Rider Dismounts*, 22–50, 95–96, 107, 156; Coulter, *William G. Brownlow*, 298; Atlanta *Christian Index*, March 13, 27, 1873.

333

feared that "a large proportion, if not a majority of Northern Methodists have become incurably radical. They teach for doctrine the commandments of men. . . . They have incorporated social dogmas and political tests into their Church creeds." There were other Southern Methodists who were willing to rejoin the Northern wing of the church if the union was on the basis of equality and not on the presumption "that men of God wish to follow the fire and sword, devastation and pecuniary ruin of the army, with an ecclesiastical guillotine that will stain the temples of God with the blood of souls." Bishop Gilbert Haven, who came south and advocated the amalgamation of the races was called by a North Carolinian an "infamous religious shyster and impostor." [47]

Though Northern Methodists were in the forefront of the onset against the South, Southerners found that all Carpetbagging preachers were alike and classed them the same. In the eyes of an Alabaman, "Perhaps the greatest liars and the most malignant slanderers that the North has spewed out upon the South since the close of the war, are the reverend blackguards that have been sent among us as ministers of religion." A Georgian declared: "Preachers blating hypocrisy with their lips, with the venom of the Devil in their hearts, missionaries of wrath, stirring up strife, kindling hate, and sowing the seeds of damnation in the soil of hate, come amongst us in clerical robes spotted with sin and dripping with crime, their Bible 'a league with hell,' their text the enmity of man with man, and the gospel of lust as their creed, only that Radical orthodoxy may be accepted and acknowledged by the South." Uncompromising Northern preachers made Southern preachers uncompromising too, as stern Robert L. Dabney, a Presbyterian, shouted out: "I do not forgive. I try not to forgive. What! forgive those people, who have invaded our country, burned our cities, destroyed our homes, slain our young men, and spread desolation and ruin over the land! No, I do not forgive them." [48]

Though the Southern churches were forced into un-Christian

[47] Farish, *Circuit Rider Dismounts*, 54–61; Nora C. Chaffin, "A Southern Advocate of Methodist Unification in 1865," in *North Carolina Historical Review* (Raleigh), XVIII (1941), 45–46; Buck, *Road to Reunion*, 59–71; Raleigh *Daily Sentinel*, December 16, 1875; Rome *Weekly Courier*, January 5, 1876.

[48] Montgomery *Weekly Advertiser*, May 19, 1868; Elberton *Gazette*, October 30, 1868; Buck, *Road to Reunion*, 66–67.

feelings by the rigorous onset of Reconstructionists, political and ecclesiastical, they maintained their old customs and beliefs uncontaminated by the new Northern notions. They held their Sunday School picnics, their ministers dressed in the conventional garb with white cravat and probably a cane, and they continued their ornate pulpit oratory. They opposed dancing and cried out against smoking and chewing tobacco, even though they themselves might be guilty of these practices. There were a few signs of something new. Instrumental music was breaking into more and more churches, though the sentinels on the watchtowers fought back vigorously and unsuccessfully against these manifestations of Satan. True enough such music might bring more people to church and "the organ of course excites people; but is it a religious excitement?" one opponent wanted to know. The Young Men's Christian Associations were beginning to spring up in the cities and led the old churches to ask what need there was for them. The Baptists especially opposed these interlopers. Slight but unsuccessful attempts were made to introduce New England Congregationalism into the South and now and then a few elders of the Church of Jesus Christ of Latter-Day Saints wandered over the countryside, producing more excitement and violence than converts.[49]

In times of unusual troubles people sometimes turn for consolation or forgetfulness either to religion or to strong drink. Some Southerners tempered their worldly thoughts and interests with more religion, others sought refuge in drink. Army life had acquainted many young soldiers with drinking, and they found little incentive to stop when the war ended. Grogshops grew up in many country settlements or crossroads and peppered the bigger cities; well-established Northern liquor houses called the attention of their Southern friends to their willingness to renew old business connections which for a quarter of a century had been uninterrupted except for the calamity of war; and illicit dis-

[49] Macon *Daily Telegraph*, May 16, 1868; Sandersville *Herald*, June 13, 1878; July 31, 1879; Atlanta *Christian Index*, December 28, 1876; July 19, 1877; June 28, 1878; Elberton *Gazette*, May 17, October 11, 1876; Alrutheus A. Taylor, "The Negro in South Carolina during the Reconstruction," in *Journal of Negro History*, IX (1924), 347.

tilleries set to work in the mountainous and backwoods parts of the country "turning out a dreary drug, in which there is little or no whisky, producing only vertigo, and ending, through all forms of violent disorder, in cholera-morbus," while big distilleries in cities cheated the government out of revenues through bribery. Churches carried on campaigns against whisky, and temperance societies grew up or old ones were renewed, run generally by women. Legal control of the sale of whisky began to appear in the form of high licenses, and a few states were beginning to adopt the principle of local option. As for the latter method, "Prohibitory statutes will not stop the traffic in spirits," warned a Georgia editor. "Morality cannot be legislated into people." [50]

The greatest difficulty the South had in handling its liquor problem related to the control of drinking by Negroes. Having been denied whisky while in slavery, they gave full reign to their appetites in freedom. With little experience in self-control they would spend their last piece of money for a drink of whisky, and they would break in and steal this article before all else. A Northern traveler declared, "I never saw man, woman, or child, reckless young scapegrace, or sanctimonious old preacher among them, who would refuse it." Many Negroes spent half their earnings for liquor.[51]

When freedom came the Negroes found in their religious organizations a jewel of great value. Being by nature highly emotional and excitable and now unrestrained by the hand of former masters, they carried their religious exercises to extreme lengths, both in time and content. Their evening services began at nightfall or later and continued frequently far into the next morning. Meetings might degenerate into blabberings, yellings, and groanings, and even into indecent orgies. Signs of voodooism were detected from the swamps of Louisiana to as far north as North Caro-

---

[50] Trowbridge, *South*, 287; Somers, *Southern States since the War*, 132–33, 245; Augusta *Daily Constitutionalist*, August 31, 1865; Nordhoff, *Cotton States*, 101; Montgomery *Weekly Advertiser*, June 23, 1868; August 24, 1869; Thompson *McDuffie Weekly Journal*, March 6, 1878; Sandersville *Herald*, March 27, 1874; Simkins and Woody, *South Carolina during Reconstruction*, 405–406; Augusta *Weekly Chronicle & Sentinel*, March 11, 1874; Columbus (Miss.) *Press*, May 2, 1874.

[51] Reid, *Southern Tour*, 553; Columbus (Miss.) *Press*, December 6, 1873; Alvord, *Letters from the South*, 9.

lina. Chants and dismal howls the Negroes called "mourning for their sins, as the angels mourn." Their services recalled to one Northerner the performances of the heathen in Africa or the rites of the savages of the Fiji Islands, leaving out the feast in human flesh. The most widespread rite was the shout, which consisted of a combination of singing and a sort of holy dance or shuffle in which the feet were dragged along the floor.[52] This is a stanza from one of their chants:

> *We's be nearer to de Lord*
> *Den de white folks; and dey knows it;*
> *See de glory-gate unbarred—*
> *Walk in, darkeys, past de guard,*
> *Bet your dollar He won't close it!* [53]

For the mass of Negroes, religion had no relation to morality. It was an emotional orgy which they enjoyed no less than did their preachers who promoted it. Dressed in their florid and ornate colors and styles Negroes passed from their day services to a night "dance break-down"; and from their night services they might likely adjourn to a watermelon patch not their own. A half hour after a Negro had left a shout he might be "begging the overseer for a drink of whiskey." Sympathetic Southerners firmly declared that good Negro workmen were ruined by their churchgoing: "Instead of assembling there together and holding services for a reasonable length of time, they frequently prolong them all night, disturbing every body in the neighborhood, and hatching up enough devilment to run a small size hot country." Sometimes the churchgoers would "get tired of listening, even to their own florid preachers, and frequently fall asleep in the midst of the most glowing descriptions of the torments of the damned." Some Negro preachers were of a degenerate and vicious character, who after their services might engage with the worst part of their congregations in carousals. A Northerner declared they were "infinitely worse than no preachers." They had great influence over their con-

---

[52] Reid, *Southern Tour*, 523; King, *Great South*, 607; *Southern Magazine*, XIII (1874), 36; Stearns, *Black Man of the South*, 350; Leigh, *Ten Years on a Georgia Plantation*, 59, 254.

[53] Marietta *Journal*, June 28, 1872.

gregations and were uniformly Republican political leaders. A Floridian said in 1868: "The colored preachers are *the great power* in controlling and uniting the colored vote, and they are looked to, as political leaders, with more confidence & sincerity, than any other source of instruction and control." [54] This characterization of Negro religious development in freedom, of course, did not fit every congregation. Some had ante-bellum foundations which stood the shock of emancipation, and undoubtedly new congregations organized after the war in certain cities and country communities carried on their worship with becoming decorum.

Before the war all Negro church members had belonged to the churches of their masters; but with the coming of freedom they wanted to run their own organizations. Various white denominations sought to secure religious control of the Negroes. Northern Methodists were the most successful, though the Southern Methodists were able to salvage a considerable number of their antebellum membership and organize them into a church of their own which they called the Colored Methodist Episcopal Church of America, but which other Negroes called the Rebel Church, the Democratic Church, or the Old Slavery Church. The Episcopalians as well as the Presbyterians in the South secured a few Negro congregations; and the Catholics for a time pondered seriously a special campaign to secure the freedmen.[55] They had little success because in fact they made little effort and because the Negro wanted more immediate access to God and a more friendly and emotional communion with Him than a Catholic priest could offer.

The Negroes wanted their own churches wherein they could do as they pleased, unchaperoned and uninstructed by Northerners or Southerners. Methodist Negroes found already in existence two colored churches of that persuasion in the African Methodist Epis-

---

[54] Dilke, *Greater Britain*, 27; Stearns, *Black Man of the South*, 121–23, 338, 500; Reid, *Southern Tour*, 523; Greensboro *Herald*, August 10, 1879; F. A. Dockray, Jacksonville, Fla., to Stevens, March 18, 1868, in Stevens Papers, XI, No. 54756; Campbell, *White and Black*, 330.

[55] Washington *New National Era*, May 25, 1871; Robert S. Henry, *The Story of Reconstruction* (Indianapolis, 1938), 127; Atlanta *Christian Index*, January 23, 1873; *De Bow's Review*, I (1866), 111; Augusta *Daily Press*, January 8, 1869; New York *Daily News*, June 16, 1866; Augusta *Weekly Constitutionalist*, May 26, 1875; Marietta *Journal*, March 22, 1872; Augusta *Weekly Constitutionalist*, October 3, November 14, 1866; Campbell, *White and Black*, 132; Carthage *Panola Watchman*, January 12, 1876.

copal Church and the African Methodist Episcopal Zion Church, both of which had been organized in the North many years before the war. These churches came South to reap a rich harvest.

The Negro had a harder task to make respectable progress in the field of religion than in politics or in the economic struggle. Having a freer hand he erected a greater independency in the field of religion than in any other endeavor, but the character of his progress recommended him no more than in other activities where the restraining hand of the whites was still felt.

CHAPTER XVI

THE DISINTEGRATION OF
RADICALISM

AS THE Radical plan of Reconstruction developed, Southerners put their hopes for honorable treatment in President Andrew Johnson. It was to no avail, however, for Radical Congressmen, drunk on their political successes, not only stripped Johnson of his power and attempted through billingsgate language to bring him into popular contempt, but finally impeached him and failed by a close vote to remove him from the presidency. The Supreme Court they intimidated and silenced. Having wooed and won the politically inept Ulysses Grant, they nominated him for the presidency in 1868 and made ready for a campaign which they hoped would lead to a thousand years of Republican supremacy. The jingle maker saw the elements in the picture and rhymed it thus:

> *High ding a-duddle,*
> *The court's in a muddle,*
> > *And Andy goes up to the moon;*
> *Little Grant laughs*
> *To see the sport,*
> > *And Butler runs away with the spoon.*[1]

Though their platform praised Radical Reconstruction and Negro suffrage, Grant said in his acceptance speech, "Let us have peace," which recalled to the South his honorable terms given Lee at Appomattox. Many Southerners had the feeling that Grant was the best choice the Radicals could have made.

The Democrats were in no compromising mood. They considered the worst Democrat infinitely better than the best Radical;

[1] Dalton *North Georgia Citizen,* June 4, 1868.

Radical Reconstruction was to them a travesty on civilized government. In seeking to restore the Union, they said in their platform that the Radicals had "dissolved it and subjected ten states, in the time of profound peace, to military despotism and negro supremacy," and that the Reconstruction acts were "usurpations, and unconstitutional, revolutionary and void."[2] The Northern Democracy thus came valiantly to the rescue of the South. It nominated for the presidency Horatio Seymour, former governor of New York.

Some Southerners felt that the South should let national politics alone, in which for a long time it could hope to play little part;[3] but the smell of political battle was too much for most of them to resist, and so they entered the campaign with a vim. "Deny peace, rest, food, and withdraw your approving smiles, from father, husband, son, brother, lover unless they should vote for Seymour," a Georgia editor counseled the women.[4] "Nothing was decided by the war, if we may trust the defiance now hurled at us by the South," retorted the New York *Tribune*.[5]

As proof that the South was loyal to the flag and that it merely wanted justice, Southerners answered the *Tribune* and all other traducers, by working whole-souled into a publicity scheme of Sergeant Gilbert H. Bates to carry the Stars and Stripes through the South. Though not conceived as part of the political campaign, the trip was made in time to have such an effect. The Sergeant, who had belonged to the First Wisconsin Heavy Artillery during the war, accepted a wager from some fellow-Wisconsinites that he could not carry the United States flag through the heart of the South without receiving insult or injury. He was to travel alone and without money. Accepting the challenge, he set out from Vicksburg in January, 1868, with a flag made by the ladies of that place, and he received the cheers of an expectant people with mounting enthusiasm wherever he went. Arriving in Washington in April, he was received at the White House by President Johnson and presented with a bouquet by his daughter. Then attempt-

2 Edward Stanwood, *A History of the Presidency from 1788 to 1897* (Boston, 1928), 324.
3 For example, see *Southern Magazine*, XIV (1874), 20.
4 Americus *Tri-Weekly Sumter Republican*, November 3, 1868.
5 New York *Tribune*, August 28, 1868.

ing to plant the flag on the capitol dome and being prevented by the Radicals, he waved it from the top of the unfinished Washington Monument. Apart from the grand entertainment he received from the Confederate Southerners throughout the trip, the only incidents of note were attacks now and then by dogs and the reputed attempt of North Carolina Radicals to bribe him with $10,000 to give up the trip with the explanation that he had been driven out of the South. When it was suggested that he try to carry the flag through New England on the same terms, he refused, as to start through that inhospitable region without money was to court starvation and to travel there with money was to risk being robbed.[6]

The South could prove that it loved and respected the flag, but it had no desire to show like feeling for Thaddeus Stevens, who died in the midst of the campaign and thereby gave opportunity for Southerners to show that his death did not mollify their feelings. According to a Georgia editor, "Living, he was abhorred by honorable men; dead, no patriot's tears will be shed for his memory."[7] "May his new iron-works wean him from earth, and the fires of his new furnace never go out!" was the prayer of a Louisianian.[8]

Aided by the United States Army, by the Negroes, and by the argument that Grant's election would bring stability and prosperity to the South, the Republicans won. Only eight of the former Confederate states voted in this election, as Virginia, Mississippi, and Texas had not yet been readmitted. In spite of every Radical impediment the Democrats carried Georgia and Louisiana. Though

[6] *Triumphal March of Sergeant [Gilbert H.] Bates from Vicksburg to Washington* (Washington, 1868), 1–36; *Land We Love*, VI (1868–1869), 256–57; Montgomery *Weekly Advertiser*, April 28, May 19, 1868; Little Rock *Weekly Arkansas Gazette*, April 21, 1868; Griffin *American Union*, April 24, 1868; Hamilton. *Reconstruction in North Carolina*, 282. Taking a leaf from Sergeant Bates's book, a Virginia youth planned to carry the Confederate flag through New England beginning at Boston. The Norfolk *Virginian* sternly objected, as the South would be "shocked at this foolish desecration of its folds." "Let its associations remain unpolluted by vulgar display and senseless bravado," the editor counseled. Quoted in Elberton *Gazette*, July 2, 1873.

[7] Augusta *Weekly Chronicle & Sentinel*, August 19, 1868.

[8] Quoted in Fleming (ed.), *Documentary History of Reconstruction*, II, 272. For a four-page letter of bitter curses on Stevens while he was still living, see J. D. Hopkins, Newberry, S.C., to Stevens, May 28, 1868, in Stevens Papers, XII, Nos. 54869–70.

Grant was elected, a majority of white Americans voted against him; only by adding the 450,000 Negro votes to the white Republicans was the Republican majority obtained.

This election showed how essential it was that the Negro vote be secured permanently for the Republican party and that the right of the Negro to vote in the North as well as in the South be imbedded in the Federal Constitution. A Southerner saw the movement to secure such an amendment in this light: "By unscrupulous, unprecedented, and unprincipled means" the Radicals had "placed the government of some of the Southern States under the absolute control of the most ignorant, most proscriptive, and most abandoned set of whites and blacks that society could spew up," and they now proposed "to perpetuate the power of these vagabonds and children of ignorance by a solemn amendment to the constitution of the United States." [9] The Fifteenth Amendment, declaring that neither the United States nor a state should deny or abridge the right of a citizen to vote "on account of race, color, or previous condition of servitude," was submitted to the states and became a part of the Constitution in March, 1870.

Southerners thought they had good reason to believe that Grant, the president, would be as magnanimous as Grant, the general. It would not take long to determine the fact; a few months would show whether this confidence was "misplaced, and whether his memorable saying—*Let us have peace*—was the mere catch-word of a trickster, or the honest utterance of a patriot." [10] Grant, somewhat confused and muddled by the political maelstrom in which he found himself, first listened to the counsel of moderation and of accommodation to realities. He began by smoothing the road to Congressional legislation providing for the submission of the constitutions of Virginia and Mississippi to their respective voters. Because of its harsh franchise clauses, Virginia's constitution had never been offered to the people, and Mississippi's had been turned down. Now, in 1869, these documents were to be submitted to the people, with or without the objectionable clauses. In both cases the milder forms were accepted, and the states were readmitted to the Union in January and February, 1870, respectively. Texas,

[9] Augusta *Daily Press*, February 11, 1869.
[10] *Scott's Monthly Magazine*, VI (1868), 888.

late in making her constitution, was also allowed to submit it. Having no harsh disqualifying and disfranchising clauses, the document was adopted, and Texas was readmitted in the following March.

After this flash of friendly understanding of the Southern problem, Grant settled down to a policy dictated by the most uncompromising and vindictive Radical leaders, to be adhered to almost to the end of his eight years in the White House. He used the United States Army, to its own disgrace, in upholding discredited corrupt Radical regimes, and he carried his program to such extremes as to nauseate the mass of people even in the North. Yet Grant's problem was not simple. Frequently he had to decide not only between contesting native white and Radical regimes, but now and then between two Radical factions. He generally supported the one which has appeared to subsequent generations to have been the worse. Having visited the South in 1865, Grant had made a report favorable to Johnson's policy of moderation; it might have been worth his time to have visited the South again when he was formulating his own policy.

In addition to the corruptions in national affairs which flourished under Grant's wing, his Southern policy went far enough during his first term to lead to a widespread reaction throughout the nation against Grantism. This movement had its first political expression in Missouri in 1869 when Schurz broke from the Republican party a liberal faction which sent him to the United States Senate. It gained in momentum until in the Presidential election of 1872 it embraced the reform Republican leadership of the North, and as the Liberal Republican party, nominated Greeley for the presidency. The Democrats accepted him as their candidate, but not without opposition.

In the South there had been growing during the same time a more liberal attitude toward the Reconstruction amendments and the so-called results of the war, which took on the name of the New Departure, from an expression first used by Clement L. Vallandigham, an Ohio Democrat. Logic inevitably pointed to the joining of the Liberal Republican and New Departure movements. Southerners were beginning to see that it availed them less than nothing to continue to attack what had been done and embedded in the

Constitution. "What we need above all things is stability in government," said a Georgian. He did not believe the people desired "to see society thrown into a state of fomentation by trying to reconstruct reconstruction." [11] Fighting the inevitable was a political trick. What the South needed was to forget politics and get down to economic rehabilitation; and this would prove "a salutary remedy for political inflamation of the brain." [12]

Benjamin H. Hill of Georgia became one of the earliest and most influential leaders in the New Departure movement. It was time for the South to admit national supremacy. Hill had surrendered to the inevitable when the Confederacy had been overcome; now he would surrender likewise to the Reconstructionists. The South's ante-bellum political background gave proof enough that a Southerner did not have to be a Democrat to be respectable. In this new economic day the South should cease its hidebound politics, and the Democrats should adapt themselves to the present. By becoming more liberal they could attract the honest man, whether Radical or Negro, and become a power in the nation again. "A black man who cannot be bought is better than a white man who can," he boldly declared, "and a Republican who cannot be bought is better than a Democrat who can." [13] Hill was a forthright leader but not a prophet, for he had said in 1867 that the Reconstruction acts would "consummate the subversion of the Republic; the destruction of the Constitution; the annihilation of individual liberty, and the ultimate but complete change of all American government from the principle of consent to the rule of force." [14] This did not happen; neither did his prediction come true that the Fourteenth and Fifteenth amendments were unescapable, for though they were never repealed, Southerners found ways to nullify them successfully.

Indeed, Greeley was hard for many Southerners to swallow, for in times past he had attacked them as bitterly as any man then living. Yet many of his acts and sayings since the war might well have pleased Southerners. He had gone on Davis' bail bond, and

11 *Weekly Columbus Enquirer*, December 20, 1870.
12 New York *Herald*, quoted in Augusta *Weekly Chronicle & Sentinel*, July 12, 1871.
13 *Weekly Columbus Enquirer*, January 5, 1869.
14 Hill, *Senator Benjamin H. Hill*, 732.

had even stirred the heart of a twelve-year-old North Carolinian who wrote Greeley not merely to ask for his signature because he could sell it for a dollar but to say, "P. S. I thank you for signing Jeff Davis' bond." [15] To quarrel with Greeley's ancient record would now be as senseless as to stop to argue about the mechanism of a fire engine hastening to put out a fire. It was now time for Southerners to amnesty Greeley and go on his bond. Greeley had made a trip through the South in 1871 and had said much to encourage its industrial development. "I am for the man that can beat Grant, be he whom he may," remarked a Georgian.[16]

There was a sprinkling of Southerners who considered Hill and all other New Departure men traitors to the South. Because they were like the French kings who never learned anything or forgot anything, the New York *Herald* called them Bourbons and the name stuck. In reply Stephens said, "We are 'Bourbon' enough to be governed by principles which never die, and from which we never depart." He also declared that the South owed Greeley no more for going on Davis' bond than it owed Grant for standing out against the arrest of Lee, forgetting that Grant had acted more to save his own honor than to help Lee. Explosive Robert Toombs thundered, "I would support the devil in preference to either of them [Greeley or Grant], because when you support the devil you support a very respectable antagonist." A Georgian who lived within the shadow of Kennesaw Mountain said he would rather have Sherman than anyone else, for he had shown himself "in the end, magnanimous, liberal and sympathetic." [17] Shortly before the election a few die-hard Southerners nominated Charles O'Conor for President, who though refusing to accept the honor, received some votes.

At first the Republicans were seriously disturbed about the inroads into their Southern membership which the Liberal Republican movement might make, especially when a Southern Republican paper could say, "The question is frequently asked, Has the Republican party accomplished its mission? And if it has, *then*

15 C. A. Taylor, Wilson, N.C., to Greeley, June 3, 1872, in Greeley Papers, "Letters to him, 1866–1872."

16 *Weekly Columbus Enquirer*, May 21, 1872.

17 Atlanta *Weekly Sun*, April 24, 1872; *Weekly Columbus Enquirer*, August 29, 1871; May 21, June 18, 1872; Marietta *Journal*, May 19, 1871.

why not disband and enter new combinations, on new and living issues?" [18] There was fear that the Negroes would weaken in their Republicanism, in the face of many Negro Democratic orators brought in, and that many Southern Scalawags would find this election an excellent opportunity to slip back into the Democratic party. The party leaders began begging the national headquarters for torches to light up processions and political meetings, copies of "Marching through Georgia" to be sung, fewer campaign documents, which Negroes could not read, and more money to buy horses for Negro preachers to ride in their work of distributing ballots and winning votes.[19] The Republicans sent flocks of Howard University students into the South to make speeches, and the government applied an extra $200,000 to the campaign in North Carolina through an increase in Federal marshals to step up the enforcement of the Ku Klux Act.[20] They also cleverly promoted as much as possible the Bourbon revolt against the Liberal Republicans. Few Southern Republicans deserted their party; but the example of Democrats voting the Liberal Republican ticket made it easier for lukewarm Republicans later to join the Democrats.[21]

This new party was disastrously defeated. Greeley carried only seven states, and all were in the South or on the border—three of them (Georgia, Louisiana, and Texas) being former members of the Confederacy. Democratic apathy had been widespread over

---

[18] *Weekly Columbus Enquirer,* August 29, 1871.

[19] G. H. White, Weldon, N.C., to Chandler, July 21, 1872, in William E. Chandler Papers, XXV, No. 4869; Allen, *Reconstruction,* 197; Marietta *Journal,* October 18, 1872; Macon *American Union,* May 9, 1872; N. B. Jones, Demopolis, Ala., to Chandler, July 9, 1872, in William E. Chandler Papers, XXIV, Nos. 4696–97.

[20] William B. Hesseltine, *Ulysses S. Grant, Politician* (New York, 1935), 282–90.

[21] "I do not know one single Republican in the entire state in favor of the Cincinnati Convention," said A. Warner, Jackson, Miss., to Chandler, April 13, 1872, in William E. Chandler Papers, XX, Nos. 4072–73. "The defection in our ranks in Tenn amount to little or nothing," reported H. H. Harrison, Nashville, to Chandler, April 2, 1872, *ibid.,* Nos. 4007–08. In discussing the return of the Scalawags, a Southerner said in 1874: "Maddened by oft-repeated disappointments, they are coming back to the White-man's party, asking to be admitted, not as office-seekers, but as humble workers. They are sincere. They are taken in, their sins are forgiven, and after being deodorized, they are freely admitted to all the rights and privileges of the party." Herbert Barnes, "The Scalawag," in *Southern Magazine,* XV (1874), 302–307.

the South. Disillusioned and pathetic, Greeley, shortly before his death soon after the election, wrote, "You knew as I did that we must stop fighting the rebels sometime. But it is now settled that we never shall." [22] So there were to be "four more years of good stealing under Grant" in the North and an equal spell of bedevilment in the South; but a danger signal arose in the Congressional election of 1874 when the Democrats elected a majority of the Representatives and for the first time since ante-bellum days secured control of a house of Congress. The Republicans had frantically waved the old "bloody shirt" in this campaign by dragging out a long list of Southern atrocities, most of which when investigated proved to be myths. Though the "bloody shirt" was to be waved hereafter, the atrocity brand was from now on less powerful. It was at this time that Edward King, a feature writer for *Scribner's Monthly*, said, "The fact that in a journey of 25,000 miles, nearly a thousand of which I traveled on horseback, through mountain regions, I saw no weapons drawn, and not a single instance of assault, lynching, or even drunken brawls, ought to be considered as good testimony in favor of the Southerners." [23] Even five years earlier the New York *Times* had said that "the amount of crime perpetrated in the South as a whole, is not greater than the amount perpetrated among a corresponding population in the North or West." [24]

Grant with his Southern policy to prevent the Southerners from controlling their governments was much like Canute trying to stay the tide. Foreign to the South in all its aspects, Radicalism was predestined to go, and not even armies could permanently maintain it. Gradually the states, one by one, and degree by degree, began to ripen and fall from the Radical tree on which they had been grafted. The Conservatives, as the Democrats were often called, took advantage of every weakness of their Radical enemies. If the Radicals developed factions, and they often did, the Conservatives joined with the least objectionable one. When the Con-

[22] Newspaper clipping, in Greeley Papers.

[23] King, *Great South*, 778. See also, William B. Hesseltine, "Economic Factors in the Abandonment of Reconstruction," in *Mississippi Valley Historical Review*, XXII (1935–1936), 208.

[24] Quoted in *Weekly Columbus Enquirer*, May 25, 1869. See also, Nordhoff, *Cotton States*, 68.

servatives like the camel got their head into the tent, they soon occupied the whole establishment—a legislature on becoming Conservative would impeach the Radical governor.

Radicalism, not being able to secure a foothold equally strong throughout the South, was shaken off more easily and quickly in some states than in others. Virginia escaped simon-pure Radical rule entirely, though, of course, she went through military Reconstruction. Here the Republicans early divided into two factions and when Virginia was readmitted in 1870 each faction put up a candidate for governor. The Conservatives seeing their chance gave up their candidate and supported the milder Republican, Gilbert C. Walker, and elected him. A disappointed and disconsolate Radical wrote Sumner that the Republican party "is destroyed here, and no power can resurrect it." [25]

The year 1870 showed a distinct break in the Radical armor in three other states. In Tennessee the overweening ambition of Parson Brownlow led him to give up the governorship in 1869 for a United States senatorship, leaving the governor's office to be filled by a special election that year. The Republicans split into two factions and nominated two candidates, and according to the successful formula, the Democrats supported De Witt C. Senter, the more conservative candidate, and elected him. A constitutional convention the next year granted universal suffrage and made the road for the Democrats from that time on smooth. A Radical, bemoaning the fate of his party, reported to Sumner that "the rebels, violently, fraudulently and wickedly acceded to the control of the State." In North Carolina the beginning of the end of Radicalism made its appearance this year. Holden, who had gained the governorship after the military Reconstruction of the state, ran wild in his irresponsible attempt to break up the Ku Klux Klan in the so-called Kirk-Holden war. With a thousand plundering soldiers Colonel George W. Kirk, acting as Holden's agent, arrested many people and fell afoul of the Federal courts. A Democratic legislature, elected this year, impeached Holden and removed him from office. Todd R. Caldwell, the lieutenant governor, succeeded to the governorship, and was re-elected in the campaign of 1872. With

[25] J. W. Woltz, Covington, Va., to Sumner, January 26, 1870, in Sumner Papers, Box 96, No. 75.

power divided in the state, the Democrats did not win complete control until 1876 when they elected former Governor Vance over Judge Thomas Settle. Georgia was the fourth of the states to break Radical control in 1870 and the first of the former Confederate states to win a clear-cut and permanent Democratic control. Her Radical governor Rufus B. Bullock, unable to prevent his legislature from expelling its Negro members in 1869, had been able to induce Congress to put Georgia under a second military Reconstruction. Out of the succeeding turmoil a bitter Radical faction grew up against Bullock, which weakened the party and led in 1870 to the election of a Democratic legislature. When this body met the next year with impeachment threats in the air, Bullock fled the state. A special election held before the end of the year put into the governorship James M. Smith, a Democrat, who in his inaugural address said, "After a long and cheerless night of misrule, let us unite in indulging the hope that a brighter day, bringing with it peace, happiness and prosperity to our stricken people, is already dawning upon our beloved State." [26]

The Liberal Republican movement in 1872 showed that many Northerners were weakening in their support of Radical misrule in the South and it enheartened and made bold the Southerners; the Congressional overturn in 1874 speeded both movements. Three more states broke away from the Radicals in 1873–1874. Inevitable Radical dissensions broke out in Texas and led to the election in 1873 of Richard Coke, a Democrat. Alabama finally secured Democratic rule in 1874. In 1870 she had elected a Democratic governor, but in 1872 the Radicals with the aid of the Ku Klux Act, Federal marshals, the army, and the poor record made by the Democrats, elected their candidate. Two years of Radical tur-

[26] Patton, *Unionism and Reconstruction in Tennessee*, 201–25; Coulter, *William G. Brownlow*, 325–48; Taylor, *Negro in Tennessee*, 64–82; A. T. Akerman, Elberton, Ga., to Sumner, April 2, 1869, in Sumner Papers, Box 94, No. 4; W. McBride, Tallapoosa, Ga., to Sumner, April 26, 1869, *ibid.*, Box 91, No. 67; Hamilton, *Reconstruction in North Carolina*, 496–533; Washington *New National Era*, January 12, 1871; Thompson, *Reconstruction in Georgia*, 183–84, 255–75; M. H. Hale, Savannah, to Chandler, March 25, 1872, in William E. Chandler Papers, XX, Nos. 3948–55; Marietta *Journal*, November 24, 1871; *Address of Rufus B. Bullock to the People of Georgia, October, 1872* (n.p., n.d.), 1–59; Elberton *Gazette*, January 24, 1872.

moil which followed drove a majority of Alabamans back into the Democratic party. In Arkansas, the Radicals, true to form, broke into two factions, who fought each other in their mad scramble for office. The Democrats themselves were muddled, and nominating no ticket in 1872 they divided their support between the Radical factions. To the utter disgrace of civilized government, Joseph Brooks and Elisha Baxter fought over the governor's office for the next two years, in the so-called Brooks-Baxter war. Deciding to support neither Radical faction in the election of 1874, the Democrats nominated their own candidate, Augustus H. Garland, and elected him. The next year the Arkansans held a solemn celebration of thanksgiving for their redemption.[27]

Mississippi, having run a lone course in rejecting by an outright vote her constitution in 1868, was alone again in being the only state to throw off Radical rule in 1875. Since her readmission into the Union in 1870, Mississippi had been the battleground between two Radical factions, with the Democrats supporting the more respectable group, only to lose each time. First it was Grant's brother-in-law, Lewis Dent, they supported against the turncoat James L. Alcorn with the latter winning; and then it was Alcorn, now receiving the Democratic support against the Carpetbagger Adelbert Ames, with Ames winning. The election of 1875 gave the Democrats the legislature by 30,000 majority; impeachment proceedings were started against Ames, but were dropped when he promised to resign. Mississippi in her peculiar way of vote getting and vote scaring, known as the Mississippi Plan, had accomplished a political miracle.[28]

There were still three states left, South Carolina, Florida, and Louisiana, awaiting the day of political redemption. Joining the more respectable Radical faction, South Carolina Democrats fought a losing fight down the line through two terms of the Carpetbagger Robert K. Scott, who used bribery to save himself from impeachment by a Radical legislature; through two years of

[27] Ramsdell, *Reconstruction in Texas*, 261–87, 295–318; Fleming, *Civil War and Reconstruction in Alabama*, 735–36, 754–55, 771, 789, 795–97; Staples, *Reconstruction in Arkansas*, 373 ff.; Nordhoff, *Cotton States*, 29.

[28] Garner, *Reconstruction in Mississippi*, 229–48, 292, 372–414.

the Scalawag Franklin J. Moses, Jr., and one term of the respectable Carpetbagger Daniel H. Chamberlain.[29] The presidential election of 1876 found South Carolina Democrats expecting victory in both state and nation. In Florida the Republican party was born twins, fighting each other from the beginning. A faction attempted four times to impeach the first governor, Republican Carpetbagger Harrison Reed. One Republican governor followed another down through the years until the trumpet blew in 1876. A gleam of light broke through in 1875 when a Democrat was sent to the United States Senate, by his own tie-breaking vote in the legislature.[30] Florida awaited the resurrection with South Carolina.

Louisiana went through a terrific crucifixion, made possible by Grant's disgraceful use of the United States Army. Henry Clay Warmoth, Illinois Carpetbagger, got control of the state in 1868, riding into the governorship with the support of the most intense Radicals. Like all the other Radical regimes, this one soon disintegrated into factions, with the Customhouse ring, promoted by Grant, contesting Warmoth's supremacy. Rather than come to terms with this faction, Warmoth in the election of 1872 supported the Democratic candidate for governor, John McEnery, and the returning board counted the Democrat in by 10,000 majority. William Pitt Kellogg, Carpetbagger Radical candidate, supported by all-powerful Stephen B. Packard, Federal marshal, and by the corrupt Federal district judge Edward H. Durell, manipulated himself into victory. Getting Warmoth impeached in a questionable procedure, Kellogg put the mulatto lieutenant governor, P. B. S. Pinchback, in as governor for the remainder of Warmoth's term. Grant drove McEnery out with the United States Army and maintained for the next four years a reign of irresponsible lawlessness unequaled in the history of civilized peoples. The election of a legislature in 1874, claimed both by the Democrats and the Radicals, led to further confusion, which resulted in the rise of the White League and its armed uprising in New Orleans. Grant

[29] Simkins and Woody, *South Carolina during Reconstruction*, 162, 448–57, 464–73; Pike, *Prostrate State*, 248.

[30] Davis, *Civil War and Reconstruction in Florida*, 523–28, 542–56, 618–37, 644, 645.

now sent to Louisiana General Sheridan, who soon shocked the whole country by asking permission to declare the disturbing Louisianians banditti and deal with them accordingly. Congress sent a committee to investigate, and through the efforts of William A. Wheeler, a New York representative on the committee, a truce was worked out, called the Wheeler Compromise, which guaranteed Kellogg's regime to the end of his term in 1877.[31] Louisiana joined South Carolina and Florida in the wait for a better day.

Undoubtedly there were forces working the destruction of Radicalism, so fundamental that even the power of the United States government could not overcome them. The weakness of the Radical system itself was decisive. The Republicans had made in the beginning a fatal mistake by grouping together all Southerners of the Confederate tradition and considering them equally bad; they must have known that they were thereby excluding the respectable South from their party. What was left or what could be acquired from the outside was the weakest part of the social creation—the freedmen, the purchasable white Southerners, some honest converts, and the political adventurers from the North. Wise Republicans early saw what was going into their Southern party. Albion W. Tourgee, Ohio Carpetbagger, declared that "ignorance, poverty, and inexperience were its chief characteristics"; [32] the editor of the *Nation* said early in 1871 that it was "largely composed of trashy whites and ignorant blacks"; [33] and *Harper's Weekly* thought the party was doomed if it did not "promptly and decisively repudiate the thieving carpet-baggers." [34] The New York *Herald* believed that if "the Republican leaders of the North understood the Southern situation those of them who . . . [were] conscientious and patriotic men would shake off those Southern barnacles, and those who . . . [were] not conscientious would still, for expediency's sake, drop these adventurers, whose alliance . . . [had] been and must continue to be an embarrassment

31 Lonn, *Reconstruction in Louisiana*, 73–109, 138–65, 256; Dunning, *Reconstruction*, 211, 217–19, 272–76; Warmoth, *War, Politics and Reconstruction*, 59 ff. "It is no wonder that 'White Leagues', in opposition to negro government, are springing up throughout Louisiana." King, *Great South*, 96.

32 Hamilton, *Reconstruction in North Carolina*, 664.

33 *Nation*, XII (1871), 192.   34 *Harper's Weekly*, XV (1871), 715.

to the national party." [35] As bad as the party membership was, Chamberlain thought that the worst element secured the offices; [36] though a Georgia Radical in opposing the advice of the national Republican chairman that Federal officeholders should not be sent to the Presidential nominating convention in 1872, argued that the men "of brains and power who are Republicans in the South fill the Federal offices and to elect a whole delegation without an office holder on it would be a mighty weak delegation to send." [37]

By making the Republican party in the South largely Negro, the color line was drawn in politics and thus powerful racial prejudice was brought into play to the advantage of the Democrats. The white Republicans, unless held in the party by office or other material considerations, soon deserted. An Alabama Radical bemoaned the fact that it was "almost impossible to persuade a 'Native' to vote for a negro, and with difficulty [to vote] for any person who did not come here with the Indians." [38] And, indeed, many Northern Republicans who came South to live soon turned away from a party that hurt their business and ruined their chances of being accepted socially by Southerners. Brownlow found many of them in Tennessee. Calling them Northern "rebels" he cried out, "May God in his mercy put it into the heads of such *cattle* to stay away from Tennessee, and especially from East Tennessee." [39]

As time went on the Negroes themselves came to be uncertain Republicans, either because they would not vote at all or be-

[35] Quoted in Rome *Weekly Courier*, October 4, 1876. See also, C. H. Lewis, Richmond, Va., to Henry Wilson, November 19, 1867, in Henry Wilson Papers (Division of Manuscripts, Library of Congress).

[36] Greenville *Enterprise*, May 10, 1871.

[37] M. H. Hale, Savannah, Ga., to Chandler, April 10, 1872, in William E. Chandler Papers, XX, Nos. 4045–46. G. K. Gilmer, of Marion Hill, Virginia, wrote John Sherman, February 26, 1877, that no Republican party could be built up in the South "that does not embody a considerable proportion of the educated and property owning class of citizens" and that "the Republican party in the South is a patent failure." Sherman Papers, CXXXVI, Nos. 3104–05. And Willard Warner, writing to Sherman from Tecumseh, Alabama, June 15, 1876, explained Republican troubles thus: "Democratic 'Bulldozing,' supplemented by Republican folly and knavery, has well nigh ruined the Republican Party in the South. . . . I repeat what I have said an hundred times—that the personnel, and not the principles of the party, ruined it in the South." *Ibid.*, CXXVIII, Nos. 4–5.

[38] R. W. Healy, Montgomery, Ala., to Chandler, March 15, 1872, in William E. Chandler Papers, Nos. 3915–18.

[39] Coulter, *William G. Brownlow*, 288–89.

cause they had decided to vote the Democratic ticket. They were getting tired of Carpetbagger leaders who would not give them what they considered their share of the offices. A South Carolina Negro exclaimed, "The colored people have been sold often enough, and they have come to the conclusion that these adventurers with white faces and black hearts shall no longer belie them and fatten off their stupidity." [40] Conventions of Negroes in both North and South began to resolve that it was time for their race to make clear to the Republican party that it could not take Negro support for granted. Frederick Douglass told his race that it had swapped economic slavery for political slavery and he advised Negroes to do their own thinking. Many Negroes were beginning to see that the Republican party had actually done little for them—Congress had provided them with neither land nor education. In fact, some disinterested Republicans advised them to quit politics altogether. Negroes were beginning to sense that dishonest and corrupt government affected themselves no less than the white people.[41] "Both races have learned that their interests are identical and the same," said a South Carolinian, "and that what is a bad government for one is a bad government for the other." [42]

Radical leaders used every device imaginable to hold Negro support. They warned that the Democrats if returned to power would re-enslave the freedmen; that they would re-establish the Confederacy and make Davis president again; that Negro women would not be allowed to wear veils and hoop skirts. Using another approach, they said Grant demanded that they vote the Republican ticket, and in South Carolina freedmen were told that the Negro militia would shoot them if they voted for Democratic candidates.[43] Negroes voting Democratic were called "renegade darkies." An Alabama Radical editor, referring to a Negro who voted with the Democrats, said, "We are sorry to see that 'nigger' in such bad

[40] Elberton *Gazette*, October 8, 1869. See also, *Nation*, XXII (1876), 2; Columbus (Miss.) *Press*, May 29, 1875; Little Rock *Weekly Arkansas Gazette*, August 15, 1871.

[41] Wesley, *Negro Labor in the United States*, 188–89; New Orleans *Weekly Times*, July 17, 1875; Leigh, *Ten Years on a Georgia Plantation*, 342; Columbus (Miss.) *Press*, November 6, 1875; Allen, *Reconstruction*, 195.

[42] Greenville *Enterprise and Mountaineer*, November 17, 1875.

[43] Campbell, *White and Black*, 330; Pike, *Prostrate State*, 186; Fleming, *Civil War and Reconstruction in Alabama*, 776.

company." [44] A Northerner observed, "The jeers, sneers, insults, and ostracism which a black man meets when he joins the Democrats are far greater than anything a white man has to endure when he joins the Republicans." [45] To make up for these deserting Negroes, a Georgia Radical advocated "the disfranchisement of about 40,000 of these dam White Rebels," adding, "with that measure of relief the Republicans will be safe." [46]

Considering the membership of the Republican party, one should not be surprised that factions grew up and tore the party to pieces. Factionalism generally arose out of rivalry between Carpetbaggers and Scalawags over a division of the offices and a contest for Negro support in their nominations—seldom from a difference in principles.

Added to all the Radicals' internal woes were the aggressions of the Democrats, who were adept in trickery and quick to make use of their economic and social positions. Some of their stratagems were more adapted to maintaining themselves in power after they had got control of the election machinery than in first establishing that power. Many tricks were played on the ignorance and credulity of the Negroes. The fact that ballots were not officially printed at this time, and were, therefore, subject to any shape, color, or decoration that the party or candidate might wish, played into the hands of the tricksters. Posing as an intense Radical, a Georgian went about among the Negroes on an election day distributing a printed slip of paper which advertised rat poison and bore the design of a dead rat. He told them it was the Radical ballot and must be shown to no one. When the ballots were counted it was found that 300 votes had been cast for Costar's Rat and Cockroach Exterminator. In an Alabama election the Negroes were told that if they voted the Radical ticket they would receive forty acres and a mule. A Democratic worker showed them a ballot just like theirs and told them that it was a receipt for his land and mule and that if it were put into the ballot box, he could no longer claim his property. Many Negroes did not vote their ballots in that election.

[44] Montgomery *Alabama State Journal*, September 9, 1870.
[45] Cincinnati *Commercial*, quoted in Richmond *Daily Dispatch*, September 14, 1876.
[46] G. H. Penfield, Atlanta, Ga., to Chandler, February 5, 1869, in Zachariah Chandler Papers, IV, Nos. 850–51.

In the Presidential elections the Radicals decorated their ballots with Grant's picture. The Democrats in some sections printed their own ballots with Grant's picture on them and easily distributed them among the Negroes who voted them. Sometimes the Radicals perforated their ballots at the top; the Democrats did their ballots the same way and fooled many Negroes into accepting them as Radical ballots. In some instances different ballots were required for each candidate and they must be deposited in specified boxes. To confuse the Negroes the relative positions of the boxes would be frequently changed on election days. In some elections more than one day was allowed, but in those where only one day was set aside, the Negroes would be told that there were three or four days and not to vote on the first day.[47] Many Negroes were prevented from registering, and, therefore, from voting, by being asked such unanswerable questions as how old they were and who were their fathers.

A Negro who was too cunning to be tricked could generally be bought. Many Negroes sold their votes for a quarter or half dollar. A correspondent of the New York *Herald* declared that they were "ready and willing to vote for the Emperor of China or the King of the Cannibal Islands, if required, for the small sum of 25 cents per head." [48] Many Negroes were bought with a few drinks of whisky or a handful of cigars. As some Negro leaders had great power over their followers, the simplest procedure was to buy the leader. A "devout" Democrat might secure the vote of a whole colored congregation, including the preacher, by contributing to the upkeep of the church. An honest Negro might be tricked into selling his vote by a clever Democrat who bet him a certain amount of money that he was afraid to vote the Democratic ticket because his wife would divorce him or the Carpetbaggers or other Negroes would whip him. The Negro would take the dare and the Democrats would get the vote. The tissue ballot trick was early used, wherein a number of thin ballots would be deposited at one time as one ballot. If any needed to be removed to make the num-

[47] Augusta *Daily Constitutionalist,* November 11, 1868; Morgan, *Yazoo,* 231; Stearns, *Black Man of the South,* 251; Fleming, *Civil War and Reconstruction in Alabama,* 795; Macon *American Union,* October 30, 1868.

[48] Quoted in Augusta *Daily Chronicle & Sentinel,* May 18, 1871.

ber in the box tally with the number of names on the registration lists, even an untrained hand could select for removal the ballots which were not tissue. To identify Negroes who had voted and prevent them from voting again under another name, a clever scheme was used in Mobile whereby a fishhook was secretly stuck into the coattail of notorious Negro repeaters when they voted.[49]

When it came to preventing Negroes from voting at all, different tactics were used. Very early the payment of a poll tax was made prerequisite to voting, and as no effort was made to collect this tax, the Negro seldom paid it. Later it was made cumulative, so that all back taxes had to be paid before voting was allowed. The most serious and dangerous method of controlling Negro voting was intimidation, and its most spectacular example was seen in the activities of the Ku Klux Klan. It reached the heights of its artistic development in the Mississippi Plan, used in the redemption of that state in 1875. Here intimidation was so cleverly organized and carried out that it violated no laws and at the same time produced remarkable results. There were organized all over the state so-called rifle clubs, which conspicuously showed themselves drilling and practicing marksmanship. They left the impressions everywhere that they believed the Negroes were arming for the election and that the whites were determined to protect themselves, and especially that they had resolved to carry the election at any cost. To make themselves more conspicuous, many members wore red shirts (a practice to be taken up in South Carolina the next year). By creating an impression that dire calamity would befall the Negroes if they should go to the polls and vote the Radical ticket, they spread terror among the colored people without having to engage in any actual violence at all. Shortly before the election the Yazoo City *Democrat* declared that the people of Mississippi were resolved "that Mississippians shall rule Mississippi, though the heavens fall. Then will woe, irretrievable woe, betide the tatterdemalions. Hit them hip and thigh, everywhere and at all times. Carry the election peaceably if we can, forcibly if we must." [50] Also, the Democrats sent to important Radical political

[49] Nordhoff, *Cotton States*, 92, 103; Augusta *Weekly Constitutionalist*, November 17, 1875; Campbell, *White and Black*, 184, 329; Somers, *Southern States since the War*, 186.
[50] Morgan, *Yazoo*, 478.

speakings a group of determined men to demand a division of time in order that they might answer the enemy's arguments.[51]

Many Negroes were able to see the economic threat which Southerners often held over them. Since most Negro laborers worked for Democrats, their employers brandished the same club over their workmen which Northern Republican industrialists wielded. Negroes were told plainly that they could not expect to hold their jobs if they voted against the planters' interests, that under corrupt government employer and employee suffered alike. The movement was carried even to the threat of boycotting any business whose proprietor voted the Radical ticket or who employed Radical workmen. In Mississippi a meeting of Democrats resolved that the Negro who voted the Radical ticket would "as certain as fate, vote meat and bread out of the mouths of his wife and children." "You have driven the white man to the verge of ruin," it declared, "and he has determined to draw the color-line, and if you can stand it, he can. Now, hunt for bread and meat among those whom you support." [52]

In dealing with white Radicals, social ostracism was added to the economic argument. Most of the Scalawags were glad to slip back into the Democratic party at the first opportunity after taking their fling with Radicalism; only a few thought they had found principles which they could not give up. Some of these sought new careers outside the South,[53] while others sought consolation in self-pity. "There are men and women here, Southern bred and born," said

---

[51] *Ibid.*, 458. Other devices were used, especially by cities, where the Negro vote could not be controlled. The Kentucky legislature moved up Lexington's first election which would have fallen under the effects of the Fifteenth Amendment and lengthened the terms of the city officials. It relocated the limits of Paris and Nicholasville, leaving out the Negro quarters, and allowed residents of counties to vote in city elections if they owned property in the city. Residents of Boyle County, in which Danville is situated, taking advantage of this law, bought parcels of land in the city four inches wide, and voting in the city elections, defeated the Radicals. Coulter, *Civil War and Readjustment in Kentucky*, 423–24.

[52] Morgan, *Yazoo*, 83. In an address to "Colored Friends," the editor of the Greenville *Daily Enterprise*, September 6, 1876, said, "If you owned land and had tenants on it, who voted against you, whenever they had a chance, and did all they could to reduce you to poverty, wouldn't you want to get rid of them, and put others on your land, who would help you live?"

[53] A. G. Hayes, Frog Level, S.C., to Stevens, July 20, 1868, in Stevens Papers, XII, Nos. 54958–60.

an Alabama Radical, "who for their loyalty, have suffered loss of property, social position, friends, and all that made the future bright, save their love of truth and the approval of a good conscience." [54]

It should not be assumed that for both black and white Radicals there were no Democratic arguments better than trickery and intimidation. Even if the Democrats had no positive program or none that was acceptable, they at least were not tarred with the blatant and flagrant corruption which had smeared the Radicals in every state where they had been in control. Negroes willingly began voting the Democratic ticket. In the famous Mississippi election of 1875 many voted for Democratic candidates, through choice as well as through fear. In black Yazoo County there were only two Radical votes in the 1875 election, and they were explained as having been cast by Democrats as it would "not do to be too d——d unanimous." [55] Reporting on the election in a Georgia county in 1870, a newspaper correspondent said: "Two hundred or more negroes had waited for their forty acres and a mule long enough, and came out boldly and said they would go with their old masters and employers." He added, "I don't suppose there was a white Radical vote cast." [56] White Radicals were becoming scarce all over the South, because the color line so successfully invoked to make the Republican party a Negro party, was now being as successfully used by the Democrats in winning for their party these Southern whites—the despised Scalawags.

The rising sympathy in the North for the native Southerner and the examples of progress in the redeemed states were powerful influences in bringing success in other states. Not only did the lower house of Congress become Democratic in 1874, but also by this time the number of states controlled by the Democrats had reached nine in the North and five in the South. It was now evident that at least for the life of this Congress there could be no more force bills or restrictive legislation against the South. This situation had a correspondingly depressing effect on Southern Radicals; not only could they not look to Congress for further aid, but they also saw in the swinging of Northern states into Democratic rule the North-

[54] Montgomery *Alabama State Journal,* May 12, 1871.   [55] Morgan, *Yazoo,* 484.
[56] Augusta *Weekly Chronicle & Sentinel,* January 4, 1871.

ern people deserting the Southern Radicals and leaving them to their own devices. A Mississippi paper exultantly declared, "There is a popular feeling in every neighborhood from Maine to Texas, against the South being further burdened and robbed and insulted." [57] Georgia, as the first state to shake off Radicalism completely, was frequently pointed to as an example. The prosperity of both whites and Negroes, as well as the honest and frugal government of the Georgians, was viewed longingly by those states still under the Radicals. South Carolinians, in their misery, looked across the Savannah River and saw their neighbors free and represented in Congress by such men as Benjamin H. Hill, John B. Gordon, and Alexander H. Stephens, and they thought, "How humble and insignificant are the South Carolina Radical delegation, when contrasted with those noble sons of Georgia." [58] The *Nation* observed that "rioting, fighting, or plundering" were least heard of in those states where the Democrats had held sway longest.[59]

The Republican party in the South was brought to its destruction not by its announced principles but by its personnel and performances. Years later chemists might make a purse out of a sow's ear and modern Americans might make bricks without straw, but no people can ever make intelligence out of ignorance or honesty out of corruption.

The Radical Reconstruction program for the South had aroused forces there which spewed it out. In the Border states, Radicalism, which could not be assisted by the Reconstruction Acts since this region had not been a part of the Confederacy, ran its course and ended even quicker. The five states making up this region bordering the free North, extending from Delaware through Missouri, had never been entirely Southern. The greatest force bringing about their affinity with the South had been slavery, an institution they had adopted and tenaciously held either because they thought their agricultural life warranted it as in Delaware and

---

[57] Yazoo (Miss.) *Democrat*, quoted in Morgan, *Yazoo*, 504. See also Raymond *Hinds County Gazette*, November 18, 1874; Morgan, *Yazoo*, 487; Fleming, *Civil War and Reconstruction in Alabama*, 771.

[58] Greenville *Enterprise and Mountaineer*, May 12, 1875.

[59] *Nation*, XIX (1874), 132.

Maryland or because in addition they had been settled largely by Southerners as in West Virginia, Kentucky, and Missouri. Their Southernism, however, had not been sufficient to lead them into the secession movement. Their economic ties with the states to the northward, their ability through proximity to both sections to see that each had valid arguments in the sectional controversy, and their fear that they would become the chief battlefields if war should come—all these had been important forces in leading them to remain in the Union in 1860–1861.

During the war these states, excepting Delaware, had suffered the ravages of marching armies and their political life had been largely directed by occupying Federal troops. As a result they emerged from the war with their state governments remade in varying degrees according to the pattern which the military authorities had set. In every Border state except Delaware, stringent political disabilities had been placed upon Confederate soldiers and they were extended even to Confederate sympathizers in Missouri and Maryland. By this method the Radicals hoped to entrench themselves against the day when the Confederate soldiers should return and when the animosities of war should be forgotten.

But by 1871 every Radical Border state had been taken over by the Democrats and joined to the Solid South to remain in that political alliance for the rest of the Reconstruction. This political transformation was caused by the excesses to which the Radical minority governments went in their proscriptions against the Confederate element and by hatred of the Reconstruction program which the Congressional Radicals were carrying out in the South. The heart of this program, Negro suffrage, was keenly resented and opposed by the majority in the Border states—even freedom for the slaves having been opposed to the bitter end by Kentucky and Delaware, both of which refused to ratify the Thirteenth Amendment. Only Missouri and West Virginia could bring themselves to ratify the Fourteenth and Fifteenth amendments. The Negro question was one of the most potent forces in aligning the Border states with the South in the Reconstruction era. For example, the Delaware legislature resolved in 1866 "That the immutable laws of God have affixed upon the brow of the white races the ineffaceable stamp of superiority, and that all attempt to elevate the negro to a social or political equality of the white man is futile and subversive of the ends and aims of which the American Government was established." [60] The next year Maryland solemnly and earnestly protested against Congress assigning the Negro a social status or endowing "him with the elective franchise, as unwarranted by the laws of his nature, and as a direct and unconstitutional interference with the rights of the States, which ought not and should not be tolerated by a free and sovereign people." [61] When Negro suffrage came in 1870 the added Radical strength was more than offset by the loss of lukewarm Republicans who were thereby turned away from their party.

In the Presidential elections from 1868 through 1880 the Border states went almost solidly Democratic. Only Missouri and West Virginia voted for Grant in 1868; unable to swallow Greeley, Delaware and West Virginia preferred Grant in 1872; and all solidly stood for Tilden in 1876 and Hancock in 1880.

Delaware emerged from the war Democratic and remained so in its state government throughout the Reconstruction period. Maryland, even with its laws disfranchising Confederates and their sympathizers, threw out its Radical minority government in 1866 and the next year repealed the restrictions and made a new constitution to supplant the Radical document of 1864. In 1869 the state became oppressively and uniquely Democratic—every state official, including all the members of the legislature, was a Democrat.[62] West Virginia, controlled by the Republicans from its inception, became Democratic in 1870. Two years later it made a new constitution removing all political disabilities and settled down to a long period of Democratic control.

In Kentucky the Conservatives (Union Democrats) in the election of August, 1865, secured a slight majority in the legislature, which swept away the restrictions on Confederates as its first act in December following. This and other acts designed to aid Confederates and harass Radicals led the Cincinnati *Daily Gazette* to exclaim, "It is a singular fact that scarce six months after the

[60] *American Annual Cyclopaedia . . . 1866*, p. 264.   [61] *Ibid., 1867*, p. 475.

[62] *Ibid., 1865*, pp. 526–27; *1866*, p. 471; *1867*, pp. 475, 476, 480; *1868*, p. 455; *1869*, p. 410.

surrender of Lee's army, the legislature of Kentucky is in the hands of as fierce set of rebels as ever thirsted for the life of the Union or ever rushed upon the bayonets of the Union army." [63] By 1866 the Democrats of the Confederate tradition had seized control of the Conservative organization, and in a minor election in August of that year, they routed completely the opposition in a clear-cut contest of Blue against Grey. In the Congressional election of the next year Kentucky sent a solid delegation of nine Democrats to Washington. So outraged with Kentucky were the Radicals both in the state and in Washington that Congress made a bold attempt to throw the commonwealth into military Reconstruction. At first its Congressmen were excluded but eventually all except two were seated.[64] In the words of a disconsolate Radical, "The election of Congressmen is over, and as might have been expected, loyal Kentucky has gone overwhelmingly for the rebels. . . . Kentucky is today as effectually in the hands of the rebels as if they had every town and every city garrisoned with their troops. With a rebel Governor, rebel Congressmen, rebel Statehouse and Senate, rebel Judges, rebel Mayors, rebel municipal officers, rebel policemen and constables, what is to become of the poor blacks and loyal white men God only knows." [65]

Missouri came out of the war with greater hostility to the Confederate element than was true in any other Border state, and probably not surpassed by Tennessee under Brownlow. The so-called Drake constitution, which became effective on July 4, 1865, pursued Confederates and their sympathizers relentlessly through an amazingly detailed and drawn-out article. They were not only disfranchised but they might not preach, teach, practice law, perform the marriage ceremony, or engage in corporate business. To make sure that no state court might interfere with the program, an "Ousting Ordinance" was passed providing for the removal of the judges and other officers from their positions and giving the governor the right to fill vacancies. In the well-known decision of *Cummings* v. *Missouri*, the United States Supreme Court declared that since that part of the Missouri constitution disqualifying Con-

---

[63] Cincinnati *Daily Gazette*, February 2, 1866.
[64] Coulter, *Civil War and Readjustment in Kentucky*, 330–39.
[65] Cincinnati *Commercial*, May 13, 1867.

federates for certain activities was *ex post facto* it was void. The Missouri Radicals had overshot the mark; they found strong antagonists not only in Conservatives like Frank Blair but also among men of their own ranks like Carl Schurz and B. Gratz Brown. In 1870 a Liberal faction split away and nominated Brown for governor. The Democrats supported him, brought about his election, and ended forever Radical rule in Missouri. A constitutional amendment removing all restrictions against Confederates was soon adopted. The Democrats now absorbed most of the Liberal Republicans and in 1874 elected the entire delegation of thirteen Congressmen.[66]

Considerable sympathy and support for the former Confederate states, now in the throes of Reconstruction, were offered them by the Border states, especially by Maryland and Kentucky. In 1866 Maryland ladies promoted the Southern Relief Fair in Baltimore and succeeded in raising $164,569, which they distributed among all the states of the old Confederacy, except Texas.[67] Kentucky distributed soon after the war much grain to the desolated and hungry parts of the South.

The Border states had not seceded and joined the South in the Civil War because they were not completely of the Southern essence, but the flavor of the South was so much upon them that after the war was over they soon identified themselves politically with that region. Though Southern in politics, the Border states continued more and more to diverge from the South in economic development. They became relatively less agricultural as industrialization made headway among them and more commercial as the three great Border-state cities, Baltimore, Louisville, and St. Louis, reached out farther for the trade that made them populous and powerful.

[66] *American Annual Cyclopaedia . . . 1865*, pp. 586–87; Eugene M. Violette, *A History of Missouri* (Boston, 1918), 406–35.

[67] *American Annual Cyclopaedia . . . 1866*, p. 469.

CHAPTER XVII

THE NEW SOUTH

M ANY signs pointed to the political deliverance of the South in the elections of 1876. There were ominous rumblings in South Carolina, Florida, and Louisiana, the three former Confederate states still remaining in the hands of the Radicals, which indicated that the native whites would seize control in the next election, and it was equally evident to Northerners and Southerners, Democrats and Republicans, that the whole country was determined to be rid of Grantism. When the Congress elected in 1874, with the lower house Democratic, should come into power after March 4, 1875, it would be impossible to pass further anti-Southern legislation. The last full fling the Radicals could take at the South must, therefore, come quickly, and it did come in the Civil Rights Act, signed by Grant on March 1, 1875. This law, which had been a particular concern of the deceased Sumner, was long in the making, and included at one time such unwise provisions as mixed schools for the South, and other plans designed to strengthen the Republican party in the Southern states through building up crumbling Negro support. In its final form it attempted to force Southerners to give Negroes equal rights with whites in hotels, theaters, on public carriers, and in all other public conveniences. Unworkable from the start it was soon declared unconstitutional by the United States Su preme Court on the ground that the Fourteenth Amendment forbade *states,* not individuals, to deny equal rights to Negroes. Congress had forbidden *individuals* to interfere with Negroes' rights. A Force Bill, giving the President the right to suspend the writ of *habeas corpus* in Alabama, Mississippi, Louisiana, and Arkansas, was passed by the lower house in February but failed to receive final action in the Senate before the end of the session.

The Republicans might win the next presidential election even if they should lose all the South, but they could not afford to lose much Northern support. To draw the attention of Northerners from the malodorous record of the party, James G. Blaine, who desired the nomination, stooped to the old trick of waving the bloody shirt. In opposing a general amnesty bill before Congress in 1876, he gave as his reason that it included Jefferson Davis, who, he affirmed, had been responsible for the death of thirteen thousand Federal prisoners at Andersonville. Refusing longer to be baited by Blaine, Benjamin H. Hill, who had returned to Congress the previous year as a sort of champion for the South, answered him in a memorable debate. Though Southerners thought Hill won the argument on the prisoners-of-war question and generally applauded him, some felt that he had played Blaine's game and had increased Blaine's chances of nomination. A Philadelphia lady, born in Blaine's state of Maine, was so carried away with admiration of Hill that she sent him a Confederate flag which had been captured in Georgia by Sherman's troops. Davis, who had tried to remain silent throughout the Reconstruction period, defended himself in a long letter.[1] Blaine's efforts did not get him the nomination but they inspired a rhymster to write:

> *"I saved the nation from the South,"*
> *Quoth war-scarred Jimmy Blaine*
> *"My weapon was my naked mouth,*
> *My battlefield in Maine."* [2]

Republican Northerners frequently waved the bloody shirt, then and later, in their attacks on the South for sending to Congress Confederate veterans—"rebel brigadiers" as they chose to call them. The most clever defense of the South was made by a Democratic Northerner, when he said: "Recollect, gentlemen of the Republican party, that the South has not the same large choice of non-combatants to select for high office which the Republican

---

[1] Augusta *Weekly Constitutionalist,* July 7, 1875; Rome *Weekly Courier,* January 26, February 16, March 8, 1876; Dunbar Rowland (ed.), *Jefferson Davis, Constitutionalist. His Letters, Papers and Speeches* (Jackson, Miss., 1923), VII, 481–85.

[2] Rome *Weekly Courier,* November 1, 1876.

party has. All her men and boys had to go into the Confederate army to meet our overwhelming numbers, while the North did not send half of her men. In this respect the Republican party has the South at a big disadvantage. They can select such men as Messrs. John Sherman and Foster, who quietly stayed at home, while the unfortunate South has no non-combatants to prefer over her soldiers for high public honors." [3] Southerners did not hold all Northerners or even all Northern Republicans responsible for these sectional attacks. A South Carolinian believed that the "great masses of the Northern people are sensible, just and patriotic," but a Virginian, less kindly disposed, thought such attacks were getting to be an old Republican custom and he insisted that "no patriot ought to support a party which bases its hopes of success upon keeping alive in the breasts of the people base passions which ought to have been allowed to burn out twelve years ago." [4]

It was inevitable that the Democrats should nominate for the presidency Samuel J. Tilden, a New York reformer, but Southerners, who could have no favorite son, had little enthusiasm for the selection. To them Tilden was too much of Tammany Hall and of the big corporations—too little able to sympathize with the money problems of Southerners. The Republicans chose Rutherford B. Hayes, Ohio's favorite son.

The campaign brought forth much of the trickery and specious arguments previously used. Republicans attempted without success to revive the Loyal League; they said that if the Democrats won the presidency they would refund cotton taxes of $100,000,000, repudiate the national debt, allow Confederate claims, and restore slavery. They still paraded "rebel atrocities," how Negroes throughout the South went to bed every night with the fear that they would have their throats cut or their cabins burnt before morning, how Christmas and election days were reserved by Southerners for killing "peart niggers" and all the other days for "robbing and personal violence." [5] Disorders were invited by

[3] Fernandina *Florida Mirror*, September 20, 1879. See also, Greenville *Enterprise and Mountaineer*, April 28, 1875.

[4] Greenville *Enterprise and Mountaineer*, January 26, 1876; Richmond *Daily Dispatch*, September 23, 1876.

[5] *Nation*, XXVIII (1879), 242.

Northern arms companies advertising "life-sized" pistols in Southern newspapers, and by Federal troops ostensibly scattered through the country to preserve order.

To rob the Republicans of their violence arguments, Southern leaders long before the election laid plans to reduce to the vanishing point all disorders that might be incident to the campaign and election; and as a result the year 1876 saw little trouble. In South Carolina the Hamburg and Ellenton riots, and disorders in Charleston and among the striking Negroes in the rice fields up and down the coast, broke out. Indeed, in South Carolina there was more violence than in any other Southern state, for South Carolinians had determined to wrest control from the corrupt ring that was running their state. Sympathetically the Baltimore *Sun* commented, "The day will come when the wrongs of the white people of South Carolina will be considered along with those of the negroes." [6] Here Daniel H. Chamberlain, the most respected of the Carpetbaggers, was running for governor against Wade Hampton, who was as wise as he was determined and who had patterned his campaign after the Mississippi Plan of 1875. Red shirts, first used in Mississippi, were worn by the so-called rifle clubs, and their bright colors coupled with the serious countenances they set off, either captivated the Negroes or filled them with fear. Outlawed by Chamberlain, these organizations changed their names to baseball clubs with 150 members or more to a team, or called themselves mother's little helpers, sewing circles, or music clubs. By demanding a division of time at Radical speakings, they either presented their arguments to Radical audiences or caused them to melt away. Social and economic pressure was fully used. Negroes and white Radicals lost their jobs unless they agreed to vote for Hampton. A petty Radical officeholder seeking to shake hands with a South Carolina gentleman was repelled with the remark, "Don't offer me your hand, sir. You have declared yourself a radical, and you may now shake hands with your associates, the negroes and thieves"; and a Radical Negro peddling door mats was turned away by a lady and told to "go to your Radical friends and let them purchase your mats." [7]

[6] Quoted in Rome *Weekly Courier*, August 30, 1876.
[7] Greenville *Enterprise and Mountaineer*, December 20, 1876.

369

In Florida the Radicals, being divided as usual, used widespread intimidation against Negroes to hold them to their party and parry the intimidations practiced by the Democrats. Radical white and Negro leaders warned wavering freedmen that they would be put on chain gangs or restored to slavery if they voted the Democratic ticket. The Radicals might well fear the results, for there were 5,000 more whites than blacks in Florida. Here there was little actual violence. Even in outraged Louisiana, which was completing four years under Kellogg's rule, there was little violence, but much "bulldozing" by both parties. Here one-eyed, one-armed, one-legged Francis T. Nicholls, whose physical dissolution to this point had been brought about by service in the Confederate armies, was running against Stephen B. Packard.

The rest of the South, already redeemed, looked with special concern on the campaigns in South Carolina, Florida, and Louisiana. Benjamin H. Hill, sure of Georgia, campaigned in Florida, and other Southerners lent their aid in the other unredeemed states. The fight to elect Democratic state officials partook of the nature of a crusade. To Southerners it was more than an ordinary election would be in the North where there was a choice between two groups of respectable candidates. In the South, "Triumph to us is *salvation*, defeat *worse than death*." [8] Many Northerners agreed. The New York *Herald* declared, "Every man, no matter whether he is Republican or Democratic, who desires to see the Southern States honestly ruled must wish that they shall be carried this fall by the Democrats." [9] Honest Negroes naturally believed in honest government and many of them voted for Democrats through choice as many others did through fear. A Mississippian wrote Tilden, "I am proud to let you know that I can control 74 of my old slaves—all of whom will go for Tilden and Hendricks— nearly all the collored [sic] voters have changed from Rad. to our party." [10]

Election day came, the votes were cast; Democrats everywhere knew Tilden was elected, Republicans feared it was so. Southerners burst forth in wild celebrations and high emotions unequaled

[8] S. B. French, Whitby, Va., to Tilden, November 21, 1875, in Tilden Papers.
[9] Quoted in Rome *Weekly Courier*, October 4, 1876.
[10] F. M. Shields, Mashulaville, Miss., to Tilden, October 22, 1876, in Tilden Papers.

since the days of secession. Guns firing, firecrackers popping, brass bands blaring, long processions with signs and banners threading the streets of cities and country hamlets, local leaders making speeches, and writers of doggerel busy:

> *Hayes is the wagon, Wheeler is the hoss,*
> *Hendricks is the driver and Tilden is the boss.*[11]

Commenting on the celebration lasting until three in the morning in a little Georgia town, the local editor exclaimed, "The oldest inhabitant never saw anything to equal it, and the youngest, we believe, will never see anything to surpass it." [12] Tilden was deluged with letters from high and low, old and young.

100,000 Majority to Dear Uncle Sam
yrs forever
Georgia

decorated a postcard from that state. A Tennessean burst forth, "Glory to God we've got you. Glory! Glory! Glory! Glory!" A grandniece of Richard Henry Lee wrote Tilden, "I want you to be President. . . . I am glad that you are going to be President, so very, very glad." An Alabama miss ten years old congratulated him, and a Virginia Negro organization wrote him, "We hope you 'hold the fort' for 8 years." [13]

And then a few flecks of clouds began to appear. No one denied that Tilden had 184 electoral votes, one short of a majority; but Republican leaders, who had determined that he should not get that vote, claimed irregularities in South Carolina, Florida, and Louisiana, which the Democrats had carried on the face of the returns. "Visiting statesmen" flocked to these states and Federal troops were on hand to assist. Republican returning boards threw out enough Democratic votes to give Hayes the victory, but by one method or another the Democrats assembled their votes and

---

[11] Rome *Weekly Courier*, November 22, 1876.

[12] Elberton *Gazette*, November 15, 1876.

[13] A. B. Lanier, Nashville, Tenn., November 9, 1876, Tilden Papers; Winifred B. Brent, Gordonsville, Va., to Tilden, December 14, 1876, *ibid.;* Colored Committee Rooms, Richmond, Va., to Tilden, November 8, 1876, *ibid.;* A. J. Dunn, Bristol, Tenn., wrote Tilden November 23, 1876, that about one eighth of the Negroes in that vicinity voted for him. *Ibid.*

sent in returns to Washington to be counted for Tilden. Many complications now arose, for there were two sets of returns from the three contested Southern states, and finally to settle the question Congress set up an Electoral Commission of fifteen members to consider the double returns. In each instance, the members voting their political prejudices, decided by eight to seven that Hayes had won.[14]

Victory had now disintegrated into the ashes of defeat; but all was not gloom in the South. What the South wanted more than anything else was home rule, unloosed from Federal interference. When there was wild talk among some Democrats, mostly in the North, that they would not be cheated out of the presidency even if they must seize it by force,[15] Southerners promptly dissented. "For the North we cannot answer," said a Southerner, "but we assert most positively that there will be no war on the part of the South. We have had our fill of that, and it's none of our business." [16] There was consolation in the fact that the South, at least, was rid of Grant and his enormities, whom an Alabaman called a monster and whose administrations he characterized as "the vilest and most corrupt that have disgraced the pages of American history." [17] Anybody was better than Grant, but Hayes had positive qualities and a program that recommended him to the South. And though Tilden was a Democrat, why should Southerners die for him? What had he done for the South? [18] And it might well be asked, What would or what could he do for the South even if he were President?

Hayes in his letter accepting the nomination had practically

14 There was a technicality in one of the electoral votes from Oregon, which gave the Democrats a claim to it, but being settled on its merits this vote was awarded to Hayes.

15 Pillow, Memphis, Tenn., to Tilden, November 18, 1876, in Tilden Papers.

16 Elberton *Gazette*, November 29, 1876. John H. Reagan wrote J. W. Truett, May 14, 1877, that the South could not have afforded to engage in armed conflict in an attempt to seat Tilden. Reagan Papers.

17 Greenville *Enterprise and Mountaineer*, March 7, 1877. Yet one Southerner wrote Tilden that "one million white men" in the South demanded his election and would "die for it." J. W. Fench, Jonesville, S.C., January 24, 1877, to Tilden, in Tilden Papers.

18 The Tilden Democrats in the North felt that the South had deserted him. Alexander C. Flick, *Samuel Jones Tilden: A Study in Political Sagacity* (New York, 1939), 403.

promised that the Federal government would cease to meddle in Southern affairs, and this promise was guaranteed fulfillment by Charles Foster and other Northern leaders who knew Hayes's mind, in a conference held in a Washington hotel with John B. Gordon and other Southerners.[19] When Hayes became President he immediately set about carrying out his Southern program. First he called to Washington the two contesting governors of South Carolina, Hampton and Chamberlain, who had set up rival governments in Columbia, and informed them that Federal troops would be withdrawn from the statehouse. Chamberlain, whose regime rested entirely on these troops, protested without avail. When the troops left, the Chamberlain government collapsed and South Carolina amidst wild rejoicing returned to the hands of the native whites after a ten-year fearful experience.[20] High colored officials returned to their old positions of streetsweepers, waiters, and field hands, and the Carpetbaggers fled the state. Chamberlain had so much that was good mixed with so much that was bad that South Carolinians were long puzzled over him. "We were satisfied at one time that he was a great scoundrel," said one, "and then he showed such high courage and honor, such determined conduct, that we thought him an honest man. He has appeared to us as a coward and a hero, a man of truth and a liar." [21]

The white Floridians came into possession of their government without a contest, but the third of the unredeemed states, Louisiana, was claimed by the Radical Packard. Like South Carolina, Louisiana set up two rival governments, but Hayes, resolving to let Louisianians run their own affairs, withdrew all Federal support from the Radicals, and as a result Nicholls became governor. Radical leaders were bought off from resisting this settlement: Kellogg was given a United States senatorship, Packard went to

[19] Charles R. Williams, *The Life of Rutherford Birchard Hayes, Nineteenth President of the United States* (Boston, 1914), I, 533–34; II, 66–67.

[20] *Ibid.*, II, 33–68; Greenville *Enterprise and Mountaineer*, April 4, 1877. A South Carolina Negro Carpetbagger wrote John Sherman: "Recognize Gov. Chamberlain and you will demoralize the Democratic Party in this state, while if Hampton should be recognized there is an end to all hope of Republican success. The imperative duty of the President is to stand by us under all circumstances." W. H. Thomas, Newberry, S.C., March 24, 1877, to Sherman, Sherman Papers, CXXXIX, No. 31676.

[21] Greenville *Enterprise and Mountaineer*, October 18, 1876.

Liverpool as consul, and lesser men were given their rewards. Yet the same vote that made Hayes President ought to have made Packard governor, as William H. Hunt of New Orleans voicing the views of many Louisiana Radicals reminded John Sherman: "The title of the Hayes electors is identically the same with that of Governor Packard." [22]

"With the establishment of Governors Hampton and Nicholls we can afford to forget Mr. Hayes and the Presidency," said a South Carolinian; "indeed, we will be very well satisfied and contented." [23] To Southern Radicals as well as to many Northern ones, Hayes had made a blunder in his Southern policy. He had deserted his party in the South, and was, therefore, not a good Republican. Southern Radicals deeply resented his appointment of a Southern Democrat to his cabinet. An Alabaman declared that he had "ignored the Republicans and Union men of sixteen contiguous states and taken a Democrat and a rebel to represent them in his counsel," and a Virginian implored Sherman to exhaust his "influence with President Hay[e]s to check the course he . . . [was] pursuing in regard to the Republican Party in the South." [24]

Some Southern Radicals saw clever strategy in Hayes's Southern policy, which would lead ultimately to the rebuilding of the Republican party in the South on an enduring basis of decency and honesty; for with kindness he could do what Federal bayonets had never been able to accomplish. He could wean away the old Whigs from their Democratic connections and with them give the Republican party respectability. Some Southern Democrats suspected that the President, in this sudden Republican generosity, was presenting the South a Trojan horse.

As Hayes's own party began to turn against him, Southerners

[22] Sherman Papers, February 21, 1877, CXXXVI, Nos. 31020–21. L. B. Packard wrote Hayes, from New Orleans, February 21, that Louisiana would be upset until he was seated as governor and that if Hayes would agree to it, Grant would act. *Ibid.*, Nos. 30988–96.

[23] Greenville *Enterprise and Mountaineer*, March 7, 1877. See also, Richmond *Daily Dispatch*, May 30, 1877.

[24] Warner, Tecumseh, Ala., March 15, 1877, to Sherman, in Sherman Papers, CXXXVIII, Nos. 31570–74; E. Nash, Heathsville, Va., March 14, 1877, to Sherman, *ibid.*, No. 31566. David M. Key of Tennessee had been made postmaster general.

forgot their suspicions and felt more kindly toward him. According to a Virginian, "When we consider the strange circumstances that a man elected as he was should turn out to be so conciliatory and just we must feel astonishment." [25] In carrying out his policy of conciliation, Hayes made a trip into the South a few months after his inauguration, accompanied by some of his cabinet members and later joined for part of his journey by Hampton. On crossing the Ohio River, he changed Greeley's famous expression into "Young man, go South." Coming as far south as Atlanta, he was received everywhere with great cordiality. He returned by way of Knoxville, Lynchburg, and Charlottesville to Washington.[26] Describing Hayes's visit to Atlanta, a Georgian declared the people "carriaged him, speeched him, musicked him, feasted him and shook hands with him." He carried "back with him the best wishes of the Southern people in his noble efforts to restore constitutional government, which Grant so badly abused." [27] If the North in 1865 could have adopted the policy of friendship and understanding which Hayes developed in 1877, much that was low and shameful would never have been written into American history. Hayes's Southern trip struck many people as a sort of miracle. According to the *Nation,* "the fact that the President whom this campaign produced should be travelling triumphantly through the South, pleading before joyous multitudes for union and conciliation, has all the look of a special Providence, and must fill the souls of those who supported him as a vessel of wrath with strange confusion." [28]

The heart of the North was with the President. It was high time for the Northern journals, thought the *Nation,* to stop their "scathing articles on Southern lawlessness" and to assist the South in its economic and educational development.[29] From Massachusetts came this sound advice: "But if we keep on treating the Southerners as our political inferiors, scoffing at them as whipped and unrepentant rebels who richly deserved all the punishment

---

[25] Richmond *Daily Dispatch,* March 10, 1877.

[26] New York *World,* September 26, 1877. At Atlanta he told the Negroes that their "rights and interests would be safer if this great mass of intelligent white men were let alone by the general Government." Williams, *Rutherford Birchard Hayes,* II, 252.

[27] Marietta *Journal,* September 28, 1877. [28] *Nation,* XXV (1877), 191.

[29] *Ibid.,* XXIV (1877), 333.

that fate has meted out, and calling them hypocrites whenever they profess any wish for the future glory and prosperity of the reunited nation—if we do this much longer, there is a dismal probability that we shall make of 'the South' a 'main question' that will vex American politics through all coming time." [30] The prosperity of the whole country now as always depended on a prosperous South. In 1878 and again in 1880 Congress forbade in the army appropriation bill the use of Federal troops at the polls. Yet there would always be a few long-tongued scolds like Wendell Phillips, of whom a Virginian said, "He is a dog. Let him be whipped to his kennel"; [31] and for political advantage there would long continue politicians who would raise the "bloody shirt" cry again. As Ben Hill said in the Senate in 1879, "Every day things are repeated upon this floor against ten millions of people which no gentlemen would dare repeat against one man. You charge a whole people with being false, untrustworthy, untrue, without evidence, against the fact, and yet you alarm the North by crying of a solid South." [32]

It was not until 1877 that the mass of Southerners could take pride in being called Americans, look upon the American flag with joy, or feel that they were a part of the United States. Now Southerners were no longer to be humiliated by being treated as inferiors in a union designed to be made up of equals. There was a deep longing in their hearts, simply expressed by Jabez L. M. Curry when he said, "I want a country I can love." [33] They had that country under Hayes. "The South now stands upon an equality with the North," said a Virginian, "and is going to continue so to stand." [34] The Fourth of July resumed its old significance; decrepit Alexander H. Stephens could now orate for two hours on the glories of his country; Texans could prematurely begin celebrating the Fourth in 1876, before the election took place; and Arkansans, this same year, could whip up enthusiasm for the Fourth in such language as this: "If the people have any life left, we should have some kind of public demonstration. If they have

[30] *Ibid.*, XXIII (1876), 198.   [31] Richmond *Daily Dispatch*, March 29, 1877.
[32] Hill, *Union and its Enemies* (speech, May 10, 1879), 42.
[33] Alderman and Gordon, *Curry*, 235.
[34] Richmond *Daily Dispatch*, May 14, 1877.

the means left after paying their taxes, we should have a grand barbecue. . . . Let the move be ushered in by the ringing of bells and the booming of cannons. Let five thousand horsemen parade our streets to the delight of both old and young." [35] Georgia could now claim to have as much right to the Fourth as did Massachusetts: "Let the minute guns of Boston shake the vine clad hills of Massachusetts," exclaimed a Georgian in 1878. "We of Georgia were represented in the famous declaration of Jefferson of '76 and have the same right to declare our rejoicing at the 102d Anniversary, then lets throw up our hats and huzza for our revolutionary fathers, and dine with our brave 'Soger' boys. . . . May each recurring national anniversary find our people, wiser men, purer patriots, better citizens." [36]

Reconstruction created as great a revolution in politics as in social and economic life. It forced the South into one party and made it solid politically—to maintain white supremacy and home rule. Its freedom of action and choice in its political life was destroyed, an evil from which it was long to suffer; for when once the necessity of its solidarity had passed it was unable to shake the old man of the sea off its neck. This movement toward solidarity began with the first enormities of Reconstruction. In 1868 an Alabaman declared, "There is but one party for true Southern men, or true National men, and that is the Democratic party." [37] A Georgian believed that if the Radicals' "infamous deeds of damning villainy had not solidified the true men" of the South, "they would have deserved to perpetually bear the degradation under which they groaned for weary years." [38] The solid South soon became a fixed fact to be railed at by some Northerners and to be misunderstood. Though the South tended to solidify along other lines than politics, there was always to remain as much diversity of thought and act in religions, occupations, and in a hundred other relationships, as there was in the North. The New York *Sun* did not marvel that there was a solid South nor did it misunderstand it. The South was solid against "public robbery such

---

[35] Dardanelle *Arkansas Independent*, March 24, 1876.
[36] Sandersville *Herald*, July 11, 1878.
[37] Montgomery *Weekly Advertiser*, November 24, 1868.
[38] Greensboro *Herald*, December 4, 1879.

as never was committed upon any other people in the world," and that newspaper thanked God that the South was "thus united for the stoppage of public plunder and the restoration of honest government." [39] The *Nation* observed, "there is but one subject on which the South is 'solid,' and that is misgovernment by an ignorant majority under the forms of law." [40]

But Southerners were solid politically only against the Republicans, not against themselves; they could fight among themselves like "tom-cats in a tow sack," and they would close their ranks only against the Republicans, who practically vanished after 1877. According to a Northern observer, all the Republicans in Texas could be hauled out in a few omnibuses, and in Florida though they showed a few signs of life, "growing out of a collection of Northern consumptives and native negroes, . . . they cannot carry the State." [41]

Independency in the Democratic party began to make its appearance soon after the Radicals were routed—in Georgia there were signs of it as early as 1874.[42] These insurgents, though avoiding as the plague any open flirting with remnants of Republicans, nevertheless accepted their votes and those of the Negroes, too. To discredit them, regular Democrats sometimes charged them with being Republicans. These breaches in the Democracy were caused partly by the common man in his economic struggle against the bigger businessman, the developer of resources, the Bourbon in politics, but also they were brought about by the party's falling into the hands of bosses, local and state, the courthouse gangs, and the statehouse rings. This insurgency was later to bloom full-grown in the Populist movement.

One of the first tasks most of the states addressed themselves to upon their deliverance from the Radicals was the adoption of new constitutions. Radical-made documents were an insult, however wise and effective they might be. In some cases, as in Georgia, the constitutions were entirely remade, and in others like North Carolina there were few changes. Virginia, South Carolina, and

[39] Quoted, *ibid.*, October 13, 1876.   [40] *Nation*, XXV (1877), 349.
[41] Sandersville *Herald*, December 13, 1877.
[42] Kenneth Coleman, "The Georgia Gubernatorial Election of 1880," in *Georgia Historical Quarterly* (Savannah), XXV (1941), 89–119.

Mississippi did not act until the last decade of the century. In every case some impress of the Radical documents remained.

The redeemed states made their most thoroughgoing onset against the debts built up by the Radicals. In varying amounts, depending upon their established fraudulence, these debts were repudiated, by law and constitutional provision. Some states, as for instance Georgia and Florida, repudiated these debts outright; others, like Tennessee and Louisiana, scaled them down to about half and reduced interest rates, either by agreement with bondholders or otherwise; and others, such as North Carolina and Virginia, scaled down not only their Radical debts but also other debts made before the war. Virginia's prewar debt became a long-standing issue in politics and was complicated by her inability to make West Virginia agree to assume her proportional part. Mississippi and Texas repudiated no Reconstruction debts. The Radical debts richly deserved the repudiation they got, and the states which so acted lost none of their financial standing.[43] In fact, Georgia's credit was higher after her repudiation than before.[44] Charles Francis Adams, Jr., advised Louisiana in 1875 to announce publicly that when responsible government should return to that state, it would repudiate the Radical debts. "Let them publicly declare that so surely as the day of relief comes," he said, "every debt contracted by the usurping government should be repudiated, every tax-title issued set aside." [45]

By 1880 the permanent effects of the Radical Reconstruction program were beginning to become clear. They fell far short of what had been intended, just as there were many developments never desired by the Radicals. Political Reconstruction was an utter failure. Radical and Republican became words to hiss at and scorn, and only the bravest or the most depraved dared join the party bearing the name. The Negro in politics had been given a miserable start, and with time his political responsibilities passed into nothingness. With corruption and depravity was the school "furnished in which our colored voters learnt their first lessons

[43] Buck, *Road to Reunion*, 158; Blake, *William Mahone*, 156–95; McGrane, *Foreign Bondholders and American State Debts*, 290–91, 296, 303–22, 344–81.
[44] *Commercial and Financial Chronicle*, XXV (1877), 173.
[45] *Nation*, XX (1875), 39.

in politics," said the *Nation*. "The United States appeared on their horizon, at the dawn of their political life, as a power which furnished artillery to bands of burglars whenever people defended their houses too stoutly." [46] Neither the South nor the North, then if ever, was prepared for Negro rule; and as Alexander K. Mc-Clure said about this time, "until all the laws of human nature and of interest shall be reversed, the white man will rule the inferior race, and he will do it better in the South at this time than the negro can rule himself. This is not the sentimental view of the race issue in the South, but it is the truth." [47] The mass of Negroes in 1880 were living in no better cabins than they possessed as slaves, nor did they have a greater sufficiency of food or clothing. A conference of missionary workers among the Negroes, held in Atlanta in 1875, pessimistically declared that the Negroes' "enthusiasm for education" was "yielding to the chilling influence of their poverty, and their innate evil propensities, uncorrected by their sensational religion" was "dragging them downward." [48] How much happier were they now than in slavery? Zebulon B. Vance oratorically exclaimed, "The ringing song of his daily work no longer awakens the echoes of his native plains; the boisterous laugh is hushed; the fiddle, without strings, hangs in silence on the cabin wall; the voice of the inspiring banjo is heard no more, and the ever famous dance—the double-shuffle —is about to be numbered with the lost arts." [49] Be that as it may, freedom has been and will always be worth its price.

Negroes easily drifted into crime, especially theft and murder. By 1880 every former Confederate state, excepting Arkansas, leased colored and white criminals to private companies which worked them in agriculture, mining, and lumbering.[50] The great majority of convicted criminals was colored, as this table of prisoners in 1880 eloquently shows:

[46] *Ibid.* [47] McClure, *South,* 208.

[48] W. E. Burghardt Du Bois, "The Negro Landowner of Georgia," in *Bulletin of the Department of Labor,* No. 35 (Washington, 1901), 666–67.

[49] *Land We Love,* VI (1868–1869), 370.

[50] *Tenth Census, 1880,* XXI, *Defective, Dependent, and Delinquent Classes,* 485; Blake McKelvey, "Penal Slavery and Southern Reconstruction," in *Journal of Negro History,* XX (1935), 153–79; Taylor, *Negro in Tennessee,* 43–44; Campbell, *White and Black,* 300; Garner, *Reconstruction in Mississippi,* 328; Beale, "On Rewriting Reconstruction History," *loc. cit.,* 817.

	White	*Colored*		*White*	*Colored*
Alabama	212	1141	North Carolina	591	979
Arkansas	298	458	South Carolina	56	570
Florida	41	228	Tennessee	759	1341
Georgia	227	1582	Texas	1585	1578
Louisiana	228	838	Virginia	348	1195 [51]
Mississippi	148	1163			

Though the Negro was not free from crime and poverty, race prejudice, and uneven justice, he was vastly better off than the mass of his race in its native Africa, and there was a closer and friendlier feeling of his employer toward him than capitalistic Northerners showed their workmen.[52]

With a new industrial life arising, in which people moved about more, and with race relations no longer regulated by slavery, the white man's crimes became of more common occurrence and of new types. Lynchings which supplanted organized government and disgraced the decencies of a civilized society were used by the lower elements of the people to regulate race relations; robbers of banks and trains down to the sneak thieves who watched "an opportunity to enter the hall and rifle a hat-rack," were beginning to make their appearances; and carrying concealed weapons, which had long been considered a Southerner's privilege, continued to be stoutly defended against legal regulation. A Georgian maintained that more lives were saved than lost by carrying pistols. He thought a law against this custom was no more logical than one against splitting fence rails, as it was possible for a person to be killed in either case, but a law against splitting rails would probably be passed "the next time a fellow is knocked in the head with one." [53] The South was happily free from the tramp problem which was beginning to beset the North. The Chicago *Tribune* thought the reason was because "a tramp would starve in the South before he had tramped any considerable distance," to which reasoning a Georgian answered that the "South may thank God, perhaps, that she is too poor to be tramped over. . . .

[51] *Tenth Census, 1880*, XXI, *Defective, Dependent, and Delinquent Classes*, 479.
[52] *Commercial and Financial Chronicle*, XXIV (1877), 383.
[53] *De Bow's Review*, I (1866), 76; V (1868), 690.

If we are to grow rich for the pickings of tramps, after the robbery of carpet-baggers, it may be just as well to remain poor." [54]

There was a New South in the making, speeded on by the enthusiastic teachings of Daniel H. Hill, Benjamin H. Hill, Lucius Q. C. Lamar, John B. Gordon, Henry W. Grady, and many others. Sentimentally it was to have a leavening but not a withering amount of the old and the traditional. It would recede a few paces from family tradition and ancestor worship, for in fact "The virtues of an ancestry wear out like the effect of vaccination." The war was not to be looked upon as wholly unfortunate; for, according to George Fitzhugh, in war there were "more generous, liberal and charitable actions performed in one day . . . than in a year of peace." [55] The people could not change their fundamental nature and characteristics. There still continued the traditions of hospitality and friendly concern one for another and for strangers, too, in private relations, and financial honesty and integrity in public life. Southerners were unchangeably conservative in every thought and relationship, and it was this conservatism which they were defending as much as anything else in their fight against Radical Reconstruction. "Isms are starting up like partridges in a stubble, each whirring off with sound and fury in a new direction," said one observer. "The office of Conservatism is to shoot these follies as they fly; if it cannot bag them all, it will cripple some, and make the others chary in its presence." Southerners were the most American part of the nation, and even the Northerners could at this time see that they themselves were "adulterated by an un-Americanized foreign element of population," and that a leaven of Southern conservatism would do the North good. [56]

The North had freed the white South as well as the black from slavery. Economically the New South should develop its own resources, mixing mining, manufacturing, and commerce with agricultural interests, and grow rich with the North. And it should cease to depend on Northern capital which it had been beckoning since 1865 but which it had not been able to attract. It would

[54] *Southern Magazine*, XIII (1873), 600; *Harper's Weekly*, XII (1868), 691; *Nation*, XX (1875), 372.

[55] Donn Piatt in the Cincinnati *Daily Commercial*, quoted in Augusta *Weekly Chronicle & Sentinel*, November 9, 1870.

[56] Greensboro *Herald*, August 7, 1879.

not put much faith in any aid the Federal government might give, for the progress it had been making came in the face of Federal hostility. Even a Northern observer could say that the Federal government had been "aggressive to the last extent, and it is no exaggeration to say that the government at Washington has wrought more injury to the South since the war than it was able to effect during the conflict of arms. It is the strangest folly that ever affected a blind people." [57] So it turned out that Southern capital was responsible for most of the manufacturing and other industrial activities that began to appear around 1880.

For a generation and more, sectional bitterness had made Southerners less than normal, the war had intensified this condition, and Reconstruction had added to their humiliation. If the South could shake itself loose from this debility, indeed would it be entering a new era. For a time it indulged itself to the fullest in the heathen sweetness of hate. According to a Virginian in 1866, "There is a mutual and inextinguishable hate between the Yankee and the Southerner. Whenever and wherever they meet, they will meet as foes at *heart!* and this feeling will live as long as there are two men on earth to bear it for each other." Happily all Southerners did not pursue this course. Even then another Virginian strongly dissented: "The South, abandoning her present hope of order, restoration, liberty, education and advancement in the arts and material progress, is to surrender herself to gloomy passions, and inextinguishable hate, and the counsels of despair! We turn with unaffected horror from such a picture and such a programme." [58]

Sectional hate had affected Northerners, too, for bitter Northerners would have no friendship with Southerners. They greeted Beauregard with hisses and epithets when he visited Chicago in 1867, and the Chicago *Republican* said all "rebels" should "be shunned by honest and loyal men. . . . They missed the deserved halter; let the rope become their lash to whip them naked through the community." [59] The Grand Army of the Republic,

[57] Augusta *Weekly Constitutionalist,* September 5, 1875.

[58] *Ibid.,* December 12, 1866. A Georgian said that "we love the South better than we love revenge." *Ibid.,* March 14, 1866.

[59] Quoted in Augusta *Daily Chronicle & Sentinel,* August 21, 1867.

organized soon after the war, rallied Northerners into hating Southerners, but it failed to win Horace Greeley, who said, "These men combine for political purposes. They propose to keep alive the wrath and bitterness of that dreadful time. They mean to control conventions and nominate men to office—to perpetuate in our civil system the bitterness of war." [60] When a local Pennsylvania post in 1869 planned to decorate Confederate as well as Federal graves, it was overruled by the national headquarters, and in 1875 when the county fair at Rockford, Illinois, invited Jefferson Davis to address the people there, the Grand Army joined other outraged Northerners in having the invitation withdrawn after it had been accepted. The invitation was "a gross insult to every decent man, woman and child in the State," said the Chicago *Inter-Ocean*. The land was dotted with the graves of Northern soldiers, "and yet the murderer and despoiler was invited to partake of the hospitalities of its people and lecture to them and their children on the duties of citizenship!" [61]

Charges of cruelty to Federal prisoners were longest and most effectively used to keep up Northern bitterness, despite the fact that published statistics of deaths in both Northern and Southern prisons showed the North had no reason to chide the South.[62] A Southern editor in 1867 aptly said, "The South can stand the ghosts of Andersonville, if the North can endure those of her many prison houses." [63] Many books were written (and many a dollar made from their sale), whipping up bitterness by portraying in lurid exaggerations the terrors of Southern prisons.

Purveyors of hatred were forced to relinquish the offensive with

[60] New York *Tribune*, quoted in Augusta *Weekly Constitutionalist*, June 23, 1869. A few posts of the Grand Army were founded in the South. *Weekly Austin Republican*, June 24, 1868; May 4, 1870; Houston *Daily Telegraph*, January 30, 1872.

[61] Quoted in Augusta *Weekly Constitutionalist*, August 25, 1875.

[62] Augusta *Weekly Constitutionalist*, July 17, 1867, quoting Secretary Edwin M. Stanton's report to President Johnson, July 19, 1866, and giving the deaths as follows: Southerners dying in Northern prisons, 26,436; Northerners dying in Southern prisons, 22,576. See also, Buck, *Road to Reunion*, 44–51; William B. Hesseltine, "The Propaganda Literature of Confederate Prisons," in *Journal of Southern History*, I (1935). 56–66. A Northern writer said of the Salisbury prison: "Salisbury,—cursed of men dying of cold and starvation, cursed of men driven mad by fiendish torture! Salisbury, —one of the horrible names an unclean and infamous usurpation carved on its sinful and loathsome monument!" Andrews, *South since the War*, 102.

[63] Augusta *Weekly Constitutionalist*, June 19, 1867.

the passing of a few years. Signs of reconciliation appeared like the growth of beautiful flowers in a garden, which gradually choke out the poisonous weeds.

There were outstanding Northerners who had bitterly attacked Southerners before the war but who were now bent on loving them into reconciliation. Greeley, appealed to by Mrs. Jefferson Davis on behalf of her husband, risked his standing in the North by signing Davis' bail bond, and Charles O'Conor, unsolicited, offered his legal services free. Gerrit Smith, forgetting his former bitterness against Southerners, and taking the Alaskan purchase as a point of departure, could say in 1867: Let the United States "buy the Southern heart, worth more to us than a thousand Alaskas, nay, than all Russia. There is one way, and only one way, by which it can be bought, and that is by proving to the South that the North loves her—that the North has a heart to give in exchange for her heart." [64] Others, like T. DeWitt Talmage, the religious statesman of the Brooklyn Tabernacle Church, visited the South and championed its cause, while many journalists, like Edward King, James S. Pike, and Charles Nordhoff, wrote healing accounts of what they saw and sensed in the South. Many Northerners who came to the South to make an honest living and become a part of their communities sought to set their Northern fellow men aright. They formed a permanent organization in Charlotte, North Carolina, to interpret the South to the North, affirming that Southerners as neighbors "visit our firesides and welcome us to the privileges of public worship, and sympathize in our sorrows and afflictions; that they admire sturdy integrity and real principle; that their definition of what these things are correspond with the idea of the same our neighbors in the North hold in common with us." [65] The more frequently Southerners and Northerners visited each other, the more they liked each other. "The constant visitations of thoughtful persons to our cities and States," said a Charleston editor, "is visibly removing the hard crust of prejudice, and acting on both sides, the generous part of peace-makers." [66]

[64] *Ibid.*, July 3, 1867.
[65] Greenville *Enterprise and Mountaineer*, January 22, 1879.
[66] *XIX Century*, I (1869), 30.

The exercise of pardon, first benignly bestowed by President Johnson, and extended to the fullest extent within his power on Christmas Day of 1868, was in the beginning retarded by Congress in laws as well as in the Fourteenth Amendment; but the better nature of Congressmen ultimately asserted itself. Congress first began by special enactments to relieve of disqualifications for office many who came under the Fourteenth Amendment, albeit those first receiving pardon were generally Radicals; and in 1872 it passed a general amnesty law which relieved all but about 500 Confederates. At this time, as far as Federal restrictions were concerned, no Southerner was denied the right to vote—restrictions applied only to officeholding. Not in all Northerners' minds was this forgiveness granted out of friendship for Southerners but rather to counteract the leadership of many Southerners, made more effective by this martyrdom. "It certainly is not to propitiate the Ku-Klux Democracy," said *Harper's Weekly*, "but it is to baffle them." [67]

Many generous acts and kind thoughts of both Southerners and Northerners, one toward the other, occurred more frequently as the years passed. Despite the program of studied hostility carried out by the Grand Army, this organization was unable to snuff out the generous impulses of many Federal soldiers; and with all the harsh words of the unreconciled and unreconstructed Southerners, there were many Confederate soldiers who felt kindly toward their brave enemies of other days. As early as 1866 Southerners began decorating the graves of Federal soldiers. When Confederate graves were decorated in Mobile in 1874, the United States troops there sent a wreath and lent Admiral Semmes a cannon to fire the salute; and when a little later in the year Federal graves were decorated, the keepers of the Confederate tradition sent a wreath. This same year the Grand Army post at Rome, New York, invited Semmes to give an address there, the proceeds from which were to be used to buy tombstones for Federal graves. Unable to accept, Semmes declined in a letter of friendly regards. In Cincinnati the Confederates were invited to join the Federals in decorating the graves of their fallen comrades, and in Madison, Wisconsin, Union soldiers decorated the graves of Confederates who had died there

[67] *Harper's Weekly*, XV (1871), 378.

as prisoners of war. In Lancaster County, South Carolina, reconciled citizens disinterred the remains of two Federal soldiers killed during the war and buried by a roadside, and a railroad whose president was an ex-Confederate soldier hauled the coffins free to Columbia to be delivered to a United States commission charged with developing a Federal cemetery at Florence. In 1875 the Soldiers' National Reunion at Caldwell, Ohio, invited Jefferson Davis and Alexander H. Stephens and through them all Confederate soldiers and sailors to be present. "Our reunion means peace and good will," said their representative. "We open our arms to receive you. We pray you all to come. The war is over forever." [68] In 1879 General Sherman made a trip to the South and was greatly pleased with his reception. In writing to a prominent citizen of Atlanta he said, "Though I was personally regarded the bete-noir of the late war in your region, the author of all your woes, yet I admit that I have just passed over the very ground desolated by the Civil War, and have received everywhere nothing but kind and courteous treatment from the highest to the lowest, and I heard of no violence to others for opinion's sake." [69] Though Southerners had been courteous to Sherman in his presence, some could not refrain from expressing some bitter words. In Sandersville, Georgia, whose courthouse had been burned by Sherman's troops, the local editor said the people had "no desire to kiss the blood stained hand of such an unfeeling monster"; and Wade Hampton in denying that he had attended a ball for Sherman in Jacksonville, Florida, said, "I would certainly have avoided meeting the man who was guilty of the cruelty of burning Columbia and the cowardice of denying it." [70]

Northerners and Southerners were clasping hands with equal eagerness. Charles Sumner, long bracketed by the South with Thaddeus Stevens as an enemy before the war as well as after, fell out with leaders of his own party and, thereby, slightly endeared himself to Southerners. When he sought to have the names of the battles of the Civil War erased from the regimental colors

[68] Nashville *Republican Banner*, May 10, 1866; New Orleans *Weekly Times*, June 6, 1874; Augusta *Weekly Chronicle & Sentinel*, March 18, April 1, 1874; June 2, 1875; Augusta *Weekly Constitutionalist*, July 21, 1875.

[69] Greenville *Enterprise and Mountaineer*, February 19, 1879.

[70] Sandersville *Herald*, January 30, 1879.

of the United States Army, he endeared himself further. So it was, then, that when he died in 1874, Lamar eulogized him in the House of Representatives and caused a tremendous sensation in the North. Up to that time it had been unbelievable that a Southerner could be so forgiving or have such generous impulses. Four years later it was also crowding human nature into a close corner when Alexander H. Stephens in the House, on the occasion of the acceptance of Carpenter's painting of Lincoln signing the Emancipation Proclamation, alluded to the war President as kindhearted and generous. Southerners were soon forgetting themselves and growing as indignant as Northerners, when foreign nations now and then insulted the Stars and Stripes, as in 1873 when Spain captured the "Virginius" and shot some of the crew.

The American Revolution having been conveniently fought one hundred years before the Reconstruction days, the centennial celebrations of its victories drew the North and South together in forgetfulness of their current bitterness as they recalled the heroic days of their birth. As the celebration of these centennials continued, a South Carolinian declared, "The bloody chasm seems 'bridged.'" "Let the centennials go on," he advised. "We can stand seven years of them. As the Revolution lasted that long, we presume the centennials will also, and from the amount of good feeling generated at each, the country will be pretty well united by that time." [71] In the celebration of the battle of Lexington, Charlestonians appeared as participants and won the heart of Boston and the North by presenting to Massachusetts the battle flag lost by Robert Gould Shaw and his Negro regiment in their disastrous assault on Battery Wagner in the siege of Charleston in 1863. A little later in the year (1875) Bostonians celebrated Bunker Hill, enthusiastically aided by the Washington Light Infantry from Charleston and by the Norfolk Blues led by General Fitzhugh Lee. Before the activities were over, it began to appear that it was not Bunker Hill but the return of good will between North and South that was being celebrated. These Southern soldiers were thrown bouquets and loudly cheered as they marched along. According to the Boston *Journal*, the South Carolinians received "an ovation grander than ever was accorded to the con-

[71] Greenville *Enterprise and Mountaineer*, June 23, 1875.

quering heroes who once met these sons of the sunny South in the stern conflict of war. 'Hurrah for South Carolina.' 'There is the flag,' and the call was responded to by a thousand husky throats, while handkerchiefs fluttered in the air and cheer upon cheer arose above the din of martial music." [72] A Georgian declared, "Every patriot has abundant reason to rejoice at a change at once so grand and so suggestive of a more glorious and lasting consummation, when the tomahawk shall be buried—the calumet smoked and peace evoked from long banishment to bless the land." [73] In 1880 the New York Seventy-first Infantry, National Guards, was invited to Mardi Gras. They received an ovation in many Southern towns as they passed through and were carried away by the hospitalities of the Crescent City.[74]

The greatest of these Revolutionary centennials—the celebration of the birth of the American nation—was held in Philadelphia in 1876. An occasion so completely engaging the attention of the country and participated in so widely drew forth much discussion in the South. Some Southern leaders opposed their section taking part; they still felt that the country was not theirs and that it might be less than dignified in themselves and lacking in respect for their heroic Revolutionary ancestors, to go to Philadelphia and be treated as less than equals in a Union which those ancestors had done a major part to found. Said J. Izard Middleton of South Carolina, "My present concern is that the prostrate State may do nothing in the present contingency that may cast the least stain upon her bright escutcheon. If she can do this and go to Philadelphia, let her go, if not, not." [75] Former Governor Benjamin F. Perry saw in the Centennial an effective way to drive home to the country the similarity of principles of the rebellion that became the Revolution and the rebellion that became the "Lost Cause." "This Centennial glorification of the rebels of '76, cannot fail to teach the Northern mind to look with more leniency on Confederate rebels who only attempted to do in the late civil war what the ancestors of the Northern people did do in the

[72] Quoted *ibid.*, June 30, 1875.   [73] Greensboro *Herald*, July 1, 1875.

[74] John F. Cowan, *A New Invasion of the South, Being a Narrative of the Expedition of the Seventy-first Infantry, National Guard, Through the Southern States to New Orleans* (New York, 1881).

[75] Greenville *Enterprise and Mountaineer*, September 15, 1875.

American revolution. . . . It shows a want of sense as well as a want of principle, and a want of truth, to call the rebels of 1776, patriots and heroes, and the rebels of 1861, traitors." [76] Other Southerners saw an even more practical benefit coming from participation. Exhibits from the South would show the progress it was making in industrial activities and might draw much Northern capital southward. Only one contingency would induce a Virginian not to take part. The Grand Army must not be represented: "It would be the death's head on the board; the skeleton in the banquet hall." [77]

The North was genuinely anxious to have the South participate. Lamar was invited to be one of the two orators for the occasion, and Sidney Lanier, to write a cantata. The editor of *Scribner's Monthly* begged: "Men of the South, we want you. Men of the South, we long for the restoration of your peace and your prosperity. We would see your cities thriving, your homes happy, your plantations teeming with plenteous harvests, your schools overflowing, your wisest statesmen leading you, and all causes and all memories of discord wiped out forever." [78] The South could not resist the Philadelphia Centennial. Railroads and steamboats made special rates, and people went to this great gathering of Americans, who before had never been out of their own communities. Parties of girls from seminaries, properly chaperoned, businessmen, planters, politicians, and semireconstructed women, flocked to "Filadelfy town" to have experiences to recount for the rest of their lives, and to return better Americans.

Though Reconstruction as designed by the Radicals had been a dismal failure, it proved that four years of civil war followed by a decade of humiliation could not blot out the old love of country implanted in North and South alike by the sacrifices of the Revolution and subsequent common problems and experiences. Never had a government that had prevailed so strongly died so completely as the Confederacy. In the days of deepest despair during Reconstruction, no Southerner ever harbored the hope of re-establishing independence. Many Northerners saw what the Radical leaders refused to admit, that the Confederate states

[76] *Ibid.,* September 8, 1875.   [77] Richmond *Daily Sentinel,* August 28, 1875.
[78] *Scribner's Monthly,* X (1875), 509.

had been ready from the day of the Surrender to resume their place in the Union; and many Southerners knew that all people in the North did not agree with the Radicals. Southerners would still be Southerners, though no less Americans. A political solidarity was forced upon the South to her detriment; a New South, tempered with much that was old, she herself devised. The nation still needed the South as much as the South needed the nation.

CRITICAL ESSAY ON AUTHORITIES

THE documentary material relating to the Reconstruction period is voluminous and widely scattered. No attempt is made here to compile either an exhaustive or an ideal list of items, but rather to indicate with some evaluation what was examined in writing this volume. The selection was, of necessity, based on the axiomatic fact that an examination of everything relating to the subject could not fall within the lifetime of any mortal and on the further consideration of availability. Not only was a fresh examination of many primary sources made and the standard works consulted but also special pains were taken to scrutinize recent monographic works and periodical material and to accept any of the newer interpretations which seemed valid.

MANUSCRIPT COLLECTIONS

To secure intimate and significant views held by contemporaries, several manuscript collections were examined. Excellent sources for opinions held by Negroes and the submerged white Southerners are their letters in the following collections of Northern Radicals: Papers of Zachariah Chandler, William E. Chandler, James A. Garfield, Joseph Holt, Charles Sumner, John Sherman, Thaddeus Stevens, Henry Wilson, and Elihu B. Washburne. All of these collections are in the Division of Manuscripts, Library of Congress, with the exception of the Sumner Papers which are in the Widener Library at Harvard University. The most valuable and voluminous of these are the William E. Chandler, Sumner, Sherman, and Stevens Papers. Important for the expression of views of the dominant Southerners are the Andrew Johnson Papers, in the Division of Manuscripts, Library of Congress, and the Papers of Samuel J. Tilden and Horace Greeley, both of which are in the New York Public Library. All of these collections contain many letters from Southerners. The dominant Southern view is also expressed in letters in the Godfrey Barnsley Papers and in the Rawlins Collection, both of which are in the University of Georgia Library; in the Jabez L. M. Curry Papers, Department of Archives and History, Montgomery, Alabama; in the Louis T. Wigfall Papers, Division of Manuscripts, Library of Congress; and in the John H. Reagan Papers, Texas State Library, Austin. Transcripts of the Wigfall and Reagan collections, in the University of Texas Library, were used. Oaths of Allegiance, Greene County, Georgia, 1865–1866, is an interesting manuscript in the University of Georgia Library.

GOVERNMENT DOCUMENTS

The official publications of the United States and of the states are vast, dealing with every side of Reconstruction, but more with the process than with the South itself. A voluminous work is "Affairs of Southern Railroads," *Reports of the Committees of the House of Representatives*, 39 Cong., 2 Sess., No. 34, Serial No. 1306. Two Federal census reports were useful in this study, the *Ninth Census of the United States, 1870*, 3 vols. (Washington, 1872), and the *Tenth Census of the United States, 1880*, 22 vols. (Washington, 1883–1888). The former is highly unreliable in much of its data, as it was a casualty of the low public morality which for political reward made census workers out of the most ignorant and dishonest Radicals. It was, therefore, used sparingly and with due care. The *Tenth Census,* containing in its twenty-two volumes a storehouse of information which could be relied on, was used extensively. The volumes on cities, cotton, the newspaper and periodical press, and transportation were especially valuable. For handy use were the *Compendium of the Ninth Census, 1870* (Washington, 1872), subject to the same limitations as the regular census for that decade, and the *Compendium of the Tenth Census, 1880*, 2 pts. (Washington, 1883). Helpful in the use of the various censuses was Carroll D. Wright, *The History and Growth of the United States Census* (Washington, 1900). For the spoken mind of Congressmen it is indispensable to examine the *Congressional Globe*, 46 vols. (Washington, 1834–1873), and the *Congressional Record* (Washington, 1873–). Of the many reports of committees and departments and other official documents, the following were examined: "Condition of the South," *Senate Executive Documents*, 39 Cong., 1 Sess., No. 2, Serial No. 1237 (Schurz's Report, pp. 2–105; Grant's Report, pp. 106–108); "Cotton Sold to the Confederate States," *Senate Documents*, 62 Cong., 3 Sess., No. 987, Serial No. 6348; W. E. Burghardt Du Bois, "The Negro Landholder of Georgia," in

Bulletin of the Department of Labor, No. 35 (Washington, 1901); "Pardons by the President," *House of Representatives Executive Documents,* 40 Cong., 2 Sess., No. 16, Serial No. 1330; Benjamin P. Poore, *Message from the President of the United States to the Two Houses of Congress . . . Third Session of the Forty-Second Congress, with the Reports of Heads of Departments and Selections from Accompanying Documents* (Washington, 1872); "Provisional Governors of States," *Senate Executive Documents,* 39 Cong., 1 Sess., No. 26, Serial No. 1237; *Regulations Relating to Army and Navy Pensions, with Statutes* (Washington, 1871); "Report of Benjamin C. Truman," *Senate Executive Documents,* 39 Cong., 1 Sess., No. 43, Serial No. 1237; *Report of the Commissioner of Agriculture,* 1866 (Washington, 1867); *ibid.,* 1867 (Washington, 1868); *ibid.,* 1869 (Washington, 1870); *ibid.,* 1870 (Washington, 1871); *ibid.,* 1871 (Washington, 1872); *Report of the Commissioner of Education,* 1867 (Washington, 1868); *Report of the Joint Committee on Reconstruction, at the First Session Thirty-Ninth Congress* (Washington, 1866); *Report of the Joint Select Committee to Inquire into the Condition of Affairs in the Late Insurrectionary States (Ku Klux Conspiracy),* 13 vols. (Washington, 1872); "Report of the Secretary of War," 1865, *House of Representatives Executive Documents,* 39 Cong., 1 Sess., No. 1, Serial No. 1249; 1866, *ibid.,* 39 Cong., 2 Sess., No. 1, Serial No. 1285; 1869, *ibid.,* 41 Cong., 2 Sess., No. 1, Pt. II, Serial No. 1412; 1870, *ibid.,* 41 Cong., 3 Sess., No. 1, Pt. II, Serial No. 1446.

NEWSPAPERS

Newspapers were used with due caution as a source for factual statements, but what public opinion was and what it demanded can nowhere else be established so clearly as through this medium. Especially in Reconstruction times the mind of the South was a factor of outstanding importance, and in determining what it was, widespread use was made of newspapers. The press in all the eleven Confederate states was consulted. As most of the papers were vehicles of the dominant Southern view, except during Congressional Reconstruction, special efforts were made to locate as many of the Radical variety as possible, in order that this despised and neglected viewpoint might have its day in court.

The following newspapers upheld the traditional Southern point of view: Virginia—Richmond *Daily Dispatch, Daily Richmond Enquirer* (changed to *Enquirer and Examiner,* July 12, 1867); North Carolina—Raleigh *Daily Sentinel;* South Carolina—Charleston *Courier,* Greenville *Southern Enterprise* (going through these successive changes in name, Greenville *Enterprise, Enterprise and Mountaineer,* and *Daily Enterprise*); Georgia—Americus *Tri-Weekly Sumter Republican* (also weekly edition), Athens *Southern Watchman,* Atlanta *Daily Sun* (also weekly edition), Atlanta *Constitution,* Augusta *Daily Chronicle & Sentinel* (also weekly edition), Augusta *Daily Constitutionalist* (also weekly edition), Augusta *Daily Press,* Columbus *Daily Enquirer* (also weekly edition), Crawford *Oglethorpe Echo,* Dalton *Cherokee Georgian,* Dalton *North Georgia Citizen,* Elberton *Gazette,* Gainesville *Eagle,* Greensboro *Herald,* Macon *Daily Journal and Messenger,* Macon *Daily Telegraph,* Marietta *Journal,* Rome *Weekly Courier* (also triweekly edition), Sandersville *Central Georgian,* Sandersville *Herald,* Thompson *McDuffie Weekly Journal,* Warrenton *Clipper;* Florida—Fernandina *Florida Mirror,* Tallahassee *Semi-Weekly Floridian* (also weekly edition); Alabama—Montgomery *Weekly Advertiser;* Mississippi—*Daily Aberdeen Examiner,* Aberdeen *Daily Sunny South,* Natchez *Democrat,* Raymond *Hinds County Gazette,* Vicksburg *Daily Times;* Louisiana—Carrollton *Times,* New Orleans *Weekly Times;* Tennessee—Memphis *Argus,* Memphis *Daily Bulletin,* Nashville *Republican Banner;* Arkansas—Dardanelle *Arkansas Independent,* Little Rock *Weekly Arkansas Gazette;* Texas—Austin *Tri-Weekly State Gazette,* Carthage *Panola Watchman,* Galveston *Tri-Weekly News,* Houston *Daily Telegraph,* San Antonio *Daily Herald.*

The Radical or near-Radical papers used were: North Carolina—Raleigh *Tri-Weekly Standard;* Georgia—Atlanta *Daily New Era,* Atlanta *Daily Opinion* (also weekly edition called *Georgia Weekly Opinion*), Dalton *North Georgia Republican,* Griffin (later Macon) *American Union,* Savannah *Journal;* Florida—Tallahassee *Sentinel;* Alabama—Montgomery *Alabama State Journal;* Mississippi—Columbus *Press;* Louisiana—New Orleans *Tribune;* Tennessee—Knoxville *Whig;* Texas—Austin *Daily State Journal, Weekly Austin Republican,* Galveston *Commercial Bulletin.*

The New York *Texas New Yorker* and the Tallahassee *Florida Immigrant* were set up to promote the economic development of the South. Other Northern newspapers used were: Boston *Liberator,* New York *Daily News,* New York *Evening Post,* New York *Tribune,* New York *World,* and Washington *New National Era.*

CONTEMPORARY PERIODICALS

The considered opinions and beliefs of people, relating more to other matters than to politics, were best expressed in periodicals—weeklies, monthlies, and quarterlies. The most learned of the Southern literary magazines, all growing up after the war and continuing only for short periods, were the *Southern Review* (Baltimore, 1867–1879), the *Southern Magazine* (Baltimore, 1868–1875), the *Land We Love, A Monthly Magazine Devoted to Literature, Military History, and Agriculture* (Charlotte, N.C., 1866–1869), the *XIX Century* (Charleston, 1869–1871), and *Scott's Monthly Magazine* (Atlanta, 1865–1869). Good for the continuing Confederate tradition was this first Southern historical journal of any importance, *Southern Historical Society Papers* (Richmond, 1876–). *De Bow's Review,* subtitle varies (New Orleans, Washington, Charleston, Columbia, Nashville, New York, 1846–1864, 1866–1870, 1879–1880) reappeared in its "After the War Series" (1866–1870) and carried on with success its ante-bellum traditions. The most valuable of the Southern agricultural journals, and the only one to continue through the war and beyond, was the *Southern Cultivator, A Practical and Scientific Newspaper for the Plantation, the Garden, and the Family Circle* (Augusta, Athens, Atlanta, 1843–1935). Others consulted were the *American Farmer: A Monthly Magazine of Agriculture and Horticulture* (Baltimore, Washington, 1819–1897); the *Plantation, Devoted to the Interests of Agriculture, Rural Economy, and the Benefits of Life Assurance* (Atlanta, 1870–1873?); *Southern Farm and Home: A Magazine of Agriculture, Manufactures and Domestic Economy* (Macon, Ga., Memphis, 1869–1873); *South Land, for Town and Country* (New Orleans, 1870–1878?); and *Southern Farmer, Devoted to Agriculture, Horticulture, Stock Raising, and All the Industrial and Mechanical Interests of the South* (Memphis, 1867–1873). The religious press was examined in two publications, *Southern Presbyterian Review* (Columbia, S.C., 1847–1908), and the *Christian Index* (Philadelphia, Washington, Ga., Atlanta, 1821–).

Northern periodicals gave much attention to conditions in the South; and some were designed entirely for the discussion of Southern affairs, as the *American Freedman, A Monthly Journal Devoted to the Promotion of Freedom, Industry, Education, and Christian Morality in the South* (New York, 1866–1869), and the *National Freedman, A Monthly Journal of the New York National Freedman's Relief Association* (New York, 1865–1866). Two journals valuable for railroad information were the *Railroad Gazette, A Journal of Transportation, Engineering and Railroad News* (Chicago, 1870–1908), and the *Railway Monitor, A Journal of Railroad Intelligence* (New York, 1873–1875). Valuable for financial news is the *Commercial and Financial Chronicle,* subtitle varies (New York, 1865–). Other magazines, of a literary and political nature, are: *Appletons' Journal* (New York, 1869–1876); *Atlantic Monthly* (Boston, 1857–); *Harper's Weekly, A Journal of Civilization* (New York, 1857–1916); the *Nation* (New York, 1865–); *Peterson's Ladies National Magazine* (Philadelphia, 1840–1894); *Scribner's Monthly, An Illustrated Magazine for the People* (New York, 1870–1881).

CONTEMPORARY PAMPHLETS

The occasion that brought forth a pamphlet often involved information or observations which did not readily find a place in print anywhere else. Though the mortality of pamphlets from their very nature has been great, the following have been found and used to advantage: John W. Alvord, *Letters from the South, Relating to the Condition of the Freedmen, Addressed to Major General O. O. Howard* (Washington, 1870), 42 pp.; *Address of Edward Atkinson of Boston, Massachusetts, Given in Atlanta, Georgia, in October, 1880 for the Promotion of an International Cotton Exposition* (Boston, 1881), 36 pp.; David Tillson, *Bureau of Refugees, Freedmen and Abandoned Lands*, Circular No. 4 (n.p., April 6, 1866), 1 p.; *Speech of Ex-Gov. Joseph E. Brown, of Georgia, Delivered in Milledgeville, Ga., June 6th, 1867, on the Present Situation and Future Prospects of the Country* (n.p., n.d.), 8 pp.; *Letter from his Excellency Governor Bullock, of Georgia, in Reply to the Honorable John Scott, United States Senator, Chairman of the Joint Select Committee to Inquire into the Condition of the Late Insurrectionary States* (Atlanta, 1871), 24 pp.; *Triumphal March of Sergeant [Gilbert H.] Bates from Vicksburg to Washington* (Washington, 1868), 36 pp.; *Address of Rufus B. Bullock to the People of Georgia, October, 1872* (n.p., n.d.), 59 pp.; John H. Caldwell, *Reminiscences of the Reconstruction of Church and State in Georgia* (Wilmington, Del., 1895), 23 pp.; *Semi-Annual Bulletin of the Georgia State Agricultural Society* (Atlanta, 1874); *Horace Greeley's Views on Virginia . . .* (n.p., n.d.), 8 pp.; *Greeley on the Ku-Klux* (n.p., n.d.), 4 pp.; *The Union and its Enemies: Speech of Hon. Benjamin H. Hill of Georgia, Delivered in the Senate of the United States, Saturday, May 10, 1879* (Washington, 1879), 43 pp.; *Maimed Soldiers in Georgia Supplied with Artificial Limbs, under the Act Approved September 20, 1879* (n.p., n.d.), 22 pp.; Mrs. A. M. Meeker, *Eliza Ross; or, Illustrated Guide of Lookout Mountain* (Atlanta, 1871), 36 pp.; Gustavus J. Orr, *The Education of the Negro, Its Rise, Progress and Present Status; Being an Address Delivered before the National Educational Association at its Late Meeting at Chautauqua, N.Y.* (Atlanta, 1880), 15 pp.; *Speech of Hon. Alex. H. Stephens, of Georgia, on*

397

the Civil Rights Bill, Delivered in the House of Representatives, January 5, 1874 (Washington, 1874), 16 pp.; Elias Yulee, *An Address to the Colored People of Georgia* (Savannah, 1868), 32 pp.

BOOKS BY CONTEMPORARIES

Many people, both from the North and from abroad, traveled through the South during Reconstruction times, and some of them wrote penetrating accounts of what they saw. These works have the virtue of being based on observations by their authors rather than on hearsay. The best-known travel books are: Sidney Andrews, *The South since the War: As Shown by Fourteen Weeks of Travel and Observation in Georgia and the Carolinas* (Boston, 1866); Sir George Campbell, *White and Black: The Outcome of a Visit to the United States* (London, 1879); Charles W. Dilke, *Greater Britain: A Record of Travel in English-Speaking Countries during 1866 and 1867* (New York, 1869); Edward King, *The Great South . . .* (Hartford, 1875); John H. Kennaway, *On Sherman's Track; or, The South after the War* (London, 1867); Charles Nordhoff, *The Cotton States in the Spring and Summer of 1875* (New York, 1876); Whitelaw Reid, *After the War: A Southern Tour, May 1, 1865 to May 1, 1866* (New York, 1866); Robert Somers, *The Southern States since the War, 1870–1* (London, 1871); John T. Trowbridge, *The South: A Tour of its Battle-Fields and Ruined Cities, A Journey through the Desolated States, and Talks with the People: . . .* (Hartford, 1866). Particularly valuable are King, Nordhoff, Reid, and Somers.

Contemporary accounts often lack reliability in factual statements but they express what no modern scholarly work can portray as well—a mental atmosphere which played an important part particularly in this period of American history. These works give the Radical viewpoint: Albert T. Morgan, *Yazoo; or, On the Picket Line of Freedom in the South* (Washington, 1884); Charles Stearns, *The Black Man of the South, and the Rebels; or, The Characteristics of the Former, and the Recent Outrages of the Latter* (New York, 1872); Albion W. Tourgee, *A Fool's Errand, By One of the Fools; The Famous Romance of American History* (New, Enlarged and Illustrated Edition, New York, 1880); a work of a reformed Radical Negro is John Wallace, *Carpetbag Rule in Florida: The Inside Workings of the Reconstruction of Civil Government in Florida after the Close of the Civil War* (Jacksonville, 1888); a particularly valuable account of a planter's attempt to use free labor is Frances Butler Leigh, *Ten Years on a Georgia Plantation since the*

398

War (London, 1883); the classic work on the outrages of Radical government in South Carolina as seen by a Northerner is James S. Pike, *The Prostrate State: South Carolina under Negro Government* (Reprint Edition, New York, 1935); and the South's answer to the Andersonville Prison charges by the North is R. Randolph Stevenson, *The Southern Side; or, Andersonville Prison* (Baltimore, 1876). An interesting speculation on what one Northerner thought was behind the Radical program and its relation to world developments is in L. B. Woolfolk, *The World Crisis* (Cincinnati, 1868).

Other useful works by contemporaries are: Myrta L. Avary, *Dixie after the War* (Reprint, Boston, 1937); John F. Cowan, *A New Invasion of the South, Being a Narrative of the Expedition of the Seventy-First Infantry, National Guard, Through the Southern States, to New Orleans* (New York, 1881); James W. Davidson, *The Living Writers of the South* (New York, 1869); Hilary A. Herbert *et al., Why the Solid South? or, Reconstruction and its Results* (Baltimore, 1890); M. B. Hillyard, *The New South, A Description of the Southern States, Noting Each State Separately, and Giving Their Distinctive Features and Most Salient Characteristics* (Baltimore, 1887); William D. Kelley, *The Old South and the New* (New York, 1888); James D. Lynch, *Kemper County Vindicated, and a Peep at Radical Rule* (New York, 1879); Alexander K. McClure, *The South: Its Industrial, Financial, and Political Condition* (Philadelphia, 1886); Edward A. Pollard, *The Lost Cause: A New Southern History of the War of the Confederates* (New York, 1866); Dennis A. Quinn, *Heroes and Heroines of Memphis, or Reminiscences of the Yellow Fever Epidemics that Afflicted the City of Memphis during the Autumn Months of 1873, 1878, and 1879, to which is Added a Graphic Description of Missionary Life in Eastern Arkansas* (Providence, 1887); Alexander L. Stimson, *History of the Express Business; Including the Origin of the Railway System in America, and the Relation of Both to the Increase of New Settlements and the Prosperity of Cities in the United States* (New York, 1881).

OTHER PUBLISHED SOURCES

Of the letters and papers of Reconstruction figures that have found their way into print, the following collections were found unusually valuable for the present study: J. G. de Roulhac Hamilton (ed.), *The Correspondence of Jonathan Worth*, 2 vols. (Raleigh, 1909); *id.* (ed.), *The Papers of Randolph Abbott Shotwell*, 3 vols. (Raleigh, 1929–1936); Dunbar Rowland (ed.), *Jefferson Davis, Constitutionalist. His Letters,*

Papers and Speeches, 10 vols. (Jackson, Miss., 1923). *The Reminiscences of Carl Schurz,* 3 vols. (London, 1909); *Memoirs of William T. Sherman. By Himself,* 2 vols. (New York, 1875); and Henry C. Warmoth, *War, Politics and Reconstruction: Stormy Days in Louisiana* (New York, 1930), were used to advantage. There is also valuable source material in Benjamin H. Hill, Jr., *Senator Benjamin H. Hill of Georgia: His Life, Speeches and Writings* (Atlanta, 1893); and in H. S. Chamberlain, *Old Days in Chapel Hill, Being the Life and Letters of Cornelia Phillips Spencer* (Chapel Hill, 1926). In the field of literary activity, useful sources are: Edwin A. Alderman *et al.* (eds.), *Library of Southern Literature,* 16 vols. and Supplement I (New Orleans, Atlanta, Dallas, 1907–1923); and William P. Trent, *Southern Writers: Selections in Prose and Verse* (New York, 1910).

Among collections of Reconstruction documents, two were indispensable: the work by a contemporary, Edward McPherson, *The Political History of the United States of America during the Period of Reconstruction* (Washington, 1875), emphasizes only one aspect of history, while the scholarly work of Walter L. Fleming (ed.), *Documentary History of Reconstruction: Political, Military, Social, Religious, Educational & Industrial, 1865 to the Present Time,* 2 vols. (Cleveland, 1906–1907), is a mine of information on various phases. Legal cases bearing upon Reconstruction problems appear in *The Federal Cases, Comprising Cases Argued and Determined in the Circuit and District Courts of the United States,* 30 vols. (St. Paul, 1894–1897). A valuable atlas for the period is Fletcher W. Hewes and Henry Gannett, *Scribner's Statistical Atlas of the United States, Showing by Graphic Methods their Present Condition and their Political, Social and Industrial Development* (New York, 1883).

Among useful annuals and manuals are: *American* (called from 1876 *Appletons'*) *Annual Cyclopaedia and Register of Important Events* (New York, 1867–1902); Henry V. Poor, *Manual of the Railroads of the United States* (New York, 1868–1924); Alexander St. Clair-Abrams, *Manual and Biographical Register of the State of Georgia for 1871–2* (Atlanta, 1872).

Historical periodicals yielded significant documents: Jessie M. Fraser (ed.), "A Free Labor Contract, 1867," in *Journal of Southern History* (Baton Rouge, Nashville, 1935–), VI (1940), 546–48; C. L. Marquette (ed.), "Letters of a Yankee Sugar Planter," *ibid.,* 521–46; Percy L. Rainwater (ed.), "Letters to and from Jacob Thompson," *ibid.,* 95–111; Robert H. Woody (ed.), "Behind the Scenes in the Reconstruction Legislature of South Carolina: Diary of Josephus Woodruff," *ibid.,* II

(1936), 78–102, 233–59; "The Proceedings of a Migration Convention and Congressional Action Respecting the Exodus of 1879," in *Journal of Negro History* (Washington, 1916–), IV (1919), 51–92; James A. Padgett (ed.), "Some Letters of George Stanton Denison, 1854–1866: Observations of a Yankee on Conditions in Louisiana and Texas," in *Louisiana Historical Quarterly* (New Orleans, Baton Rouge, 1917–), XXIII (1940), 1132–1240; *id.* (ed.), "Reconstruction Letters from North Carolina," in *North Carolina Historical Review* (Raleigh, 1924–), XVIII (1941), 171–95; Nora C. Chaffin (ed.), "A Southern Advocate of Methodist Unification in 1865," *ibid.*, 38–47.

BIOGRAPHIES

An indispensable biographical work for the study of any period of American history is Allen Johnson and Dumas Malone (eds.), *Dictionary of American Biography,* 20 vols. and index (New York, 1927–1938). Other biographical studies utilized were: Edwin A. Alderman and Armistead C. Gordon, *J. L. M. Curry: A Biography* (New York, 1911); Charles H. Ambler, *Francis H. Pierpont, Union War Governor of Virginia and Father of West Virginia* (Chapel Hill, 1937); Hamilton Basso, *Beauregard, the Great Creole* (New York, 1933); Nelson W. Blake, *William Mahone of Virginia, Soldier and Political Insurgent* (Richmond, 1935); Henry D. Capers, *The Life and Times of C. G. Memminger* (Richmond, 1893); Jaquelin A. Caskie, *Life and Letters of Matthew Fontaine Maury* (Richmond, 1928); Wirt A. Cate, *Lucius Q. C. Lamar, Secession and Reunion* (Chapel Hill, 1935); *Zachariah Chandler: An Outline Sketch of his Life and Public Services. By the Detroit* Post and Tribune (Detroit, 1880); E. Merton Coulter, *William G. Brownlow, Fighting Parson of the Southern Highlands* (Chapel Hill, 1937); Avery Craven, *Edmund Ruffin, Southerner: A Study in Secession* (New York, 1932); W. E. Burghardt Du Bois, *Dusk of Dawn: An Essay toward an Autobiography of a Race Concept* (New York, 1940); Alexander C. Flick, *Samuel Jones Tilden: A Study in Political Sagacity* (New York, 1939); Douglas S. Freeman, *R. E. Lee: A Biography,* 4 vols. (New York, 1934–1935); Armistead C. Gordon, *Memories and Memorials of William Gordon McCabe,* 2 vols. (Richmond, 1925); Phebe A. Hanaford, *The Life of George Peabody* . . . (Boston, 1870); William B. Hesseltine, *Ulysses S. Grant, Politician* (New York, 1935); Mark A. de W. Howe, *James Ford Rhodes, American Historian* (New York, 1929); Jay B. Hubbell, *The Last Years of Henry Timrod, 1864–1867* (Durham, 1941); Robert McElroy, *Jefferson Davis: The Unreal and the Real,* 2 vols. (New York, 1937); Elias Nason, *The Life and Public Services of Henry Wilson* (Boston, 1881); Raymond B. Nixon, *Henry W. Grady, Spokesman of the New South* (New York, 1943); Ellis P. Oberholtzer, *Jay Cooke, Financier of the Civil War*, 2 vols. (Philadelphia, 1907); Edd W. Parks, *Charles Egbert Craddock (Mary Noailles Murfree)* (Chapel Hill, 1941); James B. Ranck, *Albert Gallatin Brown, Radical Southern Nationalist* (New York, 1937); Dora N. Raymond, *Captain Lee Hall of Texas* (Norman, 1940); Franklin L. Riley (ed.), *General Robert E. Lee after Appomattox* (New York, 1922); George H. Smyth, *The Life of Henry Bradley Plant, Founder and President of the Plant System of Railroads and Steamships and Also of the Southern Express Company* (New York, 1898); Arndt M. Stickles, *Simon Bolivar Buckner, Borderland Knight* (Chapel Hill, 1940); Lyman B. Stowe, *Saints, Sinners and Beechers* (Indianapolis, 1934); Charles R Williams, *The Life of Rutherford Birchard Hayes, Nineteenth President of the United States*, 2 vols. (Boston, 1914); Harold F. Williamson, *Edward Atkinson, The Biography of an American Liberal, 1827–1905* (Boston, 1934).

ARTICLES IN PROFESSIONAL MAGAZINES

Valuable for modern research and points of view are the many current historical journals. Most effective use was made of the *Journal of Southern History* (Baton Rouge, Nashville, 1935–), in which these articles appear: Edward G. Campbell, "Indebted Railroads—A Problem of Reconstruction," VI (1940), 167–88; E. Merton Coulter, "What the South Has Done About Its History," II (1936), 3–28; Jonathan T. Dorris, "Pardon Seekers and Brokers: A Sequel of Appomattox," I (1935), 276–92; Paul W. Gates, "Federal Land Policy in the South, 1866–1888," VI (1940), 303–30; Fletcher M. Green, "Duff Green: Industrial Promoter," II (1936), 29–42; Harriet L. Herring, "The Clement Attachment: An Episode of Reconstruction Industrial History," IV (1938), 183–98; William B. Hesseltine, "The Propaganda Literature of Confederate Prisons," I (1935), 56–66; Albert V. House, Jr., "Northern Congressional Democrats as Defenders of the South During Reconstruction," VI (1940), 46–71; Albert B. Moore, "Railroad Building in Alabama during the Reconstruction Period," I (1935), 421–41; Walter Prichard, "The Effects of the Civil War on the Louisiana Sugar Industry," V (1939), 313–32; Roger W. Shugg, "Survival of the Plantation System in Louisiana," III (1937), 311–25; Bell I. Wiley, "Vicissitudes of Early Reconstruction Farming in the Lower Mississippi Valley," III (1937), 441–52.

The only learned historical publication conducted by Negroes is the *Journal of Negro History* (Washington, 1916-). Though all of its contributors are not Negroes, yet the general tone of this publication is one that expresses that race's views. Articles of value in this magazine are: Luther P. Jackson, "The Educational Efforts of the Freedmen's Bureau and Freedmen's Aid Societies in South Carolina, 1862–1872," VIII (1923), 1–40; Blake McKelvey, "Penal Slavery and Southern Reconstruction," XX (1935), 153–79; Louis F. Post, "A 'Carpetbagger' in South Carolina," X (1925), 10–79; William A. Russ, Jr., "The Negro and White Disfranchisement during Radical Reconstruction," XIX (1934), 171–92; Alrutheus A. Taylor, "The Negro in the Reconstruction of Virginia," XI (1926), 243–415, 425–537; *id.*, "The Negro in South Carolina during the Reconstruction," IX (1924), 241–364, 381–569; John G. Van Deusen, "The Exodus of 1879," XXI (1936), 111–29; Robert H. Woody, "Jonathan Jasper Wright, Associate Justice of the Supreme Court of South Carolina, 1870–77," XVIII (1933), 114–31.

Interesting and challenging because of an overstatement of certain views is Howard K. Beale, "On Rewriting Reconstruction History," in *American Historical Review* (New York, 1895-), XLV (1939–1940), 807–27; and in the same journal, XXXI (1925–1926), 266–84, there is a clear and concise account of the Jefferson Davis case in Roy F. Nichols, "United States vs. Jefferson Davis, 1865–1869." In the *Mississippi Valley Historical Review* (Cedar Rapids, 1914-) are these articles: Gerald M. Capers, Jr., "Yellow Fever in Memphis in the 1870's," XXIV (1937–1938), 483–502; Jonathan T. Dorris, "Pardoning the Leaders of the Confederacy, XV (1928–1929), 3–21; William B. Hesseltine, "Economic Factors in the Abandonment of Reconstruction," XXII (1935–1936), 191–210; Frank W. Klingberg, "The Southern Claims Commission: A Postwar Agency in Operation," XXXII (1945–1946), 195–214; James G. Randall, "John Sherman and Reconstruction," XIX (1932–1933), 382–93; William A. Russ, Jr., "Registration and Disfranchisement under Radical Reconstruction," XXI (1934–1935), 163–80; Wendell H. Stephenson, "A Quarter Century of a Mississippi Plantation: Eli J. Capell of 'Pleasant Hill,'" XXIII (1936–1937), 355–74; Robert H. Woody, "The Labor and Immigration Problem of South Carolina during Reconstruction," XVIII (1931–1932), 195–212.

In other current historical journals are these articles: Bell I. Wiley, "Salient Changes in Southern Agriculture since the Civil War," in *Agricultural History* (Baltimore, 1927-), XIII (1939), 65–76; Oscar Zeichner, "The Transition from Slave to Free Agricultural Labor in the Southern States," *ibid.*, 22–32; William B. Hesseltine, "Tennessee's Invitation to Carpet-Baggers," in *East Tennessee Historical Society's Publications* (Knoxville, 1929–), No. 4 (1932), 102–15; Kenneth Coleman, "The Georgia Gubernatorial Election of 1880," in *Georgia Historical Quarterly* (Savannah, 1917–), XXV (1941), 89–119; Alice B. Keith, "White Relief in North Carolina, 1865–1867," in *Social Forces* (Chapel Hill, 1922–), XVII (1938–1939), 337–55.

The following occasional papers of a historical nature were used: Robert H. Woody, *Republican Newspapers of South Carolina*, in *Southern Sketches,* No. 10 (Charlottesville, 1936); James J. Farris, "The Lowrie Gang—An Episode in the History of Robeson County, N.C., 1864–1874," in Trinity College Historical Society *Papers* (Durham, 1897–), Ser. XV (1925); William A. Mabry, "The Negro in North Carolina Politics since Reconstruction," *ibid.,* Ser. XXIII (1940); Carl R. Fish, *The Restoration of the Southern Railroads,* in University of Wisconsin *Studies in the Social Sciences and History,* No. 2 (Madison, 1919).

GENERAL AND SPECIAL HISTORIES

Modern scholarship has not been uniformly unbiased or careful in factual statements or interpretations. There has recently been an attempt to interpret American history, and especially the Reconstruction period, from the standpoint of the class struggle, which has been as unscientific as it has been farfetched. The two best examples of this effort are James S. Allen, *Reconstruction: The Battle for Democracy (1865–1876)* (New York, 1937), and W. E. Burghardt Du Bois, *Black Reconstruction: An Essay toward a History of the Part which Black Folk Played in the Attempt to Reconstruct Democracy, 1860–1880* (New York, 1935).

Reconstruction in its broader setting is taken up in these works: Charles A. Beard and Mary R. Beard, *The Rise of American Civilization,* 2 vols. (New York, 1930); Claude G. Bowers, *The Tragic Era: The Revolution after Lincoln* (Boston, 1929); Paul H. Buck, *The Road to Reunion, 1865–1900* (Boston, 1937); John W. Burgess, *Reconstruction and the Constitution, 1866–1876* (New York, 1902); William A. Dunning, *Reconstruction, Political and Economic, 1865–1877* (New York, 1907); Walter L. Fleming. *The Sequel of Appomattox* (New Haven, 1919); Robert S. Henry, *The Story of Reconstruction* (Indianapolis, 1938); William B. Hesseltine, *The South in American History* (New York, 1943); George F. Milton, *The Age of Hate: Andrew Johnson and the Radicals* (New York, 1930); Allan Nevins, *The Emergence of Modern America, 1865–1878* (New York, 1927); Ellis P. Oberholtzer, *A His-*

tory of the United States since the Civil War, 5 vols. (New York, 1917–1937); James G. Randall, *The Civil War and Reconstruction* (Boston, 1937); James F. Rhodes, *A History of the United States from the Compromise of 1850 to the Final Restoration of Home Rule at the South in 1877,* 7 vols. (New York, 1896–1906); Holland Thompson, *The New South* (New Haven, 1919).

Special state studies are: Hamilton J. Eckenrode, *The Political History of Virginia during the Reconstruction* (Baltimore, 1904); J. G. de Roulhac Hamilton, *Reconstruction in North Carolina* (New York, 1914); John S. Reynolds, *Reconstruction in South Carolina, 1865–1877* (Columbia, 1905); Francis B. Simkins and Robert H. Woody, *South Carolina during Reconstruction* (Chapel Hill, 1932); C. Mildred Thompson, *Reconstruction in Georgia, Economic, Social, Political, 1865–1872* (New York, 1915); Edwin C. Woolley, *The Reconstruction of Georgia* (New York, 1901); William W. Davis, *The Civil War and Reconstruction in Florida* (New York, 1913); Walter L. Fleming, *Civil War and Reconstruction in Alabama* (New York, 1905); James W. Garner, *Reconstruction in Mississippi* (New York, 1901); Willie M. Caskey, *Secession and Restoration of Louisiana* (University, La., 1938); John R. Ficklin, *History of Reconstruction in Louisiana (through 1868)* (Baltimore, 1910); Ella Lonn, *Reconstruction in Louisiana after 1868* (New York, 1918); Garnie W. McGinty, *Louisiana Redeemed: The Overthrow of Carpet-Bag Rule, 1876–1880* (New Orleans, 1941); Roger W. Shugg, *Origins of Class Struggle in Louisiana: A Social History of White Farmers and Laborers during Slavery and After, 1840–1875* (University, La., 1939); James W. Fertig, *The Secession and Reconstruction of Tennessee* (Chicago, 1898); James W. Patton, *Unionism and Reconstruction in Tennessee, 1860–1869* (Chapel Hill, 1934); Thomas S. Staples, *Reconstruction in Arkansas, 1862–1874* (New York, 1923); Charles W. Ramsdell, *Reconstruction in Texas* (New York, 1910); E. Merton Coulter, *The Civil War and Readjustment in Kentucky* (Chapel Hill, 1926).

Collaborative works that include essays on the Reconstruction period are: Julian A. C. Chandler *et al.* (eds.), *The South in the Building of the Nation,* 13 vols. (Richmond, 1909–1913); David K. Jackson (ed.), *American Studies in Honor of William Kenneth Boyd, by Members of the Americana Club of Duke University* (Durham, 1940); *Studies in Southern History and Politics Inscribed to William Archibald Dunning* (New York, 1914).

A few of the many special accounts are: Howard K. Beale, *The Critical Year: A Study of Andrew Johnson and Reconstruction* (New York, 1930); Horace M. Bond, *Negro Education in Alabama: A Study in Cot-*

ton and Steel (Washington, 1939); William K. Boyd, *The Story of Durham, City of the New South* (Durham, 1925); Robert P. Brooks, *The Agrarian Revolution in Georgia, 1865–1912* (Madison, 1914); Cecil K. Brown, *A State Movement in Railroad Development: The Story of North Carolina's First Effort To Establish an East and West Trunk Line Railroad* (Chapel Hill, 1928); Henry M. Bullock, *A History of Emory University* (Nashville, 1936); Gerald M. Capers, Jr., *Biography of a River Town, Memphis: its Heroic Age* (Chapel Hill, 1939); E. Merton Coulter, *The Cincinnati Southern Railroad and the Struggle for Southern Commerce, 1865–1872* (Chicago, 1922); *id., College Life in the Old South* (New York, 1928); *id., A Short History of Georgia* (Chapel Hill, 1933); Jabez L. M. Curry, *Peabody Education Fund: A Brief Sketch of George Peabody, and a History of the Peabody Education Fund through Thirty Years* (Cambridge, 1898); Howard D. Dozier, *A History of the Atlantic Coast Line Railroad* (Boston, 1920); James H. Easterby, *A History of the College of Charleston* (Charleston, 1935); Clement Eaton, *Freedom of Thought in the Old South* (Durham, 1940); Hunter D. Farish, *The Circuit Rider Dismounts: A Social History of Southern Methodism, 1865–1900* (Richmond, 1938); Walter L. Fleming, *The Freedmen's Savings Bank: A Chapter in the Economic History of the Negro Race* (Chapel Hill, 1927); *id., Louisiana State University, 1860–1896* (Baton Rouge, 1936); Douglas S. Freeman, *The South to Posterity: An Introduction to the Writing of Confederate History* (New York, 1939); Edwin L. Green, *A History of the University of South Carolina* (Columbia, 1916); Alfred J. Hanna, *Flight into Oblivion* (Richmond, 1938); Lawrence F. Hill, *The Confederate Exodus to Latin America* (Reprint from *Southwestern Historical Quarterly*, Austin, 1936); Stanley F. Horn, *Invisible Empire: The Story of the Ku Klux Klan, 1866–1871* (Boston, 1939); Augustus L. Hull, *Annals of Athens, Georgia, 1801–1901* (Athens, 1906); Edgar W. Knight, *The Influence of Reconstruction on Education in the South* (New York, 1913); Paul Lewinson, *Race, Class, & Party: A History of Negro Suffrage and White Politics in the South* (London, 1932); William P. Livingstone, *Black Jamaica: A Study in Evolution* (London, 1899); Reginald C. McGrane, *Foreign Bondholders and American State Debts* (New York, 1935); Paul S. Peirce, *The Freedmen's Bureau: A Chapter in the History of Reconstruction* (Iowa City, 1904); Charles S. Potts, *Railroad Transportation in Texas* (Austin, 1909); Perceval Reniers, *The Springs of Virginia: Life, Love, and Death at the Waters, 1775–1900* (Chapel Hill, 1941); William M. Robinson, Jr., *Justice in Grey: A History of the Judicial System of the Confederate States of America* (Cambridge, 1941); Howard W. Schotter, *The Growth and Development of the Pennsylvania Railroad Company* (Philadelphia, 1927); Samuel D. Smith, *The Negro in Congress, 1870–1901* (Chapel Hill, 1940); Edward Stanwood, *A History of the Presidency from 1788 to 1897* (Boston, 1928); Martin D. Stevers, *Steel Trails: The Epic of the Railroads* (New York, 1933); Henry L. Swint, *The Northern Teacher in the South, 1862–1870* (Nashville, 1941); Alrutheus A. Taylor, *The Negro in Tennessee, 1865–1880* (Washington, 1941); Slason Thompson, *A Short History of American Railways* (Chicago, 1925); Charles Warren, *The Supreme Court in United States History*, 3 vols. (Boston, 1922); Walter P. Webb, *The Great Plains* (Boston, 1931); *Week-End Book* (London, 1931); Thomas J. Wertenbaker, *Norfolk, Historic Southern Port* (Durham, 1931); Charles H. Wesley, *Negro Labor in the United States, 1850–1925* (New York, 1927); Alfred B. Williams, *Hampton and his Red Shirts: South Carolina's Deliverance in 1876* (Charleston, 1935); Thomas J. Woofter, Jr., *Black Yeomanry: Life on St. Helena Island* (New York, 1930).

INDEX

A. S. Barnes & Company, presents textbooks to South, 329
Adams, Charles Francis, Jr., on Reconstruction debts, 379
Adams Express Company, 242
African Methodist Episcopal Church, 338-39
African Methodist Episcopal Zion Church, 339
Agassiz, Louis, on ability of Negroes, 58
Agricultural and Mechanical Association, of Louisiana, 229
Agricultural and Mechanical Society, of South Carolina, 229
Agricultural societies, 228-29
Agricultural Society, of Georgia, 229
Agriculture, developments in, 211-32
Aiken, William, 68
Aiken, S.C., tourist center, 207, 305
Alabama, destruction of war in, 2; political developments, 350-51
Alabama Association of Base Ball Players, 302
Alabama and Chattanooga Railroad, Chinese workmen on, 105-106
Albany, N.Y., prison at, 16, 171
Alcorn, James L., Mississippi politician, 123, 124, 351
Alfriend, Frank H., author, 277
Alvord, John W., educational work of, 82; in charge of Freedmen's Bank, 88
American Colonization Society, work of resented by Negroes, 98
American Emigrant Company, 103
American Land Company, 204
American Missionary Society, 81
American Union, 287
Ames, Adelbert, Carpetbagger, 140; flees Mississippi, 351

Ames, Oakes, 302
Amnesty, proclamation, of December 8, 1863, 30; of May 29, 1865, 32; granted by Congress, 386
Andersonville, Confederate prison, 15
Andrews, John A., invests in Southern land, 205-206
Anniston, Ala., model town, 261
Appletons' Hand-Book of American Travel, 207; on Negro rule in South Carolina, 147
Arkansas, political developments, 351
Arkansas State Agricultural and Mechanical Association, 229
Arlington, home of Lee, seized, 74
Atlanta, Ga., 245; destruction of war in, education, 87
Arrests, of Confederates, 14-15
Asheville, N.C., growth, 261
Atkinson, Edward, interest in cotton, 218-19; on Southern manufactories, 266-67
Atlanta, Ga., 245; destruction of war in, 3; railroad center, 238-39, 245; economic growth, 256-57
Atlanta University, 87, 326
Atlanta and Richmond Air Line, 238, 244
Atlantic Coast Dispatch, 242
Atlantic, Mississippi, and Ohio Railroad, 236
Atrocities, Southern, 116-18; used by Radicals to discredit South, 158
Augusta, Ga., economic growth, 258-59
Austin, Texas, growth, 259
Azor, carries Negroes to Africa, 98

Baltimore, Md., center of commercial fertilizers, 215

418

Negroes *(Continued)*
330; religious developments, 336-39; effect of political experiences on, 379, 380; crimes, 380-81
New Departure, 344
New Orleans, La., historical society founded at, 182; favorite of ex-Confederate officers, 196, 197; exports and imports, 249-50; economic growth, 253-54; retarded by yellow fever, 262-63; Mardi Gras in, 299
New Orleans *Picayune*, ownership, 282; on Negro education, 324
New Orleans Riot, of 1866, 40; of 1874, 157
New Orleans *Tribune*, Negro newspaper, 288
New Orleans, Jackson, and Great Northern Railroad, 235
New Orleans and Mobile Railroad, 239
New South, 385-91
New York *Christian Advocate*, on Methodists, 332
New York City, Southerners go to, 187
New York *Herald*, on Negro land ownership, 111; on Bourbons, 346; on Southern Radicals, 353; on Negro voting, 357; on election of 1876, 370
New York *Journal of Commerce*, on Southerners in New York, 187; on Northern migration to South, 204
New York Seventy-first Infantry, entertained in New Orleans, 389
New York Southern Famine Relief Commission, 20
New York *Sun*, on Negro suffrage, 128; on Solid South, 377-78
New York *Times*, comments on relief to South, 20-21; on Reconstruction, 121; on conditions in South, 348
New York *Tribune*, on Southern violence, 158; on South, 341
Newspapers, 285-91; number, 285; Radical, 286-87; Negro, 287-88; influence, 289; country, 289-90; associations, 290-91
Nicholls, Francis T., in election of 1876, 370, 373-74
[Nineteenth] *XIX Century*, 285

Nojoque, 101
Nordhoff, Charles, journalist and author, 385
Norfolk, Va., 260
Norfolk and Petersburg Railroad, 236
Norfolk and Southern Railroad, 237
Norfolk and Western Railroad, 236
North Carolina, destruction of war in, 2; tourists in, 207; political developments, 349-50
Northern capital, in South, 266, 268, 271, 382, 390
Northern planters, in South, 205-206
"Notes on the Situation," articles by B. H. Hill, 121
Nott, Dr. Josiah C., on character of Negroes, 55; on Negro education, 85; on labor of Southern whites, 203

Oats, Joe, Negro political trickster, 63, 134
Oats, 221
Ocean Steamship Company, 249
O'Conor, Charles, in election of 1872, 346; gives legal service to Davis, 385
Officers, Confederate military, after war, 196-98; in lumber business, 271
Ogeechee River Riots, 110
Opera, at New Orleans, 292
Oranges, raising of, 207, 222
Ord, Edward O. C., military governor, 131
Orr, James L., interest in Negro education, 83; Southern Radical, 124
Oxford, Miss., destruction of war in, 3; Ku Klux trials at, 171

Packard, Stephen B., Louisiana politician, 352; in election of 1876, 373-74
Page, Thomas Nelson, author, 279
Palmer, Benjamin M., president of Southern Historical Society, 182
Panic, of 1867, 193; of 1873, 194, 236, 244
Pardons, by the President, 32-33; *see also*, Amnesty
Patrons of Husbandry, *see* Grangers
Patton, Robert M., on cotton manufactories, 265
Peabody, George, 328; at Peabody Ball,

Virginia and Kentucky Railroad, 236
Virginia and Tennessee Railroad, 236

Wade, Benjamin, Radical leader, 30-31, 114, 116; invests in Southern lands, 206
Wadsworth, James W., 68
Wages, received by freedmen, 76-77, 92-93, 99-100; of Chinese, 106; of industrial workers, 274
Walker, Gilbert C., Virginia governor, 349
Walking contests, 303-304
Wallace, John, Florida Negro, comments on Freedmen's Bureau, 91; on Carpetbaggers, 126-27
Warmoth, Henry Clay, Carpetbagger, 140, 143, 158; attends steamboat race, 303; on education, 320; political activities of, 352
Warner, William, on Southern hospitality, 208-209
Washington, Booker T., interest in education, 87
Washington College, 175, 196, 290; see also, Washington and Lee University
Washington and Lee University, 321; see also, Washington College
Water power, 272
Watermelons, 222
Watson, Thomas E., plays baseball, 301
Watterson, Harvey M., makes Southern trip, 28
Watterson, Henry, newspaper editor, 289
Wealth, per capita, of former slave states compared with that of other states, 192-93
West, migrations of Negroes to, 96, 100; alliance of South with, 189
West Virginia, organized, 31; political developments in, 363; debt settlement with Virginia, 379
West and South, 190
Western and Atlantic Railroad, in politics, 151, 237

Westmoreland, Mrs. Maria J., 312
Wheeler, Gen. Joseph, arrested, 15; criticism of, 21
Wheeler, William A., Congressman, 353
Wheeler Compromise, 353
Whigs, old, in South, 44
White Brotherhood, secret order, 169
White League, 352-53
Wilder, John T., industrialist, 272-73
Williams, George W., banker, 191
Wilmer, Bishop Richard H., 331
Wilmington, N.C., importance of, 258; ousts Negro rule, 264
Wilson, Senator Henry, on confiscation, 68; visits South, 129; on Confederate veterans, 177
Wilson, Col. Lorenzo M., 283
Wine making, 223
Wirz, Henry, hanged, 15
Wise, Henry A., on Confederate soldiers, 177
Wittemore, B. Frank, Carpetbagger, 140
Wofford College, 321
Woman suffrage, 312
Women, of the South, interest in Confederate soldiers and traditions, 178-79; occupations, 200; schoolteachers, 200-201, 326; authors, 281-83; fashions, 308-11
Woodstock Iron Company, 261
Worth, Jonathan, on Negro education, 85
Wright, Jonathan J., Negro judge in South Carolina, 143

Yazoo City Democrat, on Mississippi election, 358
Yellow fever, 259, 261; retards growth of Memphis, 258; retards growth of New Orleans, 262-63
Yerger, E. M., case of in Supreme Court, 122
Yonge, W. P. C., fish fancier, 225
Young Men's Christian Association, 335